CRITICAL THEORY AND METHODOLOGY

CONTEMPORARY SOCIAL THEORY

Series Editor:
Mark Gottdiener
University of California, Riverside

CONTEMPORARY SOCIAL THEORY books are brief, introductory texts designed to make current trends in social theory accessible to undergraduate students in the social sciences.

VOLUMES IN THIS SERIES

1. Tom Mayer, ANALYTICAL MARXISM
2. Sondra Farganis, SITUATING FEMINISM: From Thought to Action
3. Raymond A. Morrow with David D. Brown, CRITICAL THEORY AND METHODOLOGY
4. Robert Hollinger, POSTMODERNISM AND THE SOCIAL SCIENCES: A Thematic Approach

SERIES EDITORIAL BOARD

CRITICAL THEORY AND METHODOLOGY

RAYMOND A. MORROW
WITH DAVID D. BROWN

CONTEMPORARY SOCIAL THEORY

VOLUME 3

SAGE Publications
International Educational and Professional Publisher
Thousand Oaks London New Delhi

For information address:

 SAGE Publications, Inc.
2455 Teller Road
Thousand Oaks, California 91320
E-mail: order@sagepub.com

SAGE Publications Ltd.
6 Bonhill Street
London EC2A 4PU
United Kingdom

SAGE Publications India Pvt. Ltd.
M-32 Market
Greater Kailash I
New Delhi 110 048 India

Printed in the United States of America

Library of Congress Cataloging-in-Publication Data

Morrow, Raymond Allan.
  Critical theory and methodology / Raymond A. Morrow, with David
D. Brown
    p. cm. — (Contemporary social theory ; 3)
  Includes bibliographical references and index.
  ISBN 0-8039-4682-1. — ISBN 0-8039-4683-X (pbk.)
    1. Critical theory. 2. Social sciences—Philosophy.
3. Sociology—Methodology. I. Brown, David D., 1954–
II. Title. III. Series: Contemporary social theory (Thousand Oaks,
Calif.) : 3.
HM24.M622 1994
301'.01—dc20   94-10888

96 97 98 99 00 01 10 9 8 7 6 5 4 3

Sage Production Editor: Astrid Virding

CONTENTS

ACKNOWLEDGMENTS

This book had its origins in three distinct events during a number of years. Most immediately, I would like to thank Ben Agger for recommending me for this project even though his own conception of a "dialectical sensibility" lies at the Adorno-Benjamin end of the spectrum of critical theory; and I would like to commend Mark Gottdiener for taking the initiative to get this series off the ground and for having provided the patient encouragement that is so crucial for those relatively inexperienced in completing a book.

More distantly, in 1978 Peter Bruck (now at Carleton University in communications) organized a conference at Concordia University (Montreal) on "Critical Theory and Empirical Method." Although last-minute attendance precluded my preparation of a full paper on this topic, the problematic has stayed with me. The issues were sharpened as I was confronted term by term with new cohorts of skeptical graduate students. Although I could have written a somewhat different book in between, perhaps now is the most appropriate time from the ironic perspective of the subsequent ups and downs of critical theory as an intellectual force in the academic marketplace.

The crucial intermediate factor has been my association with David Brown, initially as a doctoral student in sociology at the University of Alberta, and now colleague at the University of Lethbridge. Before I became his supervisor, David had gained a reputation as a problem-solver in research methods, and our association began when I became a member of his comprehensive examination committee in "methodology." As it happens, he had set out the agenda for a comprehensive definition of the problematic that revealed he was also a theorist with a primary interest in interpretive methods. That experience revealed convergent interests and led us to explore the possibility of collaboration on a project redefining methodology from the perspective of critical theory. That collaborative project was delayed by his writing a dissertation that reconstructed Paul Ricoeur's theory of narrative for a novel conception of life history methodology; and then it was sidetracked by his subsequent relocation at Lethbridge, where various distractions undermined his ability to contribute to the extent originally envisioned. Although we collaborated directly only on Chapter 8, and I am solely responsible for all of the others, crucial aspects of my understanding of many key issues stem from our dialogue about theory and methods during the past few years.

The foundations for this slowly gestating project were laid (often unknowingly) by diverse, even contradictory, influences in Toronto in the mid-1970s: e.g., Ioan Davies, Bryan Green, John Fekete, William Leiss, Christian Lenhardt, Thelma McCormack, Dieter Misgeld, John O'Neill, Paul Piccone, Dorothy Smith, Tom Wilson, Irving Zeitlin. A DAAD fellowship to the Freie Universität in Berlin in 1976-7 exposed me in depth to German social theory. A postdoctoral fellowship at the Université de Montréal from 1981-3 facilitated understanding the problems of linking German and French theory (as exemplified in the work of the late Québécois sociologist, Marcel Rioux) and led to an ongoing intellectual exchange with Greg Nielsen (e.g., Nielsen and Morrow 1991), now at Glendon College, York University. Some recent conversations with the critical theorist and theologian Gregory Baum (now at McGill University) provided a boost of confidence at a crucial moment when I was having doubts about finishing this project. Collaboration with Carlos Alberto Torres over the past several years has been a continuous source of mutual learning that has contributed indirectly to many aspects of the present discussion.

Here at the University of Alberta, I would like to thank the members of a small Cultural Studies reading group who sensitized me to a number of interdisciplinary issues. The work of my colleague Derek Sayer has been diffusely significant for my thinking, even if it is not directly manifest in ways that would be apparent to him. Barb Marshall, a graduate of our program now teaching at Trent University, has kept me aware of the troubled aspects of the relations between critical theory and feminist theory, though that is only a theme insufficiently alluded to here.

Among recent and current graduate students here at the University of Alberta, I would like to single out several who have contributed indirectly in little ways (discussions, references, reading their work) to this project: Guy Germain and Alan Law (sociology), Michael Mauws (business), Jerry Kachur, Kelly Murphy, and Donald Plumb (educational foundations).

Occasional cappuccinos with Taras at La Gare reminded me of two themes obscured by the particular tasks of this book: that social theory needs ultimately to speak to the issues of everyday life, and in ways that do not deny the poetic origins of all critical thought. And to Marlene: Thanks for the patience and understanding at several crucial turning points.

This book is dedicated to my father—Ray Morrow, Jr.—whose natural pragmatism and principled skepticism contradicts his own deep sense of justice and human values. Although circumstances constrained him to work with his hands, he encouraged me to pursue an intellectual vocation to learn to answer the questions he could not. Mostly I have succeeded (as part of an extended community of inquirers) only in reframing some of the questions, hence the methodological focus of this book. But the outcome is, I think, quite consistent with things we implicitly learned growing up together and that I can now name: the necessary interplay between critical realist ontology, methodological pragmatism, and communicative ethics in reconstructing human understanding.

PREFACE

This book was written with different kinds of audiences in mind, resulting in certain tensions within the text itself. First, despite the prevalence of sociological issues, it is a work of social theory and methodology addressed to an interdisciplinary social scientific audience.

Second, it is oriented specifically toward upper level undergraduate and graduate students in the social sciences. Although it was conceived with the hope that it might supplement teaching in social science methodology, it more likely will be used to give the teaching of social theory a more methodological focus. Further, it could serve interested colleagues in search of a guide to recent debates and a jumping off point for more specialized reading.

Third, it seeks to address indirectly those trained in the humanities but in need of an introduction to social theory and methodology from a critical sociological perspective. In particular, proponents of cultural studies approaches in the humanities often are handicapped by a lack of ready access to the forms of sociology and social science adequate to their needs, especially in relation to methodological questions other than those of textual analysis. One manifestation of this problem is an often cavalier attitude toward questions of empirical adequacy on the basis of a wholesale rejection of "empiricism," a tendency first evident in Althusserian structuralism and now reinforced in rather different ways by the postmodernist suggestion that virtually "anything goes" with respect to knowledge claims.

In the process of this synthetic reconstruction, it was necessary to develop themes that may prove useful for ongoing debates within social theory, and critical theory in particular. The constraints of a relatively accessible format have required formulating (without fully defending or exemplifying) a number of arguments that, we hope, will be of some interest for those involved in these more specialized debates. In particular, the methodological notion of *interpretive structuralism* has an ecumenical objective: It seeks to draw out the similarities between a number of research approaches that are more often thought as either distinct or competing, a tendency reinforced by the inherently competitive character of scholarship.

Several limitations in the scope of this study should be noted at the outset. First, it does not and could not seek to provide an "applied" approach to linking critical theory and the techniques of social research. The most fundamental reason is that the pragmatic nature of inquiry precludes any general formulas or recipes. Different strategies of inquiry can be mastered only by close analyses of appropriate exemplary studies, combined with ongoing reflection on and engagement in the research process itself.

Second, it does not provide the kind of close analysis of actual empirical projects that would be appropriate for a somewhat differently conceived project (e.g., Harvey 1990). The immediate task at hand is to provide a jumping off point for direct immersion in the theoretical and methodological problems of different contexts of inquiry.

Third, various considerations have led to a relative neglect of the range of external and internal criticisms that have been directed against critical theory as a research program. Yet the whole project is directed generally toward answering much criticism that has focused on critical theory's problematic relation to empirical research. Further, it responds to the skeptical and antiscientific mood of certain postmodernist tendencies.

On the other hand, many of the most important criticisms are internal to critical theory and closely related tendencies. As a consequence, such issues constitute the central themes of ongoing debates and research controversies. Introducing too many of these more advanced questions here would only serve to further confuse the already overwhelmed reader.

The structure of the book reflects an attempt to facilitate access on the part of readers with diverse backgrounds. The chapters are highly integrated sequentially, in the sense that concepts are introduced first in contexts where their meaning is clarified. Further, the chapters are linked in that the earlier ones set up foundations for those that come later.

Nevertheless the chapters often could be read separately or in other combinations for various purposes. Half of the chapters are concerned with the reconstruction of critical theory as a specific research program (Chaps. 1, 4, 6-7, 11-12), whereas the other half treat metatheoretical and methodological issues in a manner that is not necessarily specific or unique to critical theory (Chaps. 2-3, 5, 8-10), even if broadly linked with the "new philosophy of social science" (Outhwaite 1987; Bohman 1991). The latter, in short, could be extended to analyze, justify, or criticize other research programs that focus on different aspects of domination (e.g., feminist theory) or draw on different methodological tools (e.g., analytical Marxism).

At the proof stage a couple of studies came to our attention that should be noted, partly to indicate more precisely the distinctive strategy underlying our approach. These final prefatory comments are directed primarily to readers with more specialized interests in social theory.

Derek Layder's *New Strategies of Social Research* (1993) provides a useful mediation between conventional methodological discussions (e.g., middle range and grounded theory) and a "multistrategy" conception of social analysis close to that of Giddens. As a consequence, in many respects it could be profitably used as a more "applied" sequel to our study. But his introduction is developed largely without reference to the metatheoretical issues required for grounding methodology; partly as a consequence, he fails to clearly differentiate between variable analysis and other uses of quantification. As well, the tradition of critical theory—along with discourse theory and the concept of ideology—mysteriously disappear (despite references to history and power). We do not find this sanitized approach fully consistent with Giddens' social theory, and would contend it is more productive (as we have done) to introduce the methodological implications of his work in the context of a dialogue with Habermas and critical theory generally.

For accidental reasons we did not become aware of Douglas Porpora's *The Concept of Social Structure* (1987) until the last minute, even though our project would have gained from engagement with his parallel theoretical argument. Theoretically, Porpora uses (as we do) Bhaskar's critical realism as a way of differentiating between Durkheimian (nomothetic) models of social structure and what he takes to be the Marxian conception (via Bhaskar's early work). Though he admits that much exciting recent work has focused on modes of domination "beyond Marx," he rejects the "growing chorus of voices . . . arguing that Marxian theory needs to be superseded" (1987, p.117). His point is that non-Marxian modes of domination (e.g., race and gender) "still conform to the Marxian conception of social structure. Like modes of production, they may all be interpreted as powerful particulars with underlying generating mechanisms that consist of relationships among categories of people" (Porpora, 1987, p. 132).

Though our substantive conclusions with respect to theory and research are generally convergent with Porpora's, we have framed the problematic rather differently by speaking more broadly (and ecumenically) of the *interpretive structuralist research program of contemporary critical theory*. While we would agree that this general methodological conception can be traced back to Marx (and Hegel), we would contest the suggestion that contemporary critical theory has merely "reinvented the wheel" (as Derek Sayer has argued with reference to Giddens).

But the issue at stake is not one of a priority dispute, but rather of stressing theoretical *discontinuity* as part of engaging the particulars of the present historical horizon. The omissions in Porpora's account are symptomatic of his rehabilitative strategy: no reference to Habermas or the debates on European structuralism (e.g., the later, structuralist side of Durkheim) and post-structuralism (despite a brief discussion of Foucault); and a failure to develop the more specific implications for research methods. The attempt to distance his own conception from that of Giddens (despite apparent resemblances) is not altogether convincing, though it points to some important issues requiring further clarification. The resulting theory of social structure, however compelling, is elaborated virtually without reference to one of culture and its relation to the normative presuppositions that define a critical theory of society—decisive issues for a critique and reconstruction of historical materialism. The theory of society we need today requires historical contents, normative grounding and methodological reflection that go far beyond the concept of social structure bequeathed by Marx. In short, our more comprehensive response to post-Marxist nihilism attempts to avoid the temptations of either methodological sanitization or Marxian nostalgia.

RAYMOND A. MORROW

Metatheory: Grounding Method

1

INTRODUCTION

What Is Critical Theory?

The hostility to theory as such which prevails in contemporary public life is really directed against the transformative activity associated with critical thinking. Opposition starts as soon as theorists fail to limit themselves to verification and classification by means of categories as neutral as possible, that is, categories which are indispensable to inherited ways of life. Among the vast majority of the ruled there is the unconscious fear that theoretical thinking might show their painfully won adaptation to reality to be perverse and unnecessary. (Horkheimer [1937] 1972a, p. 323)

La sociologie de la sociologie . . . est un instrument indispensable de la methode sociologique: on fait de la science—est surtout de la sociologie—contre sa formation autant qu'avec sa formation. (Bourdieu 1982, p. 9)

Why Social Science?

The social sciences have played a central part in the formation of modern, liberal democratic societies. Yet what has been described as the contemporary postmodern condition has fundamentally called into question the claims that originally inspired the Enlightenment project of social science. This book is concerned with reconstructing a social scientific perspective that has provided one of the most powerful responses to the cultural and socioeconomic crises implied by these terms of debate.

3

The notion of a scientific or scholarly discipline is linked to two basic assumptions rooted in the notion of modern science that became institutionalized—largely in universities—from the 17th century onward: (a) that knowledge can progress through specialization on the basis of an intellectual division of labor rooted in the heterogeneous nature of empirical things, and (b) that the unity of these endeavors is linked to a shared scientific method that cuts across specializations and substantive findings. Both of these assumptions have become problematic in their original form.

The contemporary university is characterized by a peculiar threefold division of labor among disciplines, based on the distinction between the natural sciences, the social sciences, and the humanities. The natural sciences are obviously distinctive with respect to what they study. But what about the division between the humanities and the social sciences? Are they not both concerned with the same object of inquiry: the social and cultural life of humanity? But, many would argue, the humanities employ distinctive methods because they do not aspire to be scientific in the strict sense as do the social sciences; instead the humanities make knowledge claims based on their ability to "interpret" culture, as opposed to constructing scientific explanations of it. But is this opposition so fundamental? Literary historians necessarily do invoke explanatory principles derived from the social sciences, and social scientists cannot escape the problems of interpreting cultural texts. Perhaps because of their shared object of inquiry and overlapping methods, the humanities and social sciences are combined most often in a single "arts faculty"; sometimes, however, the social sciences are housed in a distinct administrative unit with the unifying—and telltale—discipline of history somewhat arbitrarily allocated to either the humanities or the social sciences. The possibility of a more comprehensive notion of the human sciences gets lost in the process.

The origins of the social sciences are linked closely with transformations of society that define modernity and the rise of industrial capitalism. Whereas the humanities disciplines are rooted in philosophy, literature, and languages and can be traced backed to the Middle Ages, the forms of thought associated with the social sciences emerge only in the 18th century. The particular focus of the social sciences was the attempt to understand the massive transformations—still continuing today—that emerged initially in Europe in the form of what have been described as the "two great revolutions" of the 18th and 19th centuries: the political revolution in France in 1789 that redefined political authority in terms of human rights such a liberty, equality, and fraternity; and the industrial revolution associated with the technical innovations, transformations of economic and social life, and urbanization that accompanied the rise of capitalism (Giddens 1982b, pp. 5-6). Although sociology as a more encompassing discipline is associated most closely with the study of modern societies, its accomplishments have depended on and been shared with other disciplines and modes of thought. On the one hand, the origins of sociology are linked closely with literary forms (Lepenies 1988). On the other hand, sociology itself has depended extensively on other disciplines: history, which can only arbitrarily be separated from sociology; anthropology, which differs primarily only in the typical kind of society it studies; economics and political science, which focus on particular institutional spheres; psychology, which ranges from biology to questions of social psychology shared by all of the social sciences; and geography, which analyzes the relations between the physical features of the earth and its human populations. More recently, communications departments have emerged in response to the rise of the mass media and new communications technologies in "information societies."

Although these disciplinary distinctions and differences often are taken to be natural, it should be stressed that they often reflect accidental features of the development of modern, European universities. A quite different and more productive division of intellectual labor might have taken place, and new ones could be imagined—both within the social sciences and with respect to their relation to the humanities. The point of departure of critical theory—the social science perspective that is the focus of this study—is precisely one of questioning this existing division of labor and the social interests it serves, masks, or neglects.

Competing Scientific Perspectives

For critical theory, not only the given division of labor among disciplines is problematic. A second line of questioning concerns what it would mean to study social institutions and their transformation in a scientific manner. Here popular images of science can be very misleading, especially the medical model that psychologists often resort to or the technocratic model that economists have secured and that many sociologists enviously aspire to. The crucial point is that there are competing conceptions of what kind of scientific activity social science should be. As we shall see, if it is no longer credible to refer to "the scientific method" in the singular, our understanding of the nature of the social sciences must be profoundly transformed.

Broadly speaking, two types of answers to this question of the scientific status of the social sciences have been proposed. On the one hand, the earliest and most optimistic and influential view has been that the social sciences need only to emulate the natural sciences. Such *naturalistic* or *positivistic* approaches argue that the methodology of what are taken to be the most advanced sciences (e.g., physics, perhaps biology) should be the model. On the other hand, opposing perspectives argue that to a significant degree, social life is qualitatively different from the things studied by the natural sciences (whether physical or biological) and that consequently a *humanistic* approach based on the study of meanings is required. Other approaches—and we locate critical theory here—try to mediate between naturalistic and humanistic perspectives.

The reality of this methodological pluralism is expressed today in the notion that the social sciences are multiparadigmatic disciplines. In this context the notion of *paradigm* of research refers to the full range of assumptions and practices associated with fundamental theoretical approaches, not this or that system of abstract concepts associated with the "theory." The task of this study is to outline the basic features of what has come to be called *critical social theory*, or simply *critical theory*, as a social scientific perspective that has become the basis of a diverse research program (a paradigm of empirical research) that has influenced a number of disciplines. The term has its origins in the work of a group of German scholars (collectively referred to as the *Frankfurt School*) in the 1920s who used the term initially (*Kritische Theorie* in German) to designate a specific approach to interpreting Marxist theory. But the term has taken on new meanings in the interim and can be neither exclusively identified with the Marxist tradition from which it has become increasingly distinct nor reserved exclusively to the Frankfurt School, given extensive new variations outside the original German context.

Problems of Definition

Before we turn to a more detailed definition of critical theory, it is necessary to preface the discussion with some comments about the rather unfortunate term *critical theory* itself.[1] Beyond the obvious problem of it being confused with literary criticism, a number of other approaches to social theory could be considered "critical" in some sense. For example, Marxist research of all types could make an obvious claim to be critical. Even positivist researchers have claimed with considerable justification that empirical findings may involve criticism of existing understandings of social reality. If we follow the convention of identifying the term *critical theory* as a very specific approach to social theory, it is because no suitable alternative seems to exist.

Further, the term *critical* itself, in the context of "critical theory," has a range of meanings not apparent in common sense where critique implies negative evaluations. This is, to be sure, one sense of critique in critical theory, given its concern with unveiling ideological mystifications in social relations; but another even more fundamental connotation is methodological, given a concern with critique as involving establishing the presuppositions of approaches to the nature of reality, knowledge, and explanation; yet another dimension of critique is associated with the self-reflexivity of the investigator and the linguistic basis of representation. All of these are central to contemporary critical theory.

Two basic strategies may be used in defining a scientific approach such as critical theory: systematic and historical. We begin with a systematic presentation in this chapter by indicating in introductory terms some of the key aspects of critical theory as (a) an approach to the sciences, (b) as a conception of society, and (c) as a vision for realizing certain values. Following that, we situate contemporary critical theory in terms of its historical origins in classical sociological theory and contemporary debates in social theory. Although we seek to avoid the dogmatic presumption that any one approach (namely the one we are explicating and defending) should dominate or replace all of the

others, we will try to make the case for social science as critical
theory as having a distinctive set of tasks that make it essential to
the social sciences more generally.

Such an approach is plagued at the outset by communication
difficulties because it requires a different vocabulary, one that
runs up against both common sense and much conventional social
scientific research. But it was foreshadowed in more popular
terms in the work of C. Wright Mills (1916-1962), who almost
single-handedly pioneered the American tradition of what came
to be known as *radical sociology* by the 1960s but eventually
splintered in several directions. Mills preferred to speak of *"sociological imagination"* in trying to convey the forms of understanding often resulting from sociological knowledge (Mills
1967). The project that Mills had in mind in the 1950s is today
most widely understood under the heading of *critical theory,* a
perspective whose influence now extends throughout the social
sciences and to the humanities. In between has been an extensive reappropriation of the European tradition of social and
cultural theory that did not occur until the 1970s and 1980s. In
that context it became possible to understand more fully the
contributions of the "dialectical imagination" of the Frankfurt
School tradition of social and cultural research (Jay 1973).

Critical Theory as a Human Science

As a Human Science

Humanistic approaches to inquiry are linked closely with the
remarkable "interpretive turn" that has become visible in the
human sciences during the past decade, in which "interpretation has gained a certain currency, even prestige, in philosophical circles and in the social sciences" (Rabinow and Sullivan
1987, p. 1; Hiley et al. 1991). Such issues concerning the scientific status of social research—a central theme of this study—are
discussed under the heading of *metatheory* (theory about theory). The reason for this shift in the human sciences has been
increasing recognition that the decisive feature that separates the
practice of the human and natural sciences is the problem of

interpreting meanings in social life. Although critical theory has a distinctive position here because of its insistence on analyzing the objective structures that constrain human imagination, it is otherwise broadly allied with humanistic approaches.

According to such antipositivist or interpretive approaches, the study of the empirical character of societies differs in at least two basic ways from the natural sciences. First, "social facts" are qualitatively different from the "facts" of nature because they are created and re-created by our own actions as human beings:

> In social theory, we cannot treat human activities as though they were determined by causes in the same way as natural events are. We have to grasp what I would call the *double involvement* of individuals and institutions: we create society at the same time as we are created by it. . . . *Social systems are like buildings that are at every moment constantly being reconstructed by the very bricks that compose them.* (Giddens 1982b, pp. 13-4)

Second, because we create society, the application of sociology or social science is not really analogous to controlling physical nature. Human beings have a unique capacity to change their behavior in response to knowledge about it; as a consequence the regularities of social life are always in flux: "If we regard social activity as a mechanical set of events, determined by natural laws, we both misunderstand the past and fail to grasp how sociological analysis can help influence our possible futures" (Giddens 1982b, pp. 14-5).

This is not to say that it is impossible—and for some purposes useful—to proceed as if social facts could be analyzed in the manner of natural objects or "things." Indeed, critical theory charges that one of the failures of traditional humanistic approaches lies in their neglect of such strategies of inquiry. But it is quite a different manner to make this the exclusive definition of social inquiry that takes its method as the only scientific one.

As a Historical Science of Society

Whereas positivist approaches focus on those aspects that natural and social science may have in common, critical theory moves in the opposite direction by exploring those aspects that separate the two. A fundamental consequence is that critical theory is conceived essentially as a form of historical sociology (and in this sense a science of history). What is at issue here is how critical theory conceives the nature of its object of inquiry— that is, how it understands the nature of what it seeks to explain. To speak of critical theory as historical, therefore, does not exclude the present. The point is, rather, that the ultimate boundaries of its domain of inquiry are the unique set of events that make up world history and that are in this respect a kind of *world-historical sociology* with implications for human values, which is quite distinct from the *general theoretical sociology,* which has always been the ideal of positivist theories of science (Fararo 1989, p. 15).

These qualities are also closely associated with what Mills called "sociological imagination." More recently, Anthony Giddens— the leading contemporary British critical theorist—has specified them in terms of "several related forms of sensibility" required for understanding contemporary industrial societies: "These forms of the sociological imagination involve an historical, an anthropological, and a critical sensitivity" (1982b, p. 16). From this perspective the tasks of sociology strongly overlap with those of historians and anthropologists, among others.

Such a historical sensitivity is required to grasp imaginatively the profound transformations within human history, and our very categories of sociological conceptualization change with society itself. Anthropological insight requires coming to terms with the peculiar tension between the unity and diversity of human cultures and the difficulty of avoiding ethnocentrism—of making one's own society the lens through which all others are viewed and judged.

But critical theory has a more specific focus on the substantive problematic of *domination,* a complex notion based on a concern with the ways social relations also mediate power relations to create various forms of *alienation* and inhibit the realization of human possibilities. In this respect, critical theory is a kind of conflict theory in that it is recognized that relations of domination manifest themselves in social struggles. What is distinctive about critical theory, however, is its understanding of the complexity of domination itself (which cannot be reduced to overt oppression), as well as the methodological problems involved in studying it (Harvey 1990, p. 32).

As Sociocultural Critique

sociologic imagenation

This focus on relations of domination is connected intimately with critical theory's concern with the simultaneous critique of society and the envisioning of new possibilities. Critique in this sense is concerned with *normative theory*, theory about values and what ought to be. Critical imagination is required to avoid identifying where we live here and now as somehow cast in stone by natural laws: "But this means we must be conscious of the alternative futures that are potentially open to us. In its third sense, the sociological imagination fuses with the task of sociology in contributing to the critique of existing forms of society" (Giddens 1982b, p. 26). In a sense that will require further clarification, in short, sociocultural critique joins up here with what often has been referred to as *utopian imagination*.

Critical Theory and Interdisciplinarity

The project of critical theory is not unique to either sociology or the social sciences generally. As a consequence it is possible to identify variants of critical theory in all of the social science disciplines: for example, anthropology (Scholte 1974; Marcus and Fischer 1986), history (Poster 1989; Jay 1993), political science (Ball 1987; Dallmayr 1987; Luke 1990; White 1987), communications and cultural studies (Hardt 1992; Agger, 1990, 1992a), psychology (Sampson 1983; Sullivan 1990), geography and urban studies (Gregory 1978; Gottdiener 1985), and economics (Sherman 1987). Parallel developments can be seen also in more applied and professional fields such as education (Giroux 1981), social work (Drover and Kierans 1993), organizational studies and public administration (Dunn and Fozouni 1976; Clegg 1975, 1989), legal studies (Unger 1986), and planning and policy research (Forester 1985d).

Beyond these more specific identifications it is also possible to point to extensive influences that have reshaped somewhat differently designated research approaches. For example, certain tendencies in *feminist theory* have been influenced strongly by critical theory (Fraser 1989; Benhabib 1986; Marshall Forthcoming). As well, the humanities often have been influenced by critical social theory, thus blurring the boundaries between social and cultural criticism, especially under the heading of a *cultural studies* linking the humanities and social sciences (Brantlinger 1990; Berman 1989).

Nevertheless sociology does have a strong case for centrality. As Jürgen Habermas, the leading contemporary German critical theorist, notes, sociology's ultimate concern is with a theory of society: "Alone among the disciplines of social science, sociology has retained its relations to problems of society as a whole. Whatever else it has become, it has always remained a theory of society as well" (Habermas 1984, p. 5). Another consequence is that "sociology became the science of crisis par excellence; it concerned itself above all with the anomic aspects of the dissolution of traditional social systems and the development of modern ones" (Habermas 1984, p. 4). Nevertheless this privileged status in relation to sociology should not be allowed to obscure the inherently "supradisciplinary" character of critical theory. As the American philosopher Douglas Kellner has argued in his comprehensive synthesis of the Frankfurt tradition of critical theory:

> Yet, while there is no unitary Critical Theory, I will suggest there are features which define it in terms of method, presuppositions and positions. From the beginning to the present, Critical Theory has refused to situate itself within an arbitrary or conventional academic division of labor. It thus traverses and undermines boundaries between competing disciplines, and stresses interconnections between philosophy, economics and politics, and culture and society. . . . This project requires a collective, supradisciplinary synthesis of philosophy, the sciences and politics, in which critical social theory is produced by groups of theorists and scientists from various disciplines working together to produce a Critical Theory of the present age aimed at radical socio-political transformation. (Kellner 1989, p. 7)

political transformation

The Origins of Critical Theory

Classical Sociology

At this point it is necessary to begin the first step in the process of introducing the tradition of thought associated with the notion of critical social theory. In this initial historical presentation we will be able to provide only a very general sketch. We necessarily take for granted a certain basic familiarity with the history of sociological thought and the frame of reference for locating critical theory (Giddens 1971).

Most pertinent as a model for critical theory is the classical sociological inquiry that was the focus of Mills's account of the sociological imagination. The trio of theorists who are held (Giddens 1971) to be most crucial to the formation of contemporary sociology are Karl Marx (1818-1883), Max Weber (1864-1920), and Emile Durkheim (1858-1917). In the cases of Karl Marx and Max Weber—the most influential classical German sociologists—their decisive impact on critical theory is clear (Agger 1979). The continuity is both methodological and substantive. Marx and Weber shared a recognition of the historical character of sociology that puts them clearly outside the model of a natural science of society. To be sure, Marx has been interpreted (e.g., in Soviet Marxism) as doing a natural science of society, but modern commentators have clarified that his notion of a "science of history" cannot be made fully intelligible in positivist terms. Marxists, of course, often have been tempted by reducing Marx to his economic theory and its roots in positivist economics, but this is not usually the Marx who informs contemporary social theory.

Weber's *explicit historicism* led him to reject evolutionist and abstract theorizing and to stress the relative and changing nature of sociological concepts. Weber's type of historicism led him to be cautious about abstract laws and generalizations, as opposed to seeing social processes in specific historical contexts. Similarly, both Marx and Weber were concerned with the conflictual and contradictory features of capitalist modernity, a theme expressed in their respective complementary concern with alienation (associated with the expansion of the market system and the

comodification of social relations) and *rationalization* linked
with bureaucratization and the effects of science and technology
(Löwith [1932] 1982; D. Sayer 1991).

In contrast, the French classical sociologist Durkheim is presented in standard methodology texts as the exemplar of positivist method and founding father of "empirical methods" in his
quantitative analysis of suicide.[2] In this context his injunction to
treat "social facts" as "things" is taken more or less literally.
Further, he is recognized as the pioneer of functionalist theory
and its conservative concern with the problem of "social order"
and the division of labor. Although much truth is in this general
contrast between the two German theorists who have influenced decisively the formation of critical theory and Durkheim's
role in legitimating positivist sociology, more recent interpretations have pointed to aspects of Durkheim's work that have been
appropriated by some forms of critical theory, especially as
mediated by his influence on French social theory.[3]

Early Frankfurt Theory

Historically the notion of a critical theory of society is associated most closely with a research institute established in the
German Weimar Republic in 1923 and forced into exile by Hitler
in 1932—the so-called "Frankfurt School" (Jay 1973; Held 1980).
The term *Critical Theory* (often used in capitals to refer to this
specific German tradition) was used by its leading theorists to
identify their approach, in contrast to forms of "traditional
theory," which attempted to emulate the naturalistic objectivism of the natural sciences, an approach to methodology that the
critical theorists pejoratively labeled "positivism." Instead Critical Theory proposed that an alternative conception of social
science was required, one that could grasp the nature of society
as a historical totality, rather than as an aggregate of mechanical
determinants or abstract functions. Further, it was argued that
such analysis could not take the form of an indifferent, value-free
contemplation of social reality, but should be engaged consciously with the process of its transformation.

The three leading theorists of this original Frankfurt group were
Max Horkheimer (1895-1973), Theodor Adorno (1903-1969), and

Herbert Marcuse (1898-1979).[4] Their approach had a number of unique characteristics:

- It was the first independent research group that was able to work within an avowedly Marxist framework (though it eventually would break with key aspects of orthodox Marxism).
- It was open to the interdisciplinary appropriation of theories and methods from the social sciences, humanities, and non-Marxist philosophy.
- It represented the first systemic effort to employ traditional empirical research techniques (e.g., survey research) to the refinement and testing of propositions derived from the Marxist tradition.

Developments in the Early Frankfurt School

But this original Frankfurt tradition subsequently went through many significant changes that led it away from its original identification with classical Marxist theory. Three key phases can be identified. The first was characterized by a kind of *interdisciplinary materialism* that sought to analyze the factors that might contribute to the development of a revolutionary working class. The notion of *materialism* here referred explicitly to Marx's *historical materialism* but rejected the economic reductionism associated with orthodox Marxism. Instead it was argued that a consistent materialist approach (one that began with the assumption that consciousness could be understood only in relation to economic and social structures rooted in social being) required a more self-reflexive conception of method, a more subtle theory of culture, and a social psychological analysis of class consciousness. Development of these issues required both recourse to empirical research to assess the validity of such materialist arguments, as well as borrowing concepts from non-Marxist sources where appropriate. At this stage the early Critical Theorists still had some faith that the German working class would mobilize—along the line proposed by Marx's theory of revolution—to overthrow Hitler's Nazi dictatorship.

With the failure of overthrow, and the regression of the Soviet revolution to Stalinism, the early Critical Theorists abandoned—in the second phase in the late 1930s—a specifically Marxist political position despite their continued opposition to the destructive effects of capitalism. Instead they turned to an exploration of the new found stability of capitalism, which they attributed, in part, to the rise of the welfare state and the ability of the new mass media (what they called the "culture industries") to distract working class audiences from what was held to be their "real" interests. The outcome of this analysis was a profound pessimism.

Contemporary Critical Theory

German Continuations

The third phase involved the emergence in the 1960s of a new generation under the leadership of Jürgen Habermas (1929-), who radically revised critical theory to ensure its continuing relevance as a critique of the emergent form of advanced capitalism (McCarthy 1978). Of great strategic importance here was continuing an active engagement with the developments throughout the human sciences and philosophy, in contrast to the continuing insularity and dogmatism of much of the neo-Marxist tradition, which tended to refer to critical theory with the pejorative term *revisionism*. A number of German scholars, such as Wolfgang Bonß, Helmut Dubiel, Klaus Eder, Axel Honneth, Hans Joas, Claus Offe, and Albrecht Wellmer have continued to explore issues in ways strongly influenced by Habermas's approach. Nevertheless it should be stressed that despite a certain popularity in late 1960s, the Frankfurt tradition has always had a marginal–if quite visible–place in postwar German sociology (Meja et al. 1987; Lüschen 1979).

Today, however, the term *critical theory* has also come to be associated with various theorists in different national traditions (and disciplines) often directly influenced by this earlier tradition, but with many more recent and independent developments as well. Although until the last decade or so, many of these tendencies (e.g., Mills) would have been associated with some notion of a radical conflict theory, today the generic notion of critical theory is perhaps a more useful designation and invites a definition of the problematic that goes beyond its specific national origins or roots in debates in classical sociological theory.

French Connections

Despite a significant reception of both the earlier Frankfurt and contemporary critical theory during the past decade or so (Ferry 1987), the label "critical theory" does not apply easily to any high profile group in France, though it does in French Quebec (Rioux, 1978; Nielsen 1985). But as is evident in the influence of French debates on contemporary critical theory, many affinities and some subtle mutual influences are found. A looser definition also would include many whose work complements critical theory (often reflected in citations by critical theorists) without being explicitly identified with it: the work of the contemporary sociologists Alain Touraine (Touraine 1977) and Pierre Bourdieu (Bourdieu 1977), as well as that of the late philosopher and historian Michel Foucault (Foucault 1984).

Anglo American Adaptations

Ironically critical theory now flourishes above all in the English-speaking world. Examples of contemporary British and North American sociologists and social, political, and cultural theorists closely associated with critical theory are the work of Zygmunt Bauman, Anthony Giddens, David Held, John Keane, William Outhwaite, and John B. Thompson in Britain;[5] Ben Agger, Robert Antonio, Andrew Arato, Stanley Aronowitz, Seyla Benhabib, Richard Bernstein, Norman Birnbaum, Craig Calhoun, Jean Cohen, Fred Dallmayr, Nancy Fraser, Henry Giroux, Alvin Gouldner, Martin Jay, Douglas Kellner, Tim Luke, Tom McCarthy, Paul Piccone, Mark Poster, and Philip Wexler in the United States; Barry Adam, Gregory Baum, Ioan Davies, Rick Gruneau, Barb Marshall, William Leiss, Greg Nielsen, John O'Neill, Marcel Rioux, and Charles Taylor in Canada; and in Australia and New Zealand in work associated with the journal *Thesis Eleven* (e.g., Beilharz et al. 1992) and individuals such as Johann Arnason, Bob Connell, Michael Pusey, Robert E. Young, and Barry Smart.[6] The diversity of critical theory today is especially evident in sociologically oriented journals such as *Theory, Culture and Society,* and *Theory and Society* but also throughout the human sciences generally.[7]

Used in a looser sense, the term *critical theory* has become increasingly applicable to forms of what was earlier a quite distinctive intellectual tendency: British *cultural Marxism* (and related forms of cultural studies) associated with the literary critic and cultural theorist Raymond Williams, the social historian E. P. Thompson, and the cultural studies Stuart Hall helped define (G. Turner 1990). What is characteristic about this British tradition is that Marx is interpreted from the perspective of the Italian philosopher Antonio Gramsci (1891-1937) or as a historical sociologist concerned with the particularity and cultural aspects of social transformations, not simply explaining them in terms of abstract economic laws (Harris 1992; D. Sayer 1987). More recent work associated with such revisionist cultural materialism clearly converges with debates within contemporary critical theory (Morrow 1991a).

The Boundaries of Critical Theory

An important aspect of our approach, however, is to stress the discontinuities between contemporary critical theories of society and the neo-Marxist tradition with which they would otherwise commonly be associated. This strategy has both polemical and substantive justifications. Polemically, it is both counterproductive and misleading to conflate the variety of approaches that have been influenced by the Marxian tradition. Substantively, for more than a half century critical theories have rejected many of the most fundamental tenets of the Marxian tradition and have been influenced decisively by a number of non-Marxist contributions. Thus we would follow those who clearly differentiate between any notion of a "Marxist sociology" or "Marxism as science" from critical social theory or critical theories of society (Morrow 1992a). Whereas both could be considered forms of what often has been termed either *critical sociology* or *critical social science,* critical theory clearly is linked with a distinctive set of positions that set it apart.[8] Whether or in what sense the resulting contemporary critical theory may be post-Marxist remains highly contested—and a question to which we will return in a moment.[9]

In the present context, we employ the term *critical theory* in a broadly ecumenical manner, with the boundary of *neo-Marxist theory* on its left and *neo-Weberian conflict theory* on its right.

Neo-Marxist theory is defined by its continuing concern to establish the scientific character of Marx's theory in terms of the explanations building on a deterministic concept of modes of production (Wright 1985, 1989; Wood 1986). Critical theory, in contrast, argues that Marx's theory needs to be reconstructed in decisive ways.[10]

Neo-Weberian theory, on the other hand, provides important insights with respect to how to reconstruct Marx—for example, the need for understanding social classes with respect to their non-economic aspects, the importance of subjectivity and values in social life, the state as a form of power independent of the economy, and the significance of bureaucratization and science in modern society. But unlike critical theories, neo-Weberian theories have rejected use of such knowledge as the basis of a programmatic critique of contemporary society (Parkin 1979; Collins 1986, 1990).

Although critical theories have been influenced by the theoretical challenges and empirical findings of both of these traditions, they have resisted assimilation or identification of either of these flanking positions on a number of grounds: epistemological, methodological, analytical, and political. Yet it is important to acknowledge the affinities and the fruitful dialogue that often have taken place in the competition among these approaches.

Although critical theory in the Frankfurt tradition was never fully unified, a new configuration of differences emerged in the 1980s: "Perhaps the crucial aspect of this new constellation is the breakup of Critical Theory, particularly the separation made between Habermas, on the one hand, and Adorno and Benjamin, on the other" (Hohendahl 1991, p. 202). The work of Habermas is more popular among philosophers and social scientists because it addresses more familiar problems and largely rejects the more speculative themes found in Adorno and Benjamin's concern with the Marxian theory of history and aesthetic theory. The primary concern of this study, given the focus on the methodology of the social sciences, will be the tendency represented by Habermas.

Two social theorists are used in this study as the primary contemporary exemplars of such a project for critical theory as a form of critical social science: Jürgen Habermas (1929-) whose work originated in the trajectory of the early Frankfurt School in the late 1950s, but latter developed a systematic methodological revision of critical theory from the late 1960s; and Anthony Giddens (1938-), a British sociologist who developed an independent version of critical theory in the 1970s onward. No one would dispute Habermas's status in this regard, and his name is most strongly associated with the term *critical theory* today.[11] More problematic is the significance of his continuing affinities with the tradition of Western Marxism, an affiliation he has not found necessary to renounce. Many others have concluded, however, that "the construct of 'Western Marxism' has lost some of its usefulness for the present debate . . . Jürgen Habermas cannot be called a Western Marxist. . . . Boundaries that used to be stable have collapsed and new borderlines have emerged" (Hohendahl 1991, pp. 227-8). Accordingly the notion of contemporary critical theory used in this study recognizes the influence of the Marxist tradition but assumes that critical theory can no longer be described as a specifically Marxist approach.

The prominence of Giddens is more recent, but in the past several years an emerging secondary literature also suggests that his *structuration theory* is viewed as another major reference point for the claims of critical theory as a distinctive and influential approach to the human sciences.[12] The usefulness of Giddens stems, in part, from his sustained engagement with the issues of sociology as a discipline and its relation to other social sciences. Those who contest his status as a critical theorist (despite his self-designation in these terms) point to his explicit rejection of neo-Marxian theory, extensive use of neo-Weberian theory, and the lack of a fully workedout critique of contemporary society. Yet for the purposes of the methodological focus of this study, these aspects of Giddens's approach are often an advantage because the resulting theoretical approach is both very open-ended and methodologically self-conscious; as well, it dovetails nicely with the more philosophical orientation of Habermas and his inevitable neglect of many issues of concern to practicing social researchers.

Critical Theory Now

Ideological Crisis

Disputes about the relationship between contemporary critical theory and the Marxist tradition are linked closely to the fact that the ideological formations traditionally associated with liberalism and socialism have ceased to be adequate to the tasks of a progressive development of contemporary politics. The partial successes of neoconservatism—a return to the classical liberal notion that the invisible hand of markets will solve all of our problems—can be attributed to a great extent to the chronic inability of the prophets of 19th century progress to extend their linear visions of growth ad infinitum into the future. The question of "critical theory now" cannot escape the fundamental challenges that have eroded—or perhaps even exhausted—the utopian aspirations underlying the project of critical theory (Wexler 1991; Habermas 1989, pp. 48-70).

As a consequence a triple loss of faith is apparent in the West: (a) *politically,* the breakdown of the "great transformation" whereby free markets were to be succeeded by democratic planning, (b) *scientifically,* a loss of the faith in reason (and science) that would rationally guide this process, and (c) *morally,* pervasive challenges to the universalistic values embodied in the theories of natural rights associated with modernity.

We propose to provide an introduction to an alternative discourse that has long sought to address these issues. In the process I attempt to weave together an incredibly complex story about what has happened in the human sciences during the past few decades from the perspective of a constructive counterdiscourse.

The Post-Marxist Context and Postmodernism

The intellectual paradox of the 1990s must be confronted at the outset: Marx was fully rehabilitated in Anglo American scholarship as a fully credible empirical social scientist in the very decade—the 1980s—that culminated in the practical repudiation of Marxism as a universal, world-historical ideology of revolutionary progress. The theoretical and methodological opening

of Anglo American social science during the past two decades
has for the first time lowered the ideological resistances to a fairer
assessment of neo-Marxist and critical theories, as well as a more
acute analysis of their very important differences. But at the
same time, that lowering of boundaries has, in part, been largely
on the terms of the reigning empiricism, which, for the most
part, finds a "scientific Marx" more congenial than the form of
interpretive critical theory which is defended here.

As a consequence, contemporary critical theory, as opposed
to neo-Marxist theory, has a very different relationship to two
intellectual phenomena that have gained increasing currency in
the avant-garde intellectual marketplace: *post-Marxism* and *postmodernism*. The term *post-Marxist* has two key connotations.
The first is theoretical in the sense of suggesting approaches that
once identified themselves as part of the Marxian tradition but
have found it necessary to break with Marx on a number of
fundamental methodological and substantive issues to deal with
the intellectual "crisis of historical materialism" (Aronowitz
1981; Laclau and Mouffe 1985). Critical theory is arguably post-
Marxist in this sense, which should not be confused with the
simple obsolescence of the issues posed by the Marxian tradition. The second meaning is political and historical and is associated with the year 1989 and the fall of Soviet-style regimes as
credible models of "socialism" and "communism." Although the
term *post-Marxist* was popularized only in the 1980s, it can be
argued that critical theory has been broadly post-Marxist in both
respects for several decades.

The relationship of critical theory as a form of *modernist
theorizing* to *postmodernist social theory* is a much more complex topic, one for which only an orienting sketch can be provided here. In its most widely understood version, postmodernist
social theory is associated with the claim that totalizing theories
of society and history are obsolete and that social theory must
content itself with local analyzes that accept the essential relativity of all values and modes of cognition. Such postmodernism
is clearly incompatible with critical theory, and yet many of the
critiques by critical theorists directed against Marxism and sociological functionalism are uncannily parallel. For this reason a
number of critical theorists have argued that a critical appro-

priation of postmodernist social theory is one of the crucial challenges of contemporary critical theory (Poster 1989; Agger 1991; McCarthy 1991). Although this is not a theme that we pursue in any detail, it is consistent with our overall conception of the openness of critical theory and its break with the Marxist tradition.

Different forms of sociology serve different practical and theoretical purposes, some obviously legitimate, others problematic. *Our primary task is to carve out a niche for a particular type of sociology that is distinct from neo-Marxist theory, highly theoretical, yet attempts to link these insights to appropriate forms of evidence and reflections on social practice.* In the process we seek to address the challenge voiced by Lewis Coser, a theorist in the senior generation of American sociologists, who recently called for recognizing the "virtues of dissent in sociology": "All one can hope for . . . is that the voice of critical sociologists that has become so muted of late be again heard loud and clear. They should not monopolize the sociological forum, but they must be heard" (Coser 1990, p. 212). But the problem of "hearing" is related closely to difficulties of communication that we have attempted to address, in part, through a step-by-step introduction to the theoretical debates presupposed by understanding critical theory as a research program.

The Neglect of Methodology and the Empirical Turn

We thus seek to address one of the great points of vulnerability of the tradition of critical theory: its relation to empirical methods in the paradoxical context of the cross fire of attacks from positivists who claim it is antiscientific, on the one hand, and the postmodernists who declare its scientific and rationalistic aspirations an Enlightenment illusion on the other hand. This question of the scientific status of critical theory has been especially important from the disciplinary perspective of sociology. Many in other disciplines simply might reply that sociologists are obsessed with numbers and are best forgotten. Dealing with these foundational methodological issues, however, is of crucial long-term importance for the credibility of any marginalized

perspective. Not surprisingly these issues largely have been ignored beyond the early critique of positivism, especially on the
part of critical theories that have been skeptical of what often
has been characterized as Marxist positivism.

The present approach attempts to rescue the methodological
foundations of critical theory as a research program with empirical dimensions, but not in the classic manner of conceiving
Marxism as a positive, naturalistic science. Instead the present
strategy is linked to what has been referred to as "the applied turn
in contemporary critical theory," wherein "applied" refers "not
to instrumental application but to critical, empirically and historically oriented appropriation" (Forester 1985b, p. xvii). The
consequence is to locate actors "within more encompassing
structural settings of relations of power and control. The de-
emphasis of class analysis notwithstanding, this move distinguishes these analyses both from traditionally functionalist and
from more voluntaristic, pluralist accounts. Critical theory thus
makes possible the concrete analysis of structure and of contin-
gently staged social action" (Forester 1985b, p. xiii).

We label this methodological approach *interpretive structuralism* (or *hermeneutic structuralism*), terms designed to convey several central principles whose full implications are elaborated in the chapters that follow: that social relations and social
analysis always have an interpretive (hermeneutic) dimension;
that meaning and language (hence discourses) are the basis of
forms of reality construction that both reveal and conceal the
experiences of subjects; that structures may be species-specific
or historically constituted and sometimes consciously transformed
even if they have a kind of objective facticity that appears
independent of immediate actors; that social and cultural structures constrain human action as does a grammar language, hence
not in the way implied by variables as probalistic determinants;
and that meaning and structures constantly are reproduced
(statically) and produced (dynamically) across space and time.[13]

This neglect of methodological questions has contributed to a
fourfold vulnerability for critical theory. First, the dominance of
a restrictive conception of method patterned on the natural
sciences has made it difficult to assess the claims of other types
of methods and forms of explanation that have been either

excluded as having no scientific status or given a rather marginal place as useful as "preliminaries" to research, but not essential to doing "real" social science.

Second, the tendency has been for critical theory to be defensive—that is, to be more concerned with criticizing other approaches than outlining its own research program or even pointing to work consistent with it.

Third, the ideological context of research funding has contributed strongly to the isolation of critical theories from engagement with empirical research. Further, much research that could be considered a form of critical research does not overtly or explicitly define itself in such terms.

Fourth, there is an important sense in which the methodological approaches associated with critical theories do not provide the immediate psychological gratifications, expedient results, and marketable skills often associated with the appeal of "methods" and "techniques" in a market-oriented culture. We do not propose here to provide useful practical skills in the sense of ordinary cookbook methods texts in the social sciences. What we do seek is much closer to the spirit of so-called theory construction texts but from a rather different perspective: *the methodological implications of a critical theory of society as an interpretive structuralist research program.*

The focus of this strategy is thus methodological, rather than substantive or policy oriented. We do not propose to reconstruct in detail the specific analysis of advanced capitalism proposed by various critical theories. Nor do we propose to suggest the answers that critical theory might have about "what is to be done." Although these are important questions and we allude to contributions that deal with such issues, our immediate task is an analysis of strategies of inquiry that provide reflexive responses to this triple loss of faith in politics, science, and universal morality. For many, a methodological focus is not only unexciting, but it also appears as a distraction from "getting on" with real research, substantive theorizing, or political activism. Such impatience is understandable but ultimately not fully defensible, especially in transitional phases of scientific inquiry when nothing can be taken for granted anymore.

Critiques of Critical Theory

Given its long and complex history over more than half a century, it is not surprising that critical theory has been associated with many different—and often conflicting—images and subjected to a wide variety of criticism. One of the more remarkable aspects of critical theory—and part of its claim to scientific credibility—has been its ability to often constructively respond to criticism even if this is not always explicitly acknowledged. It is thus fitting to conclude this introductory chapter by considering three important types of criticism, two of which stretch back to the past (charges of being antiscientific and elitist) and another that has emerged more recently—the accusation of excessive rationalism.

Antiscientific?

Why the charge of being antiscientific? Because the point of departure of critical theory is to pose philosophical questions about the nature of types of knowledge, including an explicit rejection of the traditional way the sciences have understood themselves and the so-called "scientific method." So critical theory is associated justly with those who reject the characterization of sociology in natural scientific terms by reference to its ability to measure social facts and its ability to develop general laws of social life. As well, critical theory has not been clearly associated with a specific or unique method that would facilitate the development of a specialized empirical research program in the conventional sense. As a consequence it often is faulted with being irrelevant to empirical research altogether.

Given the methodological emphasis of our reconstruction of critical theory, it is consistent that we insist that critical theory be considered a form of social science—as a research program—distinct from an *ideology* in the sense of an action-oriented belief system that allows political commitments to override the criticisms of the facts. To be sure, critical research has a strong ideological content, but this is held in check by the commitment to analyze social reality.

As it happens, critical theories of society are associated closely with ideologies and, in fact, often are rejected as too ideological

to claim to be proper social science. From our perspective, this
is one of critical theory's peculiar strengths, rather than a weak-
ness to be excised in the name of objectivity. Because these
ideological assumptions are made explicit, they can be subjected
overtly to rational debate in terms of the legitimacy of the values
they embody and the social forms through which they might be
brought to life. But the tasks of critical theory are not those of
an ideology or a social movement, however much they may serve
to inform ideologies and activists. This is not to defend some
kind of abstract objectivity or purity with respect to practice,
so much as to affirm the basic autonomy required for any intellectual enterprise to form a community of understanding based
on rational assent, rather than faith, revelation, or—closer to home—
immediate implications for transformative praxis.

Too Elitist?

Why the charge of elitism? Primarily because representatives
of critical theory have been faulted with writing obscurely
(using pretentious philosophical language) and having failed to
establish the practical relevance of their ideas. Yet any form of
radical interrogation of reality requires literally going to the "roots"
of things. To engage in such fundamental inquiries often nec-
essitates asking new kinds of questions and using the resources
of the Western philosophical tradition for rethinking the
grounds of social theory. Ironically, in its first reception in
the English-speaking world in the context of student movements
and the New Left in the late 1960s, critical social theory often
was associated with anti-intellectualism and mindless political
activism (Gouldner 1971). Two decades later, however, critical
theory often is chastised as an ivory tower phenomenon jeal-
ously guided by careerist intellectual mandarins (Jacoby 1987).

Viewed more closely, the deeper aspirations of contemporary
critical theory are very different. On the one hand, critical theory
aspires to facilitate a democratization of knowledge in the sense
that every person is recognized de facto as a philosopher and
encouraged to develop the faculties of fundamental questioning.
At the same time, however, there is a refusal to identify the adequacy of theories with their immediate accessibility. A side of
scientific inquiry is also inevitably elitist in the sense that novel

interpretations of nature and society are often difficult to grasp
and translate into popular formulations. Although proponents of
critical social theory have engaged in defensive responses to critics, hence could be interpreted as elitist in the pejorative sense,
this should not obscure the more fundamental problem of communicating certain types of ideas in a culture whose fundamental categories tend to exclude philosophical and theoretical
reflection. If we focus extensively on explicating such concepts,
it is because we sympathize with the assumption that, in the
right contexts, common sense can be reconstructed through philosophical reflection. Further, it is only in this manner that the
questions of critical social theory can be brought to the level of
introductory sociology where it is otherwise largely invisible or
tucked away under a brief vulgarization of Marxist theory.[14]

Too Rationalistic?

If the self-understanding of science is questioned, it is done so
in the name of deepening our understanding of reason, not in
defense of unreason. In the current conjuncture, associated with
widespread attacks on the very notion of science, or sociology
as a scientific activity that should attempt to comprehend overall
processes, the meaning of critical theory's antipositivism can be
seen in a different light. Given the attacks on social science by
certain types of postmodernist social theory, critical theory
now, paradoxically, is charged with being too rational and scientific in its theoretical aspirations (Lyotard 1984). According to
many postmodernist theorists, the modernist and Enlightenment
emphasis on reason and science has been eclipsed, along with
"grand theories" of society, history, and human nature.[15]

As implied above, it is possible to identify a modernist and
postmodernist strain of critical theory. The modernist strain—
most visibly represented in the work of Habermas and Giddens—
identifies strongly with a revised Enlightenment concept of
reason as the basis for individual and group emancipation even
though it argues that this reason has been understood in a
superficial way by positivism. From this perspective, theories of
society still have a major role to play in explaining social life,
though they retreat from the stronger claims of positivist functionalism and structural Marxism as "grand narratives." Postmodernist

social theory in its strong forms is associated with a skeptical position that denounces not only positivism but also the whole Enlightenment project associated with ideals of human progress based on scientific reason. From this perspective all attempts to explain social life in terms of "grand narratives" is illusory even in the more modest form proposed by contemporary critical theory (Lyotard 1984; Seidman and Wagner 1992; Morrow and Torres Forthcoming).

Although this study generally defends the stance taken by Habermas and Giddens in this context, it is also important to acknowledge the significant—if often diffuse—impact of post-modernist theory on contemporary critical theory (Fekete 1987; Poster 1989; Luke 1990; Morrow 1991a; McCarthy 1991; Agger 1992b; Smart 1992). Indeed it is possible to speak of a species of *postmodernist critical theory* that, although agreeing with aspects of the critique of grand narratives, does not want to throw out altogether any basis for a critique of power and domination. Although retaining a similar political engagement in its opposition to orthodoxies of Marxism and academic disciplines, postmodern critical theory—as in the work of Michel Foucault—"indicts, sometimes explicitly, more often implicitly, the idea that modernity contains within itself the potential for human emancipation" (Leonard 1990, p. xiv). As will become apparent, the particular tasks of this book are confined largely to the modernist wing where the enlightening and transformative potentials of an empirical social science still remains central, though not in the same way as neo-Marxist positivism or mainstream social science. Nevertheless it is important to note that modernist critical theory both anticipated and increasingly has responded to questions posed by postmodernism. Further, critical theory understood in these terms has the potential to incorporate selectively the insights of postmodernist theorizing.

It is particularly significant that critical theory has been charged with being both too ideological and too rationally scientific, a tension most obvious in the case of Habermas: "Much of the criticism generated by this rather bold attempt has fallen precisely here. Either he has erred on the side of science or on the side of passion" (Rasmussen 1990, p. 7). The focus of this particular study necessarily entails defending this scientific side against critics who associate critical theory with mere ideology and ungrounded theoretical speculation.

At the outset the reader should be warned of the limits and objectives of our project. First, although attempting to avoid sectarianism and dogmatic partisanship, our approach to theory and methods is from a specific perspective that challenges many of the assumptions of "mainstream" social science. To this extent it is constructively (and dialogically) partisan: It seeks to take the principle of C. Wright Mills's notion of sociological imagination in a domain—methodology—that has been largely neglected.

Second, this strategy involves taking a specific position with respect to divisions within critical theory and its relation to both the Marxist tradition and postmodernist theory. We hope this necessary positioning will not polemically distract readers from our more fundamental theoretical arguments about methodology and social research.

Third, this is a study concerned with the relationships between theory, methodology, and empirical research, but is not a "methods" text in the strict sense, which ultimately would contradict the spirit of critical theory. Our task is thus much broader and more fundamental, one that seeks to link theory, methodology, specific research strategies, and social criticism. As a consequence much of what we present should be of value to many of those who do not directly identify with the research program of critical theory as a whole.

An Agenda

Developing this approach requires moving in sequential steps. First, in Part I, it is necessary to dwell extensively on the basic concepts necessary for talking about social theory and methodology. In this, Chapter 1, the task has been to provide an overview of critical theory as social theory, thus anticipating the issues to be covered in greater depth in the chapters that follow. Chapter 2 furthers this orienting task by reviewing the conceptual language (metatheory) usually associated with the philosophy of science and social science. Chapter 3 takes up the problem of grounding methodology through metatheoretical analysis by exploring the relationship between empiricist (positivist) and postempiricist philosophies of science.

Part II is concerned with outlining the basic assumption of critical theory as a strategy of inquiry, hence as a research program. Chapter 4 addresses the broader historical question of the development of a tradition of critical social research, one initially associated with Western Marxism but developing in various directions through the Frankfurt School tradition. Chapter 5 traces some of the key debates in the metatheory of the human sciences that influenced the reformulation of critical theory in the 1960s and 1970s. Then Chapter 6 reconstructs the central themes of the critical metatheory developed by Habermas and Giddens, whereas Chapter 7 moves on to a more systematic presentation of their conceptions of critical theory as a contemporary research program.

Part III turns to the question of how this methodological approach looks in practice. Chapter 8 is concerned with the methodological implications of critical theory's research program in the context of how it rejects the quantitative-qualitative distinction that informs contemporary approaches to methodology in sociology. Instead a distinction is made between intensive, and extensive approaches to inquiry. Chapter 9 explicates the kinds of non-empirical or reflexive procedures taken by critical theory to be central from a postempiricist perspective. Chapter 10 considers the type of empirical methods, techniques, and research designs that tend to be favored by critical social research, given its specific interests in social analysis. For the most part these are standard procedures but are organized in terms of different configurations and for distinctive purposes. In Chapter 11 three key contexts of contemporary critical research are reviewed: the state and political economy, cultural analysis, and social psychology. The concluding Chapter 12 turns to the interplay between society and social research by contrasting competing models of social science and outlining the multiple relationships of critical research to social practice.

Notes

1. Unfortunately the term *critical theory* also refers in literary studies to "theories of criticism." Partly for this reason, the term *Frankfurt School* is used in the specialized social scientific dictionaries that have become indispensable guides to the remarkable transformation of the vocabulary of the human sciences during the past two decades (Held 1983; Abercrombie et al. 1988, p. 99; Jary and Jary 1991, pp. 237-8; Honneth 1993, pp. 232-5; Angenot 1979). But the term *Frankfurt School* is no longer adequate to indicate the range of issues included under the heading of "critical theory" today (Billings 1992; Nielsen 1993a, 1993b).

2. We often will employ the term *empiricist* where others would write merely *empirical*. The reason is that in sociology the notion of *empirical methods* often is associated exclusively with variable analysis, as if ethnographic research was not empirical (an analysis of social reality), and as if participant observation was not an empirical method. Therefore an *empiricist* approach is one based on epistemological empiricism, hence forms of positivism that very narrowly construe what kinds of methods or explanatory strategies produce valid knowledge.

3. Of crucial significance here is Durkheim's use of "structuralist," as opposed to "empiricist," methods in his later work on the sociology of religion.

4. More familiar to sociologists until the past decade was the closely related contemporary work of Karl Mannheim (1936) in Frankfurt, whose *sociology of knowledge* also was concerned with the social origins of belief systems. Because Mannheim's approach was explicitly non-Marxist, his dismissal of Marx allowed him to bypass many of the important issues of concern to the original Critical Theorists. On the other hand, his eventual abandonment of the Hegelian theory of history anticipated aspects of Habermas's reconstruction of historical materialism.

5. Such labels become particularly difficult in Britain, given the extensive influence of the issues associated with critical theory in sociology generally, the decline of neo-Marxist theory, and frequent revisions of earlier theoretical positions.

6. In the United States the journal *Telos,* edited by Paul Piccone, performed an indispensable function from the late 1960s of introducing critical theory to the English-speaking world; the *New Left Review* performed a similar task in Britain, though from a more consistently neo-Marxist perspective within which critical theory often was viewed negatively or ambivalently; and the *Canadian Journal of Political and Social Theory,* edited by Arthur and Marilouise Kroker, contributed to similar debates from the late 1970s until its postmodernist about turn and more recent demise.

7. Apologies to those arbitrarily excluded (e.g., a number of philosophers and intellectual historians) and those uncomfortably included. Such listings are inevitably problematic but serve to cast a wide, interdisciplinary and international net in naming family resemblances within a recognizable community despite diffuse boundaries.

8. Some authors have linked Frankfurt type critical theory as identical with both the terms *critical sociology* (Connerton 1976) and *critical social science*

(Fay 1987). This usage is confusing, given that neo-Marxist theory generally, and analytical Marxism in particular, could be considered forms of critical social science as well.

9. For a somewhat different approach, see Antonio (1990, p. 109) who traces how Marxist theory "has changed and fragmented in response to the disjunctive pattern of social and political change," resulting in the rise of "pluralistic, discursive, and open-ended Marxism."

10. This reconstructive stance is shared in many respects with *analytical Marxism,* an approach that remains closer to positivism, defends a number of more orthodox Marxian constructs, and attempts to use rational choice theory to deal with the social psychological deficit in classical historical materialism (Roemer 1986). But analytical Marxism's focus on rational choice theories does put it in the postempiricist camp (Bohman 1991, pp. 67-76).

11. As of 1981 a bibliographical study of Habermas and the reception of his work noted nearly 1,000 items in the secondary literature (Görtzen 1982); a supplementary version can be found in Görtzen 1990. As well, several anthologies are organized around debates with Habermas and his work: Thompson and Held 1982; Bernstein 1985; Honneth et al. 1992; Calhoun 1992b. Finally, beyond more specialized studies are a number of synthetic and introductory presentations of his work: Schroyer 1975; McCarthy 1978; Roderick 1986; Pusey 1987; Ingram 1987; White 1988; Brand 1990; Braaten 1991; Holub 1991.

12. The following anthologies discuss Giddens's work and reference the secondary literature: Held and Thompson 1989; Clark and Modgil 1990; Bryant and Jary 1991. The following books also are devoted to Giddens as a social theorist: I. J. Cohen 1989; Haugaard 1992; Craib 1992. Structuration theory—the term used to characterize Giddens's approach—is an entry in some of the more recent sociological dictionaries (Abercrombie et al. 1988; Jary and Jary 1991; Cohen 1993).

13. The term *interpretive structuralism* is used synonymously with *hermeneutic structuralism* and *historical* or *historicist structuralism.* We do not know of any prior use of these terms in this way, though they appear to provide a rather natural manner of expressing the methodological framework shared by the classical historical analysis described by Mills, Habermas's theory of communicative action, Giddens's structuration theory, or Bourdieu's theory of practice. We would trace our own understanding of the reconciliation of hermeneutics and structuralism back to the seminal interventions of Paul Ricoeur in the 1960s (Ricoeur 1974). In effect we collapse into interpretive structuralism the complementary aspects of what potentially is obscured by Waters's (1994) otherwise useful typology differentiating constructionism, functionalism, utilitarianism, and critical structuralism. He locates Giddens's structuration theory as a form of constructionism and Habermas's communicationism as a form of critical structuralism. Both are somewhat anomalous in their respective categories (whose founders are respectively Weber and Marx), however, because Giddens has a serious interest in structure, as does Habermas in agency. Later we describe these complementarities as respectively "weak" and "strong" research programs for critical theory. As Waters (1994), Archer (1990), Mouzelis (1991), and others argue, there are unresolved problems with respect to the status of "structure" in Giddens's schema.

14. For exceptions, see Giddens 1982b, 1989b; Li and Bolaria 1993; Morrow 1993 and the remarkable four-volume introductory series prepared by the Open University in Britain and edited by Stuart Hall and others (Hall et al. 1992).

15. The status of "grand theory" has had its ups and downs. Attacked by Mills (1967), its return was anthologized (Skinner 1985) at about the same time its demise was celebrated (Lyotard 1984). Part of the confusion stems from the specific type of grand theory in question.

2

FOUNDATIONS OF
METATHEORY

Between Subjectivism
and Objectivism

What is "theory"? The question seems a rather easy one for contemporary science. . . . Theory for most researchers is the summary of propositions about a subject, the propositions being so linked to one another that a few are basic and the rest derive from these. . . . The real validity of the theory depends on the derived propositions being consonant with the actual facts. . . .Theory is stored-up knowledge, put in a form that makes it useful for the closest possible description of facts.
(Horkheimer [1937] 1972a, p. 188)

The preceding chapter made a number of claims about a particular kind of sociological theory defined as *critical theory*. Why should such claims be taken seriously? In other words, how does one attempt to *ground* or *justify* a theoretical approach? To answer such questions, we need to turn to the fundamental questions of the philosophy of the human and social sciences.[1]

In short, before embarking on a discussion of either critiques of positivism or a reconstruction of the approach of critical theory, it is necessary to introduce the basic concepts of *metatheory* (theory about theory) in relatively neutral terms and without all of the complications involved in defending specific positions and reviewing complex debates. Some of the positions associated

with critical theory have been introduced in the introductory
chapter, but we now need to work through some basic concepts
more carefully. Readers well versed in these basic con- cepts may
elect to move immediately on to the next chapter.

Such an introduction is necessary above all in the North American context where, aside from a few specializing in social theory
or those influenced by feminist theory, the vocabulary of metatheory—defined largely by methodologists—remains that of positivism in the social sciences. Further, other forms of philosophy have
largely been excluded from the curriculum, thus discouraging
the modes of self-reflection required to pose fundamental questions about the nature and implications of the human sciences.

This chapter is best read as a primer in metatheory or the philosophy of the social sciences or in *methodology* if this term is
understood in its philosophical sense as distinct from *methods*. Although the terms often are used synonymously, some
researchers (especially in the European tradition) have insisted
on preserving a subtle distinction between the two.[2] For example, this book is primarily a study in social methodology, not
methods. The term *methods* refers more specifically to individual
techniques (e.g., surveys, participant observation), whereas *methodology* can be construed broadly to suggest both the presuppositions of methods, as well as their link to theory and implications for society. Methodology, in short, more clearly implies a
concern, an overall *strategy* of constructing specific types of
knowledge and is justified by a variety of metatheoretical assumptions. Methodology is thus inevitably *prescriptive* because
it attempts to legitimate the use of particular methods in ways
that are consistent with the development of the specific theory in
question. Although critical theory cannot be defined exclusively
in terms of a specific method, it does suggest a distinct methodological strategy and a unique research program. How does
methodology provide this legitimation? Primarily it does so by
recourse to criteria about what science—in this case a human or
social science— should be (the problem of metatheory, or theory
about theory).

Approaching Methodology

The Conventional Literature

Three types of texts typically are referred to in the context of training in methods and methodology in social research. Most often texts in methods have taken the form of "how-to-do-it" cookbooks (Babbie 1983; Wimmer and Dominick 1983). Such texts reflect very directly the theory-methods split found throughout the social sciences and reproduced in the undergraduate curriculum. They typically begin with a ritualistic positivistic account of "the *scientific method*"–understood as a universal procedure involving the testing of theories by reference to the facts. Further, such texts are based on a problematic distinction–which we consider later in detail–between "quantitative" and "qualitative" methods, with a focus on the former. Qualitative methods are introduced peripherally and from a framework derived from the idealized model of quantitative methods. The result is a tendency to conflate methodology with statistics, given the strategic role of the latter in quantitative research. The discussion of quantitative methods tends to be rather selective (varying with the discipline) but focuses on the logic of experimental design and the practicalities of the evaluation of attitudinal survey data. For the most part, each method is presented individually as a technique even if some authors may point to the possibility of *multiple methods* or *methodological triangulation*. The nature of social science is largely taken for granted and is based on models ostensibly derived from the natural sciences and "logic." Usually a brief discussion of the ethics of research touches on problems involved in deluding experimental subjects, falsifying data, and possible misuses of social science in the wrong hands. Such texts rationalize themselves under the rubric of "the sociological method" (Cole 1980) and in the name of "the logic of science in sociology" (Wallace 1971).[3]

"Theory construction" approaches, on the other hand, attempt to break down the theory-method split, but still remain largely confined to the statistical analysis of variables and related modes of theorizing (Stinchcombe 1968; B. Cohen 1989). Here attention shifts from the testing of given theories to strategies for generating new theoretically based propositions.

A third type of text ranges more broadly under the heading of introductions to the "philosophy of social science."[4] Written primarily by philosophers, these studies often cover important recent theoretical debates but remain distant from more specific methodological questions.[5] Although such books touch on issues and concepts that should be included in introductory methodology texts, they are virtually ignored by social scientists.

The present study thus falls between the theory construction and philosophy of social science treatments along lines shared in recent accounts influenced by feminist, phenomenological, and interactionist approaches (e.g., Nielsen 1990; Kirby and McKenna 1989; Denzin 1989). Not surprisingly it is in the context of such somewhat defensive countermethodologies that we find a deeper reflection on the problematic of methodology. Although generally sympathetic with these alternative methodologies, we would seek to place them on a broader foundation and move away from the more skeptical and relativistic tendencies they often represent.

To summarize: The teaching of methodology and methods in sociology and related disciplines is characterized by a series of dominant and largely taken-for-granted assumptions: that some single, unifying scientific "method" is shared by the natural and social sciences; that this method takes two forms in social science that can be described adequately as quantitative (primarily variable analysis) and qualitative; and that questions of social scientific methodology can be reduced to the study of the different qualitative and quantitative techniques for collecting data. Before these kinds of assumptions can be questioned, however, it is necessary to develop an understanding of a number of metatheoretical distinctions useful for comparing and assessing different methodologies and theories.

Toward a Critical Theory of Methodology

Aspects of the methodology of critical theory have been discussed extensively, especially at advanced levels. Some even have claimed that "critical theory embodies the most perspicacious extant understanding of what social inquiry is and must be"

(Leonard 1990, p. xiv); as well, it has succeeded in stimulating a vast body of empirical research, as well as reinterpreting research originating in other approaches. Yet there has been very little discussion at a more introductory level of the actual consequences for methodology training and social research practice.[6] Although a number of excellent and more specialized studies in the various national traditions of critical theory touch on methodology, they are neither very accessible nor concerned with the range of issues under examination here (Fay 1975, 1987; Habermas 1988; Wellmer 1971; Giddens 1976; Morrow 1991c). Although there is clearly a *critical theory of methodology*, it does not have a visible position within the curriculum of the social sciences.

Why this absence? Why this gap between an extensive tradition of critical empirical research, on the one hand, and guidelines for how to conceptualize and conduct such research, on the other? First, a number of circumstantial, historical factors are at work here. The original body of empirical research in the Frankfurt School stems from the 1930s and 1940s and yet only became well known to social scientists in the 1970s. In between, the domination of positivism in sociology set the stage for a prolonged struggle for the legitimation of alternatives, a process that culminated in the emergence of social theory as a specialization. At the same time many others were engaged in critical empirical work in quite diverse settings, though often constrained in their theoretical and methodological self-understanding, given the reigning "norms" of social science. Only in the past decade, in short, has it become increasingly possible to reconcile critical theory and empirical research.

Even more fundamentally, however, breaking down the gap between critical theory and research requires calling into question the whole framework within which methodology normally is presented. Indeed one of the central claims of a critical theory of methodology is that these characteristics of methods and theory instruction are not accidental, inasmuch as they reveal the positivistic scientific culture in which they are embedded and cannot call into question: "Disciplinary discourse mirrors a contradictory social order and at the same time creates and recreates it . . . it presents the world implacably as a nest of 'social facts' whose depiction occupies everyday journal science" (Agger 1989, p. 3).

Orienting Definitions

What Is Theory?

The most fundamental obstacle to rethinking critical social theory and its relationship to methodology is the lack of a theoretical vocabulary—including crucial philosophical concepts—within which a critical theory of methodology can be understood and justified. The first step is to rid ourselves of some notion of a unified "scientific" language that stems from the natural sciences and that allows us to understand the human sciences. The concept of *methodology* is a difficult one, partly because it exists at the intersection of the multiple theoretical languages that constitute the *discourse* of social research. To speak of social science methodology as a discourse implies here simply that it involves a special mode of speaking that is distinct from common sense or even other "scientific" discourse, such as that in physics or chemistry. A discourse can be identified most readily and compared by analyzing its *narrative structure*—that is, the characteristic ways it tells the "stories" that make up and unify it as a particular system of meanings. For example, the narratives of scientific methodology are characterized by stories obsessed with questions about empirical evidence, proof, and validity that are quite distinct from those of theology, which focus on assessing beliefs in terms of their rational adequacy in expressing the meanings and values expressed in the Bible and a particular tradition of religious interpretation.

It is possible to distinguish three key theoretical languages (themselves distinctive discourses) that constitute and make possible the social sciences: *metatheory, empirical theory,* and *normative theory.* To view social analysis in this manner reminds us that every social scientific text is composed of forms of language that can be characterized as different types of sentences. The construction of social scientific knowledge is thus the end-product of the interplay of these different modes of analysis.

Typically the discourse of the human sciences falls along a continuum: At one pole are the *natural* or *ordinary* languages closest to common sense and everyday life account; and at the other extreme are the *formal* languages that construct abstract modes of purified symbolization, culminating in formal logic and mathematics.

Metatheory is the language of presuppositions—closely associated with the philosophy of science, or more specifically, philosophy of social science—through which a research orientation is legitimated and grounded (Ritzer 1991). For the sciences the key form of metatheory is *epistemology,* a branch of philosophy concerned with theories of knowledge or the criteria for determining whether a theory is "scientific." For example, when a researcher argues that introspection does not provide a valid basis for social psychological data collection, this conclusion requires invoking specific kinds of metatheoretical claims—that is, that such data are not adequate for the formulation of scientific propositions.

Empirical theory involves the descriptive and analytical (formal) languages through which social phenomena—what is the case—are interpreted and explained. To claim that the role of the state has changed fundamentally in the transition from early capitalism to advanced capitalism entails reference to empirical theories. This is the most common form of theorizing in the sciences.

Normative theory involves the modes of theorizing that legitimate different ethical, ideological, or policy positions with respect to what ought to be. To claim there should be more social justice or less inequality is thus a value judgment or normative statement.

What Is Science?

Implicitly we have been discussing a specific type of theory: scientific theory in the context of the special problems of social science. This qualification is important because other types of theory are essentially nonscientific, for example, theology as a rational reconstruction of a religious belief system, or political ideologies that express dogmatic beliefs about how society should be organized. Science is, of course, a belief system from a sociological point of view. In the modern world the sciences have assumed a unique and largely dominant position based on advancing knowledge claims that are held to be unique, thus taking precedence over other types of belief systems in many contexts.

The question of the distinctive nature of science can be viewed from three quite different perspectives: as a *mode of reasoning,* as a historical and institutional *form of social activity,* and as a *meaning system.* These three correspond roughly to what generally would be called the logic of science, its sociology, and its cultural implications as a worldview or *Weltanschauung.* In the past, science most often has been defined by philosophers primarily in terms of its logic, an approach that has trickled down in the common sense notion of using a scientific method. But scientific activity is a more complicated phenomenon than can be indicated by reference to some pure logic. Accordingly, throughout our study we refer again and again to these three perspectives on science.

Basic Concepts of Metatheory

Although we go into considerable in-depth discussion of all three of these languages of social theory—meta-, empirical, and normative theory—it is useful to begin some elementary definitions of metatheoretical terms. The following conceptual domains need to be introduced as a foundation for grasping the implications of our particular approach and for introducing the chapters that lie ahead:

- Empirical theory and explanation
- Types of metatheory
- Normative social theory
- Subjectivist-objectivist polarization
- Research programs and paradigms

Empirical Theory and Explanation

At this stage let us begin with a relatively simple definition of *empirical theory* (also referred to as *analytical* or *substantive theory*). Theories in this sense represent various ways of systematically organizing concepts in a manner that attempts to provide persuasively an *explanation* of phenomena. Such explanations seek to answer "why" and "how" questions about social events. So we may refer to empirical theories of suicide, of industrial society, or of self-presentation. But as we shall see, the notion of explaining something takes quite different logical forms.

The empirical is the bedrock of all sciences because it refers to what exists in human experience (ultimately, sense-data). An empirical science is thus one that refers to evidence deriving from *experience* (social reality, social facts), as opposed to *authority* (as in the case of some political or religious beliefs) or *revelation* (as in the case of some religious beliefs). An empirical question is one that bears on the "facts" held to be pertinent as evidence for a particular explanatory claim. *Empiricism* (a form of positivism) is an approach to science that stresses the primacy of the factual basis of scientific knowledge (processes of verification and confirmation), as opposed to, say, the purely rational or intuitive foundations. Often referred to as "British empiricism," this form of epistemology usually is traced to the philosophies of John Locke (1632-1704) and David Hume (1711-1776). The validity of knowledge thus is grounded in the sense-data manifest in the object studied.

Another influence on positivism—more popular in continental Europe—often is referred to broadly as *rationalism*. In its pure form as found in Descartes (1596-1650) in France and Leibniz (1646-1716) in Germany, rationalism argues that knowledge (including religion) can be grounded in pure reason, rather than in faith or appeal to factual evidence. From this perspective, truth is grounded in characteristics of the knowing subject, following Descartes's dictum, "I think, therefore I am."

Finally Immanuel Kant (1724-1804), in Germany, established the key reference point of modern philosophy by trying to avoid both rationalism and empiricism (though he usually is classified as an idealist or a rationalist). Kant began with the subject of human reason, rather than objective facts (the object) to justify the validity and uniqueness of scientific knowledge. He argued, on the one hand, that the human subject does have a form of pure reason that exists a priori—that is, as part of the basic structure of the human mind as in the capacity to perceive space and time or to make logical distinctions. On the other hand, he also gave the empirical aspect of knowledge its due by admitting that the effectiveness of pure reason depended on its capacity to discover the factual truths of nature. Despite Kant's remarkable attempt at synthesis, this split between empiricism and rationalism inevitably defined the inner tensions within the history of positivism. Should the foundations of certain knowledge be located in characteristics of the "knower" (the subject) following rationalism, or that which is to be "known" (the object) as in empiricism?

Empiricism has provided the primary justification for sociological empiricism and is evident in the fetishization of quantitative facts. Kantians, however, continually have reminded social scientists about the problematic character of social facts, given the way our concepts help construct what we observe. Social facts are particularly difficult (some say obdurate or stubborn) because they cannot be taken for granted. Naive interpretations tend to assume that facts are just there, out in the world, just sitting and ready to be harvested by an empiricist method. What this tack ignores, however, is that facts are, in practice, observable (and hence the basis for data "collection") only from the perspective of a theory. The Catholic Church in Europe collected "data" about births and deaths for centuries; only with the advent of "demography" did the information become "demographic facts," as opposed to records with familial and religious significance. Generally nobody even bothers to collect or produce data until a theory renders them of sufficient interest. This theme is talked about by reference to the *theory-laden* character of facts and is the reason why otherwise reasonable people often disagree about what the facts are or whether they effectively prove or disprove a theory.

Notice that at the outset we stress the diversity of theories and make no attempt to impose any narrow, closed definition of the logical forms explanation may take. Theory normally is taken in the social sciences to refer to a theory about something, some aspect of social life; such theory is substantive because it is about a particular type of phenomenon and attempts an explanation of it.

But what, then, is an "explanation"? Again we have to be careful here and stay with a preliminary formulation that limits itself to two key contexts of use. Most methods texts refer to an explanation as a particular kind of scientific explanation with a logical structure that parallels causal explanations in the natural science. The logical form of such explanations often is referred to as the *covering law model,* or the *hypothetico-deductive model.* To explain something in this sense is to provide an adequate and justifiable account of its necessary causes and essential determinants based on the operation of universal laws under specific conditions. In other words, the notion of *explanation* is restricted to the special case of causal explanation, and the idea of determination is limited even further by causes deduced from universal laws. One thus deduces the explanation of a specific type of event from such laws. To "explain" suicide, Durkheim proposed that the primary determinants of different rates of suicide could be correlated with types of social solidarity and integration. As we will see, some fundamental problems with this correlational notion of causation (based on *variable analysis*) pervade social science; critical theory necessarily requires a more complex, structural, and historical conception of social determination. As we shall see, from this perspective social determination operates more as structural tendencies whose effects are not strictly predictable and change over time.

But explanation also is used more loosely in other contexts with reference to *understanding* (or interpreting) social phenomena that will concern us later: Sometimes it can refer to the intentions of individuals (*intentional explanation*) or even an analysis of the ordering principles of a given meaning system or discourse (e.g., a textual or *narrative interpretation*). These kinds of questions were largely neglected in empiricism and only were given selective treatment in rationalist epistemologies. They came into their own only in the tradition of German idealism in the contexts of *hermeneutics* and also what later became known as *phenomenological philosophy.* The most famous 19th-century representative of such concerns was the German philosopher Wilhelm Dilthey (1833-1911). Within these traditions the methodological issues central to interpretive sociologies were discussed under the heading of *Verstehen*, or the interpretation of actions (derived from "understanding" in German) and of *hermeneutics* (theories of textual interpretation). The implications of these need not concern us now, beyond indicating that they are central to debates about interpretive theorizing.

Notice that to refer to an intention —or a reason— as an explanation (e.g., we are writing this book to encourage a broader conception of methodology) is to suggest an odd type of cause, one that lies in the future rather than the past. This is quite different from our normal sense of causes as operating in a temporal sequence, as when independent variable A is held to "cause" outcome B. When the cause is related to the future anticipations, on the other hand, reference is made to *teleological explanations.* These types are actually quite common even in nature wherever we observe feedback mechanisms that result in the self-regulation of systems (as in biological homeostasis or a thermostat). Such processes are especially important in functional-type explanations in social science that try to show how the existence of certain types of structures contributes to the operation of the system as a whole. A classic example is the proposition that the family exists because of the "need" of society to reproduce itself.

The point here is to recognize that it is misleading to speak of a single, uniform notion of "scientific explanation." Explanatory activities result in theories that take quite different logical forms, and there is considerable disagreement about what form explanations should take in particular contexts. Positivistic epistemologies have always recognized this diversity but have argued that this simply reflected deficient, unscientific explanations that did not live up to the ideal of physics (or other natural scientific models) usually associated with the covering law model.

Types of Metatheory

Metatheory, on the other hand, is theory about theory, where "meta" refers to that which is "beyond" theory or, more precisely, that which lies behind the theory's presuppositions. The preceding discussion of methods, methodology, and empirical theory has been metatheoretical in this sense. In effect we have already been doing metatheory. A metatheory is not concerned with explaining social reality in the manner of a substantive theory explaining specific social phenomena; rather it is a form of rational inquiry or argumentation concerned with the theory of theory or theory about theory. In contrast an analytical theoretical question, for example, might involve investigating the causes of the rise of capitalism; a metatheoretical reformulation of this substantive question might be the question of the relative significance of "material" (economic and structural), as opposed to "ideal" (symbolic and social psychological) factors in rival explanations of the rise of capitalism as, for instance, the classic debate between students of Karl Marx and Max Weber.

Metatheory is also just another way for social scientists to talk about the philosophical and methodological assumptions of their work or issues considered in the philosophy of the social sciences. Broadly speaking, then, metatheory in the social and human sciences can be associated with and draws on the major branches of philosophy: *metaphysics, ontology, epistemology, logic, aesthetics, ethics.* There is a sense in which, for example, every social theory has presuppositions or implications that touch on the questions framed by each of these philosophical domains. There is a sense in which in everyday life we are all philosophers in employing rationales for our actions from all of these branches of philosophy—even if we are not conscious of the fact.

One of the characteristics of a social scientific culture dominated by positivism, however, is that the sophisticated discussion of these presuppositions is not made an integral part of advanced training. Of course we should expect this suppression of philosophical debate in cultures dominated by dogmatic religious traditions. But one of the peculiarities of the dogmas of positivism is that they are defined as neutral and objective— beyond dogma. Yet for the most part students are socialized ritualistically into a particular metatheoretical perspective (sociology as an objective, value-free science) that is accepted as a matter of taken-for-granted "faith," rather than the outcome of sustained self-reflection and systematic argumentation. Instead social science is contrasted vaguely to nonscientific and irrational approaches, usually conjured up in "straw-man" caricatures with just enough truth to be convincing. With the alternatives logically trounced, then, real science can begin.

Further, for most purposes these metatheoretical questions are not all of equal significance for social scientists. *Metaphysical* questions about the existence of things beyond experience (e.g., the existence of an afterlife) have been marginal to social science, though they may be important for establishing the relationship between theologies and social theory. As well, *aesthetic* questions—which refer to questions about the criteria of taste that make something beautiful or artistically superior—have tended to be marginal in social science, but central to the humanities and important for the sociology of culture and cultural criticism.

In practice, four domains of metatheory are of strategic importance for the methodology of the social sciences and are our focus of attention: *ontology, epistemology, logic,* and *ethics.* Any given approach to social science inevitably makes assumptions in these domains of metatheory, and these presuppositions necessarily must be fairly consistent. Take, for example, the structural functionalist general sociology of Talcott Parsons and the experimentally based psychological behaviorism of B. F. Skinner. These are, respectively, two well-known theoretical approaches in sociology and psychology. Both are empirical theories in the sense that they make claims about explaining a particular domain of social facts. Both theories make *ontological* assumptions about the nature and existence of different kinds of things or entities in the social world. For Skinner "meanings" are introspective phenomena not accessible to science, whereas for Parsons they are central to understanding social order as a cultural system. They both also make *epistemological* assumptions because an empirical theory necessarily makes certain claims about what social scientific knowledge is and links this with certain assumptions about the logic of scientific explanation and the methodology of research, which are applied in data analysis and theory construction. For Skinner, only experimentation can generate scientific theory; for Parsons, verbal formulations of functional relations of structures suffices. Finally their theories have certain *ethical* presuppositions that make claims about values; for example, they share the assumption that science and technology have had a progressive impact on social evolution. To analyze Parsons's or Skinner's or any other theory in terms of such questions entails a metatheoretical analysis that is quite different from comparing them with respect to the fit between the theories and the empirical data invoked to confirm them.

If indeed the scientific method is based on some unified, pure logic, then presumably that should be one of the most important foundations of advanced training for researchers. The fact that it is not—that indeed even the most technically sophisticated methodologists have virtually no training in formal logic—should be interpreted as the sign of a profound discrepancy between the rhetoric and the reality of social science. Technically *logic* is the study of the rules of "correct" reasoning. But what does that mean? Do we really understand its place in scientific research? We are most familiar, however vaguely, with what is known as *formal logic.* Central to this approach is the fear of inconsistency or contradiction: If two different propositions make the same claim, they both cannot be true. Yet in real life we constantly work with inconsistencies, even in science. Hence nonformal logic is concerned with the *informal logic,* or the *practical* logics of everyday life that are central to scientific practice yet virtually ignored in traditional reconstructions of science.

As we have noted, the concept of *knowledge* is also ambiguous and constitutes the central question of epistemology—also called the "theory of knowledge" by philosophers. For positivist philosophers the ambiguity was resolved by fiat: the introduction of a logical principle of *demarcation* (e.g., correspondence to the facts) to differentiate scientific knowledge from mere beliefs. Sociologists and anthropologists have resisted this, given their need to compare and analyze the social origins of different types of beliefs as part of the *sociology of knowledge:* e.g., scientific knowledge, commonsense knowledge, religious knowledge, without initially making any assumptions about their respective validity. As a consequence, it perhaps would be useful to follow the French language and use the awkward term *knowledges* to stress the plurality of forms of knowing. For our purposes at this preliminary stage, however, we need to differentiate *empirical* knowledge and *normative* knowledge and to link these to the distinctions made by different forms of *epistemology.*

A definition of epistemology has already been noted in referring to Parsons's and Skinner's theories: how they both presuppose certain criteria that render a theory scientific. Traditional empiricist epistemology involves the investigation of the criteria for logically demarcating scientific from nonscientific knowledge. Accordingly there is a sense that science is the social enterprise that produces explanations that take a specific logical form and are linked to empirical evidence in ways characteristic of science. Hence an epistemologist can readily demarcate astronomy as a natural science and astrology as a pseudoscience on various logical grounds linked to theory and methodology.

Normative Theory

In other contexts, however, this problem of demarcation becomes more difficult and controversial as, for example, in the
distinction between empirical and normative knowledge (e.g.,
ethical inquiry). From the perspective of a strict scientific epistemology, normative knowledge is not knowledge at all, merely
a type of nonrational belief. Whereas one knows with certainty
the causes of the movements of the planets, knowledge about
the goodness of justice is in a sense just, or merely, a personal
opinion. Hence conventional philosophers make a strict logical
distinction between empirical (scientific) and normative (value)
questions. Whereas the former can be constructed and validated
in a scientific way, the latter cannot. But as we shall see later,
others contend (with critical theory) that normative questions
can be and should be subjected to rational and empirical scrutiny
in ways that a positivistic scientific approach does not encourage.

Normative theories thus are concerned with what ought to
be and, as a consequence, are associated broadly with the philosophical or metatheoretical field of ethics. Indeed normative theorizing has become recognized as so significant that it has emerged
as an important form of inquiry in its own right, one that goes
far beyond the narrower domain of philosophical ethics. Again
standard methodology texts are not very helpful here in that they
confine themselves to some brief remarks about the "ethics of
research"–that is, questions such as the confidentiality of respondents and the importance of excluding value judgments
from the research process itself. But as contemporary social
theory and political philosophy have made clear, the "ethical"
issues posed by social research are broader and more fundamental than this and have profound ideological implications.

The primary contexts in which normative theorizing becomes
central are *political philosophy, social criticism,* and *theories
of ideology.* Despite the aspirations for "value-free" social science, it is clear that value questions have always been central at
various stages of research practice. The division between political science and sociology has been especially harmful to sociology in this context. The most important context of such ethical
theorizing for social theory has been the tradition of classical
political philosophy associated originally with the ancient Greeks

(Plato, Aristotle). Such political philosophy is essentially normative because of its focus on the grounds of political authority and obligation, for example, the question of the "good society" (Taylor 1989; Kymlicka 1990). In contrast, empirical (or behavioral) political science shares with political sociology a concern with the various factors that, in fact, characterize the functioning of different political systems. Sociologists and other social scientists have engaged in similar activities in the 19th and 20th centuries in the guise of *social criticism,* an activity that joins the results of empirical research with conceptions of what ought to be. Unlike political philosophy, however, social criticism in sociology has not been organized as an academic subfield and has flourished on the margins of the discipline or outside the academy or in policy and social problems research. Political philosophy and social criticism intermingle in the context of policy analysis (whether political, social, economic, or cultural) that involves both an empirical study of public policy formation by governments, as well as an assessment of the normative implications. Such normative issues, however, have always been central to discussions about the nature of the welfare state and problems of human needs, largely through the contributions of political scientists and philosophers.[7] But such questions are not the basis of specific course offerings in sociological curricula because normative theory is not well recognized in the social sciences as a legitimate scholarly pursuit, whereas the evaluation of policies in terms of taken-for-granted values is. An important reason for this exclusion is the fine line between normative theorizing and ideologies.

The theory of *ideology* poses particular problems because it has been of concern in so many different contexts associated with normative theorizing and political action (Thompson 1984, 1990; Abercrombie et al. 1990; Larrain 1983). At various points we have much more to say about this controversial and highly contested concept, but here it is useful to distinguish two clear and important uses of the term. Most commonly, the notion of *ideology* is associated with one of the classical political ideologies: one of the well-organized, action-oriented belief systems characteristic of modern politics, for example, conservatism, liberalism, socialism, communism, fascism. What is unique about these belief systems is they contain both an empirical claim about the nature of social reality (a theory of society) and normative claims about how society should be organized (Gouldner 1976). Unlike scientific belief systems, however, the normative or political imperative predominates over the empirical dimension; even when key empirical claims of ideologies may be undermined, adherents tend to persist in ignoring them because of the priority of their value concerns.

Yet there is a second, more subtle and confusing context of use of the term. The focus of attention here is not organized ideologies, but the cultural mechanisms involved in the creation and potential distortions of consciousness and communication in everyday life. The main theme is that when individuals and groups have material or ideal interests at stake, they tend to justify them in ways that distort their perceptions of reality. In particular the concern here is with how ideological processes are a pervasive feature of the practices that make up social life and institutions even where this is not overtly associated with ideologies as organized belief systems. For example, patriarchy has long functioned as both an explicit belief system and as an implicit dimension of many social relations (even where it has been legally disenfranchised).

Many social theorists and philosophers have claimed that normative theories are, like ideologies, mere beliefs that cannot be justified rationally at all. To prefer vegetarianism over cannibalism is ultimately a simple matter of taste. In this case the important logical distinction between facts and values is used to exclude value questions from the scientific domain on the grounds that they are inherently irrational, or at least nonrational. An essential assumption of both political philosophy and critical social theory, in contrast, is that normative theorizing does admit to various degrees of rational argumentation that should be a central aspect of the critique and renewal of academic traditions and need not assume the form of simple ideological polemics between incommensurate worldviews. From this perspective, questions about justice, freedom, and equality can be subjected to critical scrutiny and strong, weak, and fallacious arguments for such values and the means to realize them can be potentially differentiated. For this reason critical theory can claim to develop a scientific research program that combines empirical and normative theorizing.

The Subjectivist-Objectivist Polarization in Metatheory

With these distinctions between metatheory, empirical theory, and normative theory in mind, let us take a closer look at the typical metatheoretical positions in contemporary social research. These can be represented conveniently in terms of a polarization between two contrasting positions—objectivism and subjectivism—a clash found throughout the social sciences (Burrell and Morgan 1979). At one pole are metatheories that strongly identify with positivism, hence natural scientific models of research as the ideal way to conduct empirical research. Here the unity or identity of natural and social science in logical and methodology is stressed. At the other extreme are those anti-positivist positions that stress the complete difference between natural and social science, holding that the latter is defined by the unique logical and methodological problems of interpreting meanings, subjectivity, and consciousness. In psychology this contrast is associated with the standoff between behaviorism and phenomenology; in sociology it is associated with the division between positivist and humanist or empiricist and interpretive sociologies.

It is instructive to see how this polarization operates at several levels of closely interrelated presuppositions: *ontology, epistemology, theory of action, nature of explanation.* For purposes of a stylized, introductory discussion, we stress the polarized extremes and avoid the complicated examples that attempt to mediate between them (a central theme of later chapters). In conclusion we allude to how critical theory tries to overcome this polarization.

Ontology

Objectivists adhere to an ontology that is broadly associated with the notion of a traditional or "naive" *realism* that stresses the reality of empirical facts independently of our consciousness of them. Scientific concepts thus seek to copy or correspond to those factual realities in some way, giving us a scientific "picture" of it, as it were. Naive realism is thus the basis of a theory of scientific *representation* or how the sciences conceptualize reality. British empiricism is associated closely with this type of ontology.

In contrast, subjectivists tend to adopt a position that philosophers have called *nominalism* (perhaps the notion of *constructivism* is more familiar in the social sciences) that argues there is a fundamental gulf between our concepts and empirical reality. This is a theme introduced by Kantian rationalism and later radicalized in phenomenology. Hence nominalists challenge that we cannot really know or represent "reality" directly because our understanding of it is mediated by the constructs of our consciousness. Indeed in strong versions nominalism (e.g., *solipsism*) is associated with the assumption that all we can really know is subjectivity and consciousness because they are immediately accessible to us, whereas nature is outside of us, hence only indirectly knowable. Subjectivism in sociology is associated most often with interpretive sociologies such as symbolic interactionism and social phenomenology; objectivism is linked with variants of positivist theories: empiricism, functionalism, and versions of materialism.

Epistemology

The consequences of these two opposing ontological positions result in dramatic differences with respect to epistemology. In other words, ontologies are linked closely to epistemologies because it is necessary to have a conception of the nature of social reality before one proposes to justify a scientific analysis of it. Traditional realism is consistent with positivist epistemologies that identify science with the discovery of invariant laws that determine the relations among observable empirical facts or objective structures outside consciousness. This approach is associated with positivism, especially in the form of *logical empiricism*.

In contrast, *antipositivist* epistemologies identify the basis of social scientific knowledge in the interpretation of what largely is excluded (or at least rendered secondary) to positivist epistemology: the meanings and consciousness of social actors. This position has been most well developed in social phenomenology and a weak version in symbolic interactionism.

One of the most well known versions of the split between subjectivism and objectivism in epistemology can be found in the opposition of *idealism* and *materialism*. In its traditional 19th-century form this conflict was defined by the clash between religion and the physicalistic materialism of the natural sciences. This clash took the form of the contrast between a view of "man" as guided by a "soul," as opposed to being a "mechanism" reducible to biology and ultimately to chemistry and physics. In the more sophisticated form found in the debate between Marxism and liberal social science, materialism refers to a historical analysis that stressed explanations based on external "material" structures (social and economic), as opposed to the voluntary actions of individuals who choose their own fate.

Theory of Action

Translated into an image of social action and the actor, positivism culminates in a fundamental determinism that views intentions and subjective states as essentially *epiphenomenal,* largely illusory phenomena, compared to their objective determinants. This is sometimes referred to by critics as the "nothing but" fallacy, as when Skinner claims that behavior is nothing but the outcome of histories of reinforcement. In other words, from this reductionist perspective the possibility that there might be other, *emergent properties* crucial for understanding social action (e.g., cognitions) is excluded at the outset.

Antipositivists, on the other hand, adopt a position of *voluntarism* that assumes that human actions do express free will and intentions. In this respect they stress that individual actions do indeed have emergent properties that cannot be reduced to or predicted from knowledge of underlying constraints and determinations. Indeed the concept of the "person" or "self" presupposes such autonomy. Antipositivists differ among themselves, however, on the degree of voluntarism assumed and the ways it becomes available to actors.

Theory of Explanation

Finally these two metatheoretical positions culminate in opposing conceptions of the nature of social scientific explanation.

For classical positivists the goal of explanation is identical to that of the natural sciences: the search for *nomothetic* explanations—that is, invariant laws (covering laws) that account for the patterns found in large populations of individual cases. Such explanations are associated with experimental methods and the quantitative analysis of statistically defined variables (e.g., in survey research).

For subjectivists, however, the ultimate goals of inquiry are *ideographic* explanations, hence interpretations of individual cases that capture their particularity and uniqueness. These kinds of explanations are based on interpretive procedures and typically are associated with what often is called (problematically, as we shall see) "qualitative methods" such as historical analysis, ethnographic description, and the use of case studies. For example, a purely ideographic approach to the Russian revolution would interpret it as a unique event that expressed the peculiar history of Czardom and Russian culture and its relation to Western Europe. In contrast a purely nomothetic approach would argue that like all other revolutions, the Russian one could be explained in terms of general laws of social change.

Three Approaches to Metatheory and Methodology

An important development in contemporary theories of scientific methodology are the related notions of *research paradigms* or *research programs*. Traditionally logicians focused on the reconstruction of the formal logic underlying a theory. The trouble with this reconstructed logic from the point of view of actual research practice is that theories change and develop. The limitations of this positivist understanding of the natural sciences became popularized in an immensely influential work in the history of science: Thomas Kuhn's *The Structure of Scientific Revolutions* (1970). To actually do research is thus to participate in a community of researchers who base their work on specific examples of research, research problems, and methodological strategies. The advantage of a focus on research paradigms is that it redirects attention away from a myopic focus on a "theory" as if it were some kind of fully unified, abstract, logical system created by an isolated individual, as opposed to the continually revised outcome of a community of researchers.

At this point we can narrow down this subjectivist-objectivist opposition in terms of three competing methodological paradigms currently competing in sociology: *positivist social science, interpretive social science,* and *critical social science* (Neuman 1991, p. 44; Braybrooke 1987). Generally speaking, *interpretive* theory in this sense can be associated with the subjectivist pole of metatheory and *positivist* with the objectivist. Positivist social scientists largely disregard the intentions and knowledge of actors as an epiphenomenon that distracts attention from the discovery of the correlated variables that apparently suggest the causes of social action. Purely interpretive approaches take the opposite strategy in largely abandoning explanatory theorizing about causality in favor of interpretive analysis of meaning systems. *Critical* social science attempts to transcend the subjectivist-objectivist split in a manner that will be developed in later chapters.

The Dominance of Objectivism

For those familiar with the standard methods texts of the social sciences, the objectivist or positivist account of metatheory remains both dominant and largely unquestioned. Even where so-called qualitative research is given some acknowledgment as a technique of inquiry, it is evaluated primarily in terms of positivist metatheory, hence its ability to facilitate the construction of nomothetic explanations. For this reason qualitative ("subjectivist") research often is acknowledged with the somewhat dismissive reference to its "heuristic" role in research: its ability to sensitize researchers to important questions and relations at the outset of inquiry, prior to the formulation of the problem in truly scientific, hence quantitative, terms.

The Interpretive Challenge

Reference to the notion of an *interpretive sociology* is ambiguous. On the one hand, it simply may apply to any sociological approach that uses *Verstehen*-type procedures, as in the case of

Max Weber's interpretive sociology. But Weber, of course, was concerned with analysis both in the context of meaning and of the causal nexus of action. In other contexts, however, interpretive sociology is associated with a stronger claim associated with strongly subjectivist approaches grounded in phenomenology and hermeneutics that argue that the interpretive analysis of meanings is the only, or at least most important, form of social inquiry. Positivist approaches are rejected because of their reductionism; the tension between subjectivism and objectivism evident in Weber is resolved in terms of the primacy of meaning in social action. This position goes back to the basic phenomenological claim that consciousness cannot be either understood or explained in terms outside of itself—that is, external social factors and processes. As expressed in the social sciences, such interpretation theory construes inquiry as purely hermeneutic, and such a research program implies that social research should be reduced to the interpenetration of meanings (Little 1991, p. 69).

In their extreme form such purely interpretive approaches often are characterized as antiscientific because of their rejection of causal explanations based on general laws. Even in their more moderate form, however, such interpretive approaches strongly limit the generalizing claims of the human sciences. For example, the American anthropologist Clifford Geertz often is cited with reference to his interpretive analysis of the cultural meaning of Balinese cockfighting. The focus of inquiry here is on how cockfighting is illuminating for understanding a wide variety of social relationships (e.g., those of kinship, status, and community) in a local context. But such an approach also rejects consideration of the objectivist aspects that might help "explain" those practices:

> Note what this account does not provide. It does not tell us what processes or mechanism brought about cockfighting (a causal explanation) and it does not attempt to show how individual Balinese men pursue their own interests or purposes through cockfighting (a rational choice explanation). This account, then, does not provide an explanation of the practice; instead it offers a reading of the practice in its context, intended to elucidate the meaning of the practice for us. (Little 1991, p. 69)

Beyond Subjectivism and Objectivism

Critical social science, to be sure, acknowledges the crucial importance of such "readings" of social practices. Yet it agrees with positivist social science that such readings fail to acknowledge adequately the social forces that act behind the backs of participants. Nevertheless it is argued that positivist social science goes about identifying these external determining factors in a very narrow and problematic manner in trying to reduce them to causal variables. In the process the subjective component of action can only be comprehended—if considered at all—in a manner restricted to the dictates of survey research methodology and correlational techniques. To analyze the interplay between meaning and structure, a very different methodological approach to social determination is required: one based on the nature of social relations, not imported from the natural sciences. Explaining the presuppositions and nature of this alternative approach is the task of the chapters that follow. At this point we need only characterize this position in general terms: its criticism of the reigning polarization between objectivism and subjectivism. A decisive aspect of critical metatheory is that it rejects the objectivist-subjectivist polarization (described above) as an adequate formulation of the problematic of the logic of social inquiry.

Let us conclude with a preliminary definition of the nature of critical social research methodology in terms of its character as a *"critical-dialectical perspective"* (e.g., Harvey 1990). Such a methodology is critical because it asks metatheoretical questions and seeks to draw attention to the relations of power that shape social reality. The question of power is largely ignored in purely interpretive approaches because they exclude the analysis of external socioeconomic structures and causality. Positivist approaches may, in principle, study objective structural relations in selective ways, but they avoid metatheory largely by restricting their methodology to the statistical analysis of variables.

The notion of something as *dialectical* is slippery and usually not very precise. As a general reference to critical methodology, however, it is useful as a way of rejecting the standoff between purely interpretive and positivist approaches. So in the present context it has the advantage of pointing to the possibility of

analyzing agency and structure as intertwined and mutually impli-
cating one another. Further, this dialectical relationship between
subjective and objective realities implies something quite distinct from dividing up the world dualistically into macro and micro
relations. These are the kinds of grounding questions posed by
a critical methodology discontent with the polarization between
objectivist and subjectivist accounts of social reality. The chapters that follow elaborate the implications of this position.

Conclusion

The task of this chapter has been to clarify the basic themes
of contemporary metatheory. We began with consideration of
the conflation of methods and methodology in the conventional
literature and then turned to an elucidation of key metatheoretical issues: the differentiation of metatheory, empirical theory,
and normative theory; analysis of science as a mode of reasoning,
type of community, and worldview; and consideration of the
various types of metatheory and the subject-objective polarization that has divided the human sciences, culminating in the
distinction between positivist, interpretive, and critical social
science.

The following chapters attempt to justify and elaborate on the
metatheoretical foundations of a critical theory of methodology
as a specific approach to critical social science. Chapter 3 considers the contribution of the shift from empiricist to postempiricist philosophies of science in order to analyze the consequences
of the decline of positivism as the metatheory of the natural
sciences as a prelude to the consideration of critical theory itself
in Part II.

Notes

1. Notice that we purposely avoid use of the term *behavioral science,* because
of its original association with a positivist research program. The more inclusive
notion of *social science* is thus preferable. The term *human sciences* is also

useful to characterize the humanities and social sciences taken together and is suggestive of many overlapping concerns, especially between interpretive sociologies and the humanities in the context of what often is referred to now as "cultural studies."

2. This distinction between methodology and methods is largely European in origin: "In the European tradition, 'methodology' refers not only to (research) techniques or to inferential procedures, but also to the epistemological reasons for their choice. Recently, the term 'metascience' has tended to replace methodology in this sense" (Gebhardt 1978, p. 512).

3. The few exceptions to these tendencies—influenced by the sociology of knowledge and a more critical approach to the philosophy of science—remain marginal to the mainstream methodology texts (Sjoberg and Nett 1968; Phillips 1971; Ford 1975) and already incorporate elements of theory construction texts and the newer philosophy of social science. These exceptions have, in part, inspired the present approach. To be sure, symbolic interactionists saw themselves as doing something different, but their efforts were hampered by attempting to justify their methodology in positivist terms (Denzin 1970).

4. Even such introductory studies presuppose a foundation in philosophy that is not a part of social scientific training. For such an introduction to philosophy from the perspective of social scientists, see Anderson et al. 1986.

5. *Metatheory* is a term increasingly used by sociologists to express the kinds of questioning that link sociology and philosophy. Despite important overlaps, the recent expansion of the philosophy of the social sciences tends to be defined primarily by more traditional philosophical problems and to remain distant from the concerns of social scientists (Kaplan 1964; Thomas 1979; Trigg 1985; Doyal and Harris 1986; Mancias 1987; Rosenberg 1988), although Little (1991) is an important exception here.

6. However, some recent works complement our approach. *Critical Social Research*, by Lee Harvey (1990), differs considerably from our approach in several ways: (a) a greater focus on British research, (b) the lack of an introduction to issues in the philosophy of social science, (c) a rather too simplified account of the theoretical and methodological issues, and (d) an almost exclusive focus on substantive research on class, gender, and race. Nevertheless it has profitably informed our approach, and its case studies of research are recommended as a follow-up for the present study. Andrew Sayer's *Method in Social Science* (1992) provides an excellent advanced introduction to many methodological issues from a critical realist perspective but does not relate these as closely to critical theory. The analysis of the structure of sociological theory by Johnson et al. (1984) develops a useful typology differentiating empiricism, subjectivism, rationalism, and substantialism (a form of critical realism). A more general formulation can be found in Donald Polkinghorne's *Methodology for the Human Sciences* (1983), but it does not focus on critical theory or critical social science per se even though it outlines a framework within which such approaches find a legitimate place.

7. For representative contemporary examples of normative theorizing, see Walzer 1987; Guttman 1988; Goodin 1988; Doyal and Gough 1991; for a spirited defense of normative theory in sociology, see Calhoun 1991.

3

POSTEMPIRICIST CRITIQUES
OF POSITIVISM
AND EMPIRICISM

The permanency of truth, too, is connected with the constellations of reality. (Horkheimer [1937] 1972a, p. 236)

Why the Critique of Positivism?

Introduction

This chapter reconstructs 20th-century debates about the nature of science and its implications for the human sciences, a dense topic that has been of concern to the philosophy, history, and sociology of science. The basic themes of the chapter can be conveyed readily at the outset, though their broader significance will become apparent only in working through this chapter and those that follow. First we must establish the broader significance of the topic and the terms of reference for analysis. Then we turn to positivist philosophies of science inspired by the ambitions of *foundationalism* (an epistemological search for certain knowledge). Karl Popper's *critical rationalism* then is discussed as a transitional approach whose contradictions point the way to *postempiricist* (or *postpositivist*) responses, culminating in varieties of *antifoundationalism.* Two varieties of postempiricism are contrasted: *skeptical postmodernism,* which calls into question all forms of social inquiry, and *critical realism,* which attempts (like critical theory) to reaffirm new bases for the credibility of scientific knowledge.

The Ideological Context
of Philosophies of Science

Why are the issues of the philosophy of science important? And why are they so neglected in the training of researchers and the curricula of higher education generally? The dominant institutions of any form of society are cemented together culturally through a set of metaphysical and ontological presuppositions that sometimes are referred to as a *Weltanschauung* or *worldview.* In the case of modern Western (or occidental) societies, science largely has replaced religion as the universalistic framework, especially in the institutions associated with education, research, and economic production. Any culture finds it inherently difficult to reflect on its most fundamental presuppositions, especially where this may involve calling them into question. The culture of positivism is no exception.

Critiques of the modern scientific worldview have taken many forms, including various dogmatic religious and irrationalist attacks. The stance of critical theory and related forms of thought toward science is distinctive in at least two ways: First, it is argued that dominant political and social interests shape the development of science and technology, hence the "autonomy" of science is always problematic; and second, it is claimed that science and technology cannot be fully neutral with respect to human values because they inevitably mediate social relations. In other words, debates about the status of science have important ideological implications. Such is the case of the otherwise esoteric discipline of the philosophy of science that is ritualistically invoked to legitimate the rationality of scientific methods and explanations against their allegedly non-scientific challengers.

This is not to say that philosophers of science are ideologists in the normal sense; to the contrary, they have defined themselves as the great defenders of universal reason, as critics of dogmatism, and generally have shown themselves willing to revise their own arguments in the light of new evidence. But certain of their earlier arguments have been institutionalized in various disciplines and have been diffused widely in a popular form that has little to do with the contemporary postempiricist theories of science actually advocated today by most historians and philosophers of science who reject empiricism and positivism:

Unfortunately, very little of the philosophical writing has been
absorbed or even noticed by the social scientists. The work of philosophers . . . is not well known outside professional philosophy.
Kuhn's *The Structure of Scientific Revolutions* has had a certain
vogue but even that is not well understood. It is surprising how
little social scientists know about the difficulties of the simple model
of observation and confirmation of theories. . . . Very little notice
has been taken of these arguments. (Garfinkel 1981, p. 135)

Today, more than a decade later, social scientists—especially
those familiar with social theory—have become increasingly aware
of these issues. Postempiricist philosophies of science and social
science have legitimated the general thrust of the various critiques of positivism originally developed within critical social
theory. But more recently, under the heading of theories of postmodernism, the very project of social science has been called
into question in ways that often go beyond—and conflict with—
the position of critical theory (Rosenau 1992). Consequently
critical theory has found it necessary to complement its critique
of positivism with one of postmodernism.

The task of this chapter is to consider recent developments
outside critical theory proper in order to legitimate indirectly
the metatheory of critical theory. In the context of the rest of this
chapter these issues can be presented only in an introductory,
illustrative, and often rather assertive manner; readers who remain
unconvinced or concerned about more elaborate formulations are
invited to pursue the more specialized sources to which we refer.

The transition from the conventional to the new view of science
is analyzed in terms of three key levels of analysis—introduced in
the previous chapter—required for understanding science as a
specialized form of discourse:

- *Its systematics or logical structure:* Logically what kind of method
  and form of explanation are or should be characteristic of a science?
- *Its history, social embeddedness, and social construction:* What is
  the nature of the community of inquiry that produces science, and
  how is this related to the nature of scientific knowledge?
- *Its cultural implications as a perspective on reality:* What is the
  broader meaning of science, what is its relation to power relations,
  ideologies, and values within a society?

These three levels of analysis can be referred to as problems deriving from, respectively, the philosophy, historical sociology, and critique of science. As we shall see, the transition from positivist to postpositivist theories of science can be grasped readily by their respective positions on the relationship between these three perspectives.

Positivist Philosophies of Science

Introduction: The Lure of Foundationalism

The point of departure for understanding the division between the traditional positivist philosophy of science and postpositivist approaches is to grasp how they diverge over a fundamental issue. The question is: How should we justify scientific theories? In short, what kind of epistemology should be used? Positivism shares with much of Western thought a foundationalist response to this question—that is, the postulation of absolute and certain (apodictic) grounds for truth claims. The underlying metaphor here is the notion that science depends on the ability of its concepts to represent reality in a manner that is analogous to "mirroring" or copying it (Rorty 1979).

The answer provided by positivism has its roots in a search for absolute truth that can be traced back to ancient Greece. The resulting quest for certainty was based on the claim that such absolute epistemological foundations for knowledge could be found, though opinions differed as to where. The resulting *foundationalism* has sought to anchor scientific knowledge in diverse ways: Plato's notion of pure ideas; the rationalism, logic, and mathematics associated with Descartes; postulation of God-given natural laws in Aquinas; the empiricist reference to sense data as in Hume; or the transcendental categories of the mind in Kant. Although few scientists selfconsciously embrace positivism (though they might refer to themselves as empiricists or naturalists), they nevertheless adhere to the unifying foundationalist themes of this classic conception of science.

Even though technical discussions of positivism differ in detail, it is possible to convey the broadly shared assumptions in terms of a basic stance with respect to the logic of science (the logic of verification), the significance of the nature of scientific institutions (the logic of discovery), and the meaning of science for modern culture.

Systematics: Reconstructed Logic

The classic positions of positivism and empiricism about science as a mode of reasoning can be summarized in three basic propositions: (a) the foundationalist claim that certain knowledge was possible because it could be based on a neutral *observation language* (facts), (b) that explanations took a logical form that made them completely universal and general (were *nomothetic*), and (c) that the reconstructed logic of the advanced sciences provided the basis for the *unity of science*.[1]

For the *logical positivism* culminating in the *Vienna Circle* in the early 20th century, the answer was the technique of analyzing the *reconstructed logic* of scientific method. The easiest way to do this was to find the most advanced form of science (presumably physics) and develop a set of techniques (ideally a value-neutral, formal or mathematical language) for finding the underlying logical structures of its explanations. It was held that neutral descriptive languages allow direct grasping of facts that are, in turn, organized into theoretical propositions. Disagreement centered around whether scientific research should be understood in terms of the inferential logic of *deduction,* where factual particulars are derived by logical necessity from general propositions, or that of *induction,* where the focus on empirical facts leads to generalizations that can be held to be probably true. Translated into research strategies, a deductive approach attempts to develop formalized theories that then can be tested and inductive ones that involve a data-driven effort to find probabilistic patterns of causal relationships.

More specifically, it was held according to the *covering law model* that valid scientific theories necessarily assumed specific deductive and inductive forms. Such *deductive-nomological models* of explanation make very stringent requirements about the determinism or necessity of events to be explained. This severity requires beginning with general premises that become the basis for deducing—within certain boundary conditions—that which is to be explained (the *explanandum*). General, invariant laws are the basis of science and demonstrate how events had to happen the way they did. These relationships can be illustrated as follows (Little 1991, pp.5-6):

L_i	(one or more universal laws)
C_i	(one or more statements of background circumstances)
=========	(deductively entails)
E	(statement of the act or regularity to be explained)

Because not all scientific explanations are universal in this sense, logicians have employed *inductive-statistical models* that focus on probabilistic statements:

L_i	(one or more statistical laws)
C_i	(one or more statements of background conditions)
=========	(makes very likely)
E	(statement of the fact or regularity to be explained)

Once this ideal reconstructed logic has been identified, it becomes possible to evaluate other scientific theories in terms of how well they live up to this model.

History: The Idealized Scientific Community

A second feature of classic positivism is the claim that the history of the sciences is, for all practical purposes, irrelevant for their practice. The *logic of justification* or *confirmation* is sharply distinguished from looking at the *logic of discovery* of theories: the psychological, historical, and social conditions through which science develops. Knowledge about history is held to have no significance for the evaluation of the validity of theories and to be largely peripheral for the discovery of better research strategies. How researchers actually went about discovering new knowledge was, strictly speaking, irrelevant, mere "personal knowledge" (Polanyi 1962).

In the light of this dictum the traditional histories of science were concerned primarily with the circumstances that lead great scientists to their discoveries, largely attributing discovery itself to the "genius" of the researcher. Disconnecting science from its history was also closely connected with the assumption of *value-freedom*—that is, the claim that scientific progress is facilitated by and dependent on the impersonality, objectivity, and lack of bias on the part of investigators. Even sociological accounts that challenged the genius myth did not question the rigid distinction between the logic of verification and that of discovery. Beginning in the 1930s, American sociologist Robert Merton (1968) began to correct the simplistic genius theory of science by looking more closely at the social context of scientific discovery and concluded that the "norms" of the scientific community were the basis of scientific progress, not the personal qualities of individual researchers. Hence all great scientists were "standing on the shoulders" of their predecessors and contemporaries. Yet Merton's position was anchored in a logical-empiricist distinction between what he termed the "history" and "systematics" of theorizing that effectively blocked asking questions about the deeper relations between science and society, including the links between science and human values.

Meaning: Science as Universal Reason

Despite the suggestion that scientists should be value-free in relation to research practices, positivism also is associated closely with a tendency to postulate science as the ultimate value. To this extent, positivism often has aspired to the metaphysical status of a universal worldview or *Weltanschauung* that claimed to have succeeded religion as the primary source of meaning and reason. As a cultural phenomenon, the scientific worldview is associated with two conflicting tendencies. On the one hand, many attempted to make claims about science as an alternative to religion, hence as embodying all of the necessary ingredients—at least potentially—for a philosophy of life. In certain respects both Emile Durkheim and Karl Marx were forced into this position by default, in that neither could escape an ultimate faith in science as universal reason and the ultimate basis of human progress. From this point of view science could become a replacement for religion in the sense of both explaining social reality and providing the rationale for the values that should guide social life.

On the other hand, a more typical consequence has been to differentiate between verifiable or scientific propositions and everything else—by default, irrational or at least nonrational. Whereas the former can be answered rationally by empirical arguments, the latter is held to be purely relativistic. For Max Weber this implied an irrational "war of the gods" with respect to values. From his skeptical perspective, scientific knowledge could not solve the problem of values that inevitably were grounded in nonrational beliefs rooted ultimately in religious systems. This is the basis of Weber's version of the value-free notion of science: Values should be excluded from science because they were not subject to rational validation. But this notion has the paradoxical effect of discouraging the use of rational procedures in value debates.

Positivism in the Social Sciences

Logical Empiricism and Unified Science

The most influential modern positivist influence on the social sciences is the *logical empiricism* of the so-called Vienna Circle. Originating in Austria in the 1920s, this group of philosophers came to have worldwide influence, especially with the flight of central European philosophers after Hitler's rise to power. The basis of this approach was a purely scientific view of the world and the assumption of the unity of the sciences. As three of its leaders noted in a pamphlet in 1929:

> The scientific world-conception knows only empirical statements about things of all kinds, and analytical statements of logic and mathematics. . . . *First,* it is *empiricist and positivist:* there is knowledge only from experience, which rests on what is immediately given. This sets the limits of or the content of legitimate science. *Second,* the scientific world-conception is marked by the application of a certain method, namely *logical analysis.* (Neurath, Hahn, and Carnap as cited in Bryant 1985, p. 111)

The Vienna Circle carried to a conclusion the Enlightenment attack on metaphysics by declaring all statements meaningless that could not be verified strictly according to their conception of the scientific method. The basis of all scientific knowledge was the elementary facts or *protocol sentences* to which sense-data could be reduced. Further, the events described by such data were ultimately physical in origin, thus making possible a unified science. The primary influence of this doctrine in the social sciences was its notion of a unified scientific method based in empirical verification; further, this was coupled with a conception of explanation based on the reconstructed logic of the natural sciences. This coupling was taken to imply that *Verstehen* or interpretation did not provide the basis for scientific explanations at all and at best was relegated to its sensitizing role—at least in the social sciences—as a preliminary to inquiry or helping to construct hypotheses, though not to test them (Abel 1977).

Popper's Critical Rationalism: Falsificationism

The obvious problems of the model of physics for the social sciences led to a number of qualifications and modifications of the logical empiricist position. The most influential alternative to Vienna Circle-type positivism was the *critical rationalism* of Karl Popper, a philosopher from Vienna who ended up at the London School of Economics. Popper radically revised logical empiricism in two key ways. First, he suggested that the focus on verification of theories detracted from the importance of theoretical innovation in the growth of knowledge; second, he stressed that the essence of scientific procedures was not logic, but a community of effective criticism.

For Popper what is more fundamental to science than verifying empirical propositions is the attempt to prove them wrong—to *falsify* them (Popper 1965a, 1965b; Radnitzky 1973; Stockman 1983). After all, endless amounts of good evidence can be found for all kinds of theories. But one crucial piece of falsifying or disconfirming evidence can potentially demolish a given theory. Because no proposition could be proven absolutely true, Popper rejected the logical empiricist focus on verification; in the light of the theory-laden character of facts, any fairly credible theory can amass a body of factual "proof." What was more important for scientific adequacy was whether propositions potentially could be proven wrong. That was the ultimate difference between astrology and astronomy, according to the principles of *falsificationism.* What is most distinctive about his approach is that it moves away from the tidy and logically ordered conception of science conveyed by traditional positivism's focus on hypothesis testing. What is more significant are forms of inquiry that falsify existing theories and propose rival new explanations for phenomena. This stress on the revolutionary or discontinuous character of scientific development has provided an important stimulus in the transition from a positivist to a postpositivist conception of science. By suggesting that theoretical innovation is not prodded by the discovery of new facts, so much as new theories that guide researchers to new facts, opens the way for completely rethinking the nature of science in nonempiricist ways.

A second key aspect of Popper's approach is that attention is shifted from the logic of inquiry to the social practices involved in guaranteeing that logic prevails over unreason. Accordingly his most general definition of scientific inquiry is a process of "conjectures and refutations" where knowledge is always recognized as fallible—always potentially in need of correction or revision (Popper 1965a). From his fallibilistic perspective, science is seen as always historically changing and its validity dependent on the social characteristics of scientific communities.

The influence of critical rationalism is evident in many current formulations of the scientific method in sociology when it is held that the scientific mode of thinking is based on "strict cultural conventions whereby the production, transformation, and therefore the criticism, of proposed items of knowledge may be carried out collectively and with relatively unequivocal results. *This centrality of highly conventionalized criticism seems to be what is meant when method is sometimes said to be the essential quality of science* [italics added]" (Wallace 1971, pp. 13-4).

The provocative character of Popper's critical rationalism contributed unintentionally to the emergence of postempiricism. In recognizing the theory-laden character of facts and the limits of formal logic, he was forced to ground science in its general critical method—its fallibilism. But this also has the effect of backing off from positivist claims about absolute, eternal truth because whatever we hold to be true today could be falsified tomorrow.

Aspects of the critical rationalist position are very pervasive; indeed many suggest that Popper saved what was valuable in the positivist tradition. To anticipate why postempiricist theories still argue that this approach remains faulty, it is useful to consider some of the fundamental problems with even a Popperian conception of science. First, despite the shift from verification to falsification, science still is identified exclusively with the ideal of deductively organized and reconstructed explanations. Much that is clearly scientific (e.g., in biology) simply does not live up to these criteria. Second, his conception of conventionalized criticism still assumes a problematic degree of rationality in scientific disputes. Third, the continuing strategy of demarcating science from nonscience leaves in limbo other types of "knowledge" and calls into question the priority of science itself, which cannot, strictly speaking, be justified scientifically. How can we even justify science as a "good" thing (a normative, not an empirical, claim) and consider it superior to other forms of knowledge?[2]

Many of these problems derive from the strict separation of the logic of discovery and that of confirmation or falsification. Postempiricists question whether the two "logics" can be separated so sharply without distorting our understanding of science. Furthermore the criteria of scientific adequacy remain so stringent that so much that is clearly "reasonable" in practical terms has no scientific status, especially in social life.

Two 20th-century streams of thinking contributed to radically revising our understanding of the nature of the foundations of knowledge: First, within philosophy itself several developments have pointed to the need to rethink the logical foundations of knowledge; second, historical and sociological studies of scientific communities pointed to the nonrational bases of knowledge construction.

Postempiricism and the Rise of Antifoundationalism

Systematics: Logics-in-Use
Versus Reconstructed Logic

Positivism and logical empiricism did not remain unchallenged in 20th-century metatheory, and three major alternative traditions can be identified: *phenomenology, pragmatism,* and *linguistic philosophy.* Because these philosophical traditions are reviewed in Chapter 5, at this point we need only summarize the shared ways they contributed (not always intentionally, to be sure) to postpositivist and antifoundationalist theories of science.

What is important at this point is to grasp the implications of the changed understanding of logic and method in postempiricist philosophies of science. First, no prescriptivist attempt is made to declare any particular logical basis for true knowledge; logical essentialism (the reconstructed logic of science as the ideal) is rejected. The covering-law model of hypothetico-deductive method is questioned as the exclusive or even primary criterion of adequate scientific explanation. Second, the focus of philosophical analysis shifts to understanding the various *logics-in-use* that guide research methods and the construction of explanations (Kaplan 1964). Science is viewed as close to everyday life as a practical and social activity.

Further, it is no longer necessary to fit the social sciences into the straightjacket of what the natural sciences appeared to look like on the basis of selective logical reconstructions. Therefore it was possible to reconsider the nature of methodology, theorizing, causality, and interpretation from the perspective of the problems unique to such sciences.[3] Whatever science is, they concluded in different ways, it could not be justified ultimately by exclusive reference to the foundational criteria (e.g., logic or correspondence with facts) suggested by positivist philosophies of science.

History: The Problematic
Rationality of Theory Choice

Although the sources of the philosophical critique of positivism were diverse, the version that proved most influential for turning the tide of academic opinion is associated with the history and sociology of science (Woolgar 1988). In the 1960s the Princeton historian of science, Thomas Kuhn, became the ritualistic point of reference for demonstrating the fallacies of the positivist theory of science. The point of departure of his *Structure of Scientific Revolutions* is a sociological one: Like Merton, he agreed that science was something that took place in a

particular type of community (Kuhn 1970). But he went beyond
Merton and radicalized this assumption by looking more closely
at the actual history of the natural sciences, especially physics.
For this purpose he employed the concept of research *paradigms* in order to describe carefully the sociological implications
of science as a social activity. This approach directed attention
away from a theory as purely logical construct to the notion of
research as part of a research program based on common (metatheoretical) assumptions about the nature of science and methodology, key research problems, and exemplars or representatives
of successful examples of science.

What was of particular concern for Kuhn was how scientific
theories changed, especially in the competition between fundamentally different theoretical perspectives or paradigms. What
he found was that the replacement of one theory by another did
not happen in the ways assumed by logical empiricists—that the
accumulation of disconfirming evidence forced researchers to
replace rationally the old theory with a new and better one.
Instead he found irrational resistance against new theories on
the part of researchers who had vested interests in the given
theories of "*normal science.*" Often science had to await the
death of an older generation to complete the process of a "scientific revolution."

But this did not happen just because researchers were not
completely rational. Something even more fundamental was at
stake, given the theory-laden character of facts. From the point
of view of one paradigm the facts confirmed its theory, whereas
another paradigm could develop its argument on the basis of
different facts. One of the consequences was that it became
logically impossible to choose between the two theories on the
grounds of notions of verification, confirmation, or even resistance to falsification. The deeper problem is that paradigms are
ultimately incommensurate with one another in the sense that
they construct scientific realities that cannot be compared because of fundamentally different uses and meanings of concepts.
To the extent that the *incommensurability thesis* is valid, translation between theoretical paradigms became virtually impossible, thus undercutting the rationality of choices between them.

In short, the "norms" of science—and "normal science"—provide only a very limited and misleading picture because they could

not explain the nature of qualitatively new knowledge—of *"revolutionary science."* For Kuhn—or at least for many of those who followed in his footsteps—such evidence about how science changes called into question assumptions about the rationality of scientific methods.[4] The stage thus was set for the emergence of postempiricist philosophies and sociologies of science that also questioned the foundational role of logic and sense-data in science, as well as science's meaning as part of the cultural system.

Meaning: The Crisis of Science as a Belief System

The consequences of postempiricist theories of science have been diverse. The unity implied by the very term *postempiricism* is defined by a shared opposition to positivism, rather than a settled agreement about the alternative. But two issues stand out with respect to the social sciences. First, these developments have contributed to influential critiques of epistemological foundationalism and have challenged the capacity of scientific knowledge to represent reality; second, they have reopened the problematic of the status of the human and social sciences, given that the positivist account of the natural sciences no longer serves as an unquestioned exemplar for other disciplines.

A decisive consequence of the new history of science was that it was no longer possible to sustain the presuppositions of positivist epistemology, for example, the unity of scientific explanation as covering laws, the indubitable character of scientific facts independent of theories, and the rational confirmation of theories by appeals to facts. Such criticisms provoked a crisis in the status of scientific knowledge. At one extreme some philosophers of science such as Paul Feyerabend celebrated these findings in writing "against method" and calling for "epistemological anarchism" (Feyerabend 1975). Others were less confident and feared that these developments would serve only to justify new attacks on scientific institutions and open the way for new forms of irrationalism. As a consequence the crisis of the sciences first announced in the 1930s (e.g., Husserl, 1970) had taken on a new form in the 1980s under the heading of *postmodernism* (a point we return to in a moment).

Postempiricist Alternatives

Implications of the Reflexive Thesis

As the preceding discussion has suggested, postempiricist positions today dominate discussion in much of philosophy of science and social theory. More contentious, however, are the consequences of postempiricist approaches for an alternative metatheory for the social sciences. The basic problem here is drawing out the implications of the "reflexive thesis" or the *constructivism* that lies at the heart of the new science studies: the notion that scientific knowledge is a social construct. Three strategies of response to this problematic have been noted: "To some it is a threat. To others it is a critical tool for use only against others. And yet to others still it is an opportunity" (Ashmore 1989, p. xxviii). As we will argue, critical realism and critical theory necessarily acknowledge that awareness of reflexivity is not merely destructive, but can advance our understanding of the sciences and open up new doors of inquiry.

Postmodernism Versus Critical Realism

One interpretation of the reflexive thesis is that it undermines faith science altogether and thus confirms the fears of its positivist critics. In its most extreme form this questioning of foundationalism has been associated with a postmodernist notion of a "dismantling of reality" that culminates in skepticism of the following type:

> If we are certain of anything, it is that we are certain of nothing. If we have knowledge, it is that there can be none. Ours is a world awash with relativism. It has seeped into our culture, it threatens to become our faith. The tide may have begun with the end of belief in a universal morality and religious code, but it has swelled with a recognition of the limited and particular perspective of our culture, our time and our society. Its full force is now being felt in the name of post-structuralism and post-modernity. . . . If relativism initiated an unsettling of truth and objectivity post-modernism is an attempt to engage in the complete dismantling of the edifice. To this extent post-modernism is a radical version of relativism. *While*

> *relativism can be described as the view that truth is paradigm-dependent, post-modernism might be described as the view that meaning is undecidable and therefore truth unattainable* [italics added]. (Lawson 1989, pp. xi-xii)

Despite the current popularity of this version of postmodernism, such drastic conclusions are either necessary or inevitable even if the logical empiricist theory of knowledge is undermined. In crucial respects radical postmodernist skepticism shares deeper assumptions with the very positivism it criticizes: The belief that to be worthy of the name, knowledge must be absolutely certain; hence both unwittingly reflect the foundationalism that lies at the origins of science, given its aspiration to provide the absolute certainty previously provided by religion. In contrast critical realism has attempted to provide a postempiricist metatheory of science that takes into account its reflexive and subjective aspects.

The Critical Realist Theory of Science

Beyond Empiricism and Subjectivism

The metatheoretical approach of *critical realism* (or *critical naturalism*) can make a strong case as the most promising basis for securing the status of critical theory in relation to the sciences as a whole.[5] Critical realism, along with critical theory, rejects the basic polarization that frames the opposition between positivism and postmodernist relativism—the standoff between empiricism and subjectivism as the only choices.[6] This rejection is achieved, in part, by redefining the relations between epistemology and ontology. It acknowledges the subjectivist (and pragmatist) point that epistemology cannot be based on some pure scientific method that is based on logic and empirical data: The methodologies of the sciences are many, and empirical evidence is always available for strong competing views. But this epistemological and methodological pragmatism does not necessarily require ontological skepticism—the suggestion that we cannot confidently posit realities independent of our consciousness.

Furthermore, without some form of ontological realism the connection between the sciences and human emancipation is jeopardized (Bhaskar 1979, 1989; Outhwaite 1987). But this form of
critical realism does not require a correspondence theory of
truth whereby concepts are held to mirror reality.

Basic Realist Assumptions

What is required to break down the empiricist-subjectivist split,
according to Roy Bhaskar, the most important British defender
of critical realism, is a fundamental distinction between thought
and objects of thought, hence between "intransitive" and "transitive" objects of scientific knowledge. *Intransitive objects* are
thus "the (relatively) unchanging real objects which exist outside and perdure independently of the scientific process," whereas
transitive objects involve "the changing (and theoretically-
imbued) cognitive objects which are produced within science
as a function and result of its practice" (Bhaskar 1986, p. 51).
Without the assumption of this enduring intransitive dimension,
the result is the kind of postempiricist relativism where "things
become a mere manifestation, expression, externalization or
embodiment of thought, devoid of extra-discursive conditions and
empirical controls"; and without a transitive dimension, "thought
becomes a mere impress, effluxion, internalization or *Doppel-
gänger* of things, bereft of intra-discursive conditions and
rational controls" (Bhaskar 1986, p. 52). In other words, the
transitive (ever-changing) concepts of science cannot be reduced
to the external objects they seek to represent and can only exist
"in more or less historically specific, symbolically mediated and
expressed, praxis-dependent, ineradicably social forms" (Bhaskar
1986, p. 52).

From this perspective the reflexive turn—the history and sociology of the sciences—becomes a necessary basis of their intelli-
gibility and justification. The continuously changing and diverse
nature of scientific concepts and practices does not, therefore,
call into question confidence in scientific knowledge because
there is no need for concepts to "correspond" to reality in order
to be justifiable.

Further, critical realism proposes an alternative way of looking
at explanation, the empirical heart of the enterprise of science.

First, the deductive-nomothetic account tied to universal laws is rejected as inadequate for even the natural sciences. Second, the postempiricist contextualist approach, based on explanation as a social process culminating in consensus, is qualified as incomplete because of its "unwillingness to admit models as hypothetical descriptions of an unknown but knowable reality" (Bhaskar 1986, p. 60). In contrast:

> For transcendental realism, explanations are quintessentially socially produced and fallible causal accounts of the unknown mode of production of phenomena, or the episodes in which such accounts are furnished. In theoretical science, explanation is accomplished by an account of the formerly unknown generative mechanism; in practical (applied and concrete) science, by an account of the formerly unknown mode of combination or interarticulation, in some specific 'conjuncture,' of antecedently known mechanisms. Realism attempts to incorporate the situated strengths of both deductivism and contextualism. (Bhaskar 1986, p. 60)

Conclusion: Rethinking Reason

From a critical modernist (or even a critical postmodernist) perspective, the postpositivist critique has been salutary by creating the conditions that might facilitate a deeper understanding of rationality and its relationship to other aspects of life. It is not merely a threat; it is also an opportunity.

In certain respects postpositivism undermines the concept of prescriptive methods in the older sense. Its objective "is not to replace positivist methodology with a new postpositivist methodology. For in the postpositivist understanding of science there is no correct method to follow" (Polkinghorne 1983, p. 3). But this postpositivist methodological pragmatism and pluralism culminates in incoherence if not coupled with something like a critical realist ontology. Even if there is no single correct method, there are distinguishable *methodological strategies* appropriate to particular questions and subject matters, depending on the nature of the object of inquiry. It is in that sense that we propose to explore further the implications of a critical theory of methodology as the point of departure for a methodological framework for critical theory.

The task of this chapter has been to explore the idea of science at three levels: (a) its logical structure (systematics), (b) as a social and historical phenomenon (the sociology of scientific knowledge), and (c) as a cultural meaning system (the critique of science). Three basic approaches to the question of the nature of science were outlined in these terms: positivism (as logical empiricism), transitional critical rationalism, and skeptical postpositivism. Critical realism was introduced as a postempiricist perspective that offers a plausible alternative to the skeptical postmodernist interpretation of the constructed character of science.

In Part II we return to the specific issues of critical theory and the social sciences. Chapter 4 introduces the research program of the early critical theory of the original Frankfurt School. Chapter 5 surveys a series of subsequent developments in metatheory that are crucial to understanding contemporary critical theory. Then Chapter 6 reconstructs the metatheoretical approach of contemporary critical theory and Chapter 7 covers the resulting research program as evident in the works of Habermas and Giddens.

Notes

1. On positivism's worship of generality, see R. Miller 1987; for a concise characterization of positivism, see Fay 1975, p. 13.

2. In this respect, Popper's falsification principle has not escaped the ironic snares of foundationalism as revealed in the *tu quoque* argument ("you too") directed originally at the verification principle: "Logical positivism demarcates meaningless from meaningful statements by the principle of empirical verification: if a statement cannot (in principle) be empirically verified, then it is meaningless; if it can be, it is meaningful. Unfortunately [or rather fortunately], a state of the verification principle cannot *itself* be so verified and is therefore meaningless" (Ashmore 1989, p. 88).

3. On the other hand, awareness of the hermeneutic and rhetorical foundations of the natural sciences has led many (like Bhaskar) to suggest a new, but quite different, basis for the unity of the sciences.

4. Kuhn himself retreated from his early formulation that implied strong incommensurability because of the resulting relativism.

5. Often critical realism (which has its origins in a theory of natural science) has been portrayed as a rival of critical theory as antipositivist strategies (Stockman 1983). This is valid with respect to the philosophy of science where Habermas, for example, relied extensively on traditional empiricist accounts, thus stressing the differences between the natural and social sciences. Given a critical realist perspective, more fundamental continuities are revealed although the unique features of social science are recognized. A more recent study (Romm 1991) contributes to this problematic polarization of the two positions in superficially contrasting what is called "Marxist realism" (Keat) and "Marxist nonrealism" (Habermas). The convergence thesis developed by Outhwaite (1987) appears more convincing and informs the present study.

6. As Bhaskar put it: "No longer can thought be conceived as a mechanical function of given things, as in empiricism; nor can the activity of creative subjects continue to be seen as constituting a world of objects, as in idealism; nor is some combination of the two possible" (Bhaskar 1986, p. 51).

PART II

Critical Theory as a Research Program

4

EARLY CRITICAL THEORY
AS A RESEARCH PROGRAM

A Historical Introduction

Just those who feel a responsibility toward theory will have to confront its doubtful aspects as relentlessly as they confront the inadequacies of mere empiricism. . . . Therefore critical reflection about empirical social research is necessary, and also an incisive familiarity with its results. (Frankfurt Institute for Social Research 1972, p. 119)

Knowledge in this traditional sense, including every type of experience, is preserved in critical theory and practice. But in regard to the essential kind of change at which the critical theory aims, there can be no corresponding concrete perception of it until it actually comes about. If the proof of the pudding is in the eating, the eating here is still in the future. (Horkheimer [1937] 1972a, p. 221)

From Western Marxism to Critical Theory

Introduction

Part I outlined many of the basic issues in metatheory and the philosophy of science. The task of Part II is to trace the origins of critical theory, a distinctive research program that became increasingly differentiated from, and eventually significantly discontinuous with, the Marxist tradition. A *research program* involves combining a metatheoretical approach with a concrete set of empirical explanatory problems.

In this chapter we are concerned primarily with the origins of early Frankfurt critical theory as a distinctive perspective that became defined as an interdisciplinary research program. The concept of a *research program* will be used as a way of analyzing the rationality of science in the wake of postempiricist critiques. In this reconstruction we stress the innovative character of early Frankfurt critical theory in relation to Western Marxism, as well as the internal shifts that ultimately culminated in contemporary critical theory. The chapter is concerned with original Frankfurt tradition from the 1920s into the 1950s.

Social Theory as a Research Program

For the purpose of analyzing social theories, the notion of *research programs,* developed initially by the British-Hungarian philosopher Imre Lakatos (Lakatos 1970), has advantages over Kuhn's notion of a research *paradigm.*[1] One problem with the paradigm concept in Kuhn's version is that it is associated with the assumption that disciplines are inherently unified. Another is that Kuhn focuses on the social psychology of research at the price of undermining how we might justify the rationality of science, given that mere appeal to empirical evidence is no longer sufficient. We have seen some of the consequences of this problem in the strands of post-empiricist metatheory that culminate in postmodernist relativism. What is required instead is a revised conception of disciplinary paradigms that can make sense of the type of research program proposed by critical theory.

Lakatos begins his sympathetic critique of Popper with a distinction between "naive" and "sophisticated" falsificationism. *Sophisticated falsificationism* proposes considerably more lenient rules for the acceptance of theories (demarcation criteria to eliminate pseudosciences) and more flexible ones for the rules for falsifying or eliminating theories.[2] Given the problems involved in devising falsifying "crucial experiments" even in the natural sciences, Lakatos proposes that the acceptance of theories should be seen comparatively (relative to the type of inquiry) and should be based on its capacity to reveal "novel facts" (Lakatos 1970, p. 116).

Crucial to the rules of falsification is attention to the adjustments that theoretical approaches make to disconfirming evidence "between rational and irrational change of theory" (Lakatos 1970, p. 117). This attention requires distinguishing ("demarcating") between those adjustments of the theory that are *rational* (e.g., new auxiliary hypotheses) and hence *progressive,* and those that are *irrational* (e.g., semantic or linguistic tricks) and hence *degenerative.* This distinction between *progressive* versus *degenerative problemshifts*–which can occur at either the theoretical or empirical level–becomes a very different way of evaluating changes within a research program. What it reveals is that theories are always undergoing change, which is why "what we appraise is a *series of theories* rather than isolated *theories*" (1970, p. 118). And it is for this reason that the original *paradigm* concept constituted a breakthrough for understanding what to evaluate in scientific research.

A research program consists of methodological rules: Some tell us what paths of research to avoid (*negative heuristic*); others tell what paths to pursue (*positive heuristic*) (Lakatos 1970, p. 132). The negative heuristic precludes attacking the "hard core" of the research program. Instead it must develop "auxiliary hypotheses" to form a "protective belt" that becomes the target of tests and readjustments. As a consequence, elements of this protective belt can be falsified without necessarily undermining the core. The positive heuristic thus requires constructing this protective belt and ignoring anomalies in order to get along with research and sustain the necessary theoretical autonomy of science: "The positivist heuristic saves the scientist from becoming confused by the ocean of anomalies. . . . He ignores the *actual* counterexamples, the available '*data*' (1970, p. 135). As Lakatos concludes, his concept of criticism is more lenient than Popper's and recognizes that one must treat emergent programs generously. Further, some of the most creative programs become visible only with hindsight and rational reconstruction (1970, p. 179).

A major limitation of Lakatos's formulation is his stress on the rigidity of the hard core and the ambiguous status of closely related competitors. To deal with these and related difficulties, the

American philosopher of science Larry Laudan suggests a notion of *research traditions* that is even more useful for the human sciences, given its openness: "Each research tradition (unlike a specific theory) goes through a number of different, detailed (and often mutually contradictory) formulations and generally has a long history extending through a significant period of time (by contrast, theories are frequently short-lived)" (Laudan 1977, pp. 78-9).

These changes cannot be understood in empiricist terms essentially as signs of increasing "truth" that is approximated through self-correction. Nor can we simply assume that science is rational because of this increasing correspondence to truth (reality), a most problematic claim from a postempiricist perspective. So rather than linking the rationality of scientific change to this slippery objectivistic "truth," Laudan suggests making it parasitic on rational, problem-solving choices (Laudan 1977, p. 125).

An important advantage of this approach is that it provides a framework for acknowledging the cumulative character of the humanistic disciplines, which "every bit as much as the sciences, have empirical and conceptual problems; both have criteria for assessing the adequacy of solutions to problems; both can be shown to have made significant progress at certain stages of their historical evolution" (Laudan 1977, p. 191). This point has been obscured, however, by the "simplistic identification of (scientific) rationality with experimental control and quantitative precision" (p. 191).

Two crucial consequences of linking the rationality of a research tradition with its problem-solving abilities have profound implications for understanding the social sciences. First, the basis of rationally choosing between research programs is expanded to include many other aspects beyond how they will appear to correspond with the facts. The focus on problem solving contributes to recognizing many other bases for rational choices about a research program: the potential richness of its theoretical insight, the significance of the problems it defines, or even its ideological implications.[3]

Second, this approach also calls into question the strict empiricist distinction between the systematics of theorizing and the history of theory (logic of discovery):

> Logicians teach us that it is a specific version of the so-called genetic fallacy to imagine that the origin or historical career of a doctrine has anything whatever to do with its cognitive well-foundedness. . . . I want to take exception with this view, even to turn it on its head, by arguing that *no sensible rational appraisal can be made of any doctrine without a rich knowledge of its historical development* (and the history of its rivals). (Laudan 1977, p. 193)

This basic insight will guide our reconstruction of the tradition of critical theory in terms of various progressive and regressive problemshifts and their impact on problem-solving capacities in research.

Of particular importance to problem solving in social theory is the role of historical events in confronting theorists with quasi-experimental evidence of a falsifying nature. In social theory this is recognized in the historicist principle of *historical respecification:* In the light of the changing structure of society and crucial historical events, it often becomes necessary to adapt concepts to the new historical realities. But this necessity of continuous revision constitutes a fundamental dilemma: At what point does historical respecification transform a theoretical approach into something qualitatively different? The core versus protective belt distinction helps clarify this problem, though it is often difficult to apply in practice, given the more diffusely organized character of social science.

Western Marxism: Scientific and Critical

The family of theories associated with the Marxist tradition has been divided in various ways, but two types of classification are perhaps most useful: (a) an epistemological-methodological one that differentiates between *Western Marxism* as "positive" science and as forms of "critical" theory and (b) a geographic-political one that differentiates between the Western Marxism of Western Europe and the *Marxist-Leninist* tradition centered in the Soviet Union. In the latter context the research program of Marxism (identified in Soviet theory as *dialectical materialism* or *Dimat*) was reduced directly to its ideological functions for a particular regime, thus culminating in degenerating problemshifts and nearly a complete loss of scientific credibility. From this perspective, Marx's theory was reduced to a totalizing dialectic of nature and history, with the former Soviet Union cast as the leading edge of historical evolution.

But Western Marxism remained a more open tradition, despite its ideological origins and the repressive effects of marginalization within bourgeois democracies. By the end of the 20th century it had become recognized in academic circles as one of the most significant traditions of modern social and political theory. Western Marxism has been divided, however, by two tendencies— scientific and critical—reflected in attempts to develop distinctive research programs from the same theoretical tradition (Gouldner 1980). Variants of the "scientific" approach or *scientific Marxism* reach back to Engels and Austro-Marxism and culminate in contemporary neo-Marxist research programs in the academy (Bottomore 1975; Morrow 1992a). Variants of the critical approach reach back to Lukacs, the Frankfurt School, and Antonio Gramsci in Italy and assume a variety of forms of critical theory and critical social science today (Held 1980; Fay 1987; Leonard 1990).

The initial basis of division between these two streams of thought reflects fundamental differences about the core argument of Marx's theory, above all of the metatheoretical assumptions of historical materialism as a theory of society and history. The key analytical concepts in dispute here are the *base-superstructure metaphor* and the theory of the evolution of *modes of production*. For *scientific* Marxism the primary object of inquiry is the discovery, in the positivist manner, of the laws of social development rooted in modes of production that are the primary reference point for revolutionary action. The status of the "subjects" of mobilization is ambiguous, however, inasmuch as they are ultimately puppets of the laws of developmental transformation, an assumption linked to the thesis of the determining economic base and the dependent cultural superstructure. The earlier versions of this model contributed to economic reductionism in the sense that, for example, the state was seen as a direct instrument of the rule of the dominant class.[4]

The point of departure of critical approaches, which rely more on Marx's early writings, is the crucial importance of analyzing the subject-object dialectic through which society as a *contradictory whole* (or *totality*) is formed. In other words, the basis of early Frankfurt critical theory is a metatheoretical rereading of Marx, based on some of the Hegelian elements in Marx's methodology. This metatheoretical position generally is referred to as a form of *critical hermeneutics.* Crucial to this reconstruction was the discovery of Marx's and Engels's early manuscripts (published in German in 1932), which established the fundamental importance of the Hegelian concept of alienation as "*alienated labor*" for Marx. On this basis it becomes possible to see Marx's approach as requiring a subject-structure dialectic, hence a model of society as a process of *social reproduction,* rather than the outcome of the linear effects of an economic base on a cultural structure (as in the base-superstructure model). Hence this model involved a way of thinking of society as a contradictory totality in which the various elements had considerable autonomy even if they ultimately expressed the contradictions of the whole (Marcuse, [1941] 1960). The resulting research program involved a fundamental revision of what Marxist theory had been understood to be until the late 1920s (though this was done in the name of faithfulness to Marx's original intentions). In any case the resulting interpretation involved a revision of the core doctrine of "economism" and related metatheoretical assumptions regarding the epistemological status of historical materialism. Nevertheless this more flexible social reproduction model still had a deterministic side in that its operation was tied to a teleological process—that is, the unfolding of world history as envisioned by Marx.

Three Problemshifts in Critical Theory

Three crucial problemshifts can be identified in the development of the critical theory tradition associated with the original Frankfurt School. In the first, neo-Marxist phase, critical theory was envisioned as a form of interdisciplinary materialism that identified with the project of working-class revolution, but from the perspective of the autonomy of a research program. It is in this first phase that the most important empirical redirection away from orthodox Marxism took place and established critical theory as an empirical research program. But this research program was divided between "inner" and "outer" circles whose differences prefigured later developments (Honneth 1987). This first phase is also characterized by significant shifts of interest from the initial Weimar phase in the 1920s to the exile period in the late 1930s. The initial period was concerned especially with explaining the lack of resistance to fascism by the German working class. In the exile phase interest shifted to rethinking the nature of the capitalist state and understanding the emergent form of society.

By the 1940s, however, critical theory had become disillusioned with its earlier interpretations and largely abandoned its concern with developing empirical methods for testing and elaborating theory. In this second phase, a decline—a degenerating problem-shift—was evident at the empirical level. This led many others away from critical theory and contributed to its near eclipse as a research program.

A third phase (to be taken up later) is represented in the work of Jürgen Habermas, who led a second generation in the early 1960s and helped stimulate a number of other theorists else-where by the end of that decade (e.g., Anthony Giddens, Alvin Gouldner) who attempted to criticize and elaborate on an approach inspired, in part, by the older Critical Theory of the original Frankfurt School.

The Hermeneutic-Dialectical Tradition

Introduction:
The Hermeneutic Tradition

Within the German tradition the methodological status of the social sciences has been debated most intensely. In France and Britain variants of positivism dominated until the post-World War II period. And in the 1930s the influx of many of the leading positivists from Europe led to positivism's dominance in the United States at the expense of the marginalization of pragmatism (the philosophical foundation of symbolic interactionist sociology) in the 1940s. The primary exception to these positivist tendencies was in 19th-century Germany, where a tradition of philosophical idealism resisted positivism in the name of hermeneutics (Mueller-Vollmer 1988; Bleicher 1980). Although these idealist philosophies contained many obscurantist elements, they did pose important questions that had been suppressed elsewhere. At the outset, however, some of the three key tendencies in this tradition need to be identified in greater detail: hermeneutics, phenomenology, and historicism.

Although the term *hermeneutics* does not appear in traditional dictionaries of the social sciences, it has become current in English language sociology during the past decade in referring to "a theory and method of interpreting human action and artifacts. It derives from the term for interpreting biblical texts, a practice which involved detailed attempts to understand the 'authentic' version of the work. Dilthey used the term (and also *Verstehen*) to refer to the method of the 'cultural sciences' " (Jary and Jary 1991, p. 272).

The hermeneutic philosopher and cultural historian Wilhelm Dilthey (1833-1911) defined the problematic in terms that have influenced German sociology by strongly differentiating between the natural sciences (or the *Naturwissenschaften*) and the "moral" or "cultural" sciences (*Geisteswissenschaften*) (Dilthey [1910] 1981; Dilthey 1976). The use of the original German terms here is advisable because of the inadequacy of translations, which cannot clearly convey the nuances of this debate. For example, in English the term *science* is already loaded with natural scientific connotations, reflecting the traditional empiricism and positivism of Anglo American scholarship. The German term *Wissenschaft* is much broader, closer to the notion of a discipline. Further, the term *Geist* is suggestive of the "spiritual" dimension of social reality, though in the sense of its cultural and moral-evaluative aspects, rather than specifically religious ones.

The differences between the natural and cultural sciences are linked with two concepts that also resist translation: *Verstehen* and *Erklären* (Apel 1984). The first of these is quite familiar in sociological theory under the heading of *Verstehen*—a term that comes from the verb meaning literally "to understand" and refers to the processes of meaning interpretation required for communication. As such, it overlaps with the methodological issues of hermeneutics or the interpretation of texts. According to Dilthey, interpretation was the task of the cultural sciences, and natural scientific causal explanation was rejected as inappropriate for understanding human action. The term *Erklären* means "explanation" in the natural scientific sense of causal explanation based on invariant (*nomothetic*) laws associated with both hypothetico-deductive and covering law models. In these German debates it was held by adherents of the *Verstehen* position that social life did not lend itself to such causal explanations, given the unique character of social life. Scientific Marxists rejected Dilthey's position and argued that Marx's historical materialism provided the basis for causal analysis in ways consistent with natural science.

Hegelian Marxism: Critical Versus Traditional Theory

Hegelian Marxism involved a very different way of looking at the relationship between interpretation and causality, one that rejected the notion of ahistorical laws. Georg Wilhelm Hegel (1770-1831) had a tremendous impact on the history of the human sciences, though known only vaguely in sociology for his influence on Marx. In contrast to his older contemporary, Immanuel Kant (1724-1804), Hegel held that the condition of possibility of knowledge was not simply the a priori structures of the human mind (Kant's transcendental categories) but also one's location in history (Kelly 1969). For Hegel the categories of thought changed from epoch to epoch. For example, for all of his wisdom Aristotle could not criticize Athenian slavery because he was a prisoner of the "spirit" of his time (his *Zeitgeist,* as Hegel would say); only later, with the development of the universal "rights of man," did this criticism become possible.

The term *Hegelian* has many meanings when applied to positions in the human sciences, but one stands out above all: the notion that social reality is thoroughly historical and can be understood only as a *totality* of contradictory elements. Such *contradictions* are distinct from ordinary conflicts because they cannot be resolved within the given form of reality and require the emergence of a new and higher form. Transferred to the analysis of capitalist political economy, it implied that the contradiction between labor and capital could not be dealt with through reform, that only a revolutionary transformation could lead to a production system based on cooperation.

The term *totality* is linked closely with a tradition of *radical historicism*—that is, the methodological approach originating in

Hegel's thesis that societies and the concepts used to describe them are relative to the historical context (D'Amico 1989; Grumley 1989). For example, historicists would tend to evaluate the meaning of any statement in terms of what it meant in the period in question. Attitudes about women or slavery, for example, would be judged as relative to what was typical at a particular point in time. Similarly any concept—such as social class—would be assumed to have quite a different meaning in analyzing, say, a feudal as opposed to a capitalist society. Consequently historicism has flirted with problems of relativism (hence is an important precursor of postempiricism) and is directed explicitly against positivist assumptions about invariant, universal laws equally applicable to any historical situation.[5]

In the context of the Marxist tradition, the term *Hegelian* Marxism is used as a code term to describe the complex and disputed process whereby Marx's theory was reinterpreted as a form of critical hermeneutics, as opposed to a natural science of society. Although opposing the traditional hermeneutics of Dilthey, the resulting *hermeneutic-dialectical tradition* interpreted society from a perspective that took into account that cultural products were conditioned by the social relations of capitalism, an approach that made the critique of ideologies the central interpretive task. And unlike positivist approaches to Marxian theory, it did not attempt to reconcile Marx with reigning empiricist conceptions of science.

Georg Lukacs (1885-1971), a Hungarian philosopher who spent much of his life in Germany until expelled by the Nazis, was one of the first (along with Karl Korsch) to introduce these kinds of metatheoretical issues as the basis of rethinking the metatheoretical foundations of Marx's theory.[6] For Lukacs the central aspect of Marx's theory was his method based on an analysis of society as a contradictory totality constituted through the subject-object dialectic (Lukacs [1923] 1968; Jay 1984). The most novel aspect of Lukacs's approach was that it demonstrated how the domination of capital was not sustained simply by external coercion, but through a process of *reification* (literally, to make into a "thing") through which social agents came to identify falsely with a social reality that they perceived as "natural"—even though it was created originally by them. For Lukacs this was the key to how the commodify form of capitalist social relations constructed the totality of capitalist society. The later discovery of Marx's early manuscripts showed that he used the notion of *alienation* (or *estrangement*) with reference to alienated labor in a similar way (Arato and Breines 1979).[7]

What defines Frankfurt critical theory (and links it to the sociology of knowledge) as a form of interpretive theory was its effort to explore this subject-object dialectic and its relation to both capitalist exchange relations analyzed by Marx and the processes of bureaucratization (instrumental rationalization) identified by Max Weber. These questions defined the "materialist" basis of its specific critical hermeneutic approach—that is, its insistence on the interplay between social being as an objective facticity and acts of interpretation as something more than a process of culture "reflecting" economics or technology (Rabinow and Sullivan 1987, pp. 16-7).

The early Frankfurt approach to social science can be reconstructed in terms of its distinction between *"critical"* and *"traditional" theory,* where the latter refers primarily to the natural scientific model or to any contemplative conception of absolute knowledge. In contrast early Critical Theory's conception often is referred to as a form of Hegelian Marxism, though this term is misleading to the extent it does not entail a full return to Hegel. What it does correctly suggest, however, is a conception of Marx's theory that cannot be subsumed in orthodox positivist conceptions of a naturalistic science. Although ambiguous on many important issues, the early Critical Theorists gave a forceful defense of the unique kind of theorizing they found in Marx, one they associated with the idea of a *dialectical method* as understood by Lukacs's analysis of society as a contradictory totality. For Horkheimer the crucial aspect here is the different relationship between subject and object in natural and social science, a difference that changes the nature of causal necessity:

> The object with which the scientific specialist deals is not affected at all by his own theory. Subject and object are kept strictly apart. . . . A consciously critical attitude, however, is part of the development of society: the construing of the course of history as the necessary product of an economic mechanism simultaneously contains both a protest against this order of things . . . and the idea of self-determination for the human race. . . . The judgment passed on the

necessity inherent in the previous course of events implies here a struggle to change it from a blind to a meaningful necessity. (Horkheimer 1972a, p. 229)

From this perspective the task of critical theory was one of *immanent critique* that merely required pointing to the discrepancy between the basic liberal values of freedom and equality proclaimed by bourgeois society and the objective realities of economic irrationality that could be subjected to human control—that is, "from a blind to a meaningful necessity." For this reason the knowledge of these contradictions produced by critical research could be presumed to inform directly the mobilization of oppositional movements. In other words, critical theory did not need to employ some kind of criticism from outside because it could employ a form of ideology critique whose message was potentially available and sensible to the subordinated classes.

Such a conception does not preclude the practical importance of the traditional theory of the positive sciences: "If such a method is applied to society, the result is statistics and descriptive sociology, and these can be important for many purposes, even for critical theory" (Horkheimer 1972a, p. 229). Critical theory also asks such "fragmentary questions" about reality in the form of general and specific hypothetical propositions about aspects of social life. But at the same time, "the critical theory of society is, in its totality, the unfolding of a single existential judgment" about social development and its relation to human reason and freedom (Horkheimer 1972a, p. 227).

The historicist aspect of this approach is the assumption that theories must change in response to fundamental changes in society: "Critical theory does not have one doctrinal substance today, another tomorrow. The changes in it do not mean a shift to a wholly new outlook, *as long as the age itself does not radically change* [italics added]" (Horkheimer 1972a, p. 234). Further, Horkheimer argued that critical theory had to rely on findings from the specialized disciplines to flesh out its "existential judgment" and to assess whether new stages of development have emerged (Horkheimer 1972a, pp. 225-6). Early critical theory was thus clearly Marxist in its insistence that the overall movement of history was revealed by the successive contradictions of modes of production. But Horkheimer still remained ambivalent about linking such truth claims to the Marxian assumption of the revolutionary role of the working class because there is no "social class by whose acceptance of the theory one could be guided" (Horkheimer 1972a, p. 242).

Interdisciplinary Materialism as a Research Program

The key aspect of the original Frankfurt Institute for Social Research was its transformation of Marxist theory into a relatively autonomous research program.[8] Until that point, despite the efforts of particular individuals, Marxism remained a political ideology despite its claims to a scientific status. Research carried out under the sponsorship of a political party could not, by definition, be sufficiently autonomous for a scientific research program. But the combination of a private endowment and affiliation with the University of Frankfurt provided such autonomy. The significance of this project to 20th-century social science did not begin to become well known in the English reading world until the 1970s, following its revival in West Germany in the 1960s (Jay 1973).[9]

Where it was noted previously in the English-speaking world, it was subsumed under the somewhat misleading rubric of "*mass society theory*," a term popular in the 1950s.[10] The term *mass society* was used by both left-wing and conservative critics to designate what was perceived to be a fundamental shift in 20th-century culture brought about by democratization (especially mass education) and the mass media, both of which had the effect of eroding the close link between class position and cultural characteristics. Left-wing critics lamented the emergence of a national "mass culture" (a pseudoconsensus) that linked all social classes because it deflected the working class from becoming aware of its collective interests and specific cultural identity; conservative critics were disturbed because in a mass culture the marketplace determined the "value" of cultural goods and the cultural elites no longer served to provide effective models for socialization (Swingewood 1977). Often the criticism of critical theory of mass and popular culture was mistaken with this elitist, conservative reaction.

We are not centrally concerned here with recounting either the history of the older Frankfurt tradition, surveying the forms of social research conducted in its name, or reviewing its reception in the social sciences. The task, rather, is to trace the shifts that culminated in the transition from the research program of early Critical Theory to the contemporary context. The distinctive feature of Max Horkheimer's research program was that it was "positivistic enough" to envision the necessity of an *interdisciplinary materialism*—that is, cooperation between Marxist theory and the social sciences (Honneth 1987, p. 349). At the time of his inauguration as director of the Frankfurt Institute, Horkheimer defined the programmatic task of Critical Theory as:

> the question of the connection between the economic life of society, the psychic development of individuals, and the changes in cultural domains in the narrower sense. To these belong not only the so-called spiritual contents of science, art, and religion, but also law, custom, fashion, public opinion, sports, leisure pastimes, life style, etc. (Horkheimer 1972b, p. 43; trans. R. M.)

From this perspective what was required was overcoming the split between empirical research and philosophy, where the latter was linked to a Hegelian Marxist conception of historical reason. Nevertheless the core of this research program was a conception of historical materialism firmly anchored in sociological analysis. But paradoxically, change in the Weimar Republic and elsewhere in the 1920s and 1930s was not clearly moving in the direction predicted by Marx's revolutionary theory. This anomaly provided the substantive problematic that defined this research program—its positive heuristic—and its central object of inquiry: the increasing integration of the working class in advanced capitalism. So for Horkheimer the investigations of the institute in the 1930s were guided by the question, "How [do] the mental mechanisms come about, by which it is possible that tensions between social classes, which feel impelled toward conflict because of the economic situation, can remain latent?" (cited in Honneth 1987, p. 353).

Answering this question required supplementing traditional Marxist *political economy*—the explanation of social forms in terms of their genesis in the capitalist mode of production—with the two new disciplinary approaches of social psychology and cultural theory. Changed historical conditions had transformed the nature of political economy. Because there was no longer the direct link between the contradictions of the economy and class action assumed by Marx, a critical social psychology based on a historical reading of Freud was required to explain the "irrational" forces that blocked the working class from recognizing its own interests. Further, a theory of culture was necessary to study the contents of the socialization process linked with the rise of the mass media (Honneth 1987, p. 353).

From the perspective of the third phase of critical theory represented by Habermas and Giddens, the crucial limitation of Horkheimer's program was that even though it avoided the economic reductionism of the base-superstructure model, it suffered from a form of *Marxist functionalism:* "Horkheimer and his collaborators could only achieve a theoretical unity in his programme by using Marxist functionalism to establish a direct dependence between the individual elements of the investigation" (Honneth 1987, p. 353). This approach was functionalist in employing strongly *teleological explanations:* Particular structures and cultural characteristics were interpreted as responding to the functional imperatives or needs of the system to reproduce itself as a capitalist society. Nevertheless reference to empirical investigations served throughout this period as a crucial basis for revision and formulation of alternative theoretical arguments in a manner that was unprecedented in the Marxist tradition.

The theoretical unity of this research program in its mature, post-Weimar phase in exile has been characterized in terms of the catchphrase *"rationalization as reification,"* a notion that provided a framework for analyzing the peculiar transformations evident in Stalinism, National Socialism, and the emergence of state capitalism. As the term suggests, classical critical theory involved a synthesis of concepts drawn from Weber and Lukacs.

The use of the notion of rationalization was originally developed by Max Weber, who distinguished between formal or instrumental rationality and substantial rationality. *Instrumental rationality* referred to the efficiency of the means realizing given ends (values), where efficiency was based on calculations and expertise was based on scientific techniques. In contrast, *substantial rationality* referred to ultimate value claims and therefore could not be based on formally rational procedures at all.[11] Although the Frankfurt theorists rejected this latter assumption, they agreed with Weber that instrumental rationalization, as evident in bureaucratization, was a theme that had not adequately been taken into account by Marx.

The term *reification* was used by Lukacs, as we have seen, to refer to the effects of the processes of commodification, which blinded social actors to the fact that they had, in fact, created the economic relations (as embodied in specific wage levels, relations of power, etc.) that otherwise would be taken as "natural" like laws of nature. From the perspective of the early Frankfurt theorists, the logic of commodification (Lukacs's reification) and that of instrumental rationalization carried out through bureaucratization (Weber) actually reinforced each other. One of the most dramatic consequences was to call into question the naive faith of Marx and Engels in the progressive effects of the growth of science and technology. From the perspective of Critical Theory's *critique of technology,* the technologies of control over nature and society naturally lent themselves to abuse by capitalism or by any other system of domination (e.g., bureaucracies in Soviet-style regimes).

Six themes dominated the resulting agenda of research: "(a) the forms of integration in postliberal societies, (b) family socialization and ego development, (c) mass media and mass culture, (d) the social psychology behind the cessation of protest, (e) the theory of art, and (f) the critique of positivism and science" (Habermas 1987, pp. 378-9). This last theme has been discussed previously in the context of the distinction between critical and traditional theory. The other, more empirical themes will be grouped under the headings of the *state and political economy, culture,* and *social psychology.*

Political Economy and the State

Although a Marxist type functionalism provided a shared framework for analyzing the emerging form of capitalist society (the postwar welfare state), the specific implications varied, depending on the sphere (the state, culture, social psychology); as well, different investigators pursued these issues on the basis of competing interpretations. In other words, there was a remarkable degree of internal dialogue and differences of opinion, often changing rapidly in response to empirical investigations and new historical events. Nowhere was this more evident than with the reassessment of the relationship between political economy and the state.

The point of departure for state theory was the assumption of a fundamental transformation of capitalism: the end of the laissez-faire *liberal capitalism*—that is, an unregulated market system. The outcome was a set of intertwined research questions about the emergent form of *state capitalism*. According to the basic argument, a new organized phase of capitalism had emerged in which the state increasingly functioned to offset or control the effects of the previously autonomous production process, for example, in Keynesian economic policies. Above all, the question was whether this new social formation would have crisis tendencies like the old one (Arato 1978, p. 13).

The details of the shifting responses to these questions are primarily of historical interest today. What is most striking for our present methodological purposes, however, was the manner in which they reformulated the research problematic in the light of various kinds of empirical evidence. During the early 1930s Critical Theory had worked within the orthodox Marxist assumption that the basic choice available was between a planned socialist economy and capitalism, which was inherently incapable (in its liberal form) of planning. A crucial step here was taken in economist Friedrich Pollock's studies of Soviet planning efforts in the late 1920s, and later his analysis of the "new structural elements within capitalist development—increasing centralization and monopolization, state intervention (as yet unplanned and arbitrary), and vast increases in the use of industrial technology" which had responded to the crisis of the old self-regulating system (Arato 1978, p. 14). Questioning the Soviet system and becoming aware of its authoritarian character put the whole thesis of planning as inherently good in a problematic light. From these studies, as well as those on Nazism, it became necessary to stress increasingly the relative "primacy of politics" and the distinctive authoritarian potentials of these different forms of planning: capitalist, fascist, communist (Arato 1978, p. 16).

Research on the structure and dynamics of neocapitalism tended to be pursued on the basis of two contrasting hypotheses: (a) that it represented a new form of manipulated, closed system (Horkheimer, Adorno, Marcuse) or, alternatively, (b) that it was opening up new democratic possibilities (Neumann, Pollock). The former position is most well known and culminated in the slogans portraying postwar capitalism as an administered (Adorno) or one-dimensional (Marcuse) society in which the welfare state and mass culture industries had succeeded in paralyzing the contradictions that otherwise would transform society. From this dominant perspective the new form of "one-dimensional" society was dominated by a depoliticized technical rationality incapable of fundamental criticism (Marcuse 1966). But in either case, these investigations established a fundamental new point of departure for the analysis of state/economy relations: "the change in the function of political economy, the end of the primacy of the economic under industrially advanced contemporary social formations and the necessity of the replacement of political economy as the framework and objective of Marxism as critique" (Arato 1978, p. 22).

Social Psychology

The central social psychological problematic in the context of the Weimar Republic was that of explaining the lack of resistance of the German working class to the fascist centralization of domination. This question was not altogether new for the Marxist left because, from World War I onward, the subjective basis of revolutionary change had not appeared even though the objective basis of crisis was clearly at hand. The question of the use of Freud for this purpose elicited diverse responses. From the turn of the century onward, those working within the Social Democratic Party had toyed with an "eclectic adaptation of Freud," the Communists had responded with the "dogmatic dissociation from Freud," and there were several "mediating positions" by practicing psychoanalysts, mostly without strong party affiliations (Bonß 1984, p. 5; I. Cohen 1982; Lichtman 1982). Erich Fromm (1900-1980) was among the latter and was recruited by Horkheimer to carry though such a reconciliation of Marx and Freud in the context of empirical research projects. The basic theoretical argument involved the development of a historical *psychoanalytic social psychology* (Dahmer 1980) concerned with the historical development of social character: "The task of social psychology is to explain the shared, socially relevant, psychic attitudes and ideologies—and their unconscious roots in particular—in terms of the influence of economic conditions on libido strivings (Fromm 1978, p. 486).

Two major research projects developed on the basis of this theoretical framework. The first, never completed and only published in its fragmentary form in 1980, involved a large-scale survey designed to "gain insights into the psychic structure of manual and white-collar workers" (Fromm cited in Bonß 1984, p. 1). To this end an overly complex 271-item questionnaire was distributed to 3,300 respondents in 1929, with about a third eventually returned.[12]

This largely exploratory survey, based primarily on open-ended questions, was plagued by methodological and theoretical problems compounded by the difficult circumstances. Nevertheless it was suggestive of possibilities that never were developed. But most importantly, it did result in a central finding that was key to the further development and revision of critical theory. The original hypothesis was that a strong correlation would be found between personality types and political orientations: "It was assumed that the authoritarian . . . would tend towards conservatism, the ambivalent towards liberalism, and the genital-revolutionary character towards socialism" (Bonß 1984, p. 27). The results, however, clearly falsified the basic assumptions of the Weimar Left. Not only was the percentage of "revolutionary" responses surprisingly low, but the authoritarian ones were too. The central tendency was thus inconsistent responses that supported an interpretation of the success of fascism after 1933 as reflecting the discrepancies between manifest and latent attitudes:

> The outward verbal radicalism of the Left was misleading with regard to the actual anti-fascist potential of the labour movement . . . in many cases a left-wing outlook was neutralized or perverted by underlying personality traits. Fromm's conclusion was that despite all the electoral successes of the Weimar Left, its members were not in the position, owing their character structures, to prevent the victory of National Socialism. (Bonß 1984, p. 29)

These general results gave impetus to the elaboration of the theoretical implications in a second project culminating in *Studies on Authority and the Family*, which appeared in 1936 with chapters by several members of the institute. Here the basic *authoritarian personality* theory was elaborated in theoretical and historical essays concerned above all with the role of the family and its patriarchal structure—a theme that anticipated the later development of feminist theory (Benjamin 1988). This basic model of the authoritarian personality was extended later in exile in the United States in a major empirical project developed by technically skilled psychologists, along with Adorno, the famous *Authoritarian Personality* study which attempted to identify the attitudinal traits of potentially fascistic personalities (Adorno et al. 1964).

The central concept here was Fromm's notion of *social character*, a concept that allowed portrayal of the collective personality of social classes in terms of psychodynamic (Freudian) theory and relations of domination (Fromm 1970; Langman and Kaplan 1981). It is in this context that the specific implications of the Frankfurt School's conception of domination (*Herrschaft*) becomes apparent. Whereas for Max Weber domination was associated with the notion of *legitimate authority* because of the voluntary character and symbolic basis of submission to political authority, for the Frankfurt theorists all authority originally was grounded in acts of violence. As a consequence, what may appear to be voluntary submission is, in fact, based on internalized fear that, in turn, distorts perceptions of reality becoming *false consciousness*. So in this context reference to domination always implies that political power is not merely coercive, but increasingly is based on internalized beliefs on the part of the ruled who unwittingly serve the interests of the rulers.

Cultural Studies

Horkheimer's original formulation of the tasks of cultural theory was not based on the assumption of the completely passive formation of socialized subjects (Honneth 1991, pp. 5-31). But this formulation was abandoned quickly in response to the pessimistic implications of the authoritarian personality thesis and "led the analysis of culture back into the functionalist reference system into which he had already previously integrated political economy and social psychology" (Honneth 1987, p. 355). Hence, with the exception of certain forms of high art, culture was associated by Horkheimer and Adorno with the purely manipulative effects of the capitalist *culture industries* (Adorno 1991). From this perspective the increasing commodification of culture brought about by the mass media largely had the effect of intensifying reification and alienation. Again the reductionism of this approach does not undermine the crucial importance of the introduction of the theories of cultural industries, but it explains some of its empirical weaknesses and its eventual partial rejection by the burgeoning cultural studies movements in the 1970s. Nevertheless the contributions of the Frankfurt Institute remain foundational for the origins of critical communications studies (Hardt 1992).

An Emergent Alternative Research Program

The "outer circle" of the Frankfurt Institute shared a certain marginality but not any other immediately visible characteristics. Franz Neumann and Otto Kirchheimer had a number of shared interests based on their legal training and contributed studies on law and the state in the exile period. Erich Fromm was concerned with social psychological issues, though he broke from the Institute in 1939 after changing directions in his interpretation of psychoanalytic theory. And Walter Benjamin, though personally close to Adorno, was a very original though eccentric figure interested in literary and cultural theory (Benjamin 1969). Although these contributors do not share theoretical orientations and thematic concerns,

> what fundamentally unites them is the overall direction of their thinking which allowed them as a body to go beyond the functionalist reference system of the original programme of the institute. The spirit of contradiction of all four authors is ignited by Marxist functionalism, against which they oppose considerations that converge

in an upward revaluation of individuals' and groups' own communicative performances. (Honneth 1987, p. 362)

As these were issues that helped provoke revision of critical theory in the 1960s and 1970s, it is important to note these earlier internal divisions. In each case (politics, culture, social psychology) the authors pointed to fundamental problems stemming from the denial of the possibility of human agency implied by the deterministic *one-dimensional society* thesis. For Neumann and Kirchheimer theories of totalitarian state control—whether in a Soviet type or state capitalist society—were problematic because of the virtual impossibility of complete central control over social groups. In the context of cultural analysis, Walter Benjamin similarly questioned the thesis developed by Adorno that culture industries dominated by large-scale capitalist enterprises would produce total homogenization. According to Benjamin, modern technology increasingly had made art forms technically reproducible (e.g., film, radio, photography), thus the *mechanical reproduction of art* had transformed the relationship between art works and publics. Previously art had been enjoyed through a

cultic aura which previously lifted them, like a sacred relic, out of the profane everyday world of the beholder. The technical media . . . destroy the aura surrounding the art produced and expose it to a remote viewing by the public; the contemplative form of the solitary enjoyment of art is suppressed by the public methods of the collective experiencing of art. (Honneth 1987, p. 366)

On this basis he argued that new technologies might allow arts and communications media to elicit new forms of what today might be called *resistance* to dominant ideologies, and even to mobilize oppositional collective action in new and unforeseen ways. Finally Fromm's reinterpretation of psychoanalysis had called into question Freud's instinct theory and turned to interactionist social psychology to develop a more sociological account of self formation. Adorno and Horkheimer reacted most directly against softening the libidinal instinctual basis of Freudian theory, charging that it betrayed therapy for the purpose of conformist therapy. Partly for this reason Fromm eventually left the Frankfurt Institute. What remained neglected in this debate, however, was the potential significance of the interactive dimensions of Fromm's new approach to social psychology in overcoming the functionalism of early critical theory's account of human agency.

The Decline of a Research Program:
The Dialectic of Enlightenment

Historical Context

With the failure of the working-class revolution in Germany to overthrow Hitler and the contradictions of Stalinism revealed by the end of the 1930s, the empirical tasks of critical theory became ambiguous. In its first phase in Weimar Germany, Frankfurt critical theory identified itself as a catalyst for the kinds of changes that would transform capitalism. Although traditional social science was held to be an obstacle to this process, there was still faith in the spontaneous ability of oppressed groups (the working class) to construct utopian visions of alternatives. But the practical failure of revolutionary movements in the 1930s led the central critical theorists—Max Horkheimer, Theodor Adorno, Herbert Marcuse—to abandon their original conception of combining research and practice in an interdisciplinary research project. Yet rather than reject their adherence to Marx altogether, Adorno and Horkheimer in particular proposed a speculative conception of history as a kind of catastrophe brought about by the failure of revolution. In terms of the theory of research programs, this apparent historical "falsification" of Marxian revolutionary theory culminated in a problematic philosophy of history that revealed the crisis of Critical Theory (Horkheimer and Adorno 1972; Held 1980).

The decline of the institute research program can be attributed to several interrelated factors: (a) the organizational consequences of exile, (b) the heavily positivist climate of the United States, which mitigated the further development of the methodological strategy that originally inspired critical theory, and (c) the disillusionment of the inner group with the potentially liberating effects of empirical research. Although this decline involved a regressive problemshift at the empirical level, there was a certain theoretical gain, but not one with any immediate significant practical consequence. The theoretical gain was insight into the autonomous contribution of science and technology to processes of domination, including the destruction of nature (thus anticipating environmental critiques). This phase of critical theory could not even sustain any convincing claim to be Marxist anymore and reflected the most well articulated analysis of the "crisis" of historical materialism.

The Logic of Disintegration

The outcome of this disillusionment was a fundamental critique of the very notion of Western reason as contaminated from its very origins with an aspiration for domination and control over nature. The result was a radicalization and generalization of Max Weber's analysis of *instrumental rationalization* that identified it with the process that Lukacs called *reification*. Hence, in contrast to the traditional Marxist argument, it is not merely capitalism (the generalization of market systems) that is the cause of problematic consequences of science and technology: Those problems are held to be rooted in the very nature of instrumental or technical reason itself, which has inherent reifying effects that distort our relation to reality through domination of external and internal (human) nature. This position generally is referred to as the thesis of the *dialectic of enlightenment*, which is a negative dialectic in that its course is regressive rather than progressive. It roots the origins of the problem of domination not in capitalism as such, but in the scientific aspiration for the domination of nature (Leiss 1974). For Adorno and Horkheimer at this pessimistic stage only the "objective reason" of philosophy could provide answers even though no one would listen. As a consequence the original interdisciplinary research program of critical theory was largely abandoned after World War II.

As Habermas puts it, "The fragility of the Marxist philosophy of history" doomed the research program to failure: "Critical theory could secure its normative foundations only in a philosophy of history. But this foundation was not able to support an empirical research program" (Habermas 1987a, p. 382). This failure also was linked to "the lack of a clearly demarcated object domain like the communicative practice of the everyday lifeworld in which rationality structures are embodied and processes of reification can be traced" (Habermas 1987a, p. 382). And of course it is precisely such a theory of communicative action that is the point of departure of Habermas's reconstruction of critical theory.

Conclusion: Beyond the Crisis

The specificity of critical theory resides in the particular manner in which it incorporates critique. Part of that critique is introduced at the metatheoretical level as an integral component of the research program, rather than as an incidental by-product. Although any form of competent social science may have critical effects, what is distinctive are those approaches in which "critique is an *integral* part of the process and those in which it is peripheral" (Harvey 1990, p. 3). Or as others have argued, critical social science has three distinctive features: "an emphasis on reflexivity, the acceptance of a methodological and ontological orientation distinct from the naturalistic paradigm, and a commitment to social criticism and advocacy" (Sabia and Wallulis 1983, p. 6).

Early Frankfurt critical theory developed its research program on the basis of a conception of critique grounded in a critical hermeneutics linked to a Hegelian-Marxist theory of totality and history. The crisis and decline of that research program can be traced to the problematic methodological functionalism underlying its model of social and cultural reproduction. The revitalization of critical theory required, as we shall see, a fundamental reconstruction of the metatheory of critical theory. In the next chapter we survey the developments in the metatheory of the human sciences that influenced the rethinking of critical theory initiated by Habermas and Giddens in the 1960s and 1970s.

Notes

1. For example, Giddens wrote: "Lakatos' formulation of 'degenerative' versus 'progressive problem-shifts' is probably the most adequate treatment of these issues yet worked out in the contemporary literature in the philosophy of science" (Giddens 1976, p. 141); Alexander also uses this model to analyze the functionalist-neofunctionalist transition (Alexander and Colomy 1990). The present discussion draws on Lakatos and Laudan here primarily as a contribution to the sociology of science, rather than as an epistemological solution to problems in Popperian empiricism.

2. For a good discussion of these issues, see A. Sayer (1992, p. 205), who recalls: "Observation is theory-laden but not necessarily theory-determined."

3. This point can be extended to choices between ideologies: "The presumption that the acceptance or rejection of ideologies can never in principle be rationally justified (a presumption at the core of the sociology of knowledge) is, on this analysis, entirely unfounded" (Laudan 1977, p. 192).

4. This understanding of the base-superstructure model was linked to what later became labeled "instrumentalist" theories of the state. In the 1960s another version of scientific Marxism emerged under the leadership of Louis Althusser in France, who proposed a complex model of social reproduction culminating in a *structuralist* theory of the state that attributed great autonomy to the state even though the economic factor was held to be determinant in the "last instance." Early Frankfurt theory worked with a similar social reproduction model a generation earlier, though its operations were understood in Hegelian, rather than French structuralist, terms.

5. A more unusual use (established by Popper) is a historical view of society that assumes a strong evolutionary form as a succession of stages based on developmental laws. The position overcomes relativism but at the price of a dogmatic theory of history.

6. A similar position was developed by Antonio Gramsci (1891-1937) in Italy in the 1920s and 1930s (Gramsci 1971; Kilminster 1979).

7. These issues were bequeathed to postwar sociological debates primarily in the context of the Anglo American receptions of Max Weber and Karl Mannheim, who represented closely related but distinctive positions on these issues in relation to the theory of ideology and instrumental rationalization (Simonds 1978; Hekman 1986). Most importantly, both generally were misunderstood because of efforts to translate the project of the sociology of knowledge into variable analysis, thus misunderstanding its hermeneutic foundations as a form of interpretive historical sociology.

8. Given our focus on classical Critical Theory as a research program, we are not concerned with a survey of the range of empirical inquiries involved (Jay 1973, 1984, 1985, 1988, 1993; Dubiel 1978; Söllner 1979; Held 1980; Bonß 1982; Wiggershaus 1987; Kellner 1989a). Also, to simplify the discussion we have not generally attempted to reconstruct these issues by reference to the more convoluted language of the original texts.

9. Most of the writing sponsored by the institute appeared in the *Zeitschrift für Sozialforschung,* published in nine volumes from 1932 until its cessation in 1941. Only the final two volumes appeared in English, thus greatly reducing international access. The key writings were not translated into English until the 1970s.

10. Even under the heading of "mass society theory" the reception of Critical Theory—that term was not even used as the label in English until the 1970s—was fragmentary (largely among a few cultural critics) and generally hostile, given the positivist climate (Bramson 1961). But an astute, if unsympathetic, critic such as Edward Shils acknowledged that "Horkheimer became in the course of several decades one of the most influential sociological writers of his time. . . . He has certainly had a much greater impact on sociological work than Mannheim" (Shils 1980, p. 190). When written in 1970, hardly any North American sociologists would have known who he was referring to, let alone that he might be more influential than Mannheim. Mentions of the Frankfurt School tradition did not regularly enter undergraduate theory texts until the 1980s.

11. Partly because differences in translations, a number of other terms are broadly synonymous with *Zweckrationalität*: instrumental rationality, *formal* rationality, *technical* rationality, *means* rationality, *purposive* rationality, *goal-oriented* rationality and contrasted with the rationality of *ultimate* ends or values (*Wertrationalität*), hence *substantial* rationality (or what Horkheimer called *objective reason,* as opposed to the *subjective reason* of instrumental rationality). For Weber substantial rationality was essentially nonrational, whereas for the Frankfurt tradition it could be subject to rational critique in the form of normative theory.

12. Much of this material was lost in the move into exile. The actual survey was executed by a woman (Hilde Weiss), and Paul Lazarsfeld was consulted for statistical advice.

5

POSTEMPIRICIST METATHEORY AND THE HUMAN SCIENCES

Interim Developments

The opposition between the universal and the unique, between nomothetic analysis and idiographic description, is a false antinomy. (Pierre Bourdieu in Bourdieu and Wacquant 1992, p. 75)

This chapter surveys some of the interim developments in social theory between the early Frankfurt School and the syntheses developed by Habermas (beginning in the early 1960s) and Giddens (beginning in the early 1970s). It complements Chapter 3, which introduced the postempiricist critiques of positivism in the natural sciences. Here the focus shifts to the broader range of debates that have impinged on the discourse of recent postempiricist metatheory in the human sciences.

This intermezzo serves several purposes. First, it introduces the kinds of debates outside the earlier critical hermeneutic tradition that defined the metatheoretical problematic of early Frankfurt critical theory. Understanding the basic issues and terms introduced by these broader and interim debates is essential background for understanding the metatheoretical approaches of Habermas and Giddens, taken up in the next chapter. We do not attempt the convoluted exegetical task of linking these influences directly with the two authors, a theme developed in the secondary literature on them. Rather our task is largely pedagogical: to familiarize readers with issues and concepts that will largely be taken for granted later on. At the same time, however, it provides an occasion to advance a central contention: that *neo*structuralist metatheory is crucial for understanding the explanatory objectives of contemporary critical theory.

Our discussion is organized around four themes. First, the challenge provided by Max Weber can be seen as having prefigured much of subsequent attempts to reconstruct historical materialism along postempiricist lines. Subsequent debates have been influenced by his effort to reconcile agency and structure, his astute and often sympathetic critique of historical materialism, his theory of rationalization, and searching questions about the status of normative theory.

Second, we consider some of the contributions that have been influential in forcing postpositivist redefinitions of conceptions of social action and language (as well as the subject or agent) inherited from historical materialism and the early Frankfurt School. Linguistic philosophy, social phenomenology, and pragmatic (symbolic) interactionism have been especially important in this context.

Third, many similar issues have been taken up in the context of French debates about metatheory, though they are mediated by the particular problematics of existentialism, structuralism, and poststructuralism. These debates provided insights for understanding the relationship between agency and structure and the nature of social determination that moved debate beyond the terms set out by Weber, social phenomenology, and critical hermeneutics generally.

Fourth, we review briefly three approaches in French sociology and social theory that have proven especially influential for debates within recent critical theory: Alain Touraine, Pierre Bourdieu, and Michel Foucault.

Finally we again take up critical realist metatheory, especially with respect to its implications for the human sciences in opposing a nonpositivist structuralism to traditional empiricism.

The Weberian Challenge

The internal conflicts within Weimar Germany precluded a productive interchange between the opposed followers of Marx and Weber despite the efforts of people like Karl Mannheim and especially Karl Löwith in the 1920s and 1930s. Mannheim, on the one hand, developed a theory of ideology under the heading of the "sociology of knowledge" that generalized Marx's method by applying it to the Marxist tradition itself. Further, he drew on Weber and hermeneutic theory in order to explore other dimensions shaping ideologies beyond those of social class (Mannheim 1936, 1952). Karl Löwith, on the other hand, first pointed to the affinities and complementarity of Marx's theory of alienation and Weber's account of rationalization (Löwith [1932] 1982). Nevertheless the theory of rationalization did become central to the second phase of the Frankfurt Institute, especially in the dialectic of Enlightenment thesis. Further, Weber also influenced the political sociology of some of the "outer circle" in the institute. The long-neglected *figurational sociology* of Norbert Elias—originally Mannheim's assistant before exile in England— also can be situated in this context (Elias 1978, 1982). Otherwise the full development of a Marx-Weber dialogue only took place more recently and has had a broad influence on critical theory (Antonio and Glassman 1985; Wiley 1987).

Neo-Weberian theory has challenged the older critical theory on a number of key issues: the dogmatism of its ideology critique, its subordination of the political to the economic, its neglect of the problems of instrumental rationalization and bureaucratization in its utopian account of alternatives to capitalism, the limits of the labor-capital class contradiction given the rise of the middle strata, and the dangers of mixing ideology and empirical research. Such Weberian influences were most evident early on in the work of Giddens, a tendency that often led him to be classified as a neo-Weberian conflict theorist (Craib 1984).[1] Similarly Habermas often has been reproached from the neo-Marxist camp for his "Weberian" revisionism (Therborn 1976). But this recognition of convergent interpretations of Marx and Weber is one of the most characteristic features of contemporary critical theory regardless of the label (D. Sayer 1991).

Action Theories

The following three approaches to metatheory and social action initially were developed independently and were long viewed as separate and even opposing. More recently, however, their similarities as critiques of positivism have been recognized, along with shared concerns in their analyses of the primacy of language in the construction of knowledge and social action. In complex and changing ways the tradition of contemporary critical theory has embraced many of these specific arguments even though not fully embracing any of these three perspectives (Bernstein 1971, 1978).

Linguistic Philosophy

The dominant style of contemporary professional philosophy in the English-speaking world often is referred to as *analytic philosophy*. With the failure of logical empiricism to carry foreword the ambitious project of positivism, most philosophers retreated even farther from the speculative traditions of European philosophy (often labeled *continental philosophy* today). Although there is a sense in which logical empiricism was earlier an important form of analytic philosophy, today analytic philosophy is open to postempiricist alternatives. Yet from the analytic perspective the questions posed by *continental philosophy*—by phenomenology, hermeneutics, and structuralism—are of little interest and are charged with lacking conceptual rigor. Even when analytic and continental philosophies are similar or refer to the same topics, "it is from different directions; and they have different methods of argument, different criteria for judging the merits of a piece of philosophizing" (Charlton 1991, p. 3). The tasks of philosophy are held to be based rather on careful logical, conceptual, and linguistic analysis, a focus that critics have charged has led to its trivialization.

In any case, the most influential form of analytic philosophy is *linguistic philosophy* (also referred to in an earlier phase as *ordinary language philosophy*). Linguistic philosophy usually is traced to the later work of eccentric Austrian philosopher Ludwig Wittgenstein (1889-1951), who eventually located in

Cambridge in the 1930s. Although a strict positivist in his early work, Wittgenstein eventually developed a philosophy of language, or more precisely, a way of doing philosophical analysis through linguistic analysis (Wittgenstein 1974). Such linguistic philosophy rejected most of traditional philosophy as based on using language in mistaken or confused ways. Above all, empiricist theories were charged with the fallacy of linking language exclusively with the function of representing "reality." From this perspective empiricist science was just another *language game* that could make no claims to objective truth in terms of the verification principle proposed by logical positivists.

More generally, linguistic philosophers have argued that much of traditional philosophy was based on confused uses of terms that can be clarified by careful linguistic and logical analysis. Crucial to this position is a *theory of meaning* quite distinct from classic positivism's search for a pure, formal language to literally represent reality. According to the pioneer British linguistic philosopher John Austin (1911-1960), meanings do not have an independent existence that can be complied in a dictionary or derived from the things they may happen to refer to; rather meaning can be determined only in the context of the sentences in which concepts are used. The use of words, in short, involves doing a kind of deed, hence is a social act. According to Austin's *speech acts theory*, words in an *utterance* (or sentence) have three kinds of uses (meanings): *locutionary* (or propositional) meaning about the truth or falsity of something; *illocutionary* meaning, related to the "force" of an utterance with respect to stating, commanding, promising, or warning; and *perlocutionary* meaning, oriented to influencing a hearer's attitudes or state of mind.

Although there has been little direct influence of linguistic philosophy on social theory, it has provided an important ally in the debate with positivism in social science, as well as complemented research on the social uses of language, for example, in the theory of speech acts. Above all, linguistic philosophy is associated with a "linguistic turn" that "could be used to show the conceptual or logical impossibility of a social science modeled on the natural sciences" (Bernstein 1978, p. 112). On the other hand, linguistic philosophy has only a rather circumscribed view of language use that simply does not address many of the questions of interest to social theory and social science.

The most direct influence of this form of linguistic philosophy in social science is evident in Peter Winch's *The Idea of a Social Science* (1958), which essentially rejects causal analysis in favor of a purely *Verstehen* or interpretive approach that embraces cultural relativism. Few in the social sciences follow these drastic conclusions, but such work has been important in undermining the pretensions of empiricism and positivism (Frisby and Sayer 1986). More constructively, linguistic philosophy has contributed to the postempiricist effort to understand science in terms of specific rhetorical strategies of argumentation and thus complements the history of science following Thomas Kuhn. Similarly the resulting studies of linguistic use have been important in rethinking the nature of human agency in nonpositivist terms. Habermas, in particular, has drawn up the theory of speech acts in his theory of *communicative action* (Habermas 1979, pp. 1-18).

As more recent observers have noted, many of these conclusions converge with the earlier tradition of European hermeneutics, which also stressed the linguistic basis of social knowledge and criticized the nomothetic model of explanation. Both have been charged, however, with a purely interpretive notion of social life that undermines analyses of social causation central to the very notion of a critical theory of society.

Social Phenomenology and Ethnomethodology

Phenomenology has roots in the tradition of German idealism and is a form of hermeneutic philosophy. Edmund Husserl (1859-1938) is recognized as its "founding father." He was concerned especially with rejecting positivist efforts to "explain" human consciousness in objectivist terms (hence his *antipsychologism*). Instead he proposed a "descriptive" science of subjectivity based on the human capacity to "bracket" the "natural attitude" of ordinary awareness and reflect on the fundamental properties of human consciousness. But Husserl's pure or *transcendental* phenomenology was initially not very helpful for social theory because of its focus on the abstract, isolated individual (Husserl's "Cartesian ego").

The link between phenomenology and sociology was elaborated initially by the Austrian Alfred Schutz (1899-1959), who attempted to work out problems in Max Weber's theory of action (Schutz 1967). Husserl provided distinctions that could clarify some aspects to Weber's account of *Verstehen* and interpretive understanding. As opposed to Husserl, however, Schutz came to stress—after his move to New York—the interactive basis of subjectivity, a theme that eventually led to an effort to combine phenomenology with aspects of symbolic interactionism (i.e., G. H. Mead).

More critical possibilities for social phenomenology were developed in an influential attempt to incorporate the theory of reification into Schutz's perspective under the heading of the "social construction of reality" (Berger and Luckmann 1967). Further, this approach provided a suggestive account of the subject-object dialectic that anticipated aspects of later critical theory despite succumbing to a Durkheimian theory of society and value-relativism.

Further, under the leadership of Harold Garfinkel's (1967) *ethnomethodology* the techniques of phenomenology were turned toward the rational properties of mundane or everyday "reasoning." Such analysis (based, in part, on the study of conversations) drew attention to the essential reflexivity—as evident in the *indexical* or contextual nature of meaning—built into social action. Again these kinds of concerns later proved useful for justifying aspects of the revitalized project of critical theory, especially in the context of its formulation of a theory of agency and communicative interaction.

Pragmatism and Symbolic Interactionism

The fortunes of American *pragmatism* as a philosophical tradition have shifted dramatically in this century. Although it enjoyed a degree of international acclaim from the turn of the century into the 1930s, pragmatism was largely eclipsed in its homeland by the arrival of logical positivism from Europe in the 1930s and the later coalescing of analytic philosophy as a style of philosophizing. Further, it was largely ignored by continental philosophy with which it otherwise had some important but generally unacknowledged affinities—a theme anticipated in W. Wright Mills's doctoral dissertation but not taken up systematically again until people such as Richard Bernstein (1971) in the United States and German philosophers and social theorists influenced by critical theory (Apel 1975; Joas 1985). But pragmatism has now come back into its own in the context of postempiricist theory.

Pragmatism is familiar to social science primarily through its offspring *symbolic interactionism,* which emerged as a form of social psychology in the 1930s under the leadership of the philosopher George Herbert Mead and the sociologist Herbert Blumer (1969). The notion of the social (interactionist) construction of the subject (self) through language provided the basis of an affinity with the tradition of historical materialism (via Hegel) and a critique of positivist behaviorism. But symbolic interactionism has been limited by its lack of an analysis of domination and power, as well as a depth-psychology of the self.

The metatheoretical contribution of pragmatism is of particular concern here because it converged broadly with linguistic philosophy and phenomenology in rejecting logical positivism. The epistemology of pragmatism is associated primarily with the work of Charles Sanders Peirce (1939-1914) and John Dewey (1859-1952). Although superficially known as the doctrine that validity or truth can be attributed to anything "that works," pragmatism is actually much more subtle (Bernstein 1971, pp. 165-229). As the most widely read neopragmatist, Richard Rorty, has demonstrated that the pragmatist tradition anticipated most of the major concerns of both contemporary analytic and continental philosophy (e.g., Rorty 1982, 1991).

Although antipositivist, pragmatism did not culminate in a fully skeptical attack on scientific knowledge; instead it stressed the importance of assessing knowledge in terms of its practical uses and justifying science in terms of its actual procedures, rather than some idealized "logic." As a consequence it was antifoundationalist because it rejected the "quest for certainty" (Dewey) as the necessary ideal of science and viewed science as merely a special kind of social practice. As noted previously, on the one hand, the pragmatic approach to the diversity of methods has been accepted generally in critical theory and critical realism. On the other hand, critical realists in particular would argue that recent neopragmatism—at least in the form represented by the contemporary work of Richard Rorty—reduces knowledge to an "endless conversation." This reduction results from the lack of a *realist* ontology and "this is responsible for his failure to sustain an adequate account of agency and *a fortiori* of freedom as involving *inter alia* emancipation from real and scientifically knowledge specific constraints, rather than merely poetic redescription of an already determined world" (Bhaskar 1991, p. ix). But as others argue, another reading of pragmatism is possible other than Rorty's "rootless" version that lacks a sense of "brute otherness in the world" and does not tap the sources of intelligence "beyond conceptual reason": "Dialogue, or 'conversation,' is a central concept of pragmatism, but the conversation is one ultimately rooted within a generalized conception of nature: a conception in which nature itself is a biocosmic, emergent dialogue" (Rochberg-Halton 1986, p. xii).

The (Post)Structuralist Revolution(s)

Introduction

In the French context the postwar debates surrounding metatheory in the human sciences were identified with three philosophical movements that have been central to continental philosophy: *existentialism, structuralism,* and *poststructuralism,* tendencies that dominated successively from the 1950s to the 1970s (with receptions in the English-speaking world delayed a decade or so). These debates had an international impact on the human sciences (especially literary theory), and critical theory in particular, but have remained quite marginal to conventional social science. We must be content here with a very stylized, oversimplified sketch to introduce certain key terms of reference of these developments—associated with the terms *structuralism* and *poststructuralism.* At stake is a new version of the subject-object polarization in metatheory that is quite distinct from the "humanist" versus "behaviorist" split in the social sciences reviewed earlier. In the French case, existentialism (with links to phenomenology and hermeneutics) took a more subjectivist position; classic structuralism responded with a new form of objectivism based in linguistics, and poststructuralism became a vague term referring to diverse efforts to overcome this dualism (though often reverting back to a new form of subjectivism).

Existentialism can be located in the trajectory of the history of phenomenological philosophy. European phenomenology eventually split into two main directions. One—most closely associated with the work of Husserl—was touched on above with reference to the work of Alfred Schutz. This tradition of "pure" phenomenology is associated with a focus on the objective description of cognitive processes within the individual (or in interaction, in the case of Schutz). This is the version most influential within the tradition of Anglo American sociology.

In Europe, and in French social theory in particular, another branch of phenomenology has been more significant. In its original German formulation it is associated with the hermeneutic phenomenology of Husserl's most famous student, Martin Heidegger (1889-1976). Whereas Husserl's phenomenology was concerned primarily with the description of the abstract cognitive structures of individual "Cartesian ego," Heidegger redirected phenomenology toward the interpretation (disclosure) of being and "lived-experience," hence an *existential phenomenology* (Heidegger 1962). In its original German form, however, Heideggerian philosophy remained rather conservative and apolitical (despite Heidegger's own brief flirtation with the Nazis).

As even some analytic philosophers have come to acknowledge, existentialism has been a major participant in overturning the "Cartesian" (and "positivist") assumptions that set the agenda for three centuries of philosophy:

> Along with American pragmatists, the later Wittgenstein and contemporary deconstructivists, existentialists reject not only any representational theory of knowledge and the search for certain foundations, but the whole idea of the isolated subject caught in an "egocentric predicament" of trying to acquire knowledge about a public world on the basis of his private experience. Where existentialist differ . . . is, first, in emphasizing the relevance of overcoming the Cartesian tradition to the conduct of life, and second, in wanting to preserve one element in Descartes' philosophy—his insis-

tence on the individual's responsibility for the stance he or she takes towards the world. (Cooper 1990, p. viii)

As a well-defined philosophical and political movement, existentialism emerged with the postwar French writings of people such as Simone de Beauvoir (1908-1986)—a founder of feminist theory—Maurice Merleau-Ponty (1907-1961), and Jean-Paul Sartre (1905-1980). The latter two have been especially important in relationship to sociology (Craib 1976; Kotarba and Fontana 1984). Above all, French existentialism involved a reception and appropriation of the phenomenology of Husserl and Heidegger, generally in association with a rereading of Marx as a theorist of alienation and an analyst of the pathologies of human existence. Rereading Hegel and Marx from the perspective of these concerns stressed the key importance of Marx's early writings and relation to Hegel and often is referred to as a version of a *humanistic* or *existential Marxism* (Poster 1975) that was, in important respects, the French equivalent of early Frankfurt critical theory.[2]

The German philosophy of Hegel's critical hermeneutics, Husserl's phenomenology, and Heidegger's existential phenomenology were used against the rationalism and positivism that had dominated French philosophy since Descartes. Given its phenomenological underpinnings, existentialism implied a very radical voluntarism for the human sciences and suggested a focus on the lived-experience of pain, suffering, and hope. In this respect existentialism embraced many of the themes traditionally only of concern to theology. It also involved forms of *existential psychology*—that is, a historicist appropriation of Freud as a theorist of anxiety (Izenberg 1976). In this respect existential theory as the basis of a theory of action complemented in some respects the role of symbolic interactionism and neo-Freudian theory in the Anglo American context (Aboulafia 1986).

Structuralism blossomed in the 1960s as the philosophical rival of existentialism and phenomenology. Whereas existentialism focused its attack on positivism and Cartesian speculative philosophy, structuralism claimed to have found a new methodological basis for grounding knowledge: in this respect it is clearly foundationalist in its aspirations. The basic explanatory principle underlying structuralism can be traced back to another stream of German philosophy—to Immanuel Kant and his critique of

British empiricism. Kant postulated that for science as we know it to exist, there must be some a priori or pre-given characteristics of the human mind (e.g., the capacity to perceive space and time).[3] Although these a priori (or *transcendental*) categories are the conditions that make knowledge possible, they cannot be observed directly and must be inferred through acts of self-reflection by the human mind. For Kant these universal structures of cognition united the human species.

From here it was a short step—taken by Emile Durkheim in France in his later work on religion—to suggest that historically specific forms of knowledge have a similar latent structure. In other words, the structuralist method is transformed from a claim about the human mind to one about the nature of social life generally. The Swiss linguist Ferdinand de Saussure (1857-1913) pushed Durkheim's intuition a crucial step further by distinguishing between the surface features of speech (*parole*) and the depth-structure of language systems (*langue*). Structuralism moved from linguistics back into the social sciences in the 1950s in the anthropological study of the structure of myths pioneered by Claude Lévi-Strauss. Under the influence of Ferdinand de Saussure's and Roland Jakobson's structuralist linguistics, as well as reinterpretations of the later Durkheim and Marcel Mauss, such classic structuralist research defined itself in explicit opposition to existentialism at every level of the subject-object polarization. Similarly Jacques Lacan reinterpreted Freud in structuralist terms by reading the subconscious linguistically as a text.

The basic method of existentialist inquiry was hermeneutic, hence involving interpretations of human experience that structuralists declared to be superficial and unscientific because they were based on the assumptions of humanistic voluntarism. To be sure, variants of existentialism influenced by Marxism (e.g., Sartre) clearly recognized the importance of historical constraints on action but still came down on the side of the radical freedom open to actors. In many ways early structuralism functioned as a kind of positivist rejoinder to existentialism, but in a form quite different from that of logical empiricism. Whereas the model for positivism was the natural sciences, structuralism was quite distinctive in that its model was part of the human sciences: the science of linguistics. This model allowed structuralism to analyze the constraints on social action in a very different way from that found in the positivist notion of deterministic laws.

It is important, therefore, to distinguish European structuralism as a specific method (based on the *linguistic analogy*) and as a fundamental metatheory. As an ontological and epistemological position, strong forms of structuralism border on a kind of idealistic positivism in that it is argued that social reality exists as a logical pattern and as a product of ideas, but that through structuralist methods these can be known in a purely objective and fully scientific manner.

In its most militant metatheoretical form, structuralist metatheory defined itself explicitly as *antihumanist, antihistoricist,* and *antiempiricist.* At the level of social action this antihumanism results in a thorough determinism often identified with the notion of the "death of the subject," a slogan that refers to the suggestion that the intentionality of agents is an epiphenomenon or illusion because all actions are constituted by structures (hence the notion that the "structures speak us," rather than we speaking for ourselves, as the existentialist would say). Notice that this argument parallels behaviorism in its objectivism but locates determination in the linguistic character of social reality, rather than some material properties external to consciousness. With respect to explanation this approach is also antiempiricist and antihistoricist. In opposition to the empiricist focus on observable features of social reality or the search for statistical relations between variables, structuralist social science seeks to uncover the generative rules evident in the depth-structure of events. The resulting method is also antihistoricist because it does not view social life in terms of the simple unfolding of history through processes of change. Applying a distinction based on structuralist linguistics, such historical or *diachronic* approaches are contrasted with the *synchronic* perspective of structuralism that reveals the underlying structure of the phenomenon at a given point in time (as a kind of snapshot).[4]

The most famous application of classic structuralism to social theory (as opposed to Lévi-Strauss's cultural analysis) can be found in Louis Althusser's (1918-1990) *structuralist Marxism* (Benton 1984), which dominated much French and British Marxist debate in the 1960s and 1970s. Although this approach had the advantage of shifting the focus in neo-Marxist theory from an economistic base superstructure model to a structuralist social reproduction model that stressed the relative autonomy of the cultural and political, the outcome was a deterministic functionalism with even graver problems than early Frankfurt theory. Although few today would defend such strongly positivist forms of structuralism or the ontological and epistemological claims made on its behalf, aspects of structuralist metatheory and methodology remain of crucial importance in the context of poststructuralist theorizing.

The Linguistic Analogy

More enduring have been some of the implications of structuralism as a method, or a type of methodological strategy appropriate for the human sciences.[5] From this more cautious perspective, the objects of such structural analysis are diverse (e.g., linguistic, psychological, historical) and develop their substantive analyzes independently, even if sharing an antiatomistic, nonempiricist metatheory:

> Structuralism is a philosophical view according to which the reality of the objects of the human or social sciences is relational rather than substantial. It generates a critical method that consists of inquiring into and specifying the sets of relations (or structures) that constitute these objects or into which they enter, and of identifying and analyzing groups of such objects whose members are structural transformations of one another. These groups jointly constitute the domains of the respective sciences. (Caws 1988, p. 1)

As a methodological strategy, structuralism is identified most often with a linguistic analogy that makes it quite distinct from empiricist uses of the term *structure* or *structuralism* in the social sciences. The basic principle, however, can be conveyed by the example of grammar as a kind of structuralist account. First, a grammar is not an observable feature of speech. Rather a grammar specifies a set of relations (rules) that describe empirical regularities than can be inferred from a system of language. These regularities are reconstructed in the form of generative rules, rather than as invariant laws. Although not visible, they can be justified empirically by reference to how their misuse produces

misunderstanding and the breakdown of the system of communication. From this perspective social phenomena can be seen
to have a surface dimension, as in the case of actual speaking as
a practical activity (*parole*), but at the same time a depth-structure
evident in the basic generative rules (*langue*) that make speaking in a particular language possible and understandable. In this
respect the rules of language can be seen to have determining
effects in a very distinctive way: They do not require speakers
to say something in particular, but they do constrain or regulate
how they have to go about the activity of speaking. This analogy
thus becomes the key to a new way of thinking about the relationship between agency and structure that gives some scope to
individual autonomy and yet takes into account the structures that
define the limits, the range of possibilities, in a given context.

But is should also be noted that the problematic of structuralism is not limited to the specific substantive features of the
linguistic model, though the two often get identified exclusively
(e.g., Petit 1977). For example, Jean Piaget's *genetic structuralism*
is the basis of cognitive developmental psychology (Piaget 1970).
Here structure is a formal property of a given state of cognitive
development, and the change from one stage to another is accompanied by complex processes that build on previous stages but
introduce new properties at higher levels. Again these kinds of
empirical regularities are not visible, must be inferred from
cognitive activity, and do not take the form of nomothetic laws.
What is of primary interest here is to illustrate what is at stake
in the differences between empiricist and structuralist conceptions of explanation:

> Briefly, and somewhat simplistically, the gist of empiricism consists
> in explaining a phenomenon in terms of its content or concrete de-
> terminations as they are attainable or observable either in external
> or internal experience. . . . [Structuralists] share a fundamental
> principle in common: they refuse to consider "experience" as a
> kind of "recording" or registering of what is immediately "given" or
> accessible to our sensory apparatus. Structuralists maintain we
> cannot understand experiential data without building formal mod-
> els—that is, without isolating from the content of experience a
> formal set of constitutive elements and relationships among the
> elements. The meaning of a phenomenon is determined not in

terms of its concrete determinations or the subjective intention of the social actors but in terms of the relational constants among the basic constitutive elements. Through this operation we can reconstruct the deep logic, or organizing principles, or compositional laws of empirical phenomena. Typically, structuralists attempt to identify the rules of the internal composition of a phenomenon and the rules which govern the possible transformations of one phenomenon into related sets of phenomena. (Rossi 1982, p. 5)

Poststructuralism as Postmodernism: A Digression

The term *poststructuralism* refers most generally to the variety of positions that emerged—primarily in the original French context—in the wake of the rejection of extravagant claims of structuralism as a general metatheory and the limitations of the specific structuralist methods employed by Lévi-Strauss and those influenced by his example. But the term *poststructuralism* now more typically refers to a very specific constellation of French theorists more concerned with the rhetorical analysis of theories or critiques of "truth," rather than developing a strategy for understanding social reality (Dews 1987). During the past decade the term *poststructuralism,* or the notion of poststructuralist social theory, has also sometimes been linked to several French theorists who are also characterized as postmodernist. In a sense postmodernist theory represents the most radical poststructuralist response to the positivistic illusions of early structuralism and often culminates in a new form of skepticism and relativism.

Four French theorists are cited most often in this context as exemplars of postmodernist theorizing. Jean-François Lyotard can be credited with popularizing the term with a book on the "postmodern condition" and the decline of what he calls the "grand narratives" of modernity associated with general theories such as Marxism, Freudians, and functionalism (Lyotard 1984).[6] Jean Baudrillard provides a controversial account of the postmodern transformations of contemporary culture as having eroded altogether the distinction between the real and the symbolic (Kellner 1989b). Jacques Derrida's *deconstructionism* develops a rhetorical strategy of reading philosophical and literary texts that reveals the rationalistic biases of Western thought, the ultimately undecidable character of interpretation and the illusions of representations of reality (Culler 1982; Agger 1991). These concerns reflect Derrida's early flirtation with existentialism and hermeneutics, hence his indebtedness to German philosophers such as Husserl and Heidegger. Most directly pertinent to sociological theory, however, is Michel Foucault, whose approach has a very ambiguous relationship to postmodernist theory (and will be taken up in a moment). The cumulative effects of such postmodernist critiques of social theory are captured by Antonio's warning with respect to the social sciences:

> The postmodernist attack on Western reason scuttles, along with the teleological baggage of the grand narrative, the necessary holistic tools for addressing increasingly "global" (regional, national, and international) social interdependencies. Perhaps Marx's greatest achievement was his compelling argument that modernity's growing networks of interdependence (linking huge social circles) have sweeping significance for human suffering and welfare and therefore ought not to be ignored. (Antonio 1990, p. 108)

Between Structuralism and Poststructuralism

Uncharacteristically this section bears an ironic, cryptic title. The reason is that the focus on poststructuralism and postmodernism during the past decade has deflected attention from the original structuralist revolution that has yet to be assimilated adequately by the social sciences (even if structuralist textual methods have become central to subfields such as media studies). Indeed one of the greatest obstacles to reading and assimilating contemporary critical theory stems from this problem, given the pervasive use of structuralist type explanatory arguments. In an intellectual culture whose common sense is grounded in empiricism, these circumstances inevitably generate profound misunderstandings and misleading interpretations.

To be sure, there has been a significant reception of French structuralist metatheory and methodology in sociology and the social sciences generally (Rossi 1982; Kurzweil 1980; Lemert 1981), as well as creative adaptations of structuralist principles (A. Sayer 1992). Further, the more sophisticated introductions to contemporary sociological theory often do provide perfunctory introductions to it as a specific (largely French) theoretical approach, but its more general significance gets lost in the text as a whole (Ritzer 1992, pp. 358-67). Only rarely is French structuralism presented in a manner that is foundational for understanding contemporary critical theory (Craib 1984). And in the context of Anglo American introductions to methodology, the problematic of French structuralism is completely absent.[7] One of the obvious consequences is the difficulty of effectively defining the problematic of methodology in anything other than empiricist terms, a process that systematically distorts the discussion of so-called "qualitative methods" (a problem we take up in a later chapter).

The overall significance of the structural-poststructuralist debates for methodology is twofold. First, it provides the basis for understanding and legitimating a wide variety of explanatory strategies that allow understanding causality or identifying empirical regularities in culture in terms other than invariant laws or correlations among variables. Second, it provides the conceptual resources necessary for overcoming the subjectivist-objectivist split that has characterized social science. As is argued later, these principles provide the key for understanding the metatheory and research programs developed by Habermas and Giddens.[8]

Our primary concern here is rather with aspects of poststructuralism that get lost with the focus on the postmodernist wing and those concerned with deconstructive analysis. From this latter perspective the primary contribution of poststructuralist thought is a critique of empiricist and naive realist accounts of representation and a reflexive theory of textual reading. That is why it is necessary to point to issues that lie between nonpositivist structuralism as the basis of strategies of social and cultural analysis and poststructuralism in its deconstructive and postmodernist modes. The problem with the prefix *post-* is that it implies some kind displacement of structuralism that is misleading (Caws 1988). Some structuralist theories may well have been decisively rejected (e.g., Althusser's structuralist Marxism), along with specific inflated ontological and epistemological claims made on behalf of positivist variants of structuralist metatheory. But inquiries based on nonempiricist, structuralist-type methodologies flourish throughout the humanities and social sciences. Partly as a consequence, the possibility and importance of a *poststructuralist structuralism*—such as exemplified very visibly in the metatheory of Paul Ricoeur, the discourse analysis of Foucault, and the theory and research of, say, Pierre Bourdieu, Anthony Giddens, or Habermas—gets lost. Perhaps the term *neostructuralism* (sometimes used in German discussions) might be appropriate here because it implicitly acknowledges that structuralist-type methods have not been abandoned altogether. We generally use the term *interpretive structuralism* (or *hermeneutic structuralism* or even *historical* or *genetic structuralism*) to characterize this programmatic position.[9]

The second aspect of poststructuralist structuralism we wish to stress is its contribution to rethinking the agency/structure relationship. It has been argued that such "relational structuralism offers the only viable alternative to the everlasting confrontation between the two predominant sociological versions of the objective versus subjective empiricist explanation—the 'natural science' and the 'interpretive' paradigms. . . . Such a confrontation is partially reflected or paralleled in the clash between structural and individualistic explanation" (Rossi 1982, p. 10). Hence "the notions of deep structure and transformational rules permits one to account both for empirical surface structures (which are the focus of traditional structuralism) and the productivity of the subject" (Rossi 1982, p. 12). As we argue later, this basic intuition—if not the precise terminology—underlies the metatheory and research program of contemporary critical theory. From this perspective such a neostructuralism is acutely aware of its own limitations:

> What we need is not an umbilical cord to some impossible origin, divine or mystical, or a vector to a similarly impossible transcendent destiny, but stabilizers, gyroscopes, devices for *local* orientation, *limited* structural connections of optimum complexity, serviceable for human needs on a human scale. The discovery and reflection on structures of language, kinship, history, mythology, literature and so on, on the one hand and of subjectivity on the other seem to me the way of providing what is needed. (Caws 1988, p. 255)

French Social Theory

Aspects of French social theory have been important for the development of critical theory in the context of both its Anglo American and German receptions. As a consequence contemporary metatheory is unintelligible without awareness of the influences of the French debates on the development of second-generation critical theory. French existentialist, structuralist, and poststructuralist theory has had a significant impact on Habermas's and Giddens's work at various points, but both have explicitly attacked postmodernism (though not necessarily post-structuralism) as either a regressive tendency or a misreading of contemporary culture and social theory.

Three critical social theorists in particular can be singled out as having strong affinities with critical social theory and its sociological concerns: Alain Touraine, Pierre Bourdieu, and Michel Foucault. Partly as a consequence, those identifying with critical theory routinely cite these theorists (and those influenced by them) as largely complementing aspects of their own work. Despite their important differences, all three can be considered to be complementing critical theory to the extent that they (a) reject positivism in favor of a poststructuralist agency-structure dialectic, (b) conceptualize social relations in structuralist terms as part of a theory of domination and power, and (c) identify social research with critical and reflexive tasks with respect to social transformation. One might be tempted to call this tradition *neo-structuralist critical sociology* to differentiate it from poststructuralism, which has too many other connotations and often is used synonymously with postmodernism.

With the waning of a specifically Marxist sociology in France, contemporary sociological theory there has been classified in terms of four basic tendencies: (a) the genetic or critical structuralism of Bourdieu, (b) the dynamic or actionalist sociology of Touraine, (c) functionalist (Michel Crozier) and strategic conflict (Raymond Aron) analysis, and (d) the positivist methodological individualism of Raymond Boudon (Touraine 1986; Ansart 1990). Of interest here are the first two forms, which in many respects are complementary. Although Foucault does not fit readily into this classification because he does not define his work in specifically sociological terms, he is, in fact, concerned with questions rooted in critical structuralism.[10]

Touraine

Alain Touraine's *actionalist theory* was elaborated under existentialist and Weberian influences, but as a sociologist Touraine was fully conscious of the need to conceptualize relations of power and domination, a theme evident in his early research on the sociology of work that developed out of a debate with classical Marxism (Touraine 1977). The central theme of Touraine's sociology is the need to reorient the object of analysis toward social action and social movements but in terms that avoid the pitfalls of naive voluntarism. Although not elaborated specifically as a critique of structuralism, this approach does point to the kind of issues neglected in hyperstructuralist accounts that lapse into determinism and economic reductionism. In particular Touraine has been interested in the struggle over the control of historicity in modern or increasingly postindustrial societies—the question of the "production of society"—as revealed in social movements. Touraine's work has been especially influential in discussions and analyses of the new social movements and his method of "sociological intervention," a theme to be discussed later (Touraine 1981).

Bourdieu

In contrast Bourdieu's concerns shift toward the structural side of the agency-structure divide, though he is interested particularly in the processes that mediate between the two. Although Bourdieu's earlier work on educational reproduction generally was associated with a strong form of structuralism and often erroneously even labeled "Marxist" in some American contexts, his sociological approach was based from the outset on a "theory of practice" that links structure and action (Bourdieu 1977; Robbins 1991; Calhoun et al. 1993). But his flexible use of structuralism as a method was not combined with a classic structuralist metatheory (Bourdieu and Passeron 1977; Bourdieu 1968). This point has been reinforced more clearly with translation of more recent work on his conception of a *reflexive*

sociology (Bourdieu 1990; Bourdieu and Wacquant 1992). Although such diverse authors as Marx, Weber, Durkheim, Lévi-
Strauss, and Goffman have influenced Bourdieu's approach, it is
synthesized through a critical structuralist perceptive—a theory
of *cultural reproduction*—that unifies his work.

The central aspects of Bourdieu's critical sociology can be conveyed in terms of three concepts: (a) society as a *system of positions* understood as social *fields,* (b) *habitus* as the mediation of
subjective and objective, and (c) *social and cultural reproduction* as a process of continuous restructuration that reproduces
relations of power (Bourdieu and Passeron 1977; Bourdieu 1984,
1988, 1989). These terms can be illustrated most readily from
his work in the sociology of education. The "educational field"
is constituted by a system of social positions defined by a struggle among social classes. Crucial to success in education is the
accumulation of *cultural capital* as defined by the hidden curriculum—that is, qualities defined by the dominant classes in
terms of their own *habitus*—that is, the kinds of classificatory
schemes and ultimate values that define the "cultural arbitrary"
of social classes. In this way the educational system exercises a
kind of symbolic violence resulting from the arbitrariness of the
qualities rewarded by success in school. Thus the habitus as a
generative structure mediates between the observable acts of
individuals and the objective structures defining a system of
social reproduction that serves the interests of dominant groups
even though "success" in school appears to be a purely individual achievement open to all. Although the term *social reproduction*—which refers to the non-economic processes required for
a society to reproduce itself, especially the construction of "workers" adapted to the demands of the market—is adapted from
Marxist theory, it is used in the context of a theory of practice
and culture that acknowledges individual agency and is not
based on any assumption of a direct "correspondence" between
the cultural and economic systems (as in structuralist Marxism).
In that respect Bourdieu's approach has contributed centrally
the notion of *cultural reproduction* as a central analytic category in social theory and one particularly important for critical
theory (Jenks 1993; Calhoun et al. 1993; Morrow and Torres 1994).

Foucault

Foucault's work defies classifications, though perhaps his approach might be called a critical *antisociology,* given his self-conscious rejection of systematic theorizing and aversion to analyzing the historical genesis of structures (Foucault 1984). Foucault was trained in philosophy, psychology, and history; his contributions primarily took the form of historical analyses of the depth-structures underlying knowledge systems and hence could be viewed as a kind of sociology of knowledge. Part of his immense interdisciplinary impact stems from the way he can mean different things to different researchers. For example, some consider that he has in effect completely undermined critical theory, and yet others see him as having provided the basis for important correctives (Smart 1983, 1985; Poster 1989).

Unlike sociologists such as Touraine and Bourdieu, Foucault can be read easily as a postmodernist largely because of his strong ambivalence toward totalizing theories. Yet he retains an interest in the use of structuralist methods and the analysis of power relations that is quite distinctive and directly applicable to sociological theory. Those in the social sciences influenced by critical theory, however, have tended to appropriate concepts selectively and critically, given the idiosyncratic character of many of his stances and formulations (Grumley 1989; Dews 1987).

To the extent that classifications are helpful, Foucault's work can be divided into two basic contributions: a structuralist methodology for the study of the history of systems of thought (the *archaeology of knowledge*), and a strategy for the analysis of the discourses of expert knowledge as "disciplinary" power relations that have defined modern social subjects (the *genealogy of knowledge*). The archaeological phase of Foucault's work has had a mixed reception in critical theory, given its ahistorical structuralism—that is, its lack of concern about the social origins of structures of thought; nevertheless it offers important insights into the structural mechanisms of disciplinary discourses that complement the sociology of knowledge. More influential in critical sociology has been the genealogy of knowledge, a mode of inquiry that claims power relations do not simply distort knowledge as suggested by the theory of ideology; rather knowledge itself is rooted in power relations, a theme originating with the 19th-century German philosopher Friedrich Nietzsche (1844-1900). According to Nietzsche's theory, all cognition has its origins in a *will to power* that defines human nature and calls into question all efforts to eliminate conflict. The task of the genealogy of knowledge thus becomes that of analyzing these *power/knowledge relations* in the context of the "disciplinary regimes" that use expertise to construct social order. From this perspective, power is not just something located in centers controlled by identifiable agents (e.g., a state apparatus), but is diffused through society and is inscribed in the very bodies of the dominated.

In significant ways, however, the genealogy of knowledge converges with the Frankfurt critique of instrumental rationalization, a point that Foucault acknowledged toward the end of his career. But Foucault's tendency to reduce all social relations to conflict and power is rejected by contemporary critical theory's insistence on the more fundamental character of communicative action, which is essentially cooperative in nature. However, his analysis of the relations between knowledge and power has brought acknowledgment of the problems entailed in oversimplified conceptions of the abolition of domination as more than a matter of merely eliminating centers of power. Resolution of these difficulties remains an important problem for the further development of Habermas's critical theory in particular.

Critical Realism and the Social Sciences

Given that realism comes in many different forms and has been associated most often with positivism, it is important to stress that critical realism as developed by Bhaskar and others is quite distinctive.[11] A crucial aspect is the influence of European structuralism and its conception of generative mechanisms, as opposed to covering laws models of explanation in the empiricist tradition. As we have already suggested, critical realism provides a postempiricist alternative that is largely compatible with critical theory and strengthens its critique of skeptical postmodernism. Critical realism's reading of the lessons of structuralism and poststructuralism is, in short, quite distinct from that of most postmodernist theories.

As critical realism makes clear, the possibility of a critical theory of society hinges on the nonrelativistic consequences of methodological pragmatism. The decisive step is the ontological claim that although we can never represent objective reality literally and absolutely, we can assume confidently that it has a consistently identifiable nature, and hence is imbued with inherent causal powers that can be represented indirectly by concepts. In the case of society, for example, we necessarily assume that basic structures operate behind the backs of agents and mediate their constructions of reality. There are no longer, of course, any historical guarantees that our knowledge of these processes is absolute or infallible. Further, it is clear there are dangers in attempting to analyze this nature in *essentialist* terms—that is, in a manner that ignores the historical construction and relativity of phenomena or the constructed nature of social inquiry itself. The most basic point is, however, that the process of historical construction is not completely arbitrary, but rather builds about some fundamental properties that define the nature of the phenomenon. In short, this fundamental rethinking of the natural sciences undertaken by postempiricism opens the way for reassessing the scientific credentials of neostructuralist critical theory in a much more positive way.

A crucial implication of this perspective for the nature of explanation will be of central importance for understanding the distinctiveness of critical theory. Recall that in the context of a theory of explanation the empiricist-idealist polarization took the form of an opposition between ideographic accounts of unique historical events and nomothetic explanations between deductively understood invariant laws. From a critical realist perspective this form merely reproduces the fallacy of the empiricist-subjectivist polarization. Ideographic approaches fail to grasp the embeddedness of particular events in broader systems of structural relations. Nomothetic explanations misconstrue the problem by focusing on the surface of causal processes as supposedly manifest in "variables" as indicators of general laws. In contrast, critical realism argues that explanations necessarily presuppose underlying generative mechanisms that cannot be directly captured through variable analysis. In this respect the social sciences are not fundamentally different from the natural sciences even though "to the extent that social phenomena are internally complex or *holistic*, the explanatory schemata . . . require adjust-ment" (Bhaskar 1986, p. 109).

Further, it should be noted that structuralist analysis is ultimately a unique form of hermeneutics (or interpretation). Although hermeneutics originally was seen as opposed to structuralism in France, this perception was misleading because structuralist analy-sis (say of a myth or economic system) is a type of interpretation. The difference is the focus on intentions and surface aspects of culture in traditional hermeneutics. But if we recall the critical hermeneutics of the early Frankfurt School, we are reminded of forms of depth-hermeneutics that also are concerned with the underlying social and economic structures as conditions of hu-man agency.[12]

Conclusion

This chapter has attempted the arduous task of tracing the highlights of key developments in the philosophy of social sci-ences since the original Frankfurt School, especially those that have influenced the reformulations of contemporary critical metatheory. It was argued that within Weberian and neo-Weberian theory could be found most of the major challenges to both classical Marxism and its reformulation in early Frankfurt critical theory. Further, three major philosophical challenges to positivism were discussed: linguistic philosophy, social phe-nomenology, and pragmatic interactionism. Each of these also provided important resources for understanding language and its relation to social action.

Under the heading of "French metatheory" the relations be-tween existentialism, structuralism, and poststructuralism were used to identify a metatheoretical alternative to empiricism. The theories of Touraine, Bourdieu, and Foucault were reviewed to illustrate some of the characteristic contributions of neostruct-uralist and poststructuralist inquiries. Finally such an interpre-tive conception of structuralist metatheory became the basis for understanding the explanatory strategy of the critical realist al-ternative to empiricism in the social sciences. With these issues in mind, we can now turn to the metatheory of Habermas and Giddens.

Notes

1. As Giddens notes, "I have often been called a 'Weberian' by critics who regard this as some sort of irreparable fault. I do not see the term, as they do, as a slur, but neither do I accept it accurately applied to my views" (1984, p. xxxvi, fn. 1).

2. It was also the French version of hermeneutics. In other words from the 1920s to the 1940s there were three historicist reinterpretations of Marx in hermeneutic terms: that of Lukacs and the Frankfurt School, Gramsci in Italy, and existentialist Marxism in France (Roth 1988).

3. Kant called such a priori phenomena *transcendental* because they could not be observed directly, as in the case of empirical phenomena manifest in sense data.

4. Others, such as the Swiss developmental psychologist Jean Piaget, extended structuralism beyond the human sciences to embrace mathematical, physical, and biological structures (Piaget 1970).

5. We also can take our point of departure here from Randall Collins, a neo-Weberian theorist not particularly enamored by critical theory; but he does have an appreciation of the problematic of structuralism that should have alerted methodologists to the problem: "In a time when prevailing intellectual fashion tends to go in the direction of relativism and idealism, structuralism provides a midway point. Science is possible, but on the level of models; reality as derived from these, on the other hand, will always have a quality of particularity and indeterminateness that we cannot overcome. . . . Structuralism's program is still valid" (Collins 1988, pp. 310-1).

6. It should be stressed, however, that many social theories acknowledge the possibility of something like a "postmodern society" as a new stage of development that should be the object of analysis, but this is not coupled with a skeptical attack on theory in general. Such theorists of postmodernity (e.g., Fredric Jameson) are not necessarily postmodern theorists in the sense of Lyotard or Baudrillard.

7. If structuralism appears at all, it is indirectly with reference to "network" theory, with which it has a certain affinity and some common origins. Along with functionalism, network explanations have been classified as nondeductive and noncausal "pattern theory" that "uses metaphors or analogies so that relationships 'make sense' " (Neuman 1991, p. 38).

8. It is in this ironic sense that Giddens can write: "Structuralism, and post-struc-turalism, are dead traditions of thought. . . . For although they did not transform our intellectual universe in the manner so often claimed, they nonetheless drew to our attention some problems of considerable and durable significance" (Giddens 1987, p. 195).

9. Although the term *genetic structuralism* is associated most closely with Piaget and Lucien Goldmann's structuralist sociology of culture, Ansart (1990) uses it to describe the critical structuralism of Pierre Bourdieu.

10. Another variant of structuralism—the genetic structuralism of Lucien Goldmann—took methodological cues from Piaget for a methodology of structure and coupled this with Lukacs's theory of society as a contradictory totality (Goldmann 1959, 1969). Although structuralists have criticized this type of approach because

of its "expressive" conception of the effects of structure, the more fundamental point is that both the Kantian-Hegelian and Durkheimian traditions legitimate forms of analysis that are "structural," rather than merely "empirical." Also in this context should be mentioned the economic anthropologist Maurice Godelier.

11. For a detailed account of some of the implications of critical realism for social science, see A. Sayer (1992), and more generally the useful introduction by Keat and Urry (1982).

12. As later commentators have pointed out, these two strategies of analysis, in fact, take up in different ways problems in Husserl's phenomenology (Holenstein 1975), and ultimately structuralism is a specific case or type of hermeneutics (Ricoeur 1974, pp. 27-61).

6

THE METATHEORY OF CRITICAL THEORY

Beyond Objectivism and Relativism

Thus positivism could forget that the methodology of the sciences was intertwined with the objective self-formative process (Bildungsprozess) of the human species and erect the absolutism of pure methodology on the basis of the forgotten and repressed. (Habermas 1971, p. 5)

The separation of subject and object is both real and illusory. True, because in the cognitive realm it serves to express the real separation, the dichotomy of the human condition, a coercive development. False, because the resulting separation must not be hypostatized, not magically transformed into an invariant. (Adorno 1978, pp. 498-9)

Rethinking Critical Theory

Introduction

As we suggested in Part I, the metatheoretical status of the research program of critical theory could be discussed only in relation to the developments in the postempiricist philosophy of science. Now we are in a better position to consider the reconstructive metatheoretical program of the research traditions associated with critical theory as a specific form of postempiricism. From this perspective critical theory's original critique of positivism from the 1930s onward was not simply the idiosyncratic response of a handful of disillusioned, antiscientific intellectuals; rather this critique both anticipated and indirectly influenced a much broader shift associated with the gradual displacement of positivism by postempiricist theories of science. The justification of critical theory as a research program thus has found independent corroboration, at least as a critique of positivism. And in the context of critical realism and certain developments in poststructuralist and feminist theory, it also finds some further complementary support (as well as constructive criticism).

We have stressed this point because critical theory often has been caricatured for its negativism (its critique of positivism), as opposed to being appreciated for its contribution as an alternative research program (Shils 1980; van den Berg 1980). We would support a rather different assessment: "It is sheer nonsense to assert that critical theorists were antiscientific. Quite to the contrary, the group relentlessly defended the sciences against neoromantic, spiritual, and idealist attacks, as well as against their positivistic reductions (Gebhardt 1978, p. 371). But the tradition of critical theory is associated with a quite distinctive position in the context of postempiricist theories of knowledge.

We find it instructive to reconstruct the metatheoretical program of critical theory in a relatively accessible form in the light of these interim developments. The distinctive aspect of our approach, however, will be to juxtapose the work of Jürgen Habermas (the focus of attention) and Anthony Giddens as rival but essentially complementary research programs for critical theory.[1] Although this complementarity is often vaguely acknowledged, comparisons of their work are few and far between. But taken together, they not only provide a profound critique of positivism (Habermas 1971, 1976; Giddens 1974, 1977) but also outline a powerful critical modernist rejoinder to skeptical postmodernist social theory (Habermas 1987b; Giddens 1984, 1991a).

The primary task of this chapter is to present the development of critical theory as metatheory beyond it origins in the form of *critical hermeneutics* associated with the Hegelian Marxist historicism of the early Frankfurt School. Here the focus is on its fundamental revision in the theory of *knowledge interests* and *communicative action* developed by Jürgen Habermas and, further, its generalization as a widely—if often loosely—shared set of metatheoretical themes associated with diverse forms of contemporary critical theory (e.g., Giddens's structuration theory), including some forms of feminist theory (Fraser 1989; Nielsen 1990; Cook and Fonow 1990; Marshall 1991). This more highly generalized form of critical theory—Giddens is our primary example here—will be referred to as a *weak research program in critical theory,* as opposed to the *strong program* associated with Habermas.[2] Although our focus is on the latter, our concluding reconstruction of the subjectivist-objectivist polarization incorporates both.

In the conclusion we argue for the distinctiveness of critical metatheory (in either variant) in simultaneously moving beyond traditional hermeneutics, reactive antinaturalism, ahistorical structuralism, and classical modernist foundationalism. In other words, the position of critical theory needs to be understood in terms of its simultaneous critique of both positivist and purely interpretive approaches to social science, hence a reaction against the unfruitful consequences of their polarization. In short, we argue that critical theory moves beyond "objectivism" and "relativism" and effectively criticizes key aspects of "the new constellation" of postmodernity (Bernstein 1983, 1992). As Habermas put it more than two decades ago, the key to social science is the relationship between analytical and interpretive methodologies:

> Whereas the natural and the cultural or hermeneutic sciences are capable of living in a mutually indifferent, albeit more hostile than peaceful, coexistence, the social sciences must bear the tension of divergent approaches under one roof, for in them the very practice of research compels reflection on the relationship between analytic and hermeneutic methodologies. (Habermas 1988, p. 3)

Habermas and the Crisis of Critical Theory

By the 1960s Habermas became disenchanted with key aspects of the tradition of critical theory, especially in its "dialectic of Enlightenment" phase: "In retrospect, what appear to me to be the weaknesses in Critical Theory can be categorized under the labels of 'normative foundations,' 'concept of truth and its relation to scientific disciplines' and 'undervaluation of the traditions of democracy and of the constitutional state' " (Habermas 1986, p. 97).[3] Of particular concern here are the first two themes: the nature of critical theory as a research program with normative implications. By the 1960s the older Frankfurt School had effectively isolated critical theory from important developments in the social sciences and elsewhere, leaving it a pessimistic and marginalized perspective with little relation to social research.

The response of Habermas to this crisis of classical critical theory is complex. A useful place to begin is with a general characterization of implications of his metatheoretical approach as a postpositivist theory of science along the lines of the dimensions discussed earlier: as a systematic account of knowledge, as a historical and sociological analysis of scientific institutions, and as an interpretation of the sciences as a meaning system. On this introductory foundation we then can turn to some of the more detailed aspects of his systematic metatheoretical program and its relations to other variants of contemporary critical theory.

With respect to epistemological credibility of critical theory, Habermas argued that it had to confront the challenge of analytic philosophy (logical and linguistic analysis) on its own ground. This required a deeper critique of positivism that could link up with non-Marxist critiques and justify a theory of knowledge that could escape the charge of being either the ideology of the working class or the dogmatic claims of elitist speculative philosophers. The systematic point of departure was the heretical charge that not only the Marxist tradition but also Marx himself was guilty of a kind of latent positivism that derived from the ultimate primacy given to work and labor in his conception of human nature and praxis. Accordingly Habermas argued that it was necessary to make a categorical distinction between work and interaction, giving primacy to the latter as the basis of the communicative and symbolic activities through which social life is constituted. This critique of Marx was coupled with an explicit epistemological alternative based on the differentiation between three knowledge-constitutive interests: an *empirical-analytical interest* in potential control, a *hermeneutic-historical interest* in understanding; and a *critical-emancipatory interest* in freedom and autonomy (Habermas 1971). We will return to these in a moment.

With respect to the history of science, Habermas largely rejects the dialectic of Enlightenment thesis and returns to the earliest position of critical theory with its stress on the strategic importance of the social context of the production and implementation of technology. The outcome was the thesis that although science and technology appeared to be neutral with respect to values, they had increasingly come to serve ideological interests (Habermas 1970). From this perspective the negative effects of science and technology were not so much inherent in scientific reason as such, as a manifestation of the contradictions of society.

Finally he redefines the nature of science as a meaning system by expanding the very concept of reason to include more than the forms of knowledge recognized by positivism. As against his Frankfurt mentor's later thesis on the dialectic of Enlightenment, however, he is reluctant to juxtapose an "objective" truth available only to the isolated philosopher and the "subjective" truth legitimated by the instrumental rationality of science and technology. The critique of instrumental rationality needed to be carried out in terms that went beyond the hermeneutics of Hegelian Marxism and could draw on some of the developments in 20th-century philosophy (broadly associated with a so-called "linguistic turn") that provided resources for a more comprehensive account of human reason, especially pragmatism, linguistic philosophy, and structuralism.

Knowledge Interests: Quasi Transcendentalism

Rethinking the Problematic: The Pragmatist Turn

The origins of the notion of knowledge interests (or cognitive interests) can be traced to questioning the positivist formulation of the problems of epistemology as ones of logical reconstruction. This latter approach begins with the assumption of a universal cognitive subject who produces knowledge. The context of this activity—the history and social psychology of discovery—is of no relevance to its scientific validity. Validity is rather an outcome of the context of justification in which the verification (or perhaps falsification) of explanations assumes a specific logical form (the covering law model). The result is a kind of logical essentialism that ignores the diversity of forms that reliable knowledge can assume.

Instead Habermas begins with the assumption guiding pragmatist theories of science (e.g., Charles Sanders Peirce, John Dewey) that science as a form of social activity cannot be separated from our understanding of its particular character as a form of knowledge (Habermas 1971). Indeed a refusal to reflect on the social origins of science becomes the ultimate basis for a definition of positivism: "That we disavow reflection is positivism" (Habermas 1971, p. vii). The key aspect of such a critique of science is to question the dogmatic assumption that science can be reduced to a single method or type of explanation, thus succumbing to logical essentialism. But Habermas is not content with the answers provided by German idealism, either, which is based on a polarization between hermeneutics and naturalism. For Dilthey, whereas natural science is concerned exclusively with general laws, the human sciences seek only to describe and interpret meanings. This position, however, turns a blind eye to the causal effects of relations of power and domination in shaping and perhaps distorting consciousness.

What, then, is the key idea behind a *knowledge-constitutive interest?* Above all, it is designed to make us wary of the claim that knowledge is identified by a single interest in knowledge, the one assumed by positivism. Instead Habermas suggested it is necessary to distinguish three basic forms of our scientific interest in knowing about the world: the empirical-analytical, the hermeneutic-historical, and the critical-emancipatory. We seek to know in order to control social and natural realities (the empirical-analytic interest), to qualitatively interpret and understand such realities (the hermeneutic-historical interest), and to transform our individual and collective consciousness of reality in order to maximize the human potential for freedom and equality (the critical-emancipatory interest).

Two important qualifications help clarify the importance of these distinctions. First, each of these knowledge interests has unique methodological problems, given the nature of its tasks in constructing and validating knowledge, a fact that precludes any single correct methodology or logic of science. Second, these interests are grounded in the inherent problems of social life; hence they should not be identified with historically contingent or psychological motivations. Habermas's argument is a much more fundamental one: These interests underlie all cognitive activities, whether we are conscious of it or not. Even the most hard-boiled positivist necessarily must presuppose the other knowledge interests in order to do science at all. For example, the observation of a fact presupposes the hermeneutic capacity to read measuring instruments; and the aspiration to control nature implies the value of human freedom from oppression by natural laws.

How can Habermas justify this ambitious epistemological claim? This strategy has its roots in a type of pragmatist *transcendentalism* that can be traced back to Kant's critique of British empiricism. For Kant, we cannot be certain about our knowledge simply by reference to the object (sense-data). Knowledge has to be rooted in the peculiar nature of the human subject, or what Kant called the *a priori* or *transcendental* structures of cognition, for example, the capacity to perceive space and time in ways that allow us to construct sciences. These transcendental structures are not empirical; as a consequence no observable facts could establish their existence. Rather they are deep structures of the human mind that we have to assume in order to have the conditions of possibility for what we in fact do know. Habermas postulates that the three knowledge interests have just such an a priori status. As we will see in a moment, Habermas came to have doubts about aspects of this way of justifying knowledge interests, hence his tendency to refer to their quasi-transcendental status.

Three Knowledge Interests

In Habermas's scheme the *empirical-analytical interest* is rooted in a desire for potential technical control over external nature (and later, internal nature as in the social sciences). In his early writings he tended to accept the reigning positivist conception defining such knowledge in terms of the nomological form of their explanations based on invariant laws, though he gave it a pragmatic twist by stressing the inherent link between deterministic explanation and the possibility of technical control over nature or social life.[4] From this perspective, even if individual scientists personally may view their research as "basic" and without any practical uses, their conception of knowledge ties them to a way of explaining in terms of invariant causes and effects that implies the possibility of control. But this tie also prejudices the possibility of forms of "knowledge" that do not exactly fit this control-oriented form, and yet may be essential for social life.

All purely interpretive or humanistic approaches–guided by the *hermeneutic-historical interest*–are based on the ostensible uniqueness of human activity that can be comprehended only through the ideographic interpretations based on the principles of hermeneutics. It is also a historical interest because the meanings that come to constitute societies are the outcome of the development of historical traditions. Analysis of causal factors along positivist lines is ruled out as reductionistic. Such methodological assumptions have, of course, always been the foundation of the humanities (as described, for example, by Wilhelm Dilthey). Within the modern university, for example, students of literature, the arts, philosophy, as well as more traditional historians, identify with the humanities, rather than the social sciences. It is also the basis of "humanistic" sociologies concerned with *Verstehen* and interpretive (cultural) anthropology.

Although appreciative of the foundational role of hermeneutics in the human sciences, Habermas is critical of its claim to self-sufficiency and universality. This issue became central in a debate with the leading contemporary representative of an ontological hermeneutics, Hans-Georg Gadamer (Gadamer 1975; Warnke 1987; Wachterhauser 1987). According to Habermas, Gadamer's grounding of all knowledge in tradition cut him off from appreciating the ways the system of social labor and power potentially distort consciousness. For this reason it was necessary to postulate a *critical-emancipatory interest* concerned with unveiling precisely the mystifications that limit any given historical tradition.

Ultimately critical-emancipatory knowledge is simply a special case of the hermeneutic-historical one.[5] The difference is that it involves a different attitude toward meanings: Rather than merely describe and understand them, the objective is to criticize and transform them. This implies that values and norms have social functions linked to social and cultural reproduction–that is, the maintenance of a particular set of social relations that disadvantages some groups relative to others. In short, *a fundamental assumption of critical theory is that every form of social order entails some forms of domination and that the critical-emancipatory interest underlies the struggles to change those relations of domination-subordination.*[6]

A unique aspect of the critical-emancipatory interest is that a cognitive activity unites both empirical and normative theorizing. Empirically, critical social science analyzes how power relations constrain the realization of human potentials in a given context. Further, this analysis argues that power relations engender forms of *distorted communication* that result in self-deceptions on the part of agents with respect to their interests, needs, and perceptions of social reality. This type of empirical analysis is, in turn, closely linked with implicit *normative claims*—that is, the necessary assumption of an *ideal speech situation* where falsifying consciousness would be reduced because communication would assume the form of authentic dialogue not based on asymmetrical relations of power. In this way analysis shifts persuasively from an empirical analysis of what *is* to a normative analysis of what *ought to be.* We cannot go into detail about all of the ramifications of this complex and highly contested concept, except to note that "from this practical hypothesis critical theory takes its start" (McCarthy 1978, p. 310).

The Master-Slave Dialectic

The simplest example of this type of distorted communication process as the basis of *ideology critique* is the pervasive tendency of slaves to identify with the legitimacy of their masters' oppression even though that clearly entails the denial of their own humanity.[7] The point of critical social science would be to construct scientifically credible causal-type explanations that would demonstrate how the coercive element defining this social relationship—often referred to as the *master-slave dialectic*—contributes to the distorted self-understanding of oppressed social actors who come to internalize a belief in the legitimacy of their own subordination and innate status as inferior humans. A further assumption would be that in the right circumstances, both master and slave alike will come to transform rationally their perceptions of reality in a manner that reflects the universal imperative of human freedom and self-respect. Although the methodological status of this mode of knowledge is clear enough in the paradigm case of slavery, it is more ambiguous with respect to forms of domination that move away from this kind of ideal-typical case (Wartenberg 1990).

The Psychoanalytic Analogy

The logic underlying the critical functions of knowledge in the master-slave dialectic is illustrated further by the *psychoanalytic analogy*.[8] The analogy of neurosis serves to illustrate the methodology of the critique of ideology, or what Habermas refers to in generalized terms as "systematically distorted communication." The neurotic (like the victim of oppression) suffers from an internal communication disturbance that is not accessible to the self; this blockage can be revealed only by the explanatory knowledge that the therapist provides to become aware of and translate these experiences, a process that requires overcoming cognitive and affective resistances: "This translation reveals the genetically important phases of life history to a memory that was previously blocked, and brings to consciousness the person's own self-formative process" (Habermas 1971, p. 228).[9] The French critical hermeneutic philosopher Paul Ricoeur has referred similarly to this translation as involving a process of *distanciation* through which the referential insight produced by any "text" that challenges taken-for-granted understandings may force cognitive transformation: "The power of the text to open a dimension of reality implies in principle a recourse against any given reality and thereby the possibility of a critique of the real" (Ricoeur 1981, p. 93).

Theory of Communicative Action: Reconstructive Sciences

Universal Pragmatics

In his later work Habermas moves away from this strategy of attempting to provide a quasi-transcendental epistemological grounding of the critical-emancipatory interest. The primary reason is that it remains too "foundationalist" in its intentions— that is, it is still caught up in the attempt to ground knowledge (following Kant) in ahistorical, a priori certainties derived from philosophical reflection. Responding to the so-called "linguistic turn" in philosophy (associated with continental hermeneutics, structuralism, pragmatism, and Wittgenstein's theory of language), he develops a different, though largely complementary, strategy to the theory of knowledge interests. This shift is evident in a concern with what he refers to as *universal pragmatics,* the task of which is "to identify and reconstruct universal conditions of possible understanding [*Verständigung*]," hence of "communicative action" (Habermas 1979, p. 1). Notice that the kind of research involving the elucidation of universal pragmatics implies a structuralist-type analysis that, in this case, is held to be universal in the sense of constituting part of the deep structure of any possible form of society. This general approach usually is referred to as Habermas's *theory of communicative action.*

From this perspective, even though processes of communication and interpretation may appear to be completely open and relative, they are, in fact, grounded and made possible by the four implicit "validity claims of comprehensibility, truth, truthfulness, and rightness" (Habermas 1979, p. 3). Whereas the theory of knowledge interests focuses on the origins of distorted communication, the theory of communicative actions shifts the emphasis to the most general conditions of intersubjective communication as such (Habermas 1984, 1987a). Assuming the existence of such universal features embedded in human social life, it becomes possible to criticize deviations. But the fundamental problem here is the status of the type of knowledge presupposed by this type of knowledge, which, though grounded in linguistics, does not have an empirical status like that of knowledge based on direct observations. However, it is not strictly philosophical and rational in the sense of the quasi-transcendental arguments grounding the theory of knowledge interests or the universalistic claims of ontological hermeneutics. The key here is the status of what he calls *reconstructive sciences* that fall between the purely empirical and the transcendental. Perhaps the most well studied example is cognitive developmental psychology's theory of innate stages and the types of generative rules studied by linguists.[10]

Communicative Ethics

The example of reconstructive science also became the basis for justifying the integral relationship between empirical and normative theorizing earlier suggested by the critical-emancipatory interest. In particular, Lawrence Kohlberg's theory of moral development is singled out as an important example of such a reconstructive science, along with other, related types (ego, social) of developmental competence (Habermas 1990). Such ontogenetic stages (universal developmental features of the species) are held to provide a universalistic basis for linking the ontological reality of stages of development with the moral imperative of realizing those possibilities. The line of reasoning here complements the earlier contrast between "ideal" and "distorted" communication in that universal pragmatic structures of human competence presuppose and imply idealized possibilities; to the extent societies fail to cultivate those potentials, they are subject to forms of criticism that are not arbitrary or culturally relative.

Such an approach seeks to challenge the moral relativism implied by both positivism and extreme antipositivism (skeptical postmodernism). For positivists the criteria of valid knowledge are such that value questions cannot be rational; for skeptical postmodernists the criteria of valid knowledge are so fluid and transitory that neither empirical nor normative knowledge can be rational. In the process the distinctive rationalities of both empirical and normative knowledge get lost in the oscillations between absolutist foundationalism and dogmatic antifoundationalism.

These issues take us in the direction of the *communicative ethics* implied by this strong form of critical theory (Benhabib and Dallmayr 1990; Kelly 1990) and away from the more immediate issue of the mediations between the interpretations of subjects and explanatory knowledge in the form of critical social science. Such an ethic is communicative because it is grounded in an analysis of the normative imperatives built into the most fundamental features of human communication and linguistic understanding. From this perspective it becomes plausible for linking *is* and *ought* in ways that allow connecting social analysis with ethical imperatives. For example, if cognitive developmental theory can reconstruct intellectual development and establish that certain groups of individuals do not attain levels of competence that are potentially available to them, that is an *empirical claim with respect to what is the case.* But this kind of empirical analysis is related intimately to the normative claim that such a restriction of real possibilities is unjust, and this implies a *value claim with respect to what ought to be.*

Transcending the Subject-Object Split

Weak and Strong Research Programs

If we return to the subjectivist-objectivist polarization in meta-theory described earlier, the distinctive contributions of critical theorists such as Habermas and Giddens becomes apparent. The basic intuition underlying their approach is the inadequacy of this very dichotomy that reproduces the original German distinction between *Verstehen* (to understand through interpretation) and *Erklären* (to explain through causal analysis based on invariant laws).[11] In identifying critical theory with the aspiration to break down or overcome this polarization, we have a useful framework for laying out the kinds of shared assumptions broadly shared by critical theorists (e.g., Giddens's structuration theory) whether or not they adhere closely to Habermas's particular formulations.

Habermas's strong program, on the one hand, is more strongly "idealistic" in its insistence on evolutionary principles of directionality in human history and its attempt to secure the bases for grounding ideology critique in normative theory (communicative ethics). Giddens, on the other hand, tends to be more "realistic" and "empirical" in his insistence on historical discontinuities and his relative indifference to epistemological questions and normative grounding. But these can be seen as tensions within the shared framework of a metatheoretical program that would transcend the opposition of interpretive and explanatory understanding in social life and would identify this with its potential contribution to the realization of the universal values of human autonomy.

The shared point of departure for both the theory of communicative action and structuration theory is a rejection of the metaphysical philosophical paradigm that has defined modern, Western philosophy: what Habermas refers to as the *philosophy of consciousness* and Giddens as *subject-object dualism*. The fundamental question involved here is how knowledge is to be grounded. According to classical modern epistemologies, there have been two basic choices: locating the certainty of knowledge in the self-reflecting subject along the lines of German idealism or French rationalism, or anchoring it in the nature of the preexisting, external object along the lines of British empiricism. These approaches remain wedded to philosophies of consciousness or reflection because debate turns on assumptions about the nature of consciousness for deciding whether to opt for subjectivism or objectivism. These thus are competing versions of foundationalist epistemology that reject other alternatives as destroying the basis of scientific knowledge.

According to the philosophy of language implied by the linguistic turn, however, the focus on consciousness and certainty of knowledge is misplaced because the ultimate basis—or rather medium—of knowledge is language itself, the means through which we have to represent reality. From this point of view the subjective and objective mutually constitute one another and cannot be elaborated as isolated, independent modes of knowing without deforming human understanding. This does not mean that we can dispense with such terms, but we must always struggle to avoid the reifications and distortions involved in one-sided characterizations. But this awareness of the linguistic and interpretive basis of all knowledge does not preclude that social science cannot effectively represent causal processes in social life, at least if these are understood in terms of structural mechanisms that constrain and enable social possibilities. Taking these two dimensions together, the metatheory of Habermas and Giddens may be described usefully as an *interpretive structuralism,* where "interpretation" refers to both the hermeneutic and historical character of structural analysis.

Ontology: Critical Realism

It is important to distinguish traditional ontology's abstract concern with the nature of being as such, and that of a scientific ontology concern with "the entities posited or presupposed by some particular substantive scientific theory" (Outhwaite and Bottomore 1993, p. 429). It is in this second context that social ontology becomes central to contemporary social theory. For this reason, although Habermas rejects the philosophical ontologies of German idealism, he nevertheless is concerned with ontological questions despite his apparent focus on epistemology. Although he has not developed an explicit ontological position, he necessarily assumes something like a critical realism, given his fundamental distinction between work and symbolic interaction, his claim that the social sciences can analyze the process of societal reproduction, and that the reconstructive sciences can describe the depth-structures of language and cognitive development.[12] Giddens has alluded specifically to viewing his own theoretical project in similar critical realist terms (Craib 1992, p. 120). A critical realism is not based on a correspondence theory of truth as in traditional realism. From the perspective of postempiricist theories of science, it has become most problematic to claim that theories somehow reflect, copy, and map reality in some kind of literal sense that becomes the basis of certain knowledge. But critical realists hold that the identification of deeper causal mechanisms does presuppose a view of reality outside discourse even if it can only be known fallibly through it. Hence for critical realists "structures are a property of being and not just a property of our discourse about being" (Baugh 1990, p. 60). From this perspective we cannot know being in-itself, of course, because our knowledge is always mediated by interpretations.

Although Giddens does not share Habermas's epistemological concerns (related to the linguistic turn and postempiricist philosophies of science), he explicitly defines the theory of structuration as a form of social ontology that challenges the dualism of subjectivism and objectivism:

Significant as these may be, concentration upon epistemological issues draws attention away from the more "ontological concerns" of social theory, and it is these upon which structuration theory primarily concentrates . . . . Those working in social theory . . . should be concerned first and foremost with reworking conceptions of human being and human doing, social reproduction and social transformation. Of primary importance in this respect is a dualism that is deeply entrenched in social theory, a division between objectivism and subjectivism. (Giddens 1984, p. xx)

Giddens's notion of the *double-hermeneutic* of social life is one of his most important contributions, one that fleshes out some of the problematic aspects of Habermas's effort to overcome the polarization between quasi-nomothetic explanation and interpretation. This is a way, of course, of drawing out the methodological implications of the interplay between the hermeneutic and analytical dimensions of social inquiry also noted by Habermas above. The first point—the notion of a double hermeneutic—refers to the way the structures of the social world were constructed originally by human agents, whereas those of nature were not. In this respect, therefore, a qualitative ontological difference exists between nature and society.

This fact has fundamental consequences for sociological methods because "the prosecution of all types of social and historical research demands communication, in some sense, with the persons or collectivities that are the 'subject-matter' of that research" (Giddens 1976, p. 151). Further, the lawlike properties of social life are essentially historical, a fact that has important implications for social explanation, given that "they are the reproduced unintended consequences of intended act, and are malleable in the light of the development of human knowledge" (1976, pp. 153-4).

As a consequence human intervention in nature is qualitatively different than in society because the nature of the control is not identical. For this reason the model of applied science as technology breaks down when applied to society where intervention is better understood as a form of social praxis. This theme was developed originally by Habermas in his critique of science and technology as ideology (Habermas 1970).

Epistemology: Pragmatism
and Historicist Structuralism

Despite a kind of realist ontology, the interpretive structuralism of critical theories is necessarily pragmatist and constructivist with respect to epistemology and methodology. In other words, nominalist and subjectivist epistemologies are granted partial validity in recognizing that science ultimately is based on a social consensus mediated through language. Hence the correspondence theory of truth associated with traditional realism is rejected. However, the constructed character of scientific knowledge and methodology does not mean that it is merely an arbitrary process. Rather it is described more accurately in terms of the *theory of argumentation*, with its pragmatic understanding of the diversity of methods and explanatory strategies used in the natural and human sciences (Morrow 1991b). The theory of argumentation, in other words, implies a pluralist stance with respect to methodological techniques, one that refers to the primacy of the logics-in-use of specific research strategies (Kaplan 1964). From this perspective, then, the ultimate basis of scientific discourse is not formal logic or factual verifications; rather it is a process of argumentation:

Post-empiricist philosophy of science has provided good reasons for holding that the unsettled ground of rationally motivated agreement among participants in argumentation is our only foundation—in questions of physics no less than in those of morality. (Habermas 1982, p. 238)[13]

But this need not imply the relativism assumed by some postmodernist critics. As Giddens puts it:

Sociological work is a core component of what I have come to see as the intrinsic reflexivity of modernity. . . . The reflexivity of modernity connects directly with Enlightenment thought, which seemed initially to be providing foundations for knowledge . . . rather than—as it has turned out—corroding the very basis of foundationalism. . . . As in my earlier work, I am not particularly interested in the epistemological aspects of this situation. I do not believe that they imply relativism or the view, sometime associated with post-structuralism, that all knowledge, or even "truth" are no more than contextual. On the contrary, in my view, those who have taken such a standpoint have misinterpreted what is essentially a set of profound institutional changes (the development and radicalizing of modernity) with the undermining of valid claims as such. Their position is as much an expression of these institutional transformations as a means of adequately comprehending them. (Giddens 1991b, p. 207)

A further shared feature of Habermas and Giddens with respect to empirical-analytical knowledge in the social sciences is the preference given to "structuralist," as opposed to "empiricist" methods, a theme that will be developed in more detail in the context of their approach to explanation. What is crucial here is the distinction between the empiricist use of variable analysis to analyze the surface correlations of phenomena, as opposed to the generalizations about deeper causal mechanisms and structural rules that operate historically.

Social Action: Praxis and Communicative Action

The hermeneutic commitments of both Habermas and Giddens ultimately require them to assume the interpretive foundations of inquiry in the manner suggested by the early Marx. In fact, Giddens explicitly defines *structuration theory* as "an extended reflection upon a celebrated and oft-quoted phrase to be found in Marx . . . 'Men [let us immediately say human beings] make history, but not in circumstances of their own choosing' " (Giddens 1984, p. xxi). But both Habermas and Giddens go beyond Marx in explicating agency more explicitly in terms of the human capacity for reflexivity and self-reflection. Whereas Giddens stresses this as a general property of the actor, Habermas has been concerned especially with the processes through which self-reflection makes possible the overcoming of suppressed forms of domination. At this point, therefore, such epistemological commitments call forth an explicit account of human agency and social action.

Habermas's concern with communicative action is directed primarily to fundamental questions about the pragmatic universals of human communication, rather than the more social psychological questions of agency-structure relations. In particular he has sought to differentiate between strategic (manipulative) and communicative action in order to isolate the latter as the basis of reconstructing various human competences with crucial normative implications. For the purpose of a theory of agency concerned with more empirically oriented questions, Giddens's structuration theory is considerably more helpful.

A distinctive and foundational aspect of Giddens's metatheory with respect to the study of social action is the notion of the *duality of structure,* as opposed to traditional dualism. The duality of structuration resides in the paradoxical fact that structures are produced by human actions and yet are simultaneously the medium of that action: "It is this dual aspect of structure, as both inferred from observation of human doings, yet as also operating as a medium whereby those doings are made possible, that has to be grasped through the notions of structuration and reproduction" (Giddens 1976, p. 122).

As a consequence the actual practice—hence the specific methodological context—of the social sciences should be differentiated from the natural sciences in two fundamental ways that are of central concern to critical theories: the relation of investigators to the object of inquiry, and the logical status of the lawlike relations involved in social life. As Giddens puts it, unlike in natural science sociologists ultimately have a subject-subject relation to the field of study, not a subject-object one (Giddens 1976, p. 146).

A further aspect of the limited voluntarism assumed by critical theory is based on the distinction between what Habermas calls *unconstrained* as opposed to *distorted communication.* Again Giddens generalizes this assumption as the basis of an institutional theory of domination:

"Domination" is not the same as "systematically distorted" structures of signification because domination—as I conceive of it—is the very condition of existence of codes of signification. "Domination" and "power" cannot be thought of only in terms of asymmetries of distribution but have to be recognized as inherent in social association (or, I would say, in human action as such). Thus—and here we must also reckon with the implications of the writings of Foucault—power is not an inherently noxious phenomenon, not just the capacity to "say no"; nor can domination be "transcended" in some kind of putative society of the future, as has been the characteristic aspiration of at least some strands of socialist thought. (Giddens 1984, pp. 31-2)

Explanation: Interpretive Structuralism

Giddens's point of departure is to challenge the priority given to explanatory theory by the positivist tradition: "The uncovering of generalizations is not the be-all and end-all of social theory. If the proponents of 'theory as explanatory generalization' have too narrowly confined the nature of 'explanation,' they have compounded the error by failing to inquire closely enough into what generalization is, and should be, in social science. (Giddens 1984, p. xix)

Further, Giddens calls into question universalistic generalizations in the social sciences, rejecting the natural scientific notion of invariant laws:

In the case of generalizations in social science, the causal mechanisms are inherently unstable, the degree of instability depending upon how far those beings to whom the generalization refers are likely to display standard patterns of reasoning in such a way as to produce standard sorts of unintended consequence. . . . In my opinion, since in natural science "law" tends to be associated with the operation of invariant relations . . . it is preferable not to use the term in social science. (Giddens 1984, p. 347)

Relaxing the requirement of invariant explanations also broadens our understanding of what most social science is about. As Giddens concludes, the role of generalizations in studying history and social change is more restricted than usually is acknowledged; indeed the notion of universal patterns of causation in social life is rejected: "This has nothing to do with historical contingency; it expresses the necessarily incomplete nature of generalizing explanations in the social sciences" (Giddens 1991b, p. 206).

A central conclusion of critical metatheory is that the polarization of the question of explanation in terms of the contrast between ideographic and nomothetic accounts does not help us understand the principal issues of social theory, ethnography, and historical sociology. For this purpose we need to recall the structuralist alternative to explanation and its emphasis on generative mechanisms that we refer to as quasi-causal. What is at stake here is not the kind of hyperstructuralism associated with the ahistorical formalism of Lévi-Strauss's structuralist theory of myths or of the structural causality entailed in Althusser's structuralist Marxism. More pertinent are the forms of genetic and historically specific structuralism grounded in the agency-structure dialectic. These can be grouped conveniently together as *interpretive structural explanations*—our term for describing what John B. Thompson has incisively characterized as the "distinctive methodological concepts" that allow "reformulating the program of depth interpretation initiated by Ricoeur and Habermas" (Thompson 1981, p. 173).[14] First, there is the generative regulation of the type associated with Bourdieu's concept of *habitus:*

> Bourdieu characterizes the habitus as "systems of durable, transposable dispositions," which regulate practice without presupposing a conscious or collective orchestration of action. Moreover, as both Ricoeur and Bourdieu rightly suggest, the form of regulation which is relevant here is peculiarly generative. Institutional schemata do not specify the course of action to be pursued in every foreseeable situation, but merely provide general principles for the creative production of particular acts. . . . The concept of schematic generation avoids the hypostatizations and reifications of role theory, insofar as it eliminates the need to posit a package of detailed instructions for every institutionalized act. The concept equally eludes the reductionism of some interpretive sociologies, for it emphasizes that social interaction is always more than the sum of its individual and ephemeral aspects. (Thompson 1981, p. 174)

Second, at the level of social structure is a further basis for explanatory structures in the "social structuration" of institutions. Here the focus is on the other end of the reproduction cycle:

> For the reconstruction of structural elements presupposes a theory of social development, and the developmental stages specify the conditions which must be satisfied by institutions of a particular type. . . . A structural analysis may facilitate the depth interpretation

of action by situating agents within a context of conditions of which they are ignorant. (Thompson 1981, p. 177)

Although Thompson is critical of aspects of Giddens's account of structuration, a crucial application for such analysis is Giddens's general theory of structural contradiction and exploitation (Giddens 1981, p. 230-52).

Unlike purely hermeneutic versions of interpretive sociology, critical theory necessarily retains a concern with social determination and causality, especially differentiating surface and depth causality. In this respect it does not differ fundamentally from those postempiricist theories of natural science that have abandoned the hypothetico-deductive and covering law models of explanation. Hence, even in the natural sciences, attention has shifted from surface to depth processes, and explanation is also ultimately viewed as a kind of reflexive social act.[15]

Where Habermas and Giddens do differ most fundamentally is with respect to the explanatory status of evolutionary-type theorizing. For Giddens the episodic and discontinuous character of social development precludes all-embracing generalizations of the type characteristic of evolutionary theories. From early on, Habermas sought, however, to rescue aspects of the Hegelian and Marxian theory of history, albeit in a scientifically credible version of social evolution as a hypothetical construct. But this first requires dropping the assumption of imitating the strict sciences and a focus on instrumental knowledge. Viewed as a special type of general interpretation, a philosophy of history with a practical interest becomes justifiable, according to Habermas. But this justification requires dispensing with a model of evolution driven by material necessity. The teleology of history is replaced by the utopian imagining of the conditions of possibility of an ideal form of society anticipated in the deep structures of human communication and competence:

> In place of the desired end-state of a self-regulating system there appears the anticipated end-state of a formative process. A functionalism that is hermeneutically enlightened and historically oriented has as its aim not general theories in the sense of strict empirical science but a general interpretation. . . . Classical social theories . . . pursued this intention more or less implicitly. . . .

Whether or not it admits this interest, sociology pursues it even today, insofar as it does not dissolve into a social-psychological behavior science, systems research, or the hermeneutics of intellectual history. . . . The truth of historically oriented functionalism is confirmed not technically but only practically, in the successful continuation and completion of a formative process. (Habermas 1988, pp. 187-9)

From Analysis to Critique: Emancipatory Self-Reflection

Despite his insistence of the universality of domination, Giddens still is concerned with the critical functions of knowledge about society and evaluative comparisons of different forms of society. Although not preoccupied with the epistemological questions driving Habermas's theory of knowledge interests and communication action, he is similarly wary of the uncritical potential of purely hermeneutic perspectives: "The tasks of social science then seem precisely limited to ethnography—to the hermeneutic endeavor of the 'fusion of horizons.' Such a paralysis of the critical will is as logically unsatisfactory as the untutored use of the revelatory model" (Giddens 1984, p. 336). As he admits, this position "presumes a definite epistemological view without supporting it in detail" (Giddens 1984, p. 338). Above all, it involves the claim that explanatory knowledge can invalidate commonsense propositions in ways that transform propositional beliefs in a critical way:

It can be shown, I think, that there is a non-contingent relation between demonstrating a social belief to be false, and practical implications for the transformation of action linked to that belief. . . . Now social beliefs, unlike those to do with nature, are constitutive elements of what it is they are about. From this it follows that criticism of false belief (*ceteris paribus*) is a practical intervention in society, a political phenomenon in a broad sense of that term. (Giddens 1984, p. 340)

The primary difference from Habermas's formulation (based on the psychoanalytic analogy) is that Habermas seeks to focus on a particular type of transformative social knowledge—that is, forms related to beliefs related to power and authority (a critique of domination) that enable a subject to overcome "self-imposed" misunderstandings that inhibit "enlightenment." Giddens again generalizes this phenomenon, referring to the full range of potentially false beliefs that can be criticized by social science, the point of those who claim that "all knowledge is critical." But Habermas's point is that positivism deflects research away from the construction of knowledge about domination, hence "critical social science" in this narrower sense.

Conclusion

Let us conclude by reiterating briefly the claims that rather assertively accompany our reconstruction of the metatheory of critical theory in its strong and weak forms. First, we suggest that critical theory pushed *beyond pure interpretivism* in a convincing way that calls into question many of the relativist claims voiced in the name of poststructuralism and postmodernist social theory. In particular we have pointed to the limits of purely interpretive theory as evident in the problematic aspects of both the universalistic claims of ontological hermeneutics and the relativism of purely interpretive social analysis; both dispense with the explanatory moment—whether causal or structures of texts—of social research.

Second, critical theory points *beyond the reactive antinaturalism* with which critical theory is often erroneously associated. Within sociology it is customary—even on the part of some of the most sophisticated commentators—to construct the metatheoretical debates in social theory in terms of a polarization between naturalist and antinaturalist positions (Collins 1989). What is missing from most of such formulations is any sense of the way critical theory does not fit easily into such dichotomies despite its antipositivism. From this perspective,

> neither strong naturalism nor strong anti-naturalism provides a credible basis for understanding the social sciences. . . . *Neither naturalism nor antinaturalism wins the field, then, and the shortcoming of each is the same. Each framework makes overly demanding assumptions about the essential features of science either natural*

or social [italics added]. . . . Methodological pluralism views the
sciences more as a fabric of related enterprises than as a single unity
activity defined by the "scientific method." (Little 1991, p. 237)

But as we have stressed, beyond merely affirming pluralism,
moving beyond this polarization also implies a kind of interpretive structuralism that is most important for the explanatory
concerns specific to a critical theory of society.

Third, Habermas's critical theory in particular points *beyond
foundationalism* to a "nonfoundationalist universalism" (White
1988, pp. 129ff). Hence the third aspect of critical theory as a
postempiricist metatheory is to justify itself in terms that avoid
the extremes of antifoundationalist postmodernism. Habermas's
version of antifoundationalism is a weak version in the sense that
he believes that rational grounds for knowledge can be formulated,
a point evident in his insistence that the theory of communicative action is "not guilty" of foundationalist claims (Habermas
1987, p. 399). It is in this very unique sense he seeks to preserve
the modernist notion of "grand narratives" of history so despised
by disillusioned postmodernists. However, he does seek to preserve a kind of grounding for critical theory in the shifting sands
of language as synthesized through fundamental structures of
human interaction as analyzed in "universal pragmatics." Similarly Giddens follows the critical realists in advocating a postempiricist ontological framework for social theory.

Finally both link the project of interpretive structuralist
metatheory with a process of critique that can, in part, be illustrated by the psychoanalytic analogy, the master-slave dialectic
and generalized as something like a critical-emancipatory interest in knowledge.

We are now in a position to ask a question that has been avoided
until this point even though it often is raised as objection to critical
theory as a research program: The Popperian retort, is not all
science "critical" (Habermas 1976)? After all, was this not implicit
in reference to Ricoeur's account of the distanciating effects of
explanation and Giddens's general characterization of social
scientific knowledge? To assert that all knowledge is critical as
a way of deflecting the claims of critical social theory is a typically
Popperian view, one that, in part, short-circuits the problem.
Above all, in the social sciences this position either privileges

forms of social explanation associated with the natural scientific model or levels out all approaches as somehow equally "critical." What is distinctive about critical theory, however, is that the relation between social analysis and critique is built into the framework of the theory of knowledge interests, not something added on afterward. The positivist interpretation of the enlightening potentials of knowledge, in short, simply does not go far enough, hence cannot reflect on its own presuppositions as an important yet truncated form of criticism:

> Critical social science asks questions that naturalistic and interpretative inquiries in social science, left to themselves, omit to ask. As normally operating social science, naturalistic and interpretative inquiries generally involved a good deal of criticism and self-criticism. They disregard, however, the questions that critical social science presses. In that sense they are *subcritical* [italics added]–not critical enough. (Braybrooke 1987, p. 68)

In the next chapter we examine the research program–the theory of society–implied by this metatheoretical approach.

Notes

1. For a somewhat different perspective, see one of the few comparisons of Giddens and Habermas (Livesay 1985).
2. This distinction is logically (but not substantively) related to the distinction between the "strong" and "weak" programs in the sociology of knowledge (Bloor 1991; Woolgar 1988, pp. 41-5).
3. To be sure, a significant number of contemporary theorists remain more or less faithful to the earlier program of Critical Theory, often to the point of rejecting Habermas's revisionism and abandonment of the dialectic. Perhaps the most fruitful version of this latter strategy is the effort of the cultural theorist Fredric Jameson to resurrect the Hegelian Marxist theory of totality for a diagnosis of postmodernist culture (Jameson 1990, 1991; Kellner 1989c).
4. Today Habermas likely would concur with Giddens's criticism of this formulation: "Science is certainly as much about 'interpretation' as 'nomological explanation' . . . 'Explanation' in science is most appropriately characterized as the clarification of queries, rather than deduction from causal laws, which is only one sub-type of explanatory procedure" (Giddens 1977, p. 149).
5. According to Ricoeur's subsequent reformulation of critical hermeneutics, the logic underlying these two interpretive perspectives (traditional and

critical) are immanent in hermeneutics itself, in the "dialectic of the recollection of tradition and the anticipation of freedom" (Ricoeur 1981, p. 100); further, "the emancipation of the text constitutes the most fundamental condition for the recognition of a critical distance at the heart of interpretation; for distanciation now belongs to the mediation itself" (Ricoeur 1981, p. 91). In short, "to understand is not to project oneself into the text but to expose oneself to it; it is to receive a self enlarged by the appropriation of the proposed worlds which interpretation unfolds. . . . Distanciation from oneself demands the appropriation of the proposed worlds offered by the text passes through the disappropriation of the self. The critique of *false consciousness* can thus become an integral part of hermeneutics, conferring upon the critique of ideology that meta-hermeneutical dimension which Habermas assigns to it" (Ricoeur 1981, pp. 94-5).

6. This is not to say, however, that all forms of domination are equal. Critical theory is based on the assumption that an overall evolutionary gain has occurred with respect to reducing traditional forms of domination, even if this has involved introducing new, more subtle forms.

7. This analogy can be traced back to Hegel's famous analysis of the master-slave dialectic, a theme that now has been explored in comparative historical terms (Patterson 1982).

8. It should be stressed that the validity of this analogy does not depend on the adequacy of any particular explanatory thesis drawn from psychoanalytic theory. The key issue, rather, is methodological: To the extent that psychoanalysis (or any similar therapeutic strategy) is effective in its own terms, these are the processes that are transformative.

9. A very similar argument was developed virtually simultaneously by the French social philosopher Paul Ricoeur, initially through a critical hermeneutic reading of Freud (Ricoeur 1965). Freud's method was analyzed as a "hermeneutics of suspicion" that was contrasted to the "hermeneutics of restoration" associated with traditional hermeneutics. The element of suspicion relates to the question of asking whether the overt consciousness of a subject may be illusory, whether for the objective psychodynamic blocs identified by psychoanalysis or for those linked to social relations of domination.

10. In Habermas's denser formulation: "I am thinking of the rational constructions of the know-how of subjects, who are entrusted to provide valid expressions and who trust themselves to distinguish intuitively between valid and invalid expressions. This is the domain of such disciplines as logic and mathematics and the philosophy of language, of ethics and the theory of action, of aesthetics, of the theory of argumentation, etc." (Habermas 1983, p. 260).

11. To be sure, certain positions within the subjectivist or objectivist camps have attempted mediating formulations that would, in effect, synthesize analysis of agency and structure, but these have largely failed. Parsonian theory in its mature form remained clearly within the objectivistic framework of systems theory. And symbolic interactionism did not succeed in uniting microsociological concerns with a theory of society despite the early suggestive formulations of Gerth and Mills (1964) and the phenomenological account of the "social construction of reality" developed by Berger and Luckmann (1967). Nevertheless this did emerge as the central theme of social theory in the 1980s with the emergence of critical

theory as a major contender. Under the heading of the "agency-structure prob-lematic," however, critical theories have staked out a number of mediating positions.

12. The question of Habermas's relationship to Bhaskar's version of critical realism goes beyond the present discussion, but we would follow the suggestion that "the examination of the recent development of Habermas's thought suggests that it is no longer right to see his version of critical theory as in fundamental opposition to a realist naturalism of the type argued for in this book" (Outhwaite 1987, p. 91).

13. It is beyond the scope of this book to defend or assess Habermas's particular form of antifoundationalist epistemology; see, however, Baynes et al. (1987) and, on the methodological implications, Morrow (1991c).

14. None of this should be confused with the American forms of empiricist structuralism identified by Giddens as "structural sociology" or the later work of Peter Blau (Giddens 1984, pp. 207ff). Nor should the notion of interpretive structuralism be confused with some logical claim about a unique type of explanation. What is suggested, rather, is simply a family resemblance between a variety of logics-in-use combining historically conceptualized structural analy-sis with the critical interpretation of agents' symbolic activities as elaborated, for example, in the rich discussions by Sewell (1992), Crespi (1992), and, more generally, Bohman (1991).

15. "We can see the overall unity and utility of this complex activity of explana-tion, if we view it as the kind of description which is most fundamentally a basis for coping with reality, i.e., for promoting or preventing change. . . . *Without the requirement of depth, we could not expect explanation generally to direct us toward a crucial point at which to intervene in order to change reality* [italics added]. When depth as necessity is lacking, it will be a waste of time to try to prevent phenomena like the explanandum, in similar cases, by preventing the shallow cause. The sequel will simply arrive by another route" (R. Miller 1987, pp. 104-5).

7

CONTEMPORARY CRITICAL THEORY AS A RESEARCH PROGRAM

Giddens and Habermas

The circle of transmitters of this tradition is neither limited nor renewed by organic or sociological laws. It is constituted and maintained not by biological or testamentary inheritance, but by a knowledge which brings its own obligations with it. And even this knowledge guarantees only a contemporary, not a future community of transmitters. The theory may be stamped with every logical criterion, but to the end of the age it will lack the seal of approval which victory brings. (Horkheimer [1937] 1972a, p. 241)

Critical social theory does not relate to established lines of research as a competitor; starting from its concept of the rise of modern societies, it attempts to explain the specific limitations and the relative rights of those approaches. (Habermas 1987a, p. 375)

This chapter reconstructs the research programs of Habermas and Giddens as respectively "strong" and "weak" versions of critical theory. First, this reconstruction requires establishing the case for the loose identity of their research programs, as well as their complementarity—that is, Giddens's weak program, which generalizes historical materialism as part of its critique,

169

and Habermas's strong program, which remains somewhat closer to Marx and aspects of Weber through reconstructing historical materialism from the perspective of the problematic of rationality. Then we turn to a brief presentation of each program with broad questions of comparison in mind relating to the following key issues: normative and methodological foundations, basic concepts, theory of social change, and central explanatory theses with respect to advanced capitalism. Finally several rival but often complementary theoretical approaches are noted briefly.

Weak and Strong
Research Programs for Critical Theory

Identifying Research Programs

The status of contemporary critical theory as an identifiable scientific research program in Lakatos's sense of the term is most obvious in the case of Habermas, who explicitly uses this terminology in reconstructing Horkheimer's approach (White 1988, pp. 5-6). However, it has been argued that Giddens's structuration theory falls short in this respect. First, the concept of a *research program* is held to imply some kind of organized research center or community of research; second, and more fundamentally, structuration theory does not lend itself to cumulative development because "there can be no trans-historical regularities in these aspects of social life as well. In principle, then, all generalisations in the social sciences must be delimited with reference to historically and spatio-temporally circumscribed domains" (I. J. Cohen 1989, p. 281). Both of these qualifications appear too restrictive and would largely exclude Habermas as well. Both theoretical programs contain universalistic claims and historically specific empirical theses and lend themselves to the kind of empirical elaboration characteristic of interpretive social research.

A further difficulty with the characterization of critical theory as a research program revolves around the differences between Habermas and Giddens. To a remarkable degree such theorists see each other's work as more complementary than antagonistic; though rivalries may exist, they do not involve fundamental differences of the type involving competing research programs. Indicative of this are the collections in which sympathetic critics have commented on the work of Habermas and Giddens who, in turn, have at times responded to their critics. Further, Giddens has commented sympathetically on various aspects of Habermas's project, though it has been argued that "he seems to learn little from Habermas and none of his concepts are directly integrated into structuration theory" (Kilminster 1991, p. 92). More mutual influences are evident on the part of people strongly influenced by Giddens (Thompson and Held 1982). Although Habermas has not been directly influenced by Giddens either, this appears to be so for circumstantial reasons. Nevertheless the explicit dialogue between these two variants of critical theory has been much less than one would have expected, but can be extended by differentiating them as strong and weak research programs.

Habermas Versus Giddens

To deal with the problem of the differences between Giddens and Habermas, we find it useful to differentiate between a "weak" and a "strong" research program for critical theory, where weak implies a minimalist program and strong a maximal. Habermas's strong program retains a closer relation, for example, to the Marxist tradition by defining itself as a *reconstructed historical materialism* (Habermas 1979). As some have argued, such a reconstruction ultimately implies a rejection of historical materialism (Rockmore 1989). In any case the point of departure is a reconstruction that challenges such basic issues as the primacy of labor in Marx's theory and suggests that epochal transitions can best be accounted for in terms of changes in normative structures, rather than relations of production.[1]

But Giddens makes it explicit that he seeks to go further: Historical materialism and evolutionary theories "cannot be reconstructed, but have to be replaced with an approach of a different character" (Giddens 1991b, p. 206). Although Giddens takes greater pains to differentiate his position from the Marxist tradition, his concern with a "contemporary critique of historical materialism" is quite complementary with Habermas in other respects:

There has been an abundance of attempts . . . written either by impla-
cable opponents of Marx or by disillusioned ex-believers. I belong
in neither of these categories, though nor do I accept the label
"Marxist." Marx's analysis of the mechanisms of capitalist production, I believe, remains the necessary core of any attempt to come
to terms with the massive transformations that have swept through
the world since the eighteenth century. But there is much in Marx
that is mistaken, ambiguous or inconsistent; and in many respects
Marx's writings exemplify features of nineteenth-century thought
which are plainly defective when looked at from the perspective of
our century. (Giddens 1981, p. 2).

Of course there is an obvious difference between these reconstructive strategies: Giddens's militant antifunctionalism and
antievolutionism do conflict with Habermas's critical appropriation of Parsons and related attempts to rehabilitate evolutionary
themes from historical materialism. Although there are some
important tensions here, Habermas's uses of functionalist and
evolutionary concepts are different in important ways from the
immediate target of Giddens's attack. Moreover, these differences
express the range of opinion within critical theory and the basis
of ongoing, unresolved debate indicative of an open-ended and
fallibilistic research program.[2]

Further, Giddens has not been concerned with grounding the
normative basis of critical theory, a tendency that has led to
charges of evasiveness (Bernstein 1989). Partly it seems that
such issues hardly require justification, though intervening postmodernist debates may give rise to some doubts here: "If Marx's
project be regarded as the furthering, through the conjunction
of social analysis and political activity, of forms of human society
in which the mass of human beings can attain freedoms and
modes of self-realisation in excess of any they may have enjoyed
before, who can dissent from it" (Giddens 1981, p. 24).

In general terms Giddens's minimal program resembles the
"outer circle" of the Frankfurt School and its more open-ended
research program in the 1930s. Giddens's antievolutionism leads
him to be suspicious of the transformative projects left over
from revolutionary Marxism, and his stress on the skills of agents
leads him away from strong formulations of false consciousness
and the enlightening role of intellectual critique. If Giddens's

structuration theory is understood in these terms, then some of the complaints about its applicability to empirical research can be reassessed in terms of what he calls "the relative autonomy of theory and research": "Theoretical thinking needs in substantial part to proceed in its own terms and cannot be expected to be linked at every point to empirical considerations" (Giddens 1989a, p. 294).

The differences between the positions of Habermas and Giddens may be built into the historicist structure of critical theory as a form of theorizing whose categories require general interpretations of historical process as the point of departure for inquiry. The strong program represented by Habermas represents the wing with deeper philosophical origins linked to the preservation of the critique of reason associated with the Hegelian tradition. The weak program developed by Giddens eschews these more fundamental problems of epistemological and normative grounding in favor of a more flexible, discontinuous, and open-ended account of historical change. As suggested by the divisions within the early Frankfurt Institute, this kind of tension may be endemic in the logic of critical theory itself.

Models of Cultural Reproduction

As theories of society, the general approach of Habermas and Giddens can be characterized as open-end models of social and cultural reproduction, a notion that recently has been revived in social theory.[3] Unlike the earlier structuralist Marxist variants based on the thesis of the correspondence between economic structure and culture, open models are based on the agency-structure dialectic and reject strong functionalist claims about the primacy of the economic in the "last instance." Outcomes rather are viewed as historically specific, and state mediations of social conflicts as of decisive importance.

The following introductory reconstruction of the research programs of Giddens and Habermas can only be sketchy and is designed primarily to give a sense of the basic elements, along with a stress on the complementarity of weak and strong programs. An extended comparison of this type would justify a major study in its own right.

Giddens: A Critique of Historical Materialism

Critique and Normative Foundations

Giddens usefully distinguishes four types of *critique* that help clarify the specific characteristics of critical theory. First, is a minimal conception of critique—*intellectual critique*—that is inherent in any disciplined inquiry. This uncontroversial form is shared with social science as a whole. Second, is *practical critique* of the type associated with the technological application of knowledge understood in positivist terms. Practical critique assumes a very different form when associated (as in structuration theory) with the reflexivity required for understanding how social science affects lay accounts. "Such practical criticism is an inherent and inescapable element of engaging in social scientific investigation. This has nothing much to do with 'critical theory' as understood by the Frankfurt School" (Giddens 1989a, p. 289). The third level, involves *ideology critique.* Although researchers cannot control what use is made of their findings, they are in a position to carry analysis further in the "role of claims to knowledge as aspects of systems of power":

> Given that social science is reflexively involved in an intimate and pervasive way with what it is about, the critique of ideology necessarily also has to concern social science itself. A further answer to the question: "who will use this knowledge, and for what ends?" is therefore that we can investigate, actually or counterfactually, how the knowledge generated from a particular research study is incorporated within asymmetrical power relations. (Giddens 1989a, p. 290)

But this purely analytic problem is distinct from the fourth level of moral critique involving "assessing the rights and wrongs of contrasting policies or courses of action" (Giddens 1989a, p. 290).

Giddens offers a very general account of the basis of the moral critique that would follow from structuration theory. Nevertheless the basic notion of *utopian realism* links *emancipatory politics* with *life politics* (Giddens 1990a, p. 156). In using the notion of utopian realism, he invokes the name of Marx but not in the sense of riding with the flow (telos) of history or controlling it. A much more stringent balance is required, one captured by the notion of "attempts to steer the juggernaut" through the "minimizing of high-consequence risks" (Giddens 1990a, p. 154). Such a critical theory "without guarantees" would be "sociologically sensitive," "geopolitically tactical," able to "create *models of the good society* which are limited neither to the sphere of the nation-state nor to only one of the institutional domains of modernity; and it must recognise that *emancipatory politics* needs to be linked with *life politics,* or a *politics of self-actualisation"* (Giddens 1990a, p. 156).

Giddens's approach thus also implies a weak program that follows from the contention that critical theory cannot be reduced to the unity of theory and practice: "In being stripped of historical guarantees, critical theory enters the universe of contingency and has to adopt a logic that no longer insists upon the necessary unity of theory and practice" (Giddens 1987a, p. 337).

Methodological Foundations

Giddens tends to reject the assumption that he is proposing a distinctive "method" or even methodological approach:

> Structuration theory is not intended as a method of research, or even as a methodological approach. The concepts I have developed do not allow one to say: "henceforth, the only viable type of research in the social sciences is qualitative field study." I have an eclectic approach to method, which again rests upon the premise that research inquiries are contextually oriented. (Giddens 1989a, p. 296)

Such a disclaimer should be read with caution, however. As we have argued with respect to defining structuration as a weak program for critical theory, he certainly does set out flexible guidelines for a methodological strategy and an agenda of research problems and hypotheses. What this seems to imply, however, is that although not all critical research needs to follow these guidelines directly, they do need to define themselves in relation to the more general program of critical theory. Structuration theory aims to facilitate this process of unification within diversity.

Although rejecting the notion that structuration theory should be directly "applied" to empirical research, Giddens suggests, for example, that it implies three basic principles of research:

contextual sensitivity, the complexity of human intentionality, and the *subtlety of social constraint* (Giddens 1990b). Further, it suggests attention to four key aspects of social life: the reproduction of practices, the dialectic of control, the discursive penetration of agents, and the double hermeneutic. Finally these orienting principles can be translated into four levels of meta-theoretical problems that have been obscured in the past by the polarization between "quantitative" and "qualitative" methods.

Although setting aside any discussion of the relevance that structuration theory may or may not have for evaluating specific types of research methods, Giddens does provide a generic account of the tasks of social research informed by it. This account is based on a continuum of four levels of investigation: (a) *hermeneutic elucidation of frames of meaning,* (b) *investigation of the content and form of practical consciousness (the unconscious),* (c) *identification of bounds of knowledgeability,* and (d) *specification of institutional orders* (Giddens 1984, p. 327). Hermeneutic inquiry not only is presupposed by quantitative research, but it also can be explanatory and generalizing when translated into comparisons. Research on practical consciousness differs in that, unlike hermeneutic research, which is not directly accessible to the subjects of such research, it "means investigating what agents already know, but by definition . . . is normally illuminating to them if this is expressed discursively, in the metalanguage of social science" (Giddens 1984, p. 328). The third level—involving the investigation of the bounds of knowledgeability of agents—requires considerable knowledge of the other three levels. In other words, it is necessary to know the "knowledge" possessed by agents drawn from the first two, and at the same time contrast it to the objective conditions of institutional orders (social and systemic integration) as understood by social science (Giddens 1984, pp. 328-9).

Basic Concepts of Structuration Theory

In outlining Giddens's theory of society, the focus of attention is his basic concepts, rather than reference to where they may have been borrowed or adapted or how they might compare with other approaches.[4] This strategy not only suggests itself because of relative simplicity (because Giddens refers to an incredible range of influences) but also avoids giving the false impression that these obviously extensive borrowings have resulted in an eclectic theoretical framework. Nor would it be accurate to credit Giddens with some kind of complete originality, given that his approach as a whole could be characterized as a kind of generalized reading of Marx and Weber; the crucial point is that the resulting synthesis breaks with both authors on crucial points and cannot be reduced to either one.

Giddens has attempted to identify the implications of a structurationist program of research as follows:

> First, it would concentrate upon the orderings of institutions across time and space, rather than taking as its object the study of human societies ... where we speak of "a" society, we have to be fully aware that this is not a "pure social form," but a politically and territorially constituted system. It is one mode of "bracketing" time and space among others, that bracketing process itself being the primary object of study in social science.
>
> Second, a structurationist programme would analyze social systems in terms of shifting modes of institutional articulation. . . . Every social system . . . gains its systemic qualities only through regularities of social reproduction. . . .
>
> Third, such a programme would be continuously sensitive to the reflexive intrusion of knowledge into the conditions of social reproduction. . . .
>
> Fourth, a structurationist programme would be oriented to the impact of its own research upon the social practices and forms of social organization it analyses. . . .
>
> To my mind, however, the empirical implications of structuration theory have to be pursued primarily through the introduction of considerations—concerned with particular types of social system and their transformation—which are not a part of the theory itself. (Giddens 1989a, pp. 300-1).

Although his schema makes the concepts of power and domination central, it avoids replacing Marx's reductionist concept of modes of production with a reduction social life to power relations in the manner currently associated with Foucault (and inherited from the philosopher Friedrich Nietzsche). The generation of power in the course of the reproduction of domination (understood as a universal property of social organization) takes two primary forms: *allocative resources,* involving domination over material resources, and *authoritative resources,* linked to control over the social world. The relative primacy of these varies in different types of societies. With Marx, Giddens would agree that allocative resources are primary in capitalism but would differ in suggesting the primacy of authoritative resources in noncapitalist societies.

Social systems are linked to systems of domination by virtue of their manner of dealing with time-space distanciation. In other words, although social systems exist in time, they also are stretched out in distinctive ways over both "space" and "time": "Time-space distanciation refers to the modes in which such 'stretching' takes place or, to shift the metaphor slightly, how social systems are 'embedded' in time and space" (Giddens 1981, pp. 4-5). For example, in small hunting and gathering societies, time-space distanciation is organized around legitimation in tradition and the social relations of kinship. Hence few social transactions involve others who are physically absent. In contrast, the modern state is characterized by precisely its capacity to organize power over long distances through the "storage" of authoritative resources that facilitate "surveillance" activities that involve the collecting of information and its use for social control.

The macro-micro distinction is rejected for two reasons: On the one hand, it pits one against the other as if one had to choose, and further, macrosociological analysts tend to regard microsociological work as trivial; on the other hand, it contributes to a division of labor in which microsociologists are concerned with "free agents" and macrosociology with "structural constraints" (Giddens 1984, p. 139). Instead "activity in microcontexts has strongly defined structural properties . . . one of the main claims which ethnomethodological research has successfully sustained" (Giddens 1984, p. 141). Most fundamentally the problem is that micro events are viewed exclusively in terms of interaction in a limited (largely face-to-face) context in space and time; but "the forming and reforming of encounters necessarily occurs across tracts of space broader than those involved in immediate contexts of face-to-face interaction" (Giddens 1984, p. 142). The importance of this difference becomes apparent when we contrast traditional societies based exclusively on interactive co-presence, as opposed to societies where electronic media create contexts of co-presence as physically far-flung.

To deal with these problems, Giddens drawn on a version of the distinction between *social integration* and *system integration,* where the former involves "interaction in contexts of co-presence" involving reciprocity, whether immediate or mediated over space and time (Giddens 1984, pp. 142-3). In contrast, system integration takes place behind the backs of actors, hence outside of co-presence, and yet also involves the reciprocal relations involving dependence and independence between actors and collectivities across time and space. Such integration does not presuppose the absence of conduct; rather it refers to continuity of social relations and the absence of their breakdown. With this framework the classical question of viewing of society is not abandoned, so much as reconstructed:

> The reproduction/transformation of globalizing systems is implicated in a whole variety of day-to-day decisions and acts. . . . The proper locus for the study of social reproduction is in the immediate process of constituting interaction, for all social life is an active accomplishment; and every moment of social life bears the imprint of totality. *"The totality," however, is not an inclusive, bounded "society," but a composite of diverse totalizing orders and impulsions* [italics added]. (Giddens 1993, p. 8)

The concept of *contradiction* is central to this analysis of the structural aspects of social systems and is defined as "an *opposition or disjunction of structural principles* . . . where those principles operate *in terms of each other* but at the same time *contravene* one another" (Giddens 1979, p. 141). Further, contradictions can be resolved in many ways, a "progressive" direction being only one possibility. In contrast, conflict operates in the context of the social integration of antagonist relations between struggling groups. Hence on this analysis the primary contradiction of capitalism involves abstract structural principles—the private appropriation of capital and the socialized character of production, whereas in the context of social integration "the relation between capital and wage-labour, as a class relations between capitalists and workers, is one of inherent conflict, in the sense of opposition of interest" (Giddens 1979, p. 138).

**Theory of Social Change:
Antifunctionalism and Antievolutionism**

The basis of Giddens's conception of society is an open model of social reproduction consistent with his antifunctionalist stance. Hence the concept of *social reproduction* "is not in and of itself an explanatory one: all reproduction is contingent and historical" (Giddens 1981, p. 27). In crucial respects, therefore, it differs from both Marxist theories of social reproduction (whether the older Frankfurt School version or more recent structuralist ones) and the structural functionalist model of a self-regulating system in dynamic equilibrium. Viewing the relation between agents, structures, and system as "situated practices" follows from the notion of the "duality of structure" understood in interpretive structuralist terms:

> A crucial move in this theory is an attempt to transcend the opposition between "action" theories and "institutional" theories . . . This move is accomplished by the concept of what I call the duality of structure. By the duality of structure I mean that the structured properties of social systems are simultaneously the medium and the outcome of social acts. . . . The concept of the duality of structure, I believe, is basic to any account of social reproduction, and has no functionalist overtones to it at all. (Giddens 1981, p. 19)

Evolutionary theories also are rejected and defined as follows: "an irreversible series of stages . . . some conceptual linkage with biological theories of evolution; and the specification of directionality through the stages indicated, in respect of a given criterion or criteria, such as increasing complexity or expansion of the forces of production" (Giddens 1984, p. xxix). Instead Giddens would restrict the analysis of social change to concrete *"episodic" transitions*—that is, as "a number of acts or events having a specifiable beginning and end, thus involving a particular sequence" (1984, p. 244). Large-scale episodes would involve processes such as the emergence of agrarian states or the modern nation-state. But he rejects linking such episodes together as part of an overall theory of history.

Central Explanatory Theses

The basic argument of Giddens's substantive, historical sociology is elaborated in three volumes: the first, *The Class Structure of the Advanced Societies* (Giddens 1973), was written prior to the elaboration of structuration theory, though its general argument (if not the terminology) is consistent with it. At that earlier point, he was concerned particularly with developing a theory of class conflict that would overcome the grave limitations of the bipolar labor-capital model of classical Marxism. The resulting conception differentiated three bases of class structuration: capital, labor power, and the ownership of educational credentials. Because this model was influenced strongly by Weber, Giddens initially was classified (however problematically) as "neo-Weberian."

A Contemporary Critique of Historical Materialism (Giddens 1981) develops the central analytical principles underlying the analysis of modern societies by using a critique of historical materialism (and to a certain extent functionalism) as the focus of argument; this theme is continued in *The Nation-State and Violence* (Giddens 1987) with a more specific focus on the rise of the modern nation-state and the global system of states. More recent volumes detail some of the implications of this argument with respect to the theme of modernity and social psychological transformations of the self, identity, and sexuality in "high" modernity (Giddens 1990a, 1991a, 1992).

The central theme of Giddens's historical sociology is the episode involving the emergence of "modern" societies and *modernity*, hence the rise of the nation-state and the world system. In expanding on Marx's emphasis on material production (allocative resources) or Weber's emphasis on bureaucratization (a form of authoritative resource), Giddens analyzes the rise of the modern nation-state in terms of four "institutional clusterings: heightened surveillance, capitalist enterprise, industrial production and the consolidation of centralized violence. None is wholly reducible to any of the others. A concern with the consequences of each moves critical theory away from its concentration upon the transcendence of capitalism by socialism as the sole objective of future social transformations" (Giddens 1987a, p. 5).

At the same time the role of the nation-state in relativized in relation to *globalization* in the form of the world system or "intersocietal systems." Indeed emphasis is placed on "the generic shortcomings of trading *any* type of society as an isolated entity" (Giddens 1981, p. 24). As a consequence he credits Wallerstein's *world system theory* for having provided an important critique of "endogenous conceptions of social change" despite reservations on a number of key points (Giddens 1987a, pp. 166ff).

Giddens's point of departure in the analysis of contemporary societies is a conception of modernity that stresses its complete discontinuity from those that proceeded; and yet he also rejects the postmodernist emphasis on the assumption of some kind of fundamental rupture within modernity. Instead he speaks of "high modernity" as a linear continuation of one of the most distinctive features of modernity, "an increasing interconnection between the two 'extremes' of extensionality and intentionality: globalising influences on the one hand and personal dispositions on the other" (Giddens 1991a, p. 2). This focus on the self and self-identity is suggestive of themes that others prefer to label as "postmodern":

> Modernity is a post-traditional order, but not one in which the sureties of tradition and habit have been replaced by the certitude of rational knowledge. Doubt, a pervasive feature of modern critical reason, permeates into everyday life as well as philosophical consciousness, and forms a general existential dimension of the contemporary social world. Modernity institutionalizes the principle of radical doubt and insists that all knowledge takes the form of hypotheses. . . . In the settings of what I call "high" or "late" modernity—our present-day world—the self . . . has to be reflexively made. Yet this task has to be accomplished amid a puzzling diversity of options and possibilities. (Giddens 1991a, pp. 2-3)

Consistent with the characterization of his research program as a weak version of critical theory, Giddens does not specifically elaborate on his analysis of contemporary societies as a crisis theory oriented to a practical strategy of transformative change, an absence closely associated with a limited concern with normative foundations. Yet his overall approach does offer insights that certainly would be of central importance for such an effort.

Habermas:
A Reconstruction of Historical Materialism

Critique and Normative Foundations

The most striking point of contrast between Habermas and Giddens is the status of normative foundations for social theory. Although normative questions are integral to Giddens's overall conception of social theory, they are not a central focus of his research program. This difference is closely related to the difference between strong and weak programs and is linked to the effects of Habermas stressing normative grounding as opposed to the openness of praxis in Giddens (Livesay 1985). We previously have discussed this aspect of Habermas in relation to his proposal for a communicative ethics and theory of distorted communication. This dialectic of relative openness and closure thus describes the inherent tensions of critical theory and has further permutations throughout the respective research programs.

Methodological Foundations

The primary methodological difference between Giddens and Habermas is that the latter has, from the outset, attempted to rescue the basis for a credible historical evolutionism conceived as a general interpretation guided by a practical interest in emancipation. This theory of history, however, explicitly rejects viewing such processes in empiricist or nomothetic terms (Habermas 1988, pp. 188-9; 1987a). In other words the primary objective of such a historically oriented structuralist functionalism is not explanatory in the strong (nomothetic) sense, so much as a heuristic for introducing evolutionary models that provide some indirect empirical justification for universalistic normative principles and developmental (directional) sequences of cultural forms. In short, Habermas's conception of critical social science takes the form of what we have called a *historically contingent interpretive structuralism*.

The basic assumptions of this position have been discussed previously in the context of how his version of critical theory attempts to overcome the subjectivist-objectivist polarization via a critique of positivism, functionalism, and hermeneutics (a theme underlying *On the Logic of the Social Sciences* [1988]). As well, Habermas's approach is coupled with a rejection of the theory of totality based on a historical materialist theory of history as assumed by early Frankfurt School theory.

In his later work, a critical engagement with French structuralism is evident in his appropriation of Piaget's and Kohlberg's developmental psychology, as well as the logic of historical materialism itself (Habermas 1979, pp. 130-177). But on the one hand, his approach to the methods of rational reconstruction is cautious and differentiated in that it is acknowledged that the ease of isolating deep structures is quite variable. For this reason structuralism is most well developed in linguistics, aspects of anthropology (kinship, myth), and developmental psychology. On the other hand, he does not preclude that "on the level of the social system we can . . . specify distinctive elementary deep structures for productive forces and for forms of social integration" (Habermas 1979, p. 168). But as he acknowledges, structuralism naturally is confronted with "the limits of all synchronic investigations" because it "limits itself to the logic of existing structures and does not extend to the pattern of structure-forming processes" (Habermas 1979, p. 169) though Piaget's genetic structuralism is a suggestive exception here.

Basic Concepts

The theory of communicative action is foundational for Habermas's overall conception in a manner similar to Giddens's conception of structuration as praxis. In both cases the traditional subject-object polarization (based on what Habermas calls the *philosophy of consciousness* dominant throughout Western philosophy) is rejected, following the linguistic turn, in favor of the primacy of an interactional subject-subject model.

But Habermas adds a distinction between two forms of rationalization: instrumental rationalization characteristic of purposive-rational systems (also called *strategic rationality*) and the *communicative rationality* within normative systems. This distinction can be traced back to Marx's implicit distinction between "work" and "symbolic interaction," though Habermas accuses Marx of having reduced the symbolic to the instrumental logic of labor.[5]

Given the assumption of the primacy of communicative rationality, it becomes possible to deflect the arguments of those such as Weber and Foucault, who point to the primacy of conflictual relations at the heart of social life. Further, it provides the framework for an evaluation of the processes whereby strategic rationality may deform and distort communication in the interest of various forms of control and domination. In this respect, the distinction serves both empirical and normative purposes.

Like Giddens, Habermas's model of society is based on the distinction between *system integration* and *social integration*.[6] But it is used somewhat differently, given Habermas's particular interest in a specific thesis relating systems of technical rationality (or the *systemic* level of systems integration) to everyday life, or what he calls (in phenomenological terms) the *lifeworld*. He holds that the characteristic feature of modernity is the selective appropriation of technical rationality mediated by the systemic constraints imposed by structure of power (bureaucratization) and money (commodification), which have the effect of *colonizing the lifeworld*, thus eliciting various social pathologies, as well as forms of resistance. This discrepancy between systemic intrusion and lifeworld experience stems from the way instrumental rationalization introduces forms of distorted communication that cannot adequately comprehend the needs expressed in the lifeworld of everyday life.

Theory of Social Change:
Reconstructing Historical Materialism

Habermas's theory of society is based on a critique of historical materialism. A key element of this process is the rejection of the classic notion of "mode of production" as insufficiently general for the purposes of a theory of social change. Instead he proposes the concept of an *organizational principle* that includes four possible (universal) combinations of social integration: kinship, lineage, political office, and formal law (Habermas 1979, pp. 150-4).

What these modifications make possible is a clear distinction between two qualitatively different kinds of learning/rationalization processes. The first is more familiar and involves the kind of rationalization associated with the development of science and technology. The second form of collective learning is less visible because it is implicated in the systems of communicative action and the normative structures that are elaborated to organized social life. Whereas "modernization" theories have tended to focus on the technical aspect, critical theory has been concerned primarily with the social and value aspects of rationality.

The extensive discussions of evolutionary theory in Habermas's work have several related functions: (a) as part of an ongoing debate with the Marxist tradition (critique of historical materialism just noted), (b) as a means of grounding critical theory in a developmental model of normative structures, and (c) as part of constructing a model of crisis adequate to the peculiarities of advanced capitalism. The second theme is based on the concept of reconstructive sciences discussed previously. For Habermas, such knowledge of depth-structures of human competence makes possible bridging the logical gap between *is* and *ought,* or human potential and actually realized form of individuals in concrete societies. Of more immediate concern, however, is the third theme relating to contemporary crisis theory—the central focus of the first phase of Habermas's explanatory arguments.

Central Explanatory Theses: A Research Agenda

Habermas is not specifically concerned about methods as techniques; his focus on methodology is attuned, rather, to the requirements of a strong program in critical theory—that is, one that responds directly to the challenge identified in the early Frankfurt School to construct a research program oriented toward the identification of change potentials. The explanatory identity of Habermas's approach in this context is that of a *"crisis" theory* of advanced capitalism that seeks to reformulate the problematic of "theory and praxis" of the Frankfurt tradition in the context of a new era (Habermas 1973). To be sure, he was quite aware of the various and practical obstacles to this goal (Habermas 1992a, 1992b), but these very real empirical constraints do not necessarily call into question the importance of theorizing the conditions of possibility of such transitions.

The initial formulation of this research problematic was carried out in the early 1970s and strongly influenced by the parallel work of Claus Offe in (then) West Germany (Offe 1984,

1985; Habermas 1975). The resulting Habermas-Offe thesis of *legitimation crisis* was based on attempting to identify the specific, emergent forms of social contradictions in the welfare state. The key theme was that crisis tendencies had been displaced from the blind operation of economic contradictions (as in liberal capitalism) to the steering responsibilities of the modern democratic state. The political economic basis of contradiction was the *fiscal crisis of the state* generated by the increasing shortfall between government revenues and demands for services necessary for democratic legitimation. What was distinctive about this interpretation was the suggestion that two new forms of crisis tendencies had become central in advanced capitalism: the *rationalization crisis* evident in overburdened administrative systems, a *legitimation crisis* for the democratic state in relation to citizens, and a *latent motivational crisis* linked to the difficulty of family and schools to socialize individuals consistent with system imperatives. Although a legitimation crisis in this sense did not emerge in quite the way hypothetically proposed as a possibility (this was not a predictive model), this thematic has formed one of the central questions of contemporary critical theories of the state (Pierson 1991).

In his more recent work, Habermas has revised this analysis of the contemporary role of the state and economy (the thesis of the colonization of the lifeworld) and explicitly connected the contemporary agenda of his version of critical theory with that of the original interdisciplinary program set out by Horkheimer in the early 1930s. The fundamental difference is that Habermas has attempted to "free historical materialism from its philosophical ballast" (Habermas 1987, p. 383) especially the teleological philosophy of history of Hegelian Marxism. That allows Habermas to take up many of the older questions in the light of intervening historical transformations. Four basic areas of inquiry are identified: (a) "the forms of integration in postliberal societies," (b) "family socialization and ego development," (c) "mass media and mass culture," and (d) "potentials for protest" (Habermas 1987a, pp. 383-97). Let us briefly discuss each of these areas as topics for explanatory and interpretive inquiry.[7]

First, the question of integration in postliberal societies involves questions about the relationship between the state and capitalist economies in advanced capitalism, a theme associated

most often with the notion of "legitimation" crisis in "disorganized" capitalism. In the more recent formulation Habermas is
concerned particularly with the selective modernization involved in the developmental path of organized (state) capitalism.
Here crisis takes the form of "systemic disequilibria" that produce "steering crises" for the state so that economic and political
performances fall below public expectations. Further, these
disturbances "call forth pathologies in the lifeworld" stemming
from the colonization of the lifeworld by the instrumental rationalization induced by systemic processes organized around money
and bureaucratic power (Habermas 1987a, p. 385).

Second, the thesis of the uncoupling of system and lifeworld
provides a new perspective on structural changes in the family,
education, and personality development. As opposed to the
authoritarian family structures associated with liberal capitalism
characterized by the coupling of system and lifeworld, organized
capitalism suggests increasingly autonomous nuclear families,
along with socialization processes (e.g., the mass media) not
directly tied to system imperatives. The consequence is a growing
discrepancy between the attitudes, competences, and motives
of youth, compared to the adult roles demanded by systemic
imperatives. This shift is manifest in the decline of Oedipal
problems of the type associated with liberal capitalism and the
increasing centrality of adolescent crises, a process fully apparent from the 1960s onward. In these circumstances the nature
of distorted communication and the reification of interpersonal
relations changes.

The outcome is that the *theory of communicative action*
suggests the need for completely revising the older Freudo-Marxist
structural model based on ego, id, and superego: "Instead of an
instinct theory . . . we have a theory of socialization that connects Freud and Mead, gives structures of intersubjectivity their
due, and replaces hypotheses about instinctual vicissitudes with
assumptions about identity formation. . . . The cognitive and
sociomoral development studied in the Piagetian tradition takes
place in accord with structural patterns that provide a reliable
foil for intuitively recorded clinical deviations" (Habermas 1987a,
p. 389).

Third, the implications of the mass media change with the
distinction between system and lifeworld because "the theory

of communicative action brings out the independent logic of socializatory interaction; the corresponding distinction between two contrary types of communication media makes us sensitive to the ambivalent potential of mass communications" (Habermas 1987a, p. 389). From this perspective the assumption of Horkheimer and Adorno that the mass media completely dominate everyday life becomes problematic, given the ability of subjects to resist those processes. Further, the mass media belong to generalized systems of communication that have a double, contradictory function: "These media publics hierachize and at the same time remove restrictions on the horizon of possible communication. The one aspect cannot be separated from the other—and therein lies their ambivalent potential" (Habermas 1987a, p. 390). Communications reception research and program analysis have revealed some of these oppositional possibilities.

Fourth, Habermas suggests that the possibility of protest potentials follow from the way in which "system imperatives *clash with* independent communication structures. . . . The analysis of lifeworld pathologies calls for an (unbiased) investigation of tendencies *and* contradictions" (Habermas 1987a, p. 391). According to the thesis of the colonization of the lifeworld, the locus of potentials for protest shifts away from class-based issues, distributional issues centering on material reproduction and increasingly assume an extraparliamentary form.

The new conflict zones involve

> cultural reproduction, social integration, and socialization . . . and the underlying deficits reflect a reification of communicatively structured domains of action that will not respond to the media of power and money. The issue is not primarily one of compensations that the welfare state can provide, but of defending and restoring endangered ways of life. In short, the new conflicts are not ignited by distribution problems but by questions having to do with the grammar of forms of life. (Habermas 1987a, p. 392)

These potentials are difficult to estimate and difficult to classify because they change rapidly and vary cross-nationally but are associated with phenomena such as the antinuclear and environmental movements and local, single-issue movements; alternative, countercultural movements; various minorities (sexual, ethnic, racial, regional); psychological self-help movements; religious fundamentalism and cults; and the women's movement. In this context of such a spectrum of protests, Habermas seeks to "differentiate emancipatory potentials from potentials for resistance and withdrawal" (Habermas 1987a, p. 393). This shift in value orientations is thus broadly compatible with what Giddens refers to as from "emancipatory politics" to "life politics." Habermas differs here because his approach begins with the rationality problematic and the two questions it poses: How could a *reason* split up between its three moments of science, law and morality, and aesthetics come to communicate with one another? and the related question, How can expert cultures be mediated with everyday practice? (Habermas 1987a, p. 398).[8]

Complementary Critical Research Traditions

Rival Theoretical Approaches

In differentiating a weak and strong research program for critical theory, we must acknowledge other variants as well, even if they are mentioned only in passing. This acknowledgment assumes, of course, that such rival research programs are essentially complementary in the dialogical sense that they mutually influence one another and share sufficient core assumptions (even if only implicitly) to participate in a common frame of theoretical discourse. To a significant degree, however, the national inflections of theoretical traditions in social theory often obscure these similarities, and competition tends to exaggerate differences. Beyond Giddens and Habermas we must acknowledge other variants of social theory that some might consider under the heading of "critical theory," even if they are mentioned only in passing. From this perspective critical theory as a research program as defined above can be seen as engaged in a fruitful, ongoing dialogue with several other rival, but not necessarily opposed, theoretical tendencies: *British neo-Gramscian cultural studies,* including its post-Marxist variants; *socialist feminism;* and *French critical sociology* and *postmodernist critical theory.* Because we do not return to these approaches in a sustained way in the remaining chapters on methodological issues, some brief comments are necessary here.

In Britain a long-standing split between those identifying with critical theory (whether of the old or new Frankfurt variety, or that of Giddens or some combination) and neo-Gramscian cultural Marxism has tended to obscure the many convergencies that have now become apparent (Hall 1992; Harris 1992), with the advent of post-Marxist tendencies on the Left (Laclau and Mouffe 1985; Morrow 1991a). This form of British cultural studies was inhibited by a break with the "bourgeois" disciplines, especially sociology, and a superficial and limited appropriation of critical theory. Exemplifying this problem is the fact that the basic program seems to "have proceeded without a single direct reference to the major works of Anthony Giddens. With omissions like this, it is easy to give the impression that sociology is naively atheoretical, ignorant of continental theory, still content with little empirical studies, and that Gramscianism is the only sophisticated theory in town" (Harris 1992, p. 15).

Variants of what usually is called "socialist feminism" converge strikingly with the research program of contemporary critical theory. Sometimes these connections are explicit (Benhabib and Cornell 1987; Nielsen 1990), but generally not. Consider the following definition, which is generally quite consistent with the research program outlined in this chapter, even if specific problems in Habermas's approach (based on gender blindness) have been identified (Fraser 1989):

> Feminist sociological theory's model of societal organization is currently anchored in these five ideas: (1) that gender, like class, is a pervasive system of stratification; (2) that stratification in any society arises from the organization of social production; (3) that social production has to be broadly construed as a multifaceted, hierarchically organized process that reproduces and maintains social life; (4) that analyzing this process effectively requires suspension of the convention of categorizing phenomena as micro- or macrosocial, and the creation of a vocabulary to describe the fluidity of the relation between interactional and structural arrangements; and (5) that ideology masks the reality of social production while reproducing stratification in the intricacies of personality and social interaction. (Lengermann and Niebrugge-Brantley 1990, p. 324)

The affinities between contemporary critical theory and the forms of sociology represented by Touraine and Bourdieu often have been noted (especially in Quebec) and perhaps require little further justification here (Morrow 1982a, 1982b, 1986). Occasionally international collections bring out surprising commonalties otherwise masked by the labels and internal debates within specific national traditions (Birnbaum 1977).

The question of *postmodernist* critical theory is considerably more complex. But the more recent work of Mark Poster represents the most elaborate effort to appropriate postmodernist themes without abandoning a basic commitment to the project of critical theory (Poster 1984, 1989, 1990). As he argues, the advent of electronic mediation requires supplementing critical theory with a less rationalistic and more visually based theory of communication and power. Foucault is the primary point of reference for this project, though Poster draws on Baudrillard, Derrida, and Lyotard as well.

Michel Foucault has been the key center of controversy because, of all of the "poststructuralist" theories, his is the closest to critical theory, a point he acknowledged late in his career. Two aspects of Foucault's approach appear most problematic from the perspective of critical social theory: first, his tendency to reject altogether the concept of ideology and aspirations to analyze the historical genesis of social structures and culture; and second, the latent critical intentions and effects of his approach are not coupled with any explicit normative rationale. The first tendency can be traced, in part, to his opposition to orthodox and structuralist Marxism's economic reductionism. But it also reflected his strong antipositivist belief in the primacy of the study of discourses for understanding social reality. The second tendency corresponded to his deep distrust of moralization and the homogeneity imposed by value systems in the name of "reason" or "enlightenment." This point is reinforced by his conception of all social relations as inevitably involving a struggle for power, and the impossibility of knowledge that is not contaminated by those power relations.

The impact of Foucault on debates in critical theory thus has been twofold. First, he has been drawn on extensively for his contributions to a structuralist methodology for studying the history of scientific disciplines. Second, he has posed fundamental questions about the nature of power, especially the assumption of classical social theory that it was to be understood as flowing from an identifiable center, and that power was something inherently objectionable. For Foucault, power was viewed as a diffuse phenomenon located everywhere, especially as inscribed in the very bodies of subjects. As a consequence a revolutionary seizure of power at the center would do little to overcome internalized domination. Further, power had to be understood as an essential aspect of realizing all human possibilities, not something simply to be abolished in the name of freedom. Indeed power was implicit in the very idea of knowledge and the desire to exert a will to power through knowledge.

Complementary Political Practices

The interplay between research and diverse political practices is also suggestive of another way of envisioning the underlying unifying principles of critical theory. As Stephen Leonard suggests, if we look at "critical theory in practice," we see examples such as "dependency theory, Paulo Freire's pedagogy of the oppressed, liberation theology, and (some forms of) feminist theory" that "are self-consciously tied to particular historical circumstances and practical contexts. Moreover, all share a commitment to the idea of empowerment and emancipation one finds in the received view of critical theory, but each in its own way provides resources that can be used for rethinking the relation between theory and practice generally, and critical theory and political practice specifically" (Leonard 1990, p. xviii). From the perspective of our concerns here, however, we would stress that awareness of the political practices of critical theory are also an important resource for rethinking the relationship between theory and research.

Conclusion

The task of this chapter has been to outline the research programs of Habermas and Giddens as respectively strong and weak variants of an analysis of social and cultural reproduction.

Habermas's approach retains a stronger relationship to historical materialism, is particularly concerned with normative foundations, and is directed more closely to an analysis of the crisis of advanced capitalism. In contrast, Giddens's weaker research program is more preoccupied with the foundations of a theory of structuration and general issues in a sociological theory of change.

At this stage we need to turn, in Part III, to the more specific methodological implications of the type of research program implicated in the work of Giddens, Habermas, and others. The first step is to deconstruct the reigning qualitative/quantitative distinction (Chapter 8). After that we consider the constructive alternatives, especially the non-empirical (Chapter 9) and empirical (Chapter 10) methodological strategies required for the kind of interpretive structuralist intensive analyses privileged by critical research. On that basis we then can review some examples of research stressing the systemic, actional, and mediational properties of social relations (Chapter 11) and the implications of such research for society (Chapter 12).

Notes

1. Brian Fay provides a useful summary of the basic scheme of a strong program for a critical social science, at least from the perspective of a focus on its task as a theory of praxis (Fay 1987, pp. 31-2). This general model applies rather well to the early form of Critical Theory advocated by Horkheimer and remains pertinent to Habermas's overall schema, but the latter's abandonment of the classical revolutionary model of transition puts greater emphasis on its educative functions as a research program.

2. This is, in essence, the conclusion of an insightful evaluation of Giddens's critique of functionalism: "However, both neo-Parsonianism and the theories of Habermas and Giddens show that the critique of functionalism does not compel us into some form of methodological individualism or its restrictive action theory. The common task, then, is to develop a social theory which is grounded in action theory; does not confuse functional analysis with causal explanation; and contains the benefits of a controlled use of systems models" (Joas 1990, p. 101).

3. " 'Cultural reproduction,' though currently not a fashionable concept, is a particularly fertile area for social theory. . . . The idea of cultural reproduction makes reference to the emergent quality of everyday life—albeit through a spectrum of interpretations. That is to say that the concept serves to articulate the dynamic process that makes sensible the utter contingency of, on the one hand, the stasis

and determinacy of social structures and, on the other, the innovation and agency inherent in the practice of social action" (Jenks 1993, p. 1).

4. See Craib 1992, pp. 13-32, for a helpful introduction to the various authors and traditions that make up Giddens's "theoretical omelette."

5. Many, including Giddens (1977, p. 152), have challenged this as an adequate portrayal of Marx himself, whose concept of praxis is not clearly reductionist, though Habermas's clearly applies to orthodox Marxism. What is more important is that both Giddens and Habermas drastically transform historical materialism as it has been known.

6. Their uses of these terms are somewhat different, the effect of which appears to be that Habermas would be more willing to theorize systemic contradictions and processes as autonomous phenomena. This would appear to be similar to the objections raised against Giddens by those who stress the importance of the systemic level (Archer 1990). As Cohen concludes: "Giddens's distinction between social integration and system integration should not be confused with the distinction employing these terms introduced by David Lockwood, and extended in the works of Jürgen Habermas. Whereas both Lockwood and Habermas maintain that for certain purposes system integration may refer to holistically conceived properties of systems, Giddens preserves his pivotal emphasis upon structured praxis by maintaining that system integration involves social reciprocities between agents at a distance" (I. J. Cohen 1990, p. 45, fn. 2). This is the basis for Waters's (1994) classification of Giddens as a "constructionist" and Habermas as a "critical structuralist." As Mouzelis acutely suggests in a complex argument, the problem may lie in the fact that "although Giddens' more empirical work does not systematically neglect considerations pertaining to hierarchy and asymmetry, his structuration theory does. . . . These intricate connections between duality and dualism on the paradigmatic and syntagmatic levels should be a major task of a reconstructed structuration theory" (Mouzelis 1991, pp. 41-2).

7. This aspect of Habermas's approach to sociological methodology is glossed over by those interpreters who seek to reduce his research program to an immediate relationship to practice that bypasses an analysis of structural constraints (Romm 1991, pp. 186-7). This characterization may refer to Marcuse, but not to the later Habermas, who does not shrink from pronouncing in "realist" terms that the traditional Marxian notion of revolution is outmoded because the integration of the state apparatus and the economy means that society "can no longer be transformed democratically from within, that is, be switched over to a political mode of integration, without damage to their proper systemic logic and therewith their ability to function. The abysmal collapse of state socialism has only confirmed this" (Habermas 1992a, p. 444).

8. Because Habermas's normative theory is built around the issues of emancipatory politics, he is not immediately in a position to consider the relations and tensions between "emancipatory" and "life" politics as does Giddens, or in rather different terms, Richard Rorty (1989). Similarly it has been argued that autonomy (freedom, emancipation) has an ethical limit that "grows out of the potential conflict between the values of autonomy and happiness" (Fay 1987, p. 198). Nevertheless Habermas frequently acknowledges the differences between his analysis of the

formal aspects of normative reasoning and the practical decisions required for constructing individual lives oriented toward happiness, and how the former can only *inform* the latter.

PART III

Critical Theory and Empirical Research

8

DECONSTRUCTING THE CONVENTIONAL DISCOURSE OF METHODOLOGY

Quantitative Versus Qualitative Methods

For sociology the question of the relation between quantitative and qualitative analysis is an immediate and timely one, because the insights which mediate between statistical methods and their adequate applicability to specific contents are to a great degree qualitative ones. (Frankfurt Institute for Social Research 1972, p. 122)

The preceding reconstruction of the research program of critical theory was incomplete in an important respect: It did not fully explicate the practical methodological implications. To do so first requires opening up the question of the role of quantification in social science and the role of empirical analysis in theory construction. At this point it is thus necessary to make a fundamental distinction—and division—between the methodological problems of strategies of theoretical inquiry based on *statistical modeling* or *variable analysis* and those oriented toward *social theorizing* and concerned with interpretive-structural interpretations and generalizations, or what Mills called "classic social analysis" (Mills 1967, p. 21). Although the strategies are not

completely mutually exclusive, they typically do have distinct research interests that often are characterized, somewhat misleadingly, by the distinction between "quantitative" and "qualitative"
research, or in other contexts, between "theory" and "empirical
research".[1] Indeed the terms *empirical research* and *quantitative
research,* based on variable analysis, are often simply equated as
if historical and ethnographic research was not "empirical." This
distinction also must be deconstructed if the full methodological
implications of the research strategies most central to critical
theory are to be clarified.

An important implication of this argument is that the gulf
between these two research strategies is so fundamental that
there is virtually no prospect that the otherwise laudable goal
of improving quantitative research designs can ever achieve the
illusory goal of reconciliation, even though in certain cases
"multimethod" approaches and "triangulation" may be possible.
The problem is greater than that of social theorists and methodologists getting together to resolve their differences, as if their
differences were a mere product of the division of academic
labor. More realistic is a better understanding of their distinctive
contributions and problems and the occasional bases for constructive mutual interplay.[2]

Despite its critique of positivism generally, critical theory has
no basis for a priori rejection of any particular methods or
techniques as such, even if some have pronounced misleading
blanket rejections of "number crunching." As we have seen,
methodological pragmatism does not justify such a conclusion,
given its essential pluralism. But critical theory does require a
critical pluralism in that it directs attention not only to how the
type of theoretical problems shapes the choice of methods but
also to the political and ideological contexts of methodological
choices as part of the process of non-empirical argumentation
(Beardsley 1980). As Galtung argues in characterizing "methodology as ideology," the structure of society tends to determine
the selection of methodologies: "Far from universal, a methodology even contributes to the definition and maintenance of a certain
social structure by being compatible with it, or to its downfall and
replacement by another by being incompatible with it" (Galtung
1977, p. 13). The prevalence and manner of use of existing techniques can be attributed to a significant extent to the relationship

between social statistics, the state, and the system or production, as opposed to their intrinsic merits for understanding social reality (Irvine et al. 1979).[3]

Accordingly:

> There is no such thing as a general, universal methodology. . . . To work with any methodology, hence, is a political act . . . the choice of a methodology is implicitly the choice of an ideology, including the mystifying, monotheistic ideology that there is but one methodology—the universal one. To the extent that we are *conscious* the choice is for us to make, not to be made for us, and to the extent that we are *free* for us to enact. (Galtung 1977, p. 40)

It is important to stress that this thesis regarding the relationship between social processes and the selection of methodological techniques is not deterministic, nor does it posit some kind of invariant relationship that assumes a certain type of theorizing automatically requires a particular type of method. We return to this point in the conclusion of this chapter.

This chapter attempts to deconstruct various aspects of the contemporary discourse on sociological methods, especially as reflected in the quantitative/qualitative methods distinction, and then goes on to reconstruct a methodological typology that we consider to be more adequate. We want to present a critical view of the conventional discourse on social research in contemporary sociology. The first objective will be to set up an argument we wish to make regarding a way of thinking and speaking about methodology that we consider to be more sophisticated, as well as more continuous with the concerns of critical social theory. To that end, we first describe the ways methodology is discussed and, more importantly, taught within the social sciences. We then critique the nature of this discourse and point toward a more viable reconceptualization.

The Conventional Methods Discourse

Although there have been many challenges to the positivist paradigm, the fundamental opposition between so-called "quantitative" and "qualitative" methods remains. For example, it is not uncommon to find the terms used to title methods courses in sociological programs at North American colleges and universities. We would contend that the use of this dichotomy serves as the rhetorical means of typification, whereby forms of social research and sociologists themselves become located. The distinction has become the primary axis of methodological discourse. We argue that the discourse ought to be aligned along a quite different, though more substantive, axis.

Those who identify themselves with one category appear to assess the other negatively on the grounds of some inadequacy. Notwithstanding many efforts at synthesis, quantitative sociologists often tend to view qualitative research as imprecise, biased by researcher subjectivity, and effective for neither prediction nor generalization. At the same time, qualitative sociologists tend to view quantitative research as grounded in a naive objectivity, ineffective for the interpretation of insider actions, and generally unable to describe the social construction of reality. In the language of Weber, one is charged with inadequacy in terms of causal explanation (*Erklären*), while the other is charged with inadequacy in terms of interpretive understanding (*Verstehen*).

Despite the conventionalized character of the debate surrounding the established opposition between quantitative and qualitative methods, the argument can be made that this discourse, as it is structured, favors the former over the latter. Conceptual oppositions are rarely, if ever, neutral. One term has, within given social contexts, a more positive loading than the other. This is particularly clear in those instances where one term is defined as the absence of the other. The main conceptual distinction in our methodological discourse displays the positive understanding of quantitative research against the relatively negative understanding of qualitative research. Although qualitative researchers are no doubt critical of quantitative methods, the prevailing language of the discipline reminds us that quantitative sociology *is* our dominant culture.

In mainstream sociology quantitative methods are packaged in such notions as objectivity, precision, and standardization; and these are presented as distinctly scientific and, therefore, positive characteristics. How are qualitative methods defined in mainstream sociology? One way to answer this question is to look at texts given currency within the discipline. For example, consider the way a leading dictionary of sociology presents qualitative as the lack of quantitative:

> Qualitative Analysis . . . refers to analysis which is not based on precise measurement and quantitative claims. Sociological analysis is frequently qualitative, because research aims may involve the understanding of phenomena in ways that do not require quantification, or because the phenomena do not lend themselves to precise measurement. (Abercrombie et al. 1988, p. 200)

Earl Babbie, who has written one of the most commonly used undergraduate introductory methods texts, appears to present the distinction in much the same manner:

> One of the most basic divisions within the field of social research is the one separating quantitative from qualitative research. Essentially, quantitative research involves numerical analysis, whereas qualitative does not. (Babbie 1983, p. 85)

At the very least we are left with no sense of what qualitative research might be, aside from its non-quantitative nature. In contrast we are given specific defining characteristics of quantitative: It is precise, and it makes certain kinds of claims. Thus the discourse is structured in such a way as to make the quantitative research the standard for comparison, and this, we would like to emphasize, is quite arbitrary.

Again we are not attempting here to set up a critique of either quantitative or qualitative methods as such. This discussion should not be taken as a critique of particular forms of sociological research, regardless of their labels. Rather it should be taken as a critical assessment of the overall discourse itself in which both terms are implicated.

From a semiotic perspective it is clear that the two terms are reciprocally defined; each must refer, at least implicitly, to the other in order to establish its own meaning. The sense of 'quantitative' is lost without a contrasting sense of 'qualitative,' just as the sense of 'qualitative' is lost without a contrasting sense of 'quantitative.' The semiotic opposition is, at root, an opposition in the ambitions of sociological practice. Continuing the German methodological dispute (*Methodenstreit*) from the earlier stages of the human disciplines, the quantitative community seeks to establish sociology as a discipline along the lines of the natural sciences, in part, by eschewing the use of natural languages. Correspondingly the qualitative community seeks to establish sociology as a discipline along the lines of the humanities, in part, by eschewing the use of formal or numeric languages. Both communities identify themselves in terms of their opposition to the other's mode of representation. Thus, although the use of the opposition might suggest two sociologies, the mutuality of its use for self-definition reminds us that both are united in a common discourse.

The arguments presented here are addressed from outside that conceptual opposition on the basis of the reconstruction of the relationship between interpretation and explanation developed in critical social theory. Despite their apparent differences, both positions together present a common way of speaking and, therefore, thinking about social scientific methods. The present discussion is a critique of the background assumptions that unite these terms as part of the common discourse of a language game, to use Wittgenstein's metaphor. By now it should be clear that our concerns are more immediately theoretical than practical. We are concerned here with how methods are conceptualized in general, rather than with how specific methods are practiced. The acceptance of the qualitative-quantitative distinction by sociologists in general serves to draw attention away from theoretical questions associated with the ontology of social life. *The consequence of this distortion is a methodology that is not atheoretical, but that is theoretical in undeclared ways.* At stake is the extent to which the theoretical foundations of social research are open to critique. The solution is to make such theoretical differences explicit by reformulating the way we speak of methods.[4]

A number of characteristics currently are used within the discipline to construct and differentiate between so-called quantitative and qualitative approaches to social research.

Quantitative Methods

For the most part, three characteristics define quantitative research in the conventional discourse: aggregation of units, meas-

urement of variables, and statistical-causal analysis. Central to
the so-called quantitative approach is its use of *aggregate analysis*–that is, the notion that we do not study individuals as such,
but rather aggregates of individuals or other social entities. It is
important to note here that such aggregates do not necessarily
represent social groups in the strong sociological sense. Rather
the analysis deals in the notion–not specific to sociology–of
populations to be described, for example, the population of
those with a criminal record in Canada. The members of such a
population to a large extent do not interact with one another. In
other words, such a set of individuals would constitute a legitimate aggregate for the purposes of most quantitative analysis in
sociology, but it clearly would not constitute any level of social
organization from a theoretical perspective.

The fact that in much quantitative research the aggregates do
not constitute social groups proper is not problematic because
the relations to be considered are not social relations. Instead,
to the extent that the quantitative analysis is statistical, the resulting *correlational analysis* pertains to studying relations between variables, rather than people. Information is collected about
relationships between varying individual attributes or, more
simply, variables. Such information typically is collected in survey research by asking people to respond to a highly structured
set of questions. The purpose of the survey instrument is to
collect data efficiently for statistical analysis. It is necessary,
therefore, that the questions asked of people during a survey be
standardized and quantified.

Within quantitative sociology the most commonly practiced
view of "cause" is borrowed directly from the natural sciences.
According to this view, causation is understood in terms of how
an antecedent condition necessarily (or probabilistically) leads
to a particular outcome. Moreover, it also is understood that cause,
in this sense, is to be revealed in patterns of statistical covaria-
tion; for example, Does age variation account for income variation? The search for causality becomes a matter of searching for
nonspurious relationships between variables (not social relationships). In ideal situations we strive to construct parsimonious
models that are both simple (based on a few correlations) and
strong (have a high predictive capacity).

Qualitative (and Historical) Methods

Similarly three characteristics also define qualitative research in the conventional discourse: *case study design,* interpretation of action (*Verstehen*), and *thick description.* Research that we conventionally refer to as qualitative tends to involve a case study design; this simply means that we examine a single case or a limited set of cases during the research, in marked contrast to the large aggregate approach discussed above. For example, the analysis of one person's autobiography would be a case study, as would an ethnographic analysis of a single community or the historical analysis of a single society.

Central to the notion of qualitative research in the conventional discourse is the non-use of formal quantitative representations in favor of natural language. It could be argued that at all levels of qualitative analysis (individual, organizational, historical) there is a reliance on the *natural language accounts* of actors concerning their actions or the actions of others within their social field. Even in historical analysis we are concerned with accounts left to us by actors and with the perspective of the so-called historical actor. Implicit, then, in the emphasis on natural language is an interest in the local interpretation of action. Furthermore it is accepted in qualitative sociology that action and its local interpretation are always imbedded within the social world of the actors themselves.

Such analysis is taken to be *idiographic.* In other words, rather than attempting to make statistical generalizations concerning a limited set of variables, the concern in a case study is with comprehending the rich complex of factors that define the case at hand—be it individual, organizational, or societal. The social context of action and interpretation, along with the emphasis on natural language, leads much qualitative research to be concerned with layers of social reality, thus requiring a depth or *thick description* of the case at hand (Geertz 1983). The basis of qualitative analysis as interpretation theory, according to the conventional discourse, is the determination and representation of meanings (Little 1991, pp. 68-86).

Critique of the Discourse

We contend that the predominant distinction between quantitative and qualitative methods in sociology serves primarily to conceal and confuse theoretical positions. This distinction focuses our attention on the *techniques* through which social life is represented in the course of research, as opposed to the process of representing social reality. As we will see, the strongest critique of accepting the quantitative-qualitative distinction as the primary way of organizing our experience of social inquiry is that it conceals another, more fundamental, distinction. Here we refer to the theoretical distinction between recognizing a set of individuals as a social group and defining a set of individuals as a sociological aggregate.

The arguments can be presented in four stages. First, the quantitative-qualitative opposition, as such, presents a false dichotomiation of actual social research practice. Second, we remind the reader that the quantitative-qualitative opposition, although appearing to reference data languages, in practice actually refers to specific analytic strategies. Third, we argue that these strategies are not simply different ways of examining the same social phenomena, but are ways of making a set of individuals into two different kinds of phenomena. Fourth, we contend that behind these different kinds of social phenomena lies an important theoretical distinction and that this distinction is revealed inadequately by the language of qualitative-quantitative.

A False Dichotomy

To begin, the dichotomy set up by the distinction between qualitative and quantitative methods lacks face validity. To the extent that it rests on the difference between the use of formal and natural language modes of representation, the dichotomy is obviously false. Simply put, nothing about qualitative research, regardless of the form it takes, necessarily precludes the use of quantitative representations or nonquantitative formal methods (Braybrooke 1987, pp. 60-66). Ethnographers and historians can and do count things. Moreover, the activities of research design, data collection, and analysis in quantitative social research necessarily are based on the interplay of constructed meanings. To imagine an appropriate question for a statistical survey is to engage in the natural language employed by both the analyst and the subjects of the research. The language of research is not an adequate criterion for a major differentiation of research forms.

Specific Analytic Strategies

The practices conventionally associated with the terms *qualitative* and *quantitative* do represent quite distinct analytic strategies. We argue that it is necessary to acknowledge these fundamental differences, rather than the more illusory language difference, in order to begin comprehending the major divisions within empirical social science.

The main underlying factor that needs to be made explicit in this regard is that for the most part quantitative research in sociology is statistical in the strong sense of bivariate and multivariate statistical modeling. Yet quantification means many different things. For example, studies may be referred to as "statistical," with the implication that they involve a specific form of theoretical analysis. So when we read that "French sociologist Pierre Bourdieu has reported on quantitative empirical research that shows . . . that there are coherent social class differences in the consumption of culture" (Hall and Neitz 1993, p. 117), we would be misled to think that Bourdieu has drawn on statistical-causal analysis. In fact, the research in question is based tangentially on surveys that are used to demonstrate striking differences (expressed in percentages) in the tastes of different occupational groups. In fact, Bourdieu explicitly rejects what he labels the "multivariate fallacy" as a theoretical strategy because "the techniques sociologist generally use to establish and measure relations implicitly contain a philosophy that is at once analytical and instantaneist . . . the structures sociology deals with are the product of transformation which, unfolding in time, cannot be considered as reversible except by a logical abstraction, a sociological absurdity" (Bourdieu and Passeron 1977, p. 88).[5]

We must ask, then, how is *statistical modeling* different from other forms of quantitative analysis in sociology. As mentioned earlier, the strategy of statistical analysis is to model the social world in terms of causal relations—understood as nonspurious correlation—between an observed system of variables. The key term here is that of "relations between variables." This term is to be contrasted with the concern of much mathematical and qualitative efforts to reconstruct social structure and processes. In other words, nonstatistical approaches in sociology—qualitative or quantitative—take as their strategy the comprehension of relations obtaining between social actors and other forms of social organization. For example, to describe the structural relationship between two social classes in a society involves a quite different epistemology than describing the statistical relationship between education and income for members of the same society.

Constructing Social Phenomena

The focus on variable relations sets the logic of statistical research at odds, to a large extent, with the focus of contemporary social theory and with that of critical theory in particular. To comprehend this point, we need to go back to the earlier description of the subjects of research. In tune with the concerns of theoretical sociology, nonstatistical research attempts to describe a society by referring to the systemic and social relations that constitute it. Subjects are subjects in *relations* with others and with forms of social organization. To study individuals in this paradigm is necessarily to study them as participants in communities, classes, institutions, and cultural discourses. In contrast, statistical-correlational research has less of a natural affinity with theoretical sociology. It does not assume at all that its analysis of variables is based on a population of subjects who interact with one another through communities and the like. It is assumed, however, that members of the sample used are independent of one another. Statistical analysis constructs a certain kind of "subject" within sociological discourse—the member of an aggregate—whereas more theoretically oriented analyses construct the "subject" as the participant in one form of social organization or another.

Theoretical Inadequacy

This incongruency with theoretical sociology is due to the fact that *statistical analysis is not a sociological method.* It is not an approach developed within sociology as a tool for its theoretical inquiries. Rather it is a tool that has been incorporated into the discipline of sociology from the natural sciences despite the incongruity with basic sociological concepts, such as the group, and basic theoretical concerns, such as the nature of social relationships constituent of a society. For this reason, Fararo, an astute formalist methodologist, carefully distinguishes between the construction of theoretical models of generative structures from statistical modeling (what he calls the "regression equation model of theorizing"):[6] *"But they are not social theoretical in character* [italics added]. . . . They are not direct instantiations of a mode of representation of the social phenomena of interest. Perhaps we can say that they are statistical theoretical models applying general statistical theory" (Fararo 1989, p. 57).

The popularity of the statistical framework can be traced, we contend, to its affinity with a modern policy- and program-oriented sociology. Statistical analysis is grounded in the values and logic of social engineering (Fay 1975) although this foundation may not be as salient for all those who practice statistical sociology. These have, in turn, come to define the dominant discourse on methods in sociology. Yet this foundation in social engineering has remained largely transparent within the discourse itself, enabling its uncritical reproduction. We would reject the qualitative-quantitative distinction as based on inadequate, misleading, and ideological assumptions.

Further, the predominance of statistical modeling is reinforced by a positivist conception of *formal logic* that presumes that the analytic ideal of formalization is always possible and most appropriate independently of the object of inquiry. It is on this basis that methods texts can outline the formal criteria of scientific explanation and then apply those to "qualitative" research showing how, inevitably, they end up defective even if often useful. What this paradox hints at is the crucial postempiricist distinction between the abstract formal criteria of mathematical logic and the values and standards characteristic of *practical logic* or *reasoning* (the logic-in-use) in a particular domain. If logic-in-use is viewed as a matter of argumentation, then it is possible to differentiate "field-invariant" and "field-dependent" criteria for constructing and evaluating arguments (Toulmin 1958, p. 15). From this perspective it is possible to differentiate the distinctive aspects—the field-dependent criteria—of the investigative concerns of statistical modeling as opposed to social theorizing.

Disciplinary Interests
and Two Research Logics

Having laid out a deconstruction of the dominant methodological discourse, we now seek to rethink methodological discourse in a manner based on the distinction between two types of *disciplinary practice*.

Social Theorizing

One can identify two fundamental disciplinary interests in sociology: world-historical *social theorizing* and the *social engineering* model—that is, the dominant form of variable-based methodology grounded in nomothetic explanations. We argue that these, in turn, provide the normative foundation for particular research logics. An interest in social theorizing, in our view, is expressed in the desire to comprehend and, in some cases, transform (through praxis) the underlying orders of social life—those social and systemic relations that constitute society. From this perspective the *raison d'être* of social theory is to construct a tenable account depicting "the underlying principle of change at work in the emergence and disappearance of the numerous forms of human life and the countless welter of human activities and relationships" (Fay 1987, p. 69). In this respect, social theorizing is interpretive, but also structural. Hence *it cannot be reduced to the ideographic interpretation;* it retains a strong quasi-causal explanatory interest, but one consistent with the nature of social reality. Accordingly we contend that the theoretically driven task of articulating underlying generative structures of social orders requires two distinct yet interdependent research logics: intensive explication and comparative generalization.

Let us first consider the logic of *intensive explication,* a strategy grounded in hermeneutic assumptions. By the term *explication* we intend the research logic of empirically lifting into view the underlying semantic, sociocultural, and structural relations that are constitutive of historically unique actors, mediations, and systems, respectively (A. Sayer 1992, pp. 236ff).[7] More specifically we can imagine (a) the interpretive explication of the self-identity and social cognitions appropriated by a given actor, (b) the interpretive or structural explication of the social interaction situated within a given mediation, and (c) the structural explication of the political and economic relations comprising a given social system. The term *intensive* implies a case study focus on specific individual actors, mediations, or systems. The logic of intensive explication includes the construction of representations such as ethnographic accounts (interpretive social psychology), componential taxonomies (cognitive anthropology), and formal models (mathematical sociology). Essential to any effort at intensive explication is the desire to discern and elaborate the substantive relations posited in social theory.

Comparative generalization is a logic complementary to intensive explication. Here the strategy is one of comparing the patterns disclosed through intensive explication across a finite set of historically comparable cases (actors, mediations, or systems). This step may be accomplished in order to make limited generalizations regarding identifiable patterns obtaining across several cases at a single point in time or for changes in the pattern of a single case over some duration of time. It is important to recall here that the patterns explicated and compared through these theoretically driven strategies are those found in the cognitive, cultural, or structural constitution of actors, mediations, or systems, respectively.

The logic is parallel to that found in structuralist linguistics. In that discipline one strives to disclose the internal orders and properties underlying the construction and transformation of meaning through explication and comparison of discourses. In the broader theory of society context, we extend this approach to include the social cognitions of actors, the sociocultural properties of mediations (collectivities, as well as discourses), and the structural properties of societal systems. In the case of both explication and comparison, we may find it useful for heuristic purposes to model such properties and processes through formal languages such as mathematics. And in some cases we may wish

to base comparisons on certain variables. But these do not sub-
stitute for the more fundamental activity of theory construction.
Taken together, intensive explication and comparative generalization are carried out in the context of intensive research designs
oriented toward case studies and nonstatistical comparative analysis—a topic discussed further in the next chapter.

Social Engineering and Causal Modeling

In contrast, statistical-causal modeling is the primary technique employed in extensive research designs based on aggre-
gating large numbers of individuals or processes. Here comparison
also takes place but involves a fundamentally different "comparative method." Hence it would be incorrect simply to equate
interpretive comparative generalization with the logic of statistical causal modeling.[8] First, statistical modeling is based on
associations between standardized variables for a large aggregate
of cases—individuals, mediations, or systems. Recall that the logics
of explication and comparison outlined thus far are concerned
with internal relations constitutive of actors, mediations, or
systems, and with the reproductive relations linking micro and
macro phenomena. As an approach, statistical modeling assumes
that the cases comprising a given aggregate are independent of
one another. The relations in questions are those obtaining
between selected variables—a much more abstract logical operation. This difference, we would suggest, creates a problematic
situation of mixed logics for analysts working from a critical
sociology perspective. Whereas the research logics of explication and comparison can be linked directly into the language of
a critical theory of society—one concerned with processes of
social reproduction and transformation—the logic implicated in
the modeling of statistical associations has a less obvious linkage
with this kind of theoretical discourse.

In principle it would require some sort of logical somersault
to transform the empirical statistical associations between variables into theoretical social relations between actors and within
or between mediations. We are concerned that such logical gym-
nastics are not made explicitly, or are even well understood. This
problem is compounded by the nomothetic requirements of statistical analysis that data be collected (a) in terms of standardized

variables and (b) across larger aggregates. Many instances of sociological inquiry may involve questions concerning phenomena
not readily standardized, such as meaning systems, or may involve cases sufficiently unique that there are only a few comparable cases.

None of this is to argue that statistical causal modeling is completely nappropriate for the purposes of theorizing or never in
the interests of critical sociology, but it is to say that the affinity
between statistical research and social theory is not at all straight-
forward. The primary reason that the conventional status of
qualitative analysis as a *heuristic* (facilitating discovery but not
its fundamental basis) for the ideal of statistical generalization
should be reversed: *Mathematics is, at best, a heuristic tool for
social research whose conceptual language is necessarily
grounded in explicative interpretations and structural generalizations.*[9]

We would suggest that this lack of clear affinity finds its
sociological source in the interest of social engineering that has
shaped, to some extent, the discipline of sociology in the latter
part of this century. The normative interest of social engineering
is distinct from the normative interest of social theorizing as we
have outlined it. Social engineering is interested in empirical
descriptions in order to conceptually reproduce, rather than to
reveal or transform, given social orders (Habermas 1970; Fay
1975). The function of research in this institutional practice is
to inform state and, in some cases, corporate policy and programming. In this rationalized milieu the "program" becomes
the means to realize a "fit" between individuals and collectivities, on the one hand, and the state, on the other hand. The
evaluation of policy decisions is based on the probability that a
given individual or collectivity will demonstrate some positively
defined attribute as a consequence of programming initiatives
and expenditures. In this context the social relations obtaining
between actors and between mediations are virtually irrelevant.
What is relevant is the ability to predict outcomes on the basis
of various inputs. Hence statistical causal modeling becomes
appropriated as the logic of choice.

The fact that the capacity of a social science to produce such
knowledge oriented toward technical control may have been
greatly exaggerated by earlier critical theory does not alter,

however, the basic critique. Indeed it calls for an explanation of *why* control-oriented social science has not lived up to its promise. In many countries the loss of faith in the technical contributions of social science have led inevitably to decline in research funding. Explanation of this anomaly is immanent in Habermas's theory of communicative action and explicit in Giddens's theory of structuration: The decontextualized analysis of controlling variables touches only on the surface of the generative causal mechanisms of social relations and cannot be translated readily into long-term, effective interventions.

We would suggest that as a consequence of the "publics of sociology"—especially state interest in social engineering—a strong sense of legitimacy arose for statistical analysis in society and, perhaps unfortunately, within the social sciences (Halliday and Janowitz 1992). The rise of statistical modeling as the dominant legitimate logic in modernity may well correspond to the decline in legitimacy of other approaches that were more theoretically grounded, for example, American pragmatism.

A Taxonomy of Social Research Strategies

The distinction between extensive research-oriented correlational accounts of causation on the one hand, and two moments of intensive accounts—individual explication and comparative generalization—on the other, allows a comprehensive typology of research strategies. In particular we wish to differentiate how each of these three types of explanatory focus has different implications for the three analytical moments of social reproduction: (a) the social psychological analysis of individual actors, (b) the systemic analysis of social structures, and (c) the sociocultural analysis of mediations (or "social practices" in Giddens's terms).

Social Psychological Analysis
of Individual Actors

The primary *naturalistic* strategy applied to individual actors can be found in various forms of behavioral social psychology, for example, Skinnerian operant conditioning. We consider to be *individual-level modeling* those forms of research that ideally seek to establish universal covering laws of behavioral processes (e.g., in Homan's exchange theory).

Interpretive social psychologies reject the thesis of universal determination even though most acknowledge the importance of external constraints on social action (even if these are ignored by the theory). Indeed interpretive social psychologies can be arranged on a continuum on this basis. Hence a fundamental tension in interpretive sociology is reflected in divergent attempts to reconstruct the logic-in-use of its research practice. Some stress its search for "rules" of action that identify regularities with explanatory significance, hence the continuity and complementarity between naturalistic and interpretive methodologies (Braybrooke 1987, pp. 47ff). Others stress the discontinuity evident from a focus on interpretation as a hermeneutic process:

> This approach is thus *hermeneutic:* It treats social phenomena as a text to be decoded through imaginative reconstruction of the significance of various elements of the social action or event. The interpretive framework thus holds that social science is radically unlike natural science because it unavoidably depends upon the interpretation of meaningful human behavior and social practices. (Little 1991, p. 68)

We account for this discrepancy by distinguishing the two aspects or moments that characterize interpretive accounts of individual focused analyses: *actor explication,* which follows the hermeneutic model in analyzing unique cases, and *actor generalization,* concerned with identifying general rules of individual action in specific causal contexts.

Macrostructural Analysis of Social Systems

System-level modeling is based on the hypothetical assumption of treating social systems as if they were relatively closed. On this basis, statistical techniques for studying collective properties can be imported from the natural sciences. The most common version in sociology is probably *aggregative compara-*

tive research, which attempts to identify crucial variables in systems dynamics on the basis of large samples of cases.

In contrast, *systemic analysis* in interpretive social theory dispenses with the organic analogy, holding that societies are open systems whose regularities are historically changeable and do not often lend themselves to formalization. On the one hand, this definition suggests analyzing systemic properties (those structures that operate behind the backs of actors) in terms of *systemic explication*—that is, defining the processing of social reproduction and contradiction within the specific historical case. On the other hand, such case studies presuppose basic structuralist concepts involving *system generalization* based on certain types of societies. Although these structural rules invoke the assumption of regularity and causality, they do so in a manner that is highly historically contingent.

Sociocultural Analysis of Mediations

Mediation-level modeling attempts the very difficult task of identifying the probabilistic conditions of social change or correlations between aggregate properties of groups and institutional orders. *Mediation-level explication* involves the attempt to identify intensively the crucial points of potential rupture, breakdown, or change in the processes of reproduction carried out at the intersection of systemic and social integration. Again such case studies presuppose *mediational generalizations* of the type associated with theories of collective behavior, social movements, and cultural change.

This comprehensive scheme has the advantage of being related directly to investigative concerns and disciplinary practices, rather than based on the more limited qualitative-quantitative distinction. The use of formal languages does not play a major role in the way we have conceptualized social methodology. Quantification could be used as part of any of the nine identified strategies, and it is certainly used in the six strategies falling under the sociocultural and macrostructural analytic moments. The reader should note, however, that although strategies involving explication and generalization employ formal languages to represent social structure and process (mathematical sociology), those strategies flowing from a social engineering paradigm of extensive analysis employ the formal language of bivariate and multivariate relationships (statistical sociology). It should also be noted that the use of mathematical models is limited by the extent to which they can be theoretically interpreted. Thus the use of mathematical models is less viable in the context of actor and, to some extent, mediation explication and generalization, which present the analyst with hermeneutic, rather than structural, phenomena.

In general we would argue that *the validity of quantitative methods is a matter of the continuity they can forge with theoretical discourse.* Techniques of a mathematical nature (e.g., network analysis) may be readily linked, as heuristic devices, to theoretical interests in explicating social structure and process. As we have argued, the logic of statistical generalizations has more of an affinity with the interests of social engineering, rather than social theorizing. Whereas the latter is geared toward the intensive explication and comparative generalization of aspects of the social world, the former is geared toward the construction of multivariable modeling intending "prediction" of variances. From a critical theory perspective the fundamental difficulty with using statistical analysis is that it is based on the relations between variables, while explicative and comparative analyses, as we have presented them, are based on discerning structural relations within and between mediations—relations that turn on the dialectic between human agency and social structure.

The Investigative Concerns of Critical Theory

Methodological Choices

At this point we wish to point to the intimate relationship between substantive and methodological choices in critical theory. On the one hand, this does not entail any necessary link, a point that would weaken the argument linking ideology and methodology that began this chapter. It is important to reaffirm, however, that this merely argues that *affinities* exist between certain types of methodological strategies and theories of society, not that this is necessarily so: Intensive methods may be used to construct knowledge that supports functionalist theories, and extensive methods may be used to provide support for causal propositions congenial to critical theory. Andrew Sayer has formulated this question carefully in terms of the "limits" of strategies

> . . . and some of the assumptions and practices which *commonly accompany* their use . . . structural analysis tends to "resonate" with marxist (and possibly some other) conceptions of society, but not with individualistic theories which portray society as a structureless aggregate of externally related individuals and causal "factors." This latter view resonates more easily with the use of quantitative methods. In noting this, I am not suggesting that structural analysis *entails* marxism or that individualistic theories entail or are entailed by quantitative approaches, but merely that there are "resonances" which encourage the clustering of certain philosophical positions, social theories and techniques. Any adequate critique of social science must go beyond piecemeal criticisms to the understanding of these resonances. (A. Sayer 1992, p. 199)

On the other hand, we would also be wary of any simplistic complementarity thesis. Giddens runs this risk in analyzing the relationship between qualitative and quantitative research. According to Giddens, awareness of the duality of structure undermines the quantitative-qualitative opposition. Although we agree with Giddens that this is a false opposition, we find that he oversimplifies somewhat and exaggerates the complementarity between quantitative and qualitative research. The crucial point is that he is talking about the complementarity of the two as "techniques" or methods, whereas we have stressed their antagonism as methodological strategies—that is, modes of theory construction.

> The idea that there is either a clear-cut division or a necessary opposition between qualitative and quantitative methods disappears. Quantitative techniques are usually likely to be demanded when a large number of "cases" of a phenomenon are to be investigated, in respect of a restricted variety of designated characteristics. But both depend upon procedures methodologically identical to the gathering of data of a more intensive, "qualitative" sort. . . . All so-called "quantitative," when scrutinized, turn out to be composites of "qualitative"—i.e., contextually located and indexical—

interpretations produced by situated researchers, coders, government officials and others . . . qualitative and quantitative methods
should be seen as complementary rather than antagonistic aspects
of social research. (Giddens 1984, pp. 333-4)

Giddens is pointing here to the essentially heuristic function
of quantification in general and the construction of all data
through interpretation. But he does not seem to appreciate the
deeper, inherent antagonism between variable analysis and the
structuration theory he advocates—that is, between extensive and
intensive research designs. One reason is that he tends to equate
quantitative approaches with macroanalysis and qualitative with
microanalysis: "It is not difficult to see in the conflict between
these two positions a methodological residue of the dualism of
structure and action" (Giddens 1984, p. 330). As suggested by
the taxonomy of methodologies above, we do not find any strong
affinities of this type. Statistical modeling is possible and well
developed at all three levels: systemic, action, mediational. After
all, on the one hand, most of social psychology is concerned with
the experimental analysis of microphenomena. On the other
hand, the qualitative approach of comparative historical sociology has always been the foundation of macrosociology. We thus
would rephrase and qualify Giddens's formulation.

The quantitative-qualitative opposition disappears only in the
sense that qualitative approaches use statistics descriptively, and
quantitative ones inevitably use interpretive procedures to construct measures. In this general sense it is perhaps possible to
speak of complementarity for the purpose of the descriptive
uses for social theorizing. But this occasional complementarity
does not eliminate the antagonism between some types of quantification (statistically based variable analysis) and interpretive
structural theorizing as modes of conceptualizing social reality.
As a consequence the relationship between the two in this case
is not one of essential or natural complementarity as if they were
equally necessary terms. Given that quantitative procedures are
heuristic, their complementarity with social theorizing is only
occasional and cannot be taken for granted. And these intrinsic
antagonisms are reinforced by the social demand for instrumental
knowledge that tends to distort the uses of variable analysis, hence
draws it away from reconciliation with interpretive sociology.

Investigative Concerns
and Analytic Moments

The theory of society underlying critical theory is based on an open-ended model of social and cultural reproduction of the type proposed by both Habermas and Giddens. Unlike older structural functionalist and structuralist Marxist approaches, however, these models avoid strong functionalism and view the attainment of reproduction of a given order as a highly historically contingent process. This analytical focus on the dynamics of stability and change, in turn, defines the investigative concerns of critical research that can for heuristic purposes be broken down in terms of three analytic moments.

Following a number of theorists (Lockwood 1964; Giddens 1984; Habermas 1987a), we can recall again *two investigative concerns* in contemporary critical sociology: questions concerning the phenomenon of *social integration* and those concerning *system integration*. The concern with social integration directs questions to the "immediate nexus of social action," whereas the concern with system integration directs questions to the "reproduction of institutions"—social orders—across time and space (Giddens 1984, pp. 139-44). The concern with questions of social integration is reflected in the various types of social psychology and microsociology (symbolic interactionism, social phenomenology, ethnomethodology, and cognitive sociology), while the concern with questions of system integration is reflected in the variants of macrostructural sociology (neofunctionalism and neo-Marxist political economy). In other words, we see action research and macrostructural research as analytic moments flowing from prior investigative concerns grounded in the intersection of social and system integration.

But we wish to introduce a third moment based on the idea of mediations (Sartre 1963). In other words, we have to incorporate a sociocultural analysis of mediations (what we refer to as *mediational analysis*) that bridges the social psychological analysis of individual actors, on the one hand, and the macrostructural analysis of social systems, on the other hand. Such mediation implies that an analysis flowing from a concern with social integration potentially can be both social psychological and sociocultural, an approach best exemplified in Bourdieu's concept of *habitus.* It can involve an analysis of actors (as agents or subjects) and an analysis of mediations (the sites of social agency and institutional reproduction). Similarly this strategy implies that an analysis based on a concern with system integration potentially can be both macrostructural and sociocultural. It can involve an analysis of a social system (as a configuration of mediations, e.g., social classes) and an analysis of particular mediations (the sites of social agency and institutional reproduction). Put otherwise, from a critical perspective, both social psychological and macrostructural analytic moments are implicitly dependent on theoretical and empirical work focused on mediations, or what Giddens would call "social practices," or Habermas, systemic-lifeworld relations.

Conclusion

In concluding, we would like to stress two key points. First, we suggest that the methodological distinctiveness of critical theory as empirical research derives from its particular fusion of an explanatory strategy (intensive analysis) with the overall substantive problematic of an open model of social and cultural reproduction characterized by three analytic moments: systemic integration, social integration, and mediational analysis.

Second, we argue that, for the purposes of a critical theory of society, the types of research developed in terms of variable-based modeling strategies is more often than not either irrelevant or peripheral for the cognitive interests of theory construction and social criticism. To an extent that is difficult to estimate, this high degree of irrelevance may be due to the current practices that happen to guide variable-based research.

To summarize our account of critical methodology in this and preceding chapters, we would point to the following conclusions:

- A conception of methodology grounded in terms of an antifoundationalist epistemology—that is, the theory of argumentation, which adequately takes into account the non-empirical aspects of method (reflexive, normative)

- A rejection of the qualitative-quantitative distinction as a way of differentiating methodologies and substituting the distinction between intensive as opposed to extensive research designs
- The claim that the typical research problems posed by critical theory (forms of structural analysis that acknowledge the knowledgeability of agents) lead to the general preference for intensive research designs
- The overall objective of intensive research designs in the context of critical theory is the construction of a theory of social and cultural reproduction
- Stress on the way all research is part of a process of social production in which particular logics-in-use specific to scientific communities come to define knowledge; hence the insistence that the history and systematic aspects of research cannot be completely severed
- The contention that given the societal demands for knowledge that can produce technical control, there has been a dominance of extensive methods under conditions that have tended to tolerate or even sanction their problematic use

The next three chapters elaborate in more detail the kind of methodological strategies implied by intensive research designs in the context of critical research. First, we consider the non-empirical, reflexive assumptions of such research (Chapter 9), followed by a discussion of some of the issues involved in deploying methods in intensive research (Chapter 10)[10] and a review of representative examples of research that touch on the analytic models of systemic integration, social integration, and mediational analysis (Chapter 11).

Notes

1. "Nowhere else is the notion of 'method' so patently out of place as in its application to sociological *theories*. . . . It is also a technical difficulty that confronts the teaching of methodology from the outset" (Baldamus 1976, p. 9). As Baldamus notes this is because *social theorizing has distinctive, implicit methods, much as methods involve distinctive, implicit forms of theorizing.*
2. Here we have in mind the kind of discussion prompted by Stanley Lieberson in *Making It Count* (Lieberson 1984) and the lament that the book would be used as ammunition for those opposed to quantification in the social sciences (Arminger and Bohrnstedt 1987). We would read it simply as a rationale

for a nonquantitative approach on the grounds that analysis of variance is difficult to reconcile with answering fundamental questions about social processes: "The focus on explained variance has had a major effect on the choice of problems to study within sociology. . . . Many, if not most, fundamental sociological questions, however, involve macrolevel, structural forces in which there is little or no variation. These problems cannot be addressed through this type of analysis (Singer and Marini 1987, p. 380). For a provocative, non-empiricist attempt to connect measurement with the study of structural mechanisms, see Pawson 1989.

3. As Baldamus argues, contrary to the usual assumption that the ideological content of theories makes them a good indicator of social change, empirical methods lend themselves more readily to study by the sociology of knowledge, "provided due attention is paid to the 'implicit theorizing' that shapes and controls the application of empirical procedures. . . . To use empirical methods instead of theories as a mirror of changes in social reality has the additional advantage that the former are much more compact and less fluctuating than the latter" (Baldamus 1976, p. 151).

4. Thus we are not making the same critique of quantification presented by Cicourel in his *Method and Measurement in Sociology* (Cicourel 1964). That argument involved an assessment of the degree to which arithmetic measures could be applied to the nonmaterial "dimensions" of social reality. Although we are essentially in agreement with Cicourel on the limits of measurement in this regard, it is not our purpose here to critique quantification per se. Rather it is our intention to question the priority given to the more basic distinction between qualitative and quantitative approaches to social research and the invidious characterization of qualitative theory as falling short of the quantitative ideal.

5. Many forms of analysis can be referred to as quantitative, of which statistical procedures represent only a part. The field of mathematical sociology, with its interest in modeling social structures and processes, covers the range of quantitative and formalized analysis not addressed by even the most advanced statistical techniques (Fararo 1989). We would argue that some of the approaches found in mathematical sociology are actually theoretically compatible with much of what we called "qualitative sociology" (e.g., network analysis).

6. Fararo (1989, pp. 53ff) thus rejects existent positivism (based on variable analysis and the covering law model) in favor of a realistic position oriented toward the construction of generative structuralist models concerned with formalized general sociological theory as opposed to the world-historical sociology and normative social theory of concern here.

7. We consider in greater detail the nature of *intensive,* as opposed to *extensive,* research designs in Chapters 9 and 10.

8. This is the basis of the important distinction between statistical and nonstatistical comparative research: "While it is true that the logic of social science is continuous from one subdiscipline to another, the peculiarities of comparative social science make it an ideal setting for an examination of key issues in methodology. . . . The most distinctive aspect of comparative social science is the wide gulf between qualitative and quantitative work. It is wider in comparative social science than in perhaps any other social science subdiscipline. In part this is because its qualitative tradition is dominant, the opposite of the situation in most other fields" (Ragin 1987, p. 2). We would argue, however,

that Ragin fails here to differentiate clearly between the field-invariant and field-dependent aspects of the logic of social science.

9. For a rigorous defense of this thesis, see Wilson (1987), who concludes: "Mathematics cannot play the same role as a vehicle for expressing fundamental concepts and propositions in the social sciences as it does in the natural sciences. The reason for this is that the basic data of the social sciences, descriptions of social phenomena, are inherently intensional in character: the social sciences cannot insist on extensional description without abandoning their phenomena. This, however, does not mean that mathematics has no place in social science; rather, that *mathematics play a heuristic rather than a fundamental role in the study of social phenomena* [italics added] (Wilson 1987, p. 402).

10. Although this also would be possible (though more difficult) to do with respect to extensive methods, that would require a very technical treatment of how to link measurement techniques to the study of causal mechanisms, a project that we leave to others (e.g., Pawson 1989).

9

NON-EMPIRICAL METHODS

Reflexive Procedures

That we disavow reflection is positivism. (Habermas 1971, p. vii)

Dialectical thought is the attempt to break through the coercive character of logic with the means of logic itself. (Adorno, cited in Gebhardt 1978, p. 396)

Thinking does not get caught up in dialectics because it disdains the rules of formal logic, but because it obstinately sticks to these rules; it employs these rules even to think about logic itself, instead of breaking off their application at this crucial point. (Habermas, cited in Gebhardt 1978, p. 396)

To argue . . . that the writing of ethnography involves telling stories, making pictures, concocting symbolisms, and deploying tropes is commonly resisted, often fiercely, because of a confusion, endemic in the West since Plato at least, of the imagined with the imaginary, the fictional with the false, making things out with making them up. The strange idea that reality has an idiom in which it prefers to talk about it without a fuss—a spade is a spade, a rose is a rose—on pain of illusion, trumpery and self-bewitchment, leads to the even stranger idea that, if literalism is lost, so is fact. (Geertz 1988, p. 140)

Future discussions of method in social science will presumably push in this direction of the examination of rhetoric, description and language. (A. Sayer 1992, pp. 265-6)

226

Having argued against the quantitative-qualitative distinction as a means of conceptualizing methodological differences, we suggested that the distinctive aspect of critical theory was its affinities with research practices oriented toward explicative interpretation and comparative generalization. This suggestion followed from the pragmatic methodological proposition that some strategies (research designs) and techniques tend to be privileged because of their appropriateness to the questions asked. The point here, however, is not to confuse the use of particular techniques (e.g., variable analysis) with strategies of theory construction.

With respect to specific techniques, critical theory is in principle much more open and innovative than empiricist social science. Not only does it embrace the possibility of all empiricist techniques, but it also introduces a number of others associated with interpretive social science. As a point of principle, therefore, critical theory is eclectic with respect to methodological techniques:

> Critical social research is clearly not constrained by its data collection techniques. . . . Empirical studies . . . include the whole gamut of research tools: observations, both participant and non-participant; formal interviews with random samples; semi-structured, unstructured and in-depth interviewing; key informants testimonies, analysis of personal and institutional documents; mass media analysis; archive searching; examination of official statistics; and reviews of published literature. Furthermore, critical social research also uses a wide variety of analytic techniques: ethnographic interpretation, historical reconstruction, action research, multivariate analysis, structuralist deconstruction and semiological analysis. (Harvey 1990, p. 196)

But this methodological pragmatism is coupled with an explicit research program whose critical realist ontology sets an agenda and priorities with respect to research problems that do tend to privilege some methods over others as part of research designs.

227

Critical theory's research program is thus quite consistent with the postempiricist theory of scientific research programs, which argues that "the rationality and progressiveness of a theory are most closely linked—not with its confirmation and falsification—but rather with its *problem solving effectiveness*" (Laudan 1977, p. 5). And of course it is the research program that selects the types of explanatory problems and the pertinent methods.

A defining characteristic of critical research methodology is that choices about linking theories and methods are an ongoing process that is contextually bound, not a technical decision that can be taken for granted through reference to the "logic of science." But what is the alternative? Critical theory's methodological uniqueness has been associated with two terms: its *reflexive* and *dialectical* character. The first is considered extensively in this chapter under the heading of "non-empirical methods"—largely ignored though implicit in empiricist research—that are crucial to the conduct of empirical inquiry and that should be a part of methodological selfconsciousness and training. With respect to the second question, we argue that although there is no distinctive "dialectical method" in the strict sense, critical theory does have a unique methodological strategy based on the agency-structure dialectic and the interpretive structural approach to historical explanation.

Logic as Rhetoric

What, then, is the methodological implication of the identification of critical theory as a "reflexive sociology" (Gouldner 1971, 1975; O'Neill 1972)? Reflexivity may be seen to operate in two contexts. First, it involves metatheoretical reflection that is a form of inquiry in its own right, a topic we considered previously under the heading of "critical metatheory." Second, reflexivity is an applied practice that, while drawing on general metatheoretical categories, is involved integrally (consciously or not) in the overall process through which research is produced.

For example, even the positivist reference to "logic" indicates a reference to non-empirical modes of persuasion that are otherwise taken for granted. Critical theories, in contrast, make reflection on non-empirical aspects of methodology a central theme of theory and research. But unlike positivist metatheory, "reason" is not reduced to deductive logic at the expense of informal logics and normative theory, which become "exiled into psychology" by default as either nonrational or irrational (Gebhardt 1978, p. 391). Again this position is consistent with the postempiricist theory of research programs that has come to recognize that "there are important *nonempirical*, even *'nonscientific'* (in the usual sense), factors which have—and should—play a role in the *rational* development of science" (Laudan 1977, p. 5).

The Logic of Argumentation

The fundamental problems of empiricism and positivism—and its unreflexive character—are rooted, as we have seen, in a worship of generality based on what has been referred to as "logicism" (Harré 1986) or "logical essentialism."[1] What this effort to reduce scientific practice to formal logic leaves in the dark is the nature of the "rationality" of the other kinds of procedures that scientists employ. Typically these simply are pushed aside as irrelevant issues that belong to the "psychology" of discovery. What is crucial about formal logic (as rules about correct thinking) is its complete indifference to the *content* of the propositions it analyzes. In other words, logic can make no claim about the relation between logically valid propositions and the real world: "Like algebra, logical systems are purely formal, neutral, timeless and contentless; the terms in the logical relations can refer to anything or nothing. A *valid* argument is one for which it is contradictory to accept the premises but reject the conclusion" (A. Sayer 1992, p. 165). As a consequence formal logic is characterized by a process of abstraction that eliminates all aspects of the proposition not related to the issues of logical entailment.

From critical realist and critical theory perspectives, formal logic cannot serve as a foundation of social scientific methodology precisely because it can say nothing about the relationship between concepts and the world, or logical relations and the substance of thinking. From a postempiricist perspective, in short, the nature of logic can be understood only from the perspective of "logical practice." Paradoxically the outcome of this kind of rethinking of logic is that it is ultimately a species of *rhetoric*, or more neutrally, as part of a *theory of argumentation* whose nature is best illustrated in linguistic philosophy by the analogy of jurisprudence:[2]

> Logic (we may say) is generalised jurisprudence. Arguments can be compared with law-suits, and the claims we make and argue for in extra-legal contexts with claims made in court, while the cases we present in making good each kind of claim can be compared with each other. . . . There is one special virtue in the parallel between logic and jurisprudence: it helps us to keep in the centre of the picture the critical function of reason. (Toulmin 1958, pp. 7-8)

The implication of this position for epistemology is that the analytic ideal of formal logic is largely irrelevant; although this may require moderating our scientific ambitions, it does not require relativism or skepticism just because everything does not match up to some logical ideal of "knowledge." From the perspective of the theory of argumentation, in short, formal logic is merely one heuristic among many for conducting argumentation, and many others are considerably more important, depending on the context of inquiry and the kind of phenomenon to be studied. Questioning the taken-for-granted dominance of formal logic thus points the way to the strategic importance of "nonlogical" and "non-empirical" methods as an explicit component of methodology in extensive research.[3]

From Empirical to Non-Empirical Methods

Accordingly it is instructive to consider those non-empirical (or perhaps, pre-empirical) methods that both complement and, in part, are presupposed by the empirical.[4] As we have argued, critical realism is able to acknowledge the interpretive foundations of inquiry while retaining a nonpositivist notion of causal explanation:

> We need to become more aware of rhetoric and the subtle interplay between object, author, reader, language, texts and moral judgments. It is not that we could ever evade rhetoric but that we need to distinguish forms of rhetoric which are better at grasping the nature of the world from those which are inferior. . . . As such the close

examination of accounts need not be merely a form of talk about talk, but a more self-aware form of talk about how we understand our world. . . . . *Future discussions of method in social science will presumably push in this direction of the examination of rhetoric, description and language* [italics added] (A. Sayer 1992, pp. 265-6)

Indeed, to speak of "non-empirical" methods may appear initially like a contradiction in terms; yet the term *empirical methods* does imply other types. Such an impression is indicative of the persuasiveness of positivist assumptions in our culture. The implication of the exclusiveness of empirical methods is that they need no recourse for justification except to themselves and their relation to the empirical facts. But the practice of social research reveals otherwise. One of the tasks of a critical theory of methodology is thus to bring these background features of research into the foreground so that they may receive the same kind of scrutiny and criticism to which other methodological procedures are subjected in the course of training and research itself. As *cognitive skills* pertinent to the production and evaluation of research, they need to be made more explicit as rational procedures of scientific practice. Our objective is primarily to identify some of the key types of such non-empirical methods and their general implications, rather than to provide an exhaustive account of their specific forms.

Types of Reflexivity:
Non-Empirical Methods

The identification of methodology with a theory of argumentation helps clarify this issue (Morrow 1991b). Clearly, non-empirical methods contribute to argumentation—and to the *rational* justification of theories, even if by different means. In other words, the notion of non-empirical methods follows from the antifoundationalist "reflexive thesis" (Ashmore 1989) about the nature of scientific knowledge discussed previously. Further, empirical argumentation is inconceivable with prior decisions about both metatheoretical and normative assumptions, as well as the existential implications of the research process for participants. To be sure, these latter assumptions do not normally come into play in the day-to-day routines of research practice, but they are necessary for beginning work and may reappear during a research crisis, the writing up of results, or the defense or use of such work in public. Recognizing the rhetorical foundations of all science, therefore, does not necessarily impugn its rationality.[5]

This section is concerned with several basic types of non-empirical argumentation or rhetorical strategies. Broadly these can all be characterized as *reflexive methods* in the sense that they involve forms of cognition (which also involve emotional responses) that go beyond research techniques narrowly understood as merely a process of matching concepts and data. The first type is familiar in that we have already introduced it indirectly with reference to aspects of *metatheoretical argumentation* or philosophical (rational) criticism, especially the status of "logic" as a part of methodology. The second form involves the contextualization and discursive reading of research—as in "reviews of the literature"—and presents the possibility of *deconstructive* and *historicist argumentation* as part of theory evaluation. The third involves self-reflexivity and the resulting *existential argumentation*. The fourth takes up another strategic concern of critical theories: *normative argumentation*. As we argue, though such types of non-empirical or reflexive argumentation are acknowledged specifically as part of social theorizing, they largely are excluded as nonscientific within the framework of logical empiricist accounts of research. An important aspect of a critical methodology as we understand it is thus the conscious use of these non-empirical methods in the setting up, execution, writing up, and application of research.

The character of these modes of interrogation as methods is evident from various perspectives, even if they obviously differ from empirical methods. First, they partake of the process of scientific argumentation. Second, they involve rational procedures that, in a meaningful sense, can be taught and learned. Third, they are related to both the process of discovery and strategies of validation, especially in their complementary relation to empirical methods. The strategic role of these non-empirical methods is revealed in histories of sociological research informed by the *sociology of knowledge*, though it is often difficult to document many aspects of research traditions. Feminist theory has been especially important in clarifying the importance of non-empirical methods in contemporary research.

Positivist Research and Non-Empirical Methods

In principle, of course, non-empirical methods are recognized in positivist conceptions of research even if they are not usually termed as such. What is most important, however, is because they are put in the background rather than the foreground, assumptions with regard to such procedures require only minimal justification due to the way they can invoke the authority of the reigning positivism in methodology training. A brief review of typical, largely implicit assumptions is thus instructive.

Logical Essentialism

Although formal logic is often almost equated with the definition of empirical methods as statistical methods, this comparison obscures the status of logic as a non-empirical method. This conflation is possible because logic and empirical research are seen as one, rather than logic simply as a rhetorical resource for research. In this context logic is associated closely with consistency even though the history of science suggests that all research programs are characterized by high levels of internal inconsistency and the results are not nearly so grave as suggested by propositional logic (Harré 1986, p. 5). The major problem here is that this characterization excessively narrows the forms of "logical" criteria that may be pertinent to assessing evidence of comparing theories. The ideological function performed by logical essentialism in scientistic discourse is perhaps evident in the fact that courses in formal logic are not required for advanced training in the social sciences.

Antihistoricism and Logocentrism

Another dogma of the logical empiricist tradition is the rigid distinction between the logic of discovery and the logic of verification. In Merton's terms the history of sociological theory must be distinguished clearly from its "systematics" as defined by theory construction and verification (Merton 1968). On these grounds all histories of social theory are regarded as ornamental and not contributing to the construction of real theories. The resulting *antihistoricism* thus deems the history of social theory and scientific disciplines as irrelevant to their current practice. In other words, the problem of grounding theory is effectively ignored by being hidden under the umbrella of formalism and logical essentialism.

Further, logical essentialism is a manifestation of *logocentrism*—a term used by the French poststructuralist philosopher Jacques Derrida to describe a foundationalist conception of truth that denies the significance of the linguistic basis of all forms of representation (Derrida 1976). According to this deconstructionist perspective, this description reflects a "metaphysics of presence" underlying Western philosophy from Plato onward. The metaphysical assumption is that language refers directly to something present and outside of itself in an unproblematic way. In other words, the referential functions of language are taken for granted, and the fluidity of meaning in all texts is ignored.

Logocentrism is another way of understanding antihistoricism: as a prohibition of reflection on the operation (and historicity) of scientific languages as part of the research process. Purification of natural language and its transformation into formal languages remains the unreflected ideal of positivism, one of the most extreme forms of logocentrism.

Existential Reflexivity:
The Objective Observer

Related to the previous three themes, all linked to the tenacious hold of logical essentialism, is the notion that science at its best is a dispassionate activity carried out at the highest possible level of decontextualization and formalization. In this muted way, positivist discourse recognizes the reality of *existential reflexivity* as an aspect of the research process. But unlike in hermeneutic theories, where "prejudices" are held to be essential to interpretation, the subjectivity of the researcher should be eliminated through acts of depersonalization, as well as decontextualization. Bias thus is associated exclusively with the distortion of reasoning powers, hence the stress on an abstract, universal, and ultimately God-like "male" subject of knowledge.

Normative Theory: Value Freedom

Of the many complex issues at stake here, three aspects of what have at times been referred as the *value-free position* can serve as illustrations of typical positivist positions in the social sciences. First, it is held that good social science cannot be combined with the value concerns of researchers. Disinterested inquiry thus becomes synonymous with good research. Second, because normative theorizing is basically a question of mere beliefs, it is held to have no logical relation to empirical theory that is strictly scientific. Accordingly, normative theorizing may have a place in the political sphere or private life, but not social science. And third, it is conceded that there are some tangential value questions for social research—that is, those relating to the problematic of the ethics of research. But ethics here is defined in rather narrow terms usually related to the rights of the subjects to be investigated (e.g., problems of confidentiality, invasion of privacy). The larger ideological implications of research are for the most part excluded from the "ethics" question in standard methodology texts. Or alternatively one often finds a form of cynicism that suggests the irrational character of value questions permits everyone to have a "point of view" that is just as good as any other—a "liberalism" that is often a mask for opportunism or irresponsibility.

Critical Theory and Non-Empirical Methods

Logics-in-Use

Although the point of departure of critical theory is a critique of positivism's logical essentialism, it does not require an outright rejection of formal logic; the consequence is rather that formal logic is conceptualized as part of a set of heuristic (and rhetorical) devices that can, in the appropriate context, instruct argumentation. But it also directs attention to context-dependent logical criteria: *logics-in-use* that are understood implicitly by practitioners, though not necessarily recognized as such. The role of informal logical procedures is especially obvious in ethnographic inquiry where establishing the communicative relations necessary for participant observation is required. And it is implicit in the experience of students whose "hands-on" instruction in research through apprenticeship is more valuable than formal exercises in theory construction or the mastery of statistical procedures. Such practical logics do not admit formalization and can only be indirectly (and generally ineffectively) presented in how-to manuals. To its credit, *ethnomethodology* has from the outset been a primary source of studies that enhance methodological reflexivity, especially in the context of analyzing the research interview as a social process (Cicourel 1964). But the basic insight is expanded and elaborated in other directions in a critical theory of methodology.

Historicist and Deconstructive Reflexivity

The basic idea underlying what we refer to as *historicist argumentation* is that knowledge of the context and conditions in which particular research findings are produced can be relevant to their evaluation and ultimate validation. The point is not to deny the partial validity of the classic distinction between the logic of justification and the logic of discovery. By itself, historicist argumentation cannot provide convincing evidence of the validity of specific theories or studies. But to take a trivial example to illustrate this point, if we are informed that a scientist has purposely falsified or fabricated data in order to produce a piece of research, we do indeed have plausible grounds for calling into question the validity of the results. Of course, even though a valid theory may be corroborated by faked evidence, this does not falsify the theory. The point is rather that issues regarding the conditions of the production of scientific knowledge provide an important reference point for comparatively weighing the relative merits of various rational and evidential criteria for deciding between rival theories. Indeed this concern with historical grounding is one of the defining characteristics of critical theory (Calhoun 1992b, pp. 258-9).

The most common (and all too often abused) traditional form of the strategy is some variant of the "blindspot" or *ad hominem* argument that aspects of a particular author's theory is deficient because of circumstances of its production (e.g., contract research) or characteristics of its producer (e.g., political party associations, sexual orientations). Again, such links by themselves cannot prove the falsity of the argument, of course, and can be subjected to misuse. But such questioning about the contexts of theoretical activity does provide primae facie evidence for difficulties and may facilitate the formulation of suggestive research questions. Such non-empirical arguments are clearly productive for methodology if properly used (as with any technique). For example, recent work on the role of "fashions" in social science is suggestive here (Sperber 1990). In other words, as Mannheim (1936) argued long ago, the sociology of knowledge—understood as a form of critical hermeneutics—should be an integral part of social research methodology.

These issues have been radicalized in a somewhat different though complementary way in so-called *deconstructionist* approaches to literary and academic discourse (Agger 1991).[6] *Deconstructive* inquiry originally was associated with the poststructuralist textual theories of Jacques Derrida (Derrida 1991).[7] A central theme of this approach is a critique of naive realism (logocentrism) as a means of understanding how we represent "reality." The application of deconstructive (and other related) techniques of reading facilities through a kind of rhetorical analysis that shows how language mediates our understanding and has provided important new interpretations of theory and research processes (Edmondson 1984; Green 1988; Simons 1989, 1990; Brown 1992; Hunter 1990). Although some have turned this ultimately "undecidable" character of interpretation and representation into postmodernist claims that social science is a rhetorical illusion, others have increasingly drawn up deconstructive techniques as a resource for methodological practice (Agger 1989, 1991).[8]

Existential Reflexivity: Insider Knowledge

All scientific knowledge is grounded in the lifeworld, common sense, and everyday life. Although the elaboration of scientific knowledge as a paramount reality requires the institutionalization of un-common sense in scientific communities, these same communities must return continually to their point of origin. But as hermeneutic theorists such as Gadamer (1975) have stressed, our interpretive skills are grounded in, and only become possible through, our experiences and prejudices; denying or suppressing them can only distort the communication process and our ability to interpret others. And as feminists have shown, absence of attention to the "experience" of women has called into question the sociological enterprise (D. Smith 1990) and has contributed to various attempts to incorporate insider knowledge as a credible technique of investigation (Lather 1991; J. Nielsen 1990). But it is also necessary to acknowledge that standpoint theorizing (or insider knowledge) can be used as a resource and claim for any social group and that mediating principles of knowledge (even if not formalized universalism) become necessary for a comprehensive understanding of social life across existential differences.

Further, there is the potential danger of infinite regress into expressions of difference within a given interpretive community. The interpretive character of knowledge does produce the apparent paradox of the *hermeneutic circle,* which involves an endless process of interpretation and precludes any absolutely "correct" one. These matters are complicated further by the epistemological differences that separate distinctive standpoints defined by the interplay of historical contexts and social positions. But as Gadamer argues, such interpretive differences do not altogether preclude the possibility of a *fusion of horizons* that allows otherwise apparently incommensurate and incompatible viewpoints to come to recognize shareable understandings that are the foundations of a social science that would aspire to speak only in terms of fragmented voices. To be sure, the positivist dream of purely ahistorical, decontextualized, formal, and invariant social theory fails to understand the essential historical character of social inquiry.

Normative Theory:
The Rationality of Critique

As a discursive practice, normative argumentation is so pervasive that we rarely stop to consider that it is a *rational* technique of persuasion. And when we do become aware at moments, normative argumentation usually is associated with the irrational—the intrusion of emotionally and blindly held beliefs.

But this exclusive stress on the irrationality of value judgments is misleading when we consider that in the context of *practical* reasoning we continuously uphold normative or value propositions that are entirely unproblematic and without doubt rational in every sense: Children should not play with fire; fraud is unjust. And yet even positivist accounts of methodology give value judgments a marginal place under the heading of the "ethics of research," thus implying that such questions can be subject to rational debate, at least at the level of "professional ethics." Such examples imply, in short, that different types of value claims—as with the case of empirical knowledge—admit to different degrees of consensual validation in different contexts and that, most crucially, such claims are more or less subject to rational argumentation. After all, when scientists have committed their entire research career to the defense of particular theory, should we consider them to be any less liable to an emotional distortion of evidence than someone whose religious belief is challenged rationally? Moreover, if a particular stubbornness facilitated the original discovery in the first place, should we expect scientists to suddenly abandon it every time falsifying evidence is brought forward? In short, *if the postempiricist philosophy of science has downgraded the formal rationality of scientific practice, it has also implicitly upgraded the (potential) practical rationality of normative reasoning and related social practices.*

With respect to the three issues taken up in the context of positivism's typical stances toward normative issues, critical theory has taken opposing positions. First, it is argued that knowledge is inherently interested (as in the case of the theory of knowledge interests). Second, it is generally acknowledged that normative and empirical reasoning have much more in common than generally held and that social theory and normative theory are inevitably intertwined. Whatever dangers to empirical research may be involved can be dealt with most adequately by confronting them directly, rather than arguing abstractly for an impossible exclusion of normative questions. Third, it is argued that the conventional "ethics of research" approach tends to trivialize many crucial larger value questions and has in important ways served more to protect research institutions from controversy than to protect innocent clients.

An implication of the importance of normative theorizing is that it should become a more systematic part of the curriculum of the social sciences, rather than fragmented as ad hoc evaluations added on in some domains and largely ignored in others. For example, discussions about the welfare state, women, and social problems generally are rife with explicit and implicit value judgments, but rarely coupled with an examination of the relevant theoretical discourses (e.g., theories of justice) implicated. Because these more technical normative theoretical discussions have tended to be carried by philosophers and political scientists, other social scientists—especially sociologists—have virtually no systematic training in normative theory (Kymlicka 1990; Goodin 1988; Doyal and Gough 1991). Feminist theory is the primary exception here, partly because its interdisciplinary character has allowed it to take into account the work of philosophers and political theorists (Hanen and Nielsen 1987). And for critical theory the issues of normative theorizing are implicated from the outset, especially in the form of a *communicative ethics* (Benhabib 1986, 1992; Benhabib and Dallmayr 1990). The tasks involved in the relationship between empirical social science, as opposed to ethical theory and social policy, have been defined comprehensively as those of a *social ethics* that at present has no official status in the curriculum of the social sciences even though bioethics is now recognized in the medical field (T. Smith 1991, pp. ix-x).

Is There a Dialectical Method?

Critical Theory Versus Analytical Marxism

At this point we wish to return to several questions that have been lurking in the background: Does critical theory have a distinctive method? and if so, is it usefully called "dialectical"? Recall that at the outset we did refer to the metatheory of critical theory as a hermeneutic-dialectical one. But in what sense does that imply, if at all, *dialectical methods*? Although this is a term we generally avoid due to the confusion it generates, it is not irrelevant to our project.

Ironically the dominant contemporary neo-Marxist theory has attempted to salvage some of the core analytical elements of historical materialism through abandonment of any assumptions about its methodological uniqueness understood in dialectical terms. For example, *analytical Marxists* are characterized by the assumption that Marxist theory cannot be defined in methodological terms where this refers "to strategies for concept formation, theory construction, the 'logic' of justification and discovery, and related issues that contemporary philosophers of science conventionally designate 'methodology.' So understood, most analytical Marxists implicitly reject the view that Marxism is distinguished by its method"(Levine 1989, p. 34). The reason is that "Marxists aim to provide causal explanations in the familiar sense" (Levine 1989, p. 35).[9] For these kinds of reasons, critical theory as an alternative to classical Marxism is summarily rejected: "The ideas of a critical, directly emancipatory or otherwise 'practical' theory—and *a fortiori* of less developed extra-scientific explanatory agendas—has yet to be satisfactorily defended" (Levine 1989, p. 38). Accordingly any definition of either Marxism or critical theory "would be distinguished, at most, by the *particular configuration of methodological postures it embraces*" [italics added] (Levine 1989, p. 38), hence not a "unique" methodology that defines the approach as such.

We feel quite comfortable with the suggestion that critical theory can be defined by the "particular configuration of methodological postures it embraces," and indeed this has been the central theme of this book. But Levine's dismissive response to critical theory links the uniqueness of method to the monolithic logic of causal theorizing and obscures the practical significance of particular configurations of methodological postures of the type that help define a research program. As previously noted, critical theory is eclectic with respect to the use of techniques of investigation. What is distinctive is their use within a particular "system of inquiry":

> Methods, then, take their validity and reliability from their participation in a particular system of inquiry. . . . Particular methods do not operate independently of a system of inquiry; the use of a method changes only as a researcher uses it in different systems of inquiry. . . . The meaning of a particular research conduct is

determined by the context of its system of going after 'knowledge.' " (Polkinghorne 1983, p. 6)

On our account, for example, interpretive structural explanations are the basis of theorizing in critical theory. As such, this
basis is not unique to critical theory as it was practiced widely
by classical and historical sociologists and even is by some neo-
functionalist researchers today. *The claim to methodological
distinctiveness lies, rather, at the level of the research program
within which such explanatory strategies are privileged.* As a
research program ultimately linked to a critical-emancipatory
knowledge interest, critical theory is distinguished clearly by a
distinctive approach to methodology as a set of metatheoretical
assumptions and privileged research design strategies, a core set
of substantive commitments related to the analysis of crisis tendencies in advanced capitalism, and an explicit approach to normative
theory and its relation to critique of ideologies. In this weaker
sense, critical theory clearly has a distinctive methodology, and
one that goes beyond any strict definition of "science" even if a
number of other orientations closely approximate this, for example, certain types of feminist research, and cultural Marxism.

This methodological strategy is dialectical primarily in the sense
that it presupposes an ontology of social reality that recognizes
peculiar properties of social phenomena that are largely ignored
by naturalistic ontologies. For example, Ollman identifies these
dialectical properties with moving from the whole to parts, a
process that "is primarily directed to finding and tracing four
kinds of relations: identify-difference, interpenetration of oppo-
sites, quantity/quality, and contradiction" (Ollman 1993, p. 13).
Further, he recognizes that many non-Marxist thinkers' work
with similar ontological assumptions (e.g., Hegel and the process philosophy of Alfred North Whitehead) and that "elements
of dialectics can be found in other social science methods, such
as structural functionalism, systems theory, and ethnomethodology" (Ollman 1993, p. 18).

A fundamental problem here is the tendency of those attempting to justify a dialectical methodology in the strong sense to fall
back on a logical essentialist strategy—that is, the search for a
unified, reconstructed dialectical logic and linking this with
Marx's analysis of capital. More fruitful would seem to be a more

pragmatic understanding of many logics-in-use involving a dialectical understanding of social reality. Hence it appears problematic to start out with a search for "dialectical methods," as opposed to methods (of many different kinds) that may, in fact, illuminate an object of inquiry with dialectical properties. Or, as we have done, address the configuration of methodological postures that contribute to this end without implying—as does Ollman's orthodox stance—that all of the crucial aspects of contemporary society can be derived from understanding the logic of capital, however dialectically carried out.

Beyond Totality as "The Dialectic"

Is, therefore, this system of inquiry—what we have called a strategy of theorizing based on interpretive structuralist models of social and cultural reproduction—itself "dialectical"? The functionalist theory of totality developed by Lukacs and early critical theory was clearly dialectical in this strong sense. In the original version of Critical Theory developed by Max Horkheimer, the notion of a *dialectical methodology* was associated explicitly with the Hegelian concept of *totality* as the basis for a philosophy of history that would guide sociological research. In the version of critical theory proposed by Habermas, however, the classic theory of totality is abandoned for a more attenuated reference to dialectical concepts, primarily at the level of metatheory of the subject-object relation:[10]

> The concept of dialectic is explicated in a number of ways. The unifying thread seems to be "the insight that the research process organized by subjects belongs—through the very act of knowing itself—to the complex that is supposed to be known." . . . Critical theory is doubly reflective: it is self-conscious of its origins in the historical development of society, and it is self-conscious of its role in the further development of society. (McCarthy 1978, p. 135)

Similarly Giddens's notion of the double hermeneutic of social theory is dialectical in this sense:

> Sociology, unlike natural science, stands in a subject-subject relation to its "field of study," not a subject-object relation; it deals with

a pre-interpreted world, in which the meanings developed by active
subjects actually enter into the actual constitution or production
of that world; the construction of social theory thus involves a
double hermeneutic that has no parallel elsewhere; and finally the
logical status of generalizations is in a very significant way distinct
from that of natural scientific laws. (Giddens 1976, p. 146)

For these kinds of reasons we have preferred to speak of the
methodology of critical theory in terms of an interpretive structuralist approach to social history (social and cultural reproduction) coupled with a normative framework for assessing the
relations of domination revealed by such investigations. Further,
although critical theory in principle aspires to inform transformative action, there is no historical guarantee of this. In short,
on the one hand, the analytical Marxist rejection of "the dialectic" in the form presupposed by the Marxist tradition's theory
of history from Marx through Horkheimer is shared by critical
theory. On the other hand, critical theory also necessarily insists
that the latent positivism of analytical Marxism blinds it to the
multiple logics-in-use that make up creative and credible social
research. In this respect the debate about dialectics is far from
over but goes beyond our present purposes.[11]

Conclusion

Reflexive methods are more central to the formation and self-
criticism within a research community than to the typical conduct of a particular research project. This is one reason that such
issues have been neglected; they can routinely be taken for granted
as part of the socialization process of membership within a
particular discipline and research approach. However, during
times of internal debate and change, such concerns often become
central to day-to-day activities within a research community.
Also much of the reflexive methodological work is carried about
by specialists in those kinds of activities: Historians of disciplines, theorists, and methodologists all may contribute frequently
to these kinds of debates. Also outsiders (in applied fields, or a
discipline such as philosophy or intellectual history) may be

crucial to this process and feed back on a discipline itself. In other words, all research communities use reflexive methods whether self-consciously or not. Critical theory, however, makes such issues a central concern of social inquiry and attempts to link them up to the more visible issues of empirical techniques and strategies of inquiry.

Further, critical theory is not only distinctive in its concern with reflexive methods but also dialectical in its use of empirical techniques. This statement does not imply a specific dialectical method, but it does suggest a distinctive theoretical strategy based on the agency-structure dialectic. This strategy involves the form of theorizing that we previously have labeled "interpretive structuralism" and whose theoretical reach was considered briefly under the heading of limited "comparative generalization." The task of the next chapter is to explore some of the ramifications of this approach with respect to the empirical procedures of social inquiry in the context of intensive research designs.

Notes

1. "The giving of primacy to logical structures as the inner essence of discourse has had a disastrous effect in philosophy of science, vividly illustrated by the implausibility of Hempel's account of scientific explanation. The same doctrine appears again in Popper's early form of fallibilism . . . Logic does have a place in the creation of scientific discourse, but not at its core. That is formed by semantic structures, and relations of likeness and difference. A clear-eyed look at the cognitive and material practices of the scientific community will reveal that logic is a socially motivated addition, a rhetorical contribution to persuasive power" (Harré 1986, pp. 4-5).

2. Versions of this postempiricist "logic as rhetoric" argument have been developed by critical realists (Harré), post-Wittgensteinian linguistic philosophy (Toulmin), and the tradition of rhetoric developed in Chaim Perelman's argumentation theory: "The formalization of language, far from being natural to it, is the result of a previous effort of understanding, rooted in contextual implications, which one does away with in order to clarify. . . . Perelman does not grant privilege to the logico-mathematical aspect because there is no discourse without an audience; hence, no argumentation without rhetorical effect. Argumentation and rhetoric are linked. The relation to the audience is the search for its agreement; and the rhetorical strategies are the means" (Meyer 1986, pp. 92-4). Such conceptions of logic also can be traced back to Dewey's pragmatism (Dewey 1938) and, in the German tradition, to the constructivist conception of the "logic of

reflection" and its "dialogical interpretation of logic. Particular knowledges are things done, or constructed. They have a primary location, in other words, in *practice*; they do not hover in a depersonalised realm based on pure description" (Roberts 1992, p. 285).

3. This is not to say that non-empirical methods are insignificant in extensive research, so much as trivialized by the methodological canons associated with most statistically based research, which, by design, attempt to eliminate their need as much as possible. On the contrary, intensive research designs require, by their very nature, greater concern with these issues; further, from a postempiricist perspective, concern with non-empirical issues becomes a requirement of the rational problem solving in a research tradition (e.g., Guba 1990).

4. In a pioneering exploration of these issues, Baldamus notes that he originally was driven to ask such questions because of concern about the ideological evaluation of theories, independent of evidence. Only later did he realize this was not only a fundamental problem but also a resource for a more reflective methodological concern with political and politically neutral "*non-empirical* procedures" (Baldamus 1976, p. vii), a topic opened up by Ludwig Fleck's work (which later influenced Thomas Kuhn) on the role of collective error in scientific discovery.

5. Hence as a sociologist recently concludes, consistent with postempiricist critical realism: "It is not that Science is 'reduced' to rhetoric and thus rendered corrupt and useless. It is rather that the rhetorical component seems to be unavoidable if the work is to have a theoretical or policy relevance. Thus an analysis of scientific work should also include its rhetorical as well as its empirical component" (Gusfield, cited in Simons 1990, p. 10).

6. Moreover, these arguments often are presented as completely novel, when in fact they have been with the social sciences for more than half a century; one would have only to replace Mannheim's sociology of knowledge with "postmodernism" to agree with Lather that "postmodernism foregrounds an awareness of our own structuring impulses and their relation to the social order" (Lather 1991, p. 89). To be sure, many of these issues can now be taken up in a more sophisticated way and, more importantly, gender has been added to the arsenal of understanding "structuring impulses."

7. The term *deconstruction* is used increasingly loosely to refer to virtually any type of rhetorical analysis that calls into question naively realistic and unreflexive conceptions of representation. But the more technical sense refers to Derrida's approach, which has been defined succinctly as follows: "To deconstruct a discourse is to show how it undermines the philosophy it asserts, or the hierarchical oppositions on which it relies, by identifying in the text the rhetorical operations that produce the supposed ground of argument, the key concept or premise" (Culler 1982, p. 86).

8. In some discussions the concept of *deconstructive methods* (e.g., Lather 1991, p. 90) has been expanded somewhat to incorporate a broad range of reflexive issues that we separate out under distinctive headings.

9. In practice, however, the methodology of analytical Marxism has tended to imply two basic and often conflicting research strategies: attempts to rigorously justify the explanatory value of the base-superstructure model in functional terms (G. A. Cohen) or to revitalize a reconstructed production-based class analysis (E. O. Wright); and the application of the methods of neo-classical economics

(e.g., game and rational choice theory, optimization theory, general equilibrium theory) to issues posed by Marxist theory (Jon Elster, John Roemer). All of these strategies remain vulnerable to the limitations of positivist methodologies generally. The present study contends that there are a number of other credible methodological postures besides these and that they are generally more relevant to the research program of critical theory. This contention does not preclude, to be sure, that the latter may incorporate selectively findings or theoretical propositions developed by analytical Marxists (e.g., Carlin 1991).

10. For a useful reconstruction of such a defensible conception of a "rehumanized dialectic" compatible with both Giddens's structuration theory and Habermas, see Rachlin 1991.

11. See most recently, Rachlin (1991), Ollman (1993), T. Smith (1993), and, above all, the recent study by Roy Bhaskar (1993) on dialectics.

10

EMPIRICAL PROCEDURES
IN CRITICAL RESEARCH

The cult of technical specialization cannot be overcome by abstract and irrelevant humanistic demands. . . . The path of true humanism leads thorough the midst of the specialized and technical problems, insofar as one succeeds in gaining insight into their significance within the societal whole and in drawing conclusions from this. (Frankfurt Institute for Social Research 1972, p. 127)

The following proposition recommends itself as essentially true: methodology can only bring us reflective understanding of the means which have demonstrated their value in practice by raising them to the level of explicit consciousness; it is no more the precondition of fruitful intellectual work than the knowledge of anatomy is the precondition for "correct" walking. . . . Such discussions can become important for the enterprise of science only when, as a result of considerable shifts of the "viewpoint" from which a datum becomes the object of analysis, the idea emerges that the new "viewpoint" also requires a revision of the logical forms in which the "enterprise" has heretofore operated, and when, accordingly, uncertainty about the "nature" of one's work arises. (Weber 1949, pp. 115-6)

Explanation and Interpretation in Social Science

Introduction

As we have seen in the discussion of metatheory and reflexive procedures, critical theory attempts to avoid the extremes of the interpretivist reduction of explanation to meaning descriptions and

248

the positivist search for invariant laws. At this point we need to flesh out this question more fully with reference to the types of research this kind of approach to explanation suggests. Another way of characterizing social explanations is to note that they are "relatively incomplete, approximate and contestable" (A. Sayer 1992, p. 232). The problem here is not so much that some methods are intrinsically "appropriate" and others not, so much as "what is or isn't appropriate can only be decided by reference to judgments about the nature of the thing to be explained" (A. Sayer 1992, p. 232). It is in this context that this chapter *privileges* certain research designs and techniques of analysis; if so, it is because they are more appropriate for answering the questions posed by the theoretical program of contemporary critical theory. Obviously the search, say, for a formalized "general theoretical sociology" would privilege quite different research designs and techniques (Fararo 1989).

As the postempiricist theory of science suggests, explanations come in a wide variety of forms. As a kind of social act based on demands within a society for making sense of things, social scientific explanations are significantly differentiated from those of common sense, despite significant overlaps. This chapter is concerned with two different types of explanatory strategies in the context of intensive research designs.

The first type assumes a basically causal form in that the object of inquiry is to identify the generative mechanisms underlying the historically contingent production of a particular phenomenon. As noted previously, the objective of *causal depth*—a notion consistent with structuralist-type explanations—has particular importance for critical theory, given its concern with the fundamental contradictions within social life.

The second explanatory strategy is not strictly causal and involves, first, the identification of empirical regularities as represented in the narrative structures of texts and actions. Such accounts go beyond the purely descriptive approach of *Verstehen*-type analysis by introducing theoretical accounts of the mechanisms involved in meaning production and reception. Second, such accounts in the sociology of culture also may involve historical interpretations of the genesis of particular meaning systems, but not in a way that makes any claim to be a strictly causal explanation.[1]

Extensive Versus Intensive Research Designs

In standard methodology texts, research design usually is reduced to a single type, ultimately related back to the logic of experimentation: aggregate analysis of variables in the form of what we have—following Andrew Sayer—termed *extensive research designs*. This strategy defines the objects of research in a very distinctive way, requiring a very large number of cases (a representative sample), a process that also demands reducing the number of their properties analyzed. If we construct a national survey, for example, it is possible to consider only a few characteristics of individuals as the basis for comparison and generalizations. Because of all of the potentially relevant properties of diverse individuals, it becomes problematic to attribute causality (despite sophisticated statistical techniques) to the few actually chosen as the basis for comparing these diverse individuals. Such research designs are linked closely with the social engineering model of theorizing discussed previously.

In contrast *intensive research designs* take the opposite path by considering small numbers of cases in terms of a great number of individual properties. The primary question becomes that of explicating the operations of causal processes and meaning structures in a single or limited number of cases. This procedure requires asking very different questions and employing very different methodological techniques, largely (but not exclusively) qualitative in nature. The concept of *variables* may be employed but not in a statistically defined way. Such an explicative approach to critical theory—and what we previously called *social theorizing*—can be described usefully in terms of the research work that would provide an alternative to both "abstracted empiricism and positivist grand theory" without falling into the abyss of postmodernist relativism.[2]

Intensive Research Designs

Research Designs and Case Study Methods

A research design is "the logical sequence that connects the empirical data to a study's initial research questions and, ultimately to its conclusions" (Yin 1984, p. 29). More specifically that involves five components: "(1) a study's questions; (2) its propositions, if any; (3) its unit(s) of analysis; (4) the logical linking of the data to the propositions; and (5) the criteria for interpreting the findings" (Yin 1984, p. 29). In this section we consider four types of intensive research designs based on case studies: historical analysis, ethnography, participatory action research, and discourse analysis.[3]

At this point it is appropriate to reiterate the systematic significance of the crucial point made in the preceding chapter regarding the *comparative* nature of all social knowledge, a point lost by the ideographic-nomothetic polarization. The *ideographic approach* assumes a completely unique case as the unit of analysis, thus obscuring that we can comprehend a case only through our knowledge of similar ones. In contrast, *nomothetic theorizing* reduces "cases" to representative samples of artificial characteristics such that the individual instance becomes a manifestation of a universal law. From the perspective of intensive research designs, each case resembles others of that type, which allows construction of limited generalizations, as well as explications of the individual case.

Further, we wish to link this point closely with the primacy of case study methods in intensive research. Recent indications are that the centrality of the case study to social research has been rediscovered (Hamel 1992; Ragin and Becker 1992). Although the question of identifying "cases" has provoked considerable disagreement, the extensive/intensive research design distinction allows a clear-cut association of variable analysis with extensive designs, and case study methods with intensive ones.

Obviously case studies are not unique to critical research and become associated with the latter only when they address theoretical questions within its research program. Further, it needs to be stressed that the case study is at the heart of a number of research strategies that have been central to critical theory. For example, analytic case studies differ from historical research primarily in having contemporary access to the phenomenon, thus making systematic observation and interviewing possible (Silverman 1985). And they differ from traditional ethnographies due to a stronger "explanatory" (as opposed to interpretive) focus and do not necessarily depend on detailed participant observation (e.g., a largely quantitative archival analysis may be the base of a case study). Similar problems emerge in comparative ethnographic studies in anthropology (Holy 1987).

At the same time, the complementarity of individual explication (an ostensibly ideographic exercise) and comparative generalization (a weakly nomothetic activity) lies in their mutual necessity: One cannot even begin to describe a "case" without a sense of "types" of cases and their shared properties (including explanatory generalities, even if historically specific to a type). Some of the issues involved in the interplay between critical research and case study methods can be reviewed by reference to several influential research strategies that have been used by critical researchers: historical and comparative sociology, ethnography and participant observation, and participatory action research. Of these, only the last could be seen in some sense as specific to critical theory, and indeed is sometimes identified with it. As we argue later, however, the significance of a research method is closely related to the theoretical problematic within which it is elaborated.

Historical and Comparative Sociology

Historical sociology is the method most closely associated with the tradition of Marx's historical materialism; today it remains the most common strategy associated with empirical research influenced by critical theory. Indeed it is possible to reconstruct Marx's original method as a form of undogmatic historical sociology whose attention to historical contingency makes it largely compatible with the non-Marxist approach of Anthony Giddens (D. Sayer 1983, 1987, 1991). Similarly more recently Max Weber's comparative historical sociology has been reconstructed as a "configurational" macrosciological method capable of identifying the interaction of institutional and cultural factors, as well as the carriers of social transformation (Kalberg 1992). Only from the perspective of a positivist search for nomothetic laws could history and sociology be held to be quite separate activities: one in search of general laws, the other of unique events or their succession in time: "But this kind of separation has no rational justification: with the discovery of temporality as integral to social theory, history and sociology become methodologically indistinguishable" (Giddens 1979, p. 8).

Such considerations suggest a somewhat different perspective on the nature of case study research, especially the contrast between qualitative and quantitative uses of the comparative method. Our central contention is that *case study methods coupled with nonstatistical comparative case studies are most compatible with the research problems identified by critical theory and its concern with intensive research designs.* As recent debates have suggested, the holistic nature of comparative research has led to the dominance of intensive, small comparisons over statistical analysis of large samples.[4]

The logic of small comparisons can be understood in terms of the *comparative method* as originally defined by John Stuart Mill: the methods of agreement and difference. In the first case, two otherwise different cases have a common outcome. Here explanation involves a search for the shared characteristic that is the effective cause of similarity. In the case of difference, two otherwise similar cases have a different outcome. Again the problem is finding the factor of difference that produces the difference. Either of these strategies can be effective for generating theories (Ragin 1987, pp. 44-5).

But the "comparative method" in this classic sense is only one possibility, given the three other main types of comparative historical analysis that have been identified: (a) applications of a general model to history, (b) the use of concepts for a meaningful historical interpretation, and (c) analysis of causal regularities in history (Skocpol 1984, p. 362). The first two of these are related directly to the research program of critical theory, which in its strong form presupposes a general model of societal evolution along the lines suggested by Habermas, though not one based on nomothetic explanatory assumptions. In the weak version proposed by Giddens, general models are limited to specific historical "episodes," given the reluctance to assume that such historical epochs fall into some kind of overall set of stages. Further, both of these assumptions about general models, then, become the basis for case studies—concrete historical investigations. In terms of our previous terminology, meaningful historical interpretation corresponds to our notion of explicating an individual case, whereas the general model or the analysis of causal regularities constitute variants of the generalizing case study method. In short, authors such as Habermas and Giddens have provided major contributions to a general model in their critiques of historical materialism. As well, they have provided suggestive discussions pertinent to pursuing case studies employing the other two strategies.

Ethnography and Participant Observation

Generally speaking, the explanatory problems posed by historical sociology are analogous to those of ethnography. Both may involve a focus on the structural, action, or mediational levels of social inquiry; and both employ an implicit comparative method when they invoke limited generalizations. In the context of ethnography, however, researchers are confronted through actual participation with "live" events whose meaning has immediate practical (and political) significance. In this connection, the notion of a "critical" ethnography poses different questions than in the case of historical research where this designation can be inferred from the explicit focus on relations of domination and resistance in the past.

Considerable ambiguity surrounds the question of the relationship between critical theory and ethnography, for example, what makes "critical" ethnography critical? The descriptive and contemporary focus of much ethnographic analysis would appear to be rather distant from the concerns with critical theory. The apparent exception might be ethnographic investigations linked with immediate social practice, but this does not serve well as a defining characteristic. Much of what is taken to be critical ethnography clearly is not praxis oriented in this sense. The decisive methodological aspect is perhaps that cultural description is carried out from the perspective of a *critical hermeneutics,* a theme developed in recent anthropological debates. As in the case of historical research, our necessary point of departure is situating critical theory in relation to complementary developments with respect to reflection on ethnographic methods (Clifford and Marcus 1986; Manganaro 1990), a question related to sociology's traditional concern with participant observation (Denzin 1989; Baugh 1990).

We thus are concerned here initially with ethnographic and case study analysis as a general research practice broadly shared by anthropology, sociology, and other disciplines. In the process we will be concerned with two overlapping contributions of critical ethnography beyond its descriptive and explanatory value: *cultural critique as defamiliarization* and *cultural critique as ideology critique*. Although these are in principle shared with historical research, they assume a more direct poignancy as part of field research, as opposed to the more arcane process of reconstructing historical processes through the interrogation of remote documents.

The contribution of ethnography to ideology critique assumes various more familiar forms in the context of the analysis of relations of imperial domination found in the formation of postcolonial societies, as well as the internal dynamics of class-divided, largely agrarian (peasant-based) societies. Both derive their critical force from particular strategies of comparison and ultimately are grounded in a critical hermeneutics oriented toward the demystification of hegemonic power relations.

The more general strategy of defamiliarization is less well known and has been reconstructed from recent work on ethnographic writing (Marcus and Fischer 1986). Such work (sometimes misleadingly labeled "postmodern ethnography") is interesting, in part, because of its demonstration of the uses of poststructuralist themes for critical purposes. In this respect it serves as a reflexive contribution to methodology, though one distinctive from the normative context of ideology critique.

More specifically, it is argued that realistic analysis of cultural forms, even when carried out in the name of empirically grounded ideology critique, has its limits. In other words, experimental forms of representation may be more insightful or effective, given the dialogical character of the reception and comparison of different forms of knowledge and perceptions of reality. This theme has long been recognized in various expressionist and surrealist critiques of realism in the arts. In this context two basic strategies of defamiliarization have been identified for ethnography. "Defamiliarization by epistemological critique" stems from travel to the exotic worlds on the margins of the Eurocentric universe and how this reacts back "to raise havoc with our settled ways of thinking and conceptualization" (Marcus and Fischer

1986, p. 138). "Defamiliarization by cross-cultural juxtaposition," on the other hand, "offers a more dramatic, up-front kind of cultural criticism. It is a matching of ethnography abroad with ethnography at home" (Marcus and Fischer 1986, p. 138). For example, Margaret Mead juxtaposed adolescence in Somoa and America in this provocatively critical way.

Defining critical ethnography in terms of strategies of ideology critique and defamiliarization helps make sense of a number of misunderstandings that swirl around the methodological status of critical ethnography. A circumstantial factor here is perhaps the tendency of some defenders of critical ethnography to stress its distinctiveness by focusing on political practice and breaking down the gap between researcher and object of research. Feminist exponents of critical ethnography express these elements most strongly in making ideology critique and praxis the defining moment of methodology (Lather 1991). This tactic sets the stage for an unsympathetic critic to define the problem in a problematic way: "The term 'critical ethnography' refers to a form of qualitative research that contrasts with more traditional approaches in being closely, perhaps one should say organically, linked to socialist and/or feminist politics" (Hammersley 1992, p. 97). Although this definition may be applicable to some forms of action research (as we will see in a moment), it scarcely touches on the deeper issues involving the intensive analysis concerned with combining interpretive understanding, causal analysis, and critique. As we have just seen, the deeper sources of ethnography's critical potential lies in its capacity for ideology critique and defamiliarization, not its immediate link with political causes.

Further, such a concretely politicized definition allows setting up a simplistic "known-down" set of arguments ultimately based on relativist and positivist premises. Above all, both critics and some defenders of an activist version of ethnography leap from general epistemological claims about the ultimate grounding of inquiry in knowledge interests in Habermas to a conception of the immediate transformative effects of the practice of such research—all in a manner quite inconsistent with Habermas's own intentions. This leap allows quasi-positivist critics to show how politicized approaches inherit most of the problems of validity in conventional research and then add some new ones: It presupposes a complex theory of society and its potential for transformation; it is supposed to be immediately political when ethnography takes time and corrective follow-up studies; in using the concept of *ideology* it cannot suspend judgments necessary for understanding the beliefs of others; and critical theory presupposes quasi-causal laws that are "given no attention in the discussions of their approach by critical ethnographers" (Hammersley 1992, p. 118). As Habermas explicitly warns, however, though a critical sociology necessarily resists reducing intentional action to behavioral responses, its hermeneutic dialogical approach still requires "discipline" and autonomy in the research process that is not adequately addressed by "action research" oriented toward immediate enlightenment.[5]

Participatory Action Research

By defining critical historical, case study, and ethnographic research in methodological terms that include reference to interpretation, explanation, and critique, we would also reaffirm the autonomy required of any research program. The specificity of critical research lies in its non-empirical reflexivity, combined with the use of case study methods for the purposes of the kind of comparative generalization and intensive explication involved with models of social and cultural reproduction.

At this point, however, we turn to the critical functions of ethnographic research in a stronger sense linked to political practice. One of the distinctive characteristics of critical research is that the kinds of questions asked relate to the dynamics of power and exploitation in ways that potentially are linked to practical interventions and transformations. Accordingly, from this perspective, engaged, *participatory action research* becomes a legitimate possibility, though not the exclusive basis for defining critical ethnography (Kemmis and McTaggart 1988a, 1988b; Lather 1991). Participatory action research is also closely related to *standpoint methodologies* in the sense that the researchers may, in fact, be studying themselves, or at least others in a similar situation (D. Smith 1990). This notion has been invoked most commonly for women, racial and ethnic groups, and alternative sexual orientations. Such possibilities perhaps are built into the very nature of *autobiographical* and *life history methods,* given the intimate relationship between the critical-emancipatory knowledge interest and individual development as mediated by collective awareness.

In this respect such inquiries may break with some of the methodological restrictions of participant observation by pushing the question of participation even further because the researcher no longer is assumed to be merely an "outsider" looking in. Standpoint methodologies thus assume that researchers are capable of full membership in the community to be observed, hence further eroding the expert/subject distinction. Further, this assumption is coupled with a moral obligation to participate, given awareness of the lived-experience of specific dominated groups. This approach has been most well developed in standpoint methodologies concerned with the unique "experience" of race and gender. And it is here that "action" research (a topic taken up in the concluding chapter) comes into its own in the dialogue of methodological strategies, as a special case of critical ethnography.

Narrative and Discourse Analysis

Introduction

Previously we have spoken of the "linguistic turn" as having had a decisive impact on the formulation of contemporary critical metatheory, especially as the basis of a critique of the traditional subject-object polarization. But a parallel development—what sometimes has been called a "narrative turn"—has had more practical consequences with respect to methodologies for the study of the production, interpretation, and reception of meanings in social life.

A limitation of Andrew Sayer's account of types of extensive and intensive explanation discussed above is that he does not adequately address the problems specific to interpretive research of the type associated with cultural and social psychological analysis whose "explanatory" objectives do not fully coincide with causal explanations of the origins of events. This limitation is also evident in efforts to make sense of the analysis resulting from the intensive explication involved in case studies prior to

and independently of their possible uses for comparative generalization. To be sure, he acknowledges that "interpretive understanding is presupposed by all these types of research, though
the extent to which it is problematized will depend on the topic:
e.g., cultural studies as opposed to economics" (A. Sayer 1992,
pp. 236-7). The concern here is neither with this question nor
the larger claim that ultimately all forms of social explanation
are narrative in character; instead we wish to address *narrative
analysis* of *discourse* as a specific methodological approach
central to ethnography, social psychology, and cultural studies—
issues that go beyond Sayer's consideration of intensive research
designs. He does address some of these issues in an appendix
concerned with the textual character of the presentation of knowledge in "a discussion of the narrative versus analysis debate, the
neglect of description and the influence of rhetoric" (A. Sayer
1992, p. 258). Perhaps Sayer's stress on structural explanations
is salutary, given the pervasiveness of postmodernist "textuali-
zation" of reality.

The study of narrative and discourse is concerned with the
analysis of meanings in social life. To the extent that such research
is allied with critical theory, however, it necessarily resists either
the interpretivist temptation to reduce meanings to free-floating
discourses and the positivist imperative of reducing them to
structural variables. The problem of meaning is not entirely
absent in most empiricist research (the primary exception being
radical behaviorism) but is handled in quite a different way,
primarily "attitude research." This problem represents perhaps
the most central concern of empiricist quantitative (extensive)
sociology, which attempts to measure attitudes and correlate them
with variables indicating social structures (e.g., income, education). As we shall see, however, the strategies for analyzing meaning in intensive research begin from very different assumptions.

To the extent that positivist approaches to methodology have
incorporated a concern with techniques specific to cultural analysis and texts, the method of *content analysis* has been the focus
of attention (Holsti 1969). Content analysis, of course, is defined
in empiricist methodological terms as a "research technique for
the objective, quantitative and systematic study of communications content. It involves charting or counting the incidence, or
co-incidence, of particular items belonging to a set of (usually)

predetermined categories" (Jary and Jary 1991, p. 117). For example, endless studies of advertising and television show the frequency with which particular racial or gender groups are depicted (or not) in particular roles.

The questions related to a non-empiricist analysis of meaning (whether in the context of social action or cultural texts) were broached in important ways in symbolic interactionism, the concern with interpretive understanding in the theory of *Verstehen* in the German tradition (Dilthey, Weber), and the nature of ideology critique in the Hegelian Marxist tradition's concern with critical hermeneutics (Adorno, Mannheim). And indeed these represent the foundations of interpretive social science. But these early debates within sociology where limited in important respects because of the absence of an adequate theory of language. The revitalization of such issues during the past three decades under the headings of "structuralism," "poststructuralism," "discourse analysis," and "narrative theory" are linked to the impact of various types of linguistic theory and the extensive use of narrative techniques in the humanities, especially literature.

What is meant today by *discourse* and, more specifically, *narrative* as discourse, especially as related to debates in the social sciences? *Narrative* refers to the primary basis of the making of meaning. As a cognitive process it organizes experience into temporal episodes that can only be indirectly studied with structuralist-type methods because they cannot be observed as such: "However, the individual stories and histories that emerge in the creation of human narrative are available for direct observation. Examples of narrative include personal and social histories, myths, fairly tales, novels, and the everyday stories we use to explain our own and other's actions" (Polkinghorne 1988, p. 1).

Two features of this definition are crucial to note, both relating to the way narrative as an "object" of inquiry is not available to direct observation (the primary criterion of factuality in empiricism). The definition stresses the difference between "invisible" narratives as cognitive processes, as opposed to those that take a written form—as *texts*. "Everyday stories" have an ambiguous status here because they occur in contexts of social action and yet could be "written down" (transcribed) to become texts. What this slippage between the analysis of action and narratives suggests is that narrative analysis is concerned with both the analysis of social action and texts even though these methods originally were elaborated for the purposes of textual analysis. In other words, cognitive narratives do become partially observable in the context of interaction. For this reason Paul Ricoeur has written of "meaningful action considered as a text" (Ricoeur 1981, pp. 197-221).[6]

But all narratives are also not subject to direct observation in another sense that is familiar from the basic problem faced by structuralist-type analysis: The rules governing narrative structures must be inferred from interpretive analysis and cannot be observed as social facts. It is this feature that has led to the virtual exclusion of such methodological issues from empiricist accounts of social scientific methodology.

The term *discourse,* in contrast, refers to the issues involved in defining *units of analysis* in narrative inquiry. A discourse is not just any collection of words or sentences: "A discourse in an integration of sentences that produces a global meaning that is more than that contained in the sentences viewed independently. There are various kinds of discourses, and each kind links the sentences that compose it according to distinct patterns" (Polkinghorne 1988, p. 31). For example, in the preceding chapter, concerned with non-empirical methods, we were, in effect, concerned with sociological research as a kind of *social scientific discourse.* In that context it was suggested that certain types of reflexive procedures should be used to analyze that discourse as part of the research process itself. Reflexive methods (rhetorical, historical, and deconstructive analysis) were given particular attention because of their specific applicability to the analysis of social scientific discourse. We do not pursue these forms of analysis any further here largely because, on the one hand, they are less central to the issues of narrative structure, ideology, and interpretation that have been central to the sociology of culture and communications. On the other hand, they remain more central in literary analysis, though in ways that often are problematic from the perspective of literary critics informed by critical social theory (Norris 1990).

Two traditions have contributed to the development of theories of texts that have been of more central concern to substantive inquiries influenced by critical theory: hermeneutics and structuralism/poststructuralism. Critical hermeneutics provided (as we have seen) the original basis of the theory of ideology as developed within the Hegelian Marxist tradition, one limited by its dogmatic theory of history. We begin by discussing these separately in order to gain some historical perspective. Then we turn to some specific types of *discourse analysis* that currently are influential in the social sciences and have proven instructive for the problems posed by critical theory.

It should be pointed out, however, that "discourse has become one of the most widely and often confusingly used terms in recent theories in the arts and social sciences, without a clearly definable single unifying concept" (Meinhof 1993, p. 161). The forms of discourse analysis that have been drawn on by critical theory have been characterized by two defining traits: first, interpretations of meaning are sensitized to detecting forms of distorted communication linked to power and strategic (or manipulative) forms of interaction; second, discourses eventually are recontextualized with reference to the historical social relations through which they are constituted. Most recently, the methodology of discourse analysis of this type has been synthesized usefully in terms of a three-dimensional model:

> Any discursive "event" (i.e., any instance of discourse) is seen as being simultaneously a piece of text, an instance of discursive practice, and an instance of social practice. The "text" dimension attends to language analysis of texts. The "discursive practice" dimension . . . specifies the nature of the processes of text production and interpretation. . . . The "social practice" dimension attends to issues of concern in social analysis such as the institutional and organizational circumstances of the discursive event and how that shapes the nature of the discursive practice. (Fairclough 1992, p. 4)

Hermeneutics and Ideology Critique

The methodological problems now associated with the notion of discourse analysis in critical theory can be traced back to the critical hermeneutics of Georg Lukacs, Karl Mannheim, and the early Frankfurt School. This type of analysis was based on a theory of totality and the assumption that the underlying contradictions of the material foundations of society were expressed and reflected in its cultural reproduction. The focus of such analysis was elucidating the ideological dimensions of ideological processes both through a *transcendent critique* based on the viewpoint of the revolutionary working class or an *immanent critique* (more characteristic of the Frankfurt School) based on the internal contradictions of bourgeois culture—that is, its inability in practice to live up to its universalistic ideas of freedom and equality. These issues entered into sociological theory through the largely marginalized discussions in the sociology of knowledge and culture originally associated primarily with Mannheim's hermeneutic *sociology of knowledge* (Simonds 1978; Longhurst 1989; Dant 1991). Mannheim, for example, turned the critique of ideology on the Marxian tradition itself by demonstrating that it could not ground its claim to a privileged perspective (that of the working class) except through an arbitrary, metaphysical theory of history. But Mannheim also pointed to the general methodological importance of a hermeneutic sociology of knowledge as a basis for understanding the social genesis of ideas and the evaluation of ideologies.

Such strategies remain a central part of critical cultural research but have been complemented by the shift toward understanding ideology as *distorted communication* as opposed to *false consciousness,* and by more recent developments in narrative theory. Classical ideology critique based on the theory of totality suffered from the problematic epistemological assumption of claiming objective "truth," hence allowed a strategy of reading off other viewpoints as merely "false." Further, the theory of language implicated by this approach was inadequately developed. Both the theory of communicative action and structuration theory, in contrast, require a conception of the active subject that goes beyond any assumption of mere "dupes" of ideology and extensively incorporates linguistic theory (Thompson 1990).

From Structuralist Semiotics
to Social Semiotics

Under the heading of "structuralism," an (initially) distinctively different tradition developed under the influence of Durkheimian sociology (especially his analysis of religious thought systems) and the structuralist linguistics of Ferdinand de Saussure.[7] This tradition is also often associated with the term *semiotics* or *semiology*. The most famous exemplification of this approach can be seen in the work of Claude Lévi-Strauss on kinship systems and tribal myths (Lévi-Strauss 1967) and Roland Barthes on the mythical structures of contemporary mass culture (Barthes 1972). But the changes within this tradition, as well as its complex process of reception elsewhere, have contributed to a rather messy situation with respect to the status of such methods in the sociology of culture.

At times the notion of a "semiotic" approach to culture has been used in an offhand and potentially misleading way as, for example, in the influential case of the interpretive anthropologist Clifford Geertz, who conflates it with any symbolic (hence nonbehaviorist, nonfunctionalist, or nonmaterialist) approach:

> The concept of culture I espouse . . . is essentially a semiotic one. Believing with Max Weber, that man is an animal suspended in webs of significance he himself has spun, I take culture to be those webs, and the analysis of it to be therefore not an experimental science in search of law but an interpretive one in search of meaning. . . . What defines it is the kind of intellectual effort it is: an elaborated venture in, to borrow a notion from Gilbert Ryle, "thick description" (Geertz 1973, pp. 5-6)

In fact, Geertz's approach is a hermeneutic one quite at odds with the traditional association of semiotics (and semiology) with structuralist linguistics, which is associated for Geertz with the mixtures of "intuition and alchemy" that would quickly "discredit a semiotic approach to culture" (Geertz 1973, p. 30).

Further, the status of semiotic approaches has been blurred in the context of poststructuralist theories of discourse that move freely among the hermeneutic traditions. Although in the French context the hermeneutic and structuralist traditions were viewed as diametrically opposed approaches to the study of meaning, more recently their complementarity has become evident, a thesis introduced by Paul Ricoeur (Ricoeur 1974). From this latter poststructuralist perspective, structuralist or semiotic text interpretation is simply a special type of hermeneutics involving high levels of distanciation.

Considerable confusion is evident in discussions of semiotics because of the profound shifts from the 1950s through the 1970s associated with the advent of poststructuralism as a successor to structuralism. This confusion is perhaps most obvious in the career of Roland Barthes, who was most responsible for popularizing the term in his early work and then largely abandoned it in his later "poststructuralist" phase. The term *social semiotics* is useful as a designation of the form of semiotic analysis that has retained credibility in a poststructuralist context where it is crucial to be sensitive to history, interaction, and the reflexivity of the researcher (Hodge and Kress 1988). Such strategies have become an indispensable complement to the older forms of ideology critique based in hermeneutics (Thompson 1990).

Textual Discourse Analysis and Power

Sometimes the term *discourse* (and *discourse formation*) is used synonymously with the specific approach of Michel Foucault and narrowed to scientific disciplines, as in the following definition: "the particular 'scientific' and specialist language(s), and associated ideas and social outcomes, which, according to Foucault, must be seen as a major phenomenon of social power, and not simply a way of describing the world" (Jary and Jary 1991, p. 166). Foucault's version of discourse analysis is associated closely with a critique of notions of power as a centralized form of control, rejection of the use of the concept of *ideology,* and skepticism regarding the possibility of tracing the historical origins of knowledge systems.

But more commonly *discourse analysis* is acknowledged as a general strategy (Parker 1992) incorporating a wide variety of techniques (e.g., critical hermeneutics, social semiotics, conversation analysis), as well as types of discourse (e.g., scientific, interactional, popular and elite culture). But a focus on questions of *power, ideology,* and *historical genesis* defines the link to critical methodologies even though Foucault's contributions have called into question conventional formulations of these questions in instructive—and often completely devastating—ways.

More recently, an emergent major influence in discourse analysis is associated with the work of Mikhail Bakhtin (1895-1975), a Russian philosopher and literary theorist who has become recognized during the past decade as perhaps the most significant social theorist in the Soviet tradition (Gardiner 1992). But many of his works were lost and the rest (along with the Bakhtin Circle he inspired) suppressed under Stalinism, and were for the most part only recently translated. What is most distinctive about his approach in the present context is that he developed a critique of structuralism from a critical hermeneutic perspective in the late 1920s (Volosinov 1986). Although he preserved the concept of *narrative structure* as crucial to the theory of ideology, he developed a *dialogical model* that anticipates many of the basic insights in Habermas's theory of distorted communication as an approach to the problem of ideology and the analysis of cultural texts.

Conclusion

The Decentered Identity of Critical Research

Although the theoretical tradition of critical theory has a relatively coherent identity extending beyond the Frankfurt School tradition, as we have seen, the same cannot be said of the forms of substantive research that exemplify the intentions of this research program. First, there is a body of empirical research directly associated with the early Frankfurt School tradition, as well as more recent work that labels itself with reference to contemporary theorists such as Habermas or Giddens.

But it would be a mistake to limit the identification of the link between critical theory and empirical research to these explicit indications of working within a "school" of research. The primary reason is that many of the central themes and assumptions of critical theory have been embraced implicitly by people who do not directly identify with the key theoretical figures discussed in this study, or perhaps fall back on the inspiration of others (e.g., Foucault, Bourdieu, feminist theory) indirectly related to this tradition. Furthermore much good research carried out under the influence of theoretical debates in substantive domains does not necessarily link itself back to the general theoretical debate. Although we would not go so far as to label all good research as "critical" in this stronger sense, we would not want to restrict the tradition of critical research to explicit connections. The increasingly diverse and international character of social research has increasingly eroded the stronger "school" ties of various kinds that contributed to more solid identifications of research orientations. Again this is not to fall back on some kind of postmodernist pluralism to suggest that many complementary things are being done under slightly different labels.

As a consequence, critical theory as a research program makes no claim to be self-sufficient or define itself as a "school" in the traditional sense strongly associated with a "master thinker." As a glance at the more substantive writings of Giddens and Habermas shows, they make reference to a wide range of empirically based literature that is not directly inspired by critical theory. Further, their work is open-ended and fallibilistic in ways quite distinct from the totalizing theoretical "systems" that have filled the intellectual graveyard of Western thought. Accordingly Giddens suggests that the "empirical implications of structuration theory have to be pursued primarily through the introduction of considerations—concerned with particular types of social systems and their transformation—which are not part of the theory itself" (Giddens 1989a, p. 300). At other points, those who may appear to be "critics" may be taken to exemplify the intentions of a theoretical approach. For example, Giddens cites R. W. Connell's study on *Gender and Power* (Connell 1987) as "a major contribution" but adds: "Connell is critical of my approach and makes use of it only at a few junctures in his argument. Yet these seem to me pivotal to the overall claims of the work and results in a standpoint that I find persuasive" (Giddens 1991a, p. 215). Much the same can be said of the diffuse influence of Habermas, many of whose apparent critics could be viewed, from a broader perspective, in terms of participating in the tradition of critical theory. It is thus important to differentiate family squabbles or issues derived from exploring different empirical contexts of research from more fundamental differences.

Basic Assumptions of Critical Methodology

Similar problems of identification become apparent in outlining the basic assumptions of critical methodology. For example, the implications of the critical theory of methodology developed in the preceding chapters for research practice can be distinguished from empiricist approaches in the following ways:

- The choice and manner of using methods (logics-in-use) cannot be separated from the theory-informing method and the problem to be clarified.
- Critical theory is dialectical in its recognition of the double hermeneutic of social inquiry, hence social structures are preconstituted by human agents.
- The non-empirical aspects of methodology (crucial to the logic of discovery) are made explicit components of research practice.
- Because research within a given society cannot be ideologically neutral, it is legitimate to justify rationally the definition of forms of research guided by critical-emancipatory cognitive interests.
- The empirical dimensions of methodology are differentiated as extensive and intensive, rather than quantitative and qualitative; and intensive methods are considered primary for social theorizing understood in interpretive structuralist terms.
- Extensive and intensive research designs can be differentiated with respect to their focus on processes at the level of system integration, social integration, and sociocultural mediation.

It would be possible to identify forms of research that fall within these guidelines without making them fully explicit or making reference to the critical theory tradition (through explicit citation) as we have defined it here. Much postcolonial anthropology would fall into this category. Similarly most social scientific definitions of *feminist methodology* are clearly a species of critical methodology whose identity stems from its focus on gender/power issues as the object of inquiry.[8]

Three Moments of Inquiry

An obstacle to understanding critical theory as a research program has been the tendency to reduce its methodology to these particular characteristics. For example, the critical-emancipatory interest may be invoked to require every individual investigation to have immediate transformative effects. Or, alternatively, the ultimate focus on social practices may be interpreted to preclude the analysis of systemic properties of social institutions.

Viewed as a research program with many rooms, critical theory's analysis of the processes of social and cultural reproduction and change embraces a wide variety of intensive research designs; the activist and interactionist options are in this respect exemplary but not definitive. In other words, although the research program itself does entail certain kinds of quasi-totalizing ambitions as a regulative ideal, every specific methodological strategy entails focusing on some aspects of reality at the expense of others; any given investigation cannot attempt to do everything at once. This is one practical reason for the traditional qualitative-quantitative split, even if it obscures more fundamental bases for selecting strategies. Similarly the macro-micro split reflects the practical problems in "slicing up" social reality in manageable portions for inquiry. In both cases the resulting reification of techniques and theoretical distinctions becomes an obstacle to inquiry.

Although we sympathize with Giddens's suggestion that analysis should focus on social practices in a manner that bypasses the dualism of agency and structure (as in the macro-micro distinction), we find convincing the suggestion that there are *practical methodological grounds* for research designs that focus on one or other of these dimensions, at least as long as their ultimate unity in mutual constitution is never completely forgotten. Such possibilities are built into the distinction between system and social integration shared by Habermas and Giddens, one distinct from the macro-micro distinction, given its implication in the understanding of the *duality of structure* underlying critical theory.

Analysis at the level of *system integration* may involve concepts involving functional-type part-whole relations. This involvement entails the macrosociological assumption that society, as a contradictory totality, must be analyzed structurally as a process of reproduction and transformation of agency/structure relations over time. But system integration here is understood in terms of an interpretive structuralism that rejects the analogy of organic systems in favor of open, historical social formations.

In contrast, analysis at the level of *social integration* is processual and interactionist, involving both individual and group processes. Such investigations are carried out with the implicit awareness of the conditional nature of social action—that is, that it ultimately is embedded in constraints imposed by systemic relations. But the focus here is on skilled actors constructing reality through praxis; hence it entails the phenomenological assumption that the formation and transformation of individual subject or self is the constitutive principle underlying all social inquiry, without falling back into methodological individualism. Hence Giddens suggests that *Verstehen* must be understood "not as a special method of entry into the social world peculiar to the social science, but as the ontological condition of human society as it is produced and reproduced by its members" (Giddens 1976, p. 151).

Finally what we have called *sociocultural mediation* is analogous to what Giddens calls *social practices,* a form of analysis that seeks to realize the nearly impossible task of transcending dualism, a task perhaps possible only for rather unique types of social settings and contexts. Only in crucial conjunctures do the ruptures of social reproduction become studiable in the mediations between systemic structure and social action, the points of *dereification* in which nascent forms of awareness are either increasingly elaborated in a collective learning process or temporarily (or permanently) silenced as a failed questioning. It is here that the dialectic of domination and resistance becomes momentarily visible in forms that reveal the fragile foundations of social order and potential change. The next chapter explores the contexts of critical research in terms of these three moments of inquiry: *systemic, actional,* and *mediational.*

Notes

1. There has been much recent discussion of the methodology of the sociology of culture that we cannot review here, for example, Griswold 1987; Denzin 1991; Münch and Smelser 1992. For informative overviews of issues in qualitative methodology, see Silverman 1989, Atkinson 1990, and Guba 1990.

2. Our approach is consistent with Craig Calhoun's formulation: "One of the problems of many epistemological critiques is that they have seemed to endorse or entail a relativism so thoroughgoing as to make empirical research—and most scholarly discourse—meaningless. . . . My argument is not just for the virtues of history and ethnography, but for the virtues of a theory which can take both of them seriously. Yet . . . this is an argument for theory—including both empirical

and normative theory, and theory of very broad reach. . . . The kind of theory I advocate would be continuous with cross-cultural and historical description, but not identical to them because the explanations the theory proposes would purport to anticipate or account for cases beyond those for which they were developed" (Calhoun 1992a, p. 246).

3. See Andrew Sayer's text (1992) for a detailed elaboration of the methodology of intensive research applied to problems of structuralist causal analysis in case studies and, more generally, two studies that became available only after completion of this manuscript: Layder (1993), which provides a useful sequel to the present study; and Blaikie (1993), which covers much of the same ground as we do in the philosophy of social sciences, but somewhat confusingly and schematically stresses the differences among interpretivism, critical theory, realism, structuration theory, and feminism—as opposed to the broader convergence stressed here.

4. Ragin's formalization of what he calls the "qualitative comparative method" reinforces our previous argument about the problems of the qualitative-quantitative distinction, as well as the distinctiveness of interpretive generalization and variable analysis: "The principle guiding the formulation of this approach was that the essential features of case-oriented methods should be preserved as much as possible. . . . This is important because mainstream statistical methods disaggregate cases into variables and distributions before analyzing them. This practice makes historical interpretive work very difficult, if not impossible." (Ragin 1987, p. x).

5. As Habermas stresses: "In place of controlled observation, which guarantees the anonymity (exchangeability) of the observing subject and thus of the reproducibility of the observation, there arises a participatory relation of the understanding subject to the subject confronting him [*Gegenüber*] (alter ego). The paradigm is no longer the observation but the dialogue—thus, a communication in which the understanding subject must invest a part of his subjectivity, no matter in what manner this may be controllable, in order to be able to meet confronting subjects at all on the intersubjective level which makes understanding possible. To be sure (as the example of the ground rules for the psychoanalytic dialogue shows) this makes disciplinary constraints more necessary than ever. The fashionable demand for a type of 'action research,' that is to combine political enlightenment with research, overlooks that the uncontrolled modification of the field is incompatible with the simultaneous gathering of data in that field, a condition which is also valid for the social sciences" (Habermas 1973, pp. 10-11).

6. Over the past decade the concept of discourse as narrative analysis has been proposed—in opposition to attitude theory and cognitive science—as an alternative paradigm for a constructionist social psychology (Potter and Wetherell 1987; Bruner 1990; Parker 1992). A parallel development is evident in Norman Denzin's effort to revise symbolic interactionism as part of a critical cultural studies (Denzin 1992).

7. The differences between the critical hermeneutic and structuralist traditions are most striking in the positivist phase of structuralism; in the poststructuralist form represented by Ricoeur and Bourdieu, their potential complementarity becomes apparent.

8. "From a review of the literature we have identified five basic epistemological principles discussed by scholars who have analyzed feminist methodology in the field of sociology. They include: (1) the necessity of continuously and reflexively

attending to the significance of gender and gender asymmetry as a basic feature of all social life, including the conduct of research; (2) the centrality of consciousness-raising as a specific methodological tool and as a general orientation or 'way of seeing'; (3) the need to challenge the norm of objectivity that assumes that the subject and object of research can be separated from one another and that personal and/or grounded experiences are unscientific; (4) concern for the ethical implications of feminist research and recognition of the exploitation of women as objects of knowledge; and (5) emphasis on the empowerment of women and the transformation of patriarchal social institutions through research" (Cook and Fonow 1990, pp. 72-3).

11

CONTEXTS OF CRITICAL EMPIRICAL RESEARCH

The concrete is concrete because it is the concentration of many determinations, hence unity of the diverse . . . the method rising from the abstract to the concrete is the only way in which thought appropriates the concrete, reproduces it as the concrete in the mind. (Marx cited in Tucker 1978, p. 237)

The problem of the relation between the constitution (or, as I shall often say, production and reproduction) of society by actors, and the constitution of those actors by the society of which they are members, has nothing to do with a differentiation between micro- and macro-sociology; it cuts across any such division. (Giddens 1976, p. 22)

The world is systematized horror, but therefore it is to do the world too much honor to think of it entirely as a system; for its unifying principle is division, and it reconciles by asserting unimpaired the irreconcilability of the general and the particular. (Adorno 1974, p. 113)

The Range of Critical Research

The task of this chapter is to give some indications of the influence of contemporary critical theory on empirical research. By that we do not refer exclusively to the specific influence of people such as Habermas, Giddens, or others, or even an explicit identification with "critical theory" or "critical social science" as a research program. As any close investigation of research fields would show, so many of the concepts and methodological stances originally associated with critical theory in the narrower sense have become part of the common culture of the human sciences, at least among researchers engaged in work falling outside the traditional boundaries of empiricist or purely interpretive inquiry. The names given to such tendencies and the authors cited follow a wide variety of patterns reflecting specific national traditions and the diversity of contemporary research.

The most common strategy of a comprehensive research review has the advantage of providing a compendium of the theoretical approaches and "results." For example, Kellner surveys critical theory from the early Frankfurt School to the present under the heading of early state and political economy debates, authoritarian personality theory, culture industries research, along with more recent trends: needs and consumption theory, state crisis theory, the new social movements and radical politics (Kellner 1989a). In contrast, Harvey surveys a small number of examples of empirical research studies drawn from the substantive domains of class, race, and gender (Harvey 1990). That approach has the advantage of the concreteness of a substantive problem focus, for which a variety of methodological strategies can be illustrated by topic in some detail.

We propose yet another alternative for the purposes of this chapter, one that lies between the above strategies. In the 1990s the influence of critical theory and critical social science cuts across so many disciplines in complex ways that it has become virtually impossible to survey without arbitrary boundaries. Kellner does so in a manner that adheres closely to the Frankfurt tradition and its more or less direct influences in North America, but even there crucial sociological contributors such as Norman Birnbaum and Alvin Gouldner are neglected, along with Giddens and all of those influenced by his example in Britain.[1] Further, if we were to extend the criteria of inclusion only slightly, one would have to consider extensive debates stimulated by critical theory in fields such as anthropology, history, law, education, social work, social psychology, cultural studies, feminist theory, and theology—to name just a few of the disciplinary domains largely neglected.

In the present study we have argued, however, that broadly shared metatheoretical and substantive issues cut across these disciplinary practices. Sociology has been perhaps the most well situated in mediating this process, even as it has benefitted from the seminal contributions of those in other fields or on the margins of sociology as a discipline (Morrow 1985). That is the justification for referring to critical theory as a "supradisciplinary" project even though in practice most researchers have had to code their work in more disciplinary terms that facilitate communication with specific audiences. Similarly we have focused more on the notion of "critical theory as sociology" as part of defining an ecumenical framework, rather than as any kind of imperial claim for the disciplinary primacy of sociology.

The objectives of our review in this chapter thus are dictated by attempting to come to terms with the intrinsic tensions within critical research arising from the effort to study agency and structure without the dualism of micro-macro. For purposes of convenience, therefore, we organize our discussion around the classic three domains in which critical research has focused: *political economy and state theory, cultural analysis,* and *social psychology.* These broad, overlapping domains conceal many topics that also might illuminate critical research. So, for example, the focus on gender, race, and class usefully focuses on the primary contexts of asymmetrical power relations, topics that might appear in any of the domains in our more general schema.

In the case of gender, however, the limitations of this basic schema—deriving from the interdisciplinary research program of the early Frankfurt School and extended by Habermas—run deeper than the incidental constraints inevitably imposed by any organizing framework (Fraser 1989; Marshall Forthcoming). Despite the pioneering analysis of authority in the patriarchal family in early critical theory, as Nancy Fraser has argued, an "unthematized gender subtext" of Habermas's theory of communicative action contributes to relegating the issues of the family and gender to issues of socialization and social psychology that obscure fundamental issues. Such an analysis "reveals the inadequacy of those critical theories that treat gender as incidental to politics and political economy. It highlights the need for a critical theory with a categorical framework in which gender, politics, and political economy are internally related" (Fraser 1989, p. 128). These gender blindspots are especially consequential for the theorization of the welfare state and the problematic effects of the private/public distinction with respect to Habermas's theory of the democratic public sphere (Calhoun 1992b).

Such issues would be central to a discussion of the internal critiques of critical theory, as well as new points of departure for research. For the purposes at hand, however, we necessarily focus on simply illustrating the *range* of critical research from the generalized perspective of the relationship between theory and methodology. Hence, our primary purpose here is an *analytical* presentation of the relationship of critical theory, methodological strategies, and various contexts of empirical research. For that purpose we isolate the three moments of the research process that define focal points for research strategies: (a) structural analyses of *system integration,* (b) interpretive analyses of *social action* by individual and group agents, and (c) *mediational analyses* that reveal the simultaneous operation of agency and structure—the ideal outcome of inquiry according to Giddens's theory of structuration. Further, our objective here is illustrative rather than evaluative; that is, we are not directly concerned with the various internal disputes that define the ongoing development of such a multifaceted research program.[2]

What is distinctive about critical research when well done is that even if it focuses on any one of these moments (or substantive domains), it tries to remain conscious of the other two in framing and executing the research process. The resulting tension stems from the assumption that "you can't do everything at once." Built into any methodic procedure is the heuristic need to break up the flow of reality—here society as a multidimensional, historical totality—for analytic purposes. To be sure, on the one hand, the positivist model so prioritizes the moment of the technical control of data that reality itself is fully reified and fragmented. On the other hand, purely interpretive models run the risk of an immersion in reality that does not allow analytic distance. And purely activist approaches risk being swallowed up in the present moment in a search for resistance and change.

A key assumption is that each of these modes of analysis presupposes the other even though polemical priority disputes often obscure this complementarity. Differences among critical researchers largely reflect these different research emphases: Those concerned with systemic structures lean in a positivist direction (we reinterpret their objectives in critical realist terms) to be able to identify structural determinations; those focusing on social action give priority to an interpretive stance concerned with agents; and those who attempt the most challenging forms of mediational inquiry often make no one happy because neither agency nor structure is assigned center stage.

An Extended Example:
Gottdiener's Critique of Urban Sociology

Given the volume of the material to be reviewed and the resulting cursory indications of the research strategies, it is useful to begin with a more detailed presentation of a representative example of empirically oriented critical theory. For this purpose Mark Gottdiener's *The Social Production of Urban Space* (1985b) cross-cuts the issues at stake in a manner that nicely illustrates most of the basic methodological concerns of research influenced by critical theory.[3] The point of departure is a critique of mainstream urban sociology (and related forms of geography) based on positivist methodologies and simplistic evolutionary models of universal and inexorable urban development, for example, the sequence of preindustrial, urban-industrial, and metropolitan stages. In such mainstream analysis fundamentally new forms of settlement spaces either have been ignored or their implications have been theoretically misrecognized.

The focal point of empirical analysis in Gottdiener's critical theory of urban sociology is the reorganization of settlement spaces, especially the process of "deconcentration"–the expansion of high-density populations outside traditional city regions and urban centers. Although a generalized process, deconcentration is nevertheless historically specific (at this point) to postwar developments in the United States. Political economy, with its emphasis on class conflict and the logic of capital accumulation, provides some crucial initial clues for a fundamental reconceptualization of urban science directed toward explaining

CRITICAL THEORY AND EMPIRICAL RESEARCH

deconcentration. Yet there are limitations to these analyses that are endemic to Marxist theory generally, for example,

> the inability . . . to break away from the ideological categories of mainstream economic reasoning . . . ; the scourge of positivism, in particular the penchant for replacing monocausal, deterministic arguments on the mainstream side with marxian versions of the same thing; and, finally, the imprecise way in which the state-society articulation is specified, which undercuts the ability of the marxian approach to address political phenomena within settlement space. (Gottdiener 1985b, p. 20)

As against the positivism underlying this form of political economy, the example of critical realism and its understanding is invoked as an alternative metatheory for redirecting inquiry of this type (Gottdiener 1985b, pp. 158-9). More specifically, an analysis of space is introduced at the deep level of capitalist relations to show "how such processes of development affect spatial phenomena in a way marxists cannot explain" (Gottdiener 1985b, p. 160).

Developing a synthetic and constructive alternative, he continues with a critical review of the rich, more specific discussions of spatiality in the Marxian tradition as found in the works of Manuel Castells (a Spanish sociologist who studied in France) and Henri Lefebvre, a French Marxist philosopher who pioneered the theme of "everyday life" and the "production of space" as sociological topics. In the course of Gottdiener's discussion, on the one hand, the problematic elements of Castells's Althusserian-type structuralism become apparent; and on the other hand, suggestive aspects of Lefebvre's "humanistic" approach lead directly into consideration of structure and agency in the production of space. What is required is to see that the relations involved are "*simultaneously* economic, political and cultural . . . that social phenomena are contingent rather than predetermined, following a realist epistemology" (Gottdiener 1985b, p. 207). From this perspective, "sociospatial patterns and interactive processes are seen as constituting contingent outcomes of the many *contradictory* relations interacting in the capitalist mode, rather than as direct products of either capitalist intentions or structural machinations" (1985b, p. 23).

On the basis of this synthesis, Gottdiener's attention shifts back to the empirical analysis of deconcentration as a form of uneven development in the United States, a process that has undercut the previous city-country opposition still relevant elsewhere. The outcome of deconcentration is thus a profound transformation of the social landscape:

> The action of abstract space fragments *all* social groups, not only the least powerful, so that local community life loses the street and public areas of communion to the privacy of the home. . . . The new areas of communion are encapsulated within social worlds engineered by the logic of consumption—the malls, shopping centers, singles bars, amusements parks, and suburban backyards. (Gottdiener 1985b, p. 272)

The mainstream literature's account of the "natural" process of urbanization "is unveiled as an uncoordinated form of profit taking aided by the state and involving the manipulation of spatial patterns by vested interests operating within the property sector" (1985b, p. 23). Thus the empirical analysis of deconcentration has direct implications for policy critique, especially the standoff between neoconservatives and leftist liberals who remain locked within the same mainstream framework of assumptions about economic growth and urbanization. In this context "Marxists differ from mainstreamers only through the reformist schemes proposed, which seek to ameliorate the inequities of economic patterns of development. This eludes the transformative role of social thought" (1985b, p. 271). Further, mainstream ecologists focus on the "value problematic" and thus neglect the historical processes that have created these outcomes. In short, "through the ideological devices of conventional thought, the causes of society's problems are advocated as their cures" (1985b, p. 288).

As opposed to the "utopian schemes of left-liberal reformers," another form of utopian thought is required, one based on a very different diagnosis of the realities of capitalist urbanization. This form requires a shift of attention to "unprivileged" spaces, new social movements, contradictions of the ideology of growth, and to "changing the existing property relations of society and redesigning both the workplace and community accordingly"

(1985b, p. 289) even though "this project, tying production and consumption relations together in a liberated space, remains undeveloped in radical thought" (1985b, p. 291).

In short, Gottdiener's study combines virtually all of the features we have linked with uniting critical theory and empirical research: a critical metatheory that stresses interpretive structuralism and the agency-structure dialectic; a critique of existing knowledge claims coupled with an alternative synthesis based on a historical, interpretive structural model that links systemic analysis (e.g., political economy, the state) with cultural analysis and social psychology; the use of a wide range of empirical evidence (case studies that are often quantitative, but not driven by statistical modeling) based on historical, ethnographic, demographic, and cultural materials; and a normative critique grounded in an understanding of the generative causal mechanisms underlying the phenomena to be transformed in the name of generalizable and justifiable needs and hopes as expressed and reflected—often is distorted form—in the everyday lives of members of urban "communities."

The following overview somewhat artificially organizes an extensive body of material in terms of a substantive focus on political economy and the state, cultural theory, and social psychology. Within each, discussion touches on representative analyses reflecting, respectively, the systemic, actional, and mediational emphases of critical research. The three substantive domains identified correspond with (though also slightly reorganized) the four domains of empirical inquiry that Habermas sees as the contemporary agenda of critical theory: "interdisciplinary research on the selective pattern of capitalist modernization" (Habermas 1987a, p. 397). What he calls "the forms of integration in postliberal societies" corresponds to our analysis of the state and economy; "mass media and mass culture" to the domain of the sociology of culture and cultural studies; and "family socialization and ego development" along with "protest potential" to social psychology. Our more standard and generic terms help preserve the distinction between Habermas's strong program for critical theory and the range of complementary topics that might be and have been of concern to those working within a "weaker" program.

State and Economy

Introduction: Political Economy and Political Sociology

The use of statistical modeling for studies of systemic properties has been the basis of modern economic theory (econometrics) and has been employed widely in various forms of "systems" analysis. The most compelling versions appear to be those in domains that most closely touch on the interface between nature and society—that is, areas where statistical regularities are grounded in the nature of the phenomenon: economic and demographic processes and their relationship to the environment. Formal system models of society have been much less convincing and largely without influence. Formalization of systems models is achieved at the price of an extremely high level of abstraction (Freeman 1973). The more influential systems models within sociology (structural functionalism and neofunctionalism) are qualitative in nature (Alexander 1985). In other words, the use of statistical modeling largely took the form of confirming theoretical arguments generated by structural functionalist theory, rather than participating in the construction of the theory.

Systemic analysis in the political economy and critical theory traditions is most similar to qualitative functionalist theory, though it may employ economic modeling procedures for certain purposes. In fact, functionalist Marxist accounts are methodologically parallel to structural functionalism in their attribution of system needs and teleological mechanisms; they differ because the "needs of capital" replace the illusory "needs of society." The development of a more historically contingent interpretive structural crisis theory as a theory of social and cultural reproduction, however, has allowed analysis of systemic contradictions in a more plausible manner consistent with recognition of the communicative basis of social integration and the possibilities of transformation.

Systemic Models: Crisis Theory

Classical *political economy* was used in basically determinist ways based on simplistic assumptions about the inexorable unfolding of systemic contradictions. As we have seen, early Frankfurt Critical Theory was plagued by a Marxist functionalism of this kind, though one creatively used to analyze the transition from laissez-faire to state capitalism in the 1930s and 1940s. Contemporary critical theories of the state can be characterized, in contrast, with having pioneered research based on the assumption of the limitations of political economy, a strategy employed today by many who otherwise might be labeled "neo-Marxist."

The limits of political economy have been explicitly and constructively addressed in the work of Offe and Habermas, as we have seen, in their attempt to construct a crisis theory for the form of advanced capitalism evident by the 1970s. In this context the thesis of the *fiscal crisis of the state* is rooted in a political economic model of systemic contradiction (O'Connor 1987). In this revised form, systemic analysis informed by political economy remains a key aspect of critical social research and has been expanded in creative ways by a number of researchers not directly connected (despite important influences) to the Frankfurt critical theory tradition. Despite stress on the need to revise the older political economy, critical theories differ sharply from the tendency of theories of postindustrial society and postmodernity to deny the continuing significance of key elements of the capitalist organization of production.

A distinctive theme of classical critical theory was the selective way technology was appropriated in the capitalist production process, a form of analysis influenced by Weber's theory of instrumental rationalization. From this perspective technology and bureaucratization had to be analyzed as independent sources of domination that had been neglected within the Marxist tradition. Today this type of question has been preserved under the heading of the *critical theory of technology*. Another focal point for mediational analysis related to the state and economy has been research on the social uses and shaping of technology (Leiss 1974, 1990; Aronowitz 1988) and the implications for feminist theory (Wajcman 1991). In moving back from the abyss of the technological determinism and fatalism implied by authors as diverse as Adorno, Heidegger, and Ellul, critical theory nevertheless rejects the thesis of the neutrality of technology:

> The dominant form of technological rationality is neither an ideol-
> ogy (an essentially discursive expression of class self-interest) nor is it
> a neutral requirement determined by the "nature" of technique. . . .
> Critical theory argues that technology is not a thing in the ordinary
> sense of the term, but an "ambivalent" process of development
> suspended between different possibilities. This "ambivalence" of
> technology is distinguished from neutrality by the role it attributes
> to social values in the design, and not merely the use, of technical
> systems. On this view, technology is not a destiny but a scene of
> struggles. It is a social battlefield, or perhaps a better metaphor
> would be a *parliament of things* on which civilization's alternatives
> are debated and decided. (Feenberg 1991, p. 14)

A remarkable illustration of the role of technology as part of a
social battlefield is provided by David Noble's study of how
engineering in America early came under the sway of corporate
capitalism, a process that dramatically shaped industrial design
around issues of power and control in the workplace (Noble 1977).

Transformations of technology also are implicated in the
emerging form of "techno-capitalism," where "what Marx calls
the 'organic composition of capital' shifts toward a preponder-
ance of constant over variable capital, as machines and technologies progressively and often dramatically replace human labor
power in the production process" (Kellner 1989a, p. 179). A
related political economic argument that has influenced critical
theory is the notion of *post-Fordism*—that is, the suggestion that
a fundamental shift is occurring in the production process. In
contrast to the "Fordist" strategies of the past based on rigid
specialization along assembly lines, post-Fordist production
processes increasingly are built around decentralization and
flexibility. These changes have far-reaching effects in all spheres
of society and culture, including the phenomenon of postmodernism (D. Harvey 1989). The post-Fordist theme, for example,
is central to the *disorganized capitalism* thesis of Lash and Urry
(1987).[4] In their comparative study of five countries (Germany,
Sweden, Britain, France, and the United States) they attempt to
demonstrate the shifting relations between liberal, organized,
and disorganized capitalism, especially the latter two. Changes
are compared along three axes: the predominant organizational
structures, changes within territories, and the predominant

methods of transmitting knowledge and carrying out surveillance. Disorganized capitalism is associated with a global, transnational economy, the decline of distinct national and regional economies built around major industrial cities, and the role of electronic communication in reducing the time-space distances between people, as well as enhancing capacities for surveillance. What is especially significant methodologically about this study is the way it incorporates political economic arguments within a framework sensitive to transformations of culture.

Another theme that has emerged as central in critical theories is the phenomenon of *globalization:*

> The challenge for sociology . . . is to both theorize and work out modes of systematic investigation which can clarify these globalizing processes and distinctive forms of life which render problematic what has long been regarded as the basic subject matter for sociology: society, conceived almost exclusively as the bounded nation-state. (Featherstone 1990, p. 2)

As we have seen, this theme has been especially central to Giddens's critique of historical materialism and an acknowledged strength of *world system theory* despite its problematic aspects (Wallerstein 1990; Boyne 1990). Finally in political science the field of international relations has been influenced increasingly by debates in critical theory and poststructuralism (Linklater 1990; Der Derian and Shapiro 1989).

Another disputed theme originating in political economy has been the status of the analysis of social class in advanced capitalism. Research guided by neo-Marxist assumptions (Miliband 1987; Wright 1985, 1989) continues to define the problematic in terms of class positions and their relation to the mode of production. Hence the primary focus of such research has been to map class positions defined in this way despite modifications that acknowledge intermediate middle strata and the significance of subjective class awareness. But it has proven most problematic to connect that kind of structural analysis to actual processes of and potential for change. As a consequence, the status and functions of class analysis have been transformed fundamentally in contemporary critical theory. The classic Marxian thesis that reduces class dynamics to the systemic features of the capitalist mode of production is rejected as a failure. A pioneering contribution of this kind was Giddens's analysis of the class structure of advanced societies (Giddens 1973). More recently an alternative *critical stratification theory* is suggested that seeks to reestablish the links between stratification processes and social action as suggested by the work of Habermas, Offe, Touraine, and others:

> A "post-Marxist" approach to stratification should be able to *identify* the structural contradictions, crisis tendencies, and mechanisms of stratification within contemporary social systems; to *assess* the potentials for and of social movements without presupposing the primacy of either the economy or socioeconomic class struggles. It must also be able to *justify* the principles guiding the partisanship for a given social and political project against others. (I. J. Cohen 1982, p. 195)

Action Analysis:
Political Actors and Civil Society

Research concerned with social integration can be pursued by a number of different interpretive perspectives, and hence is not specific to critical theory as such. The most important body of such work is Weberian in inspiration because, for Weber, a focus on concrete group struggles was the primary concern of sociological analysis. In this connection *social closure theory* has proven especially fruitful for the analysis of group-based strategies of exclusion both within social classes and outside of them (Murphy 1988; Manza 1992). Somewhat more broadly, interpretive studies of actual and potential political actors have been important for critical researchers. In this context the primary focus of analysis has been *civil society*—that is, the non-state institutions not directly linked to the economy. For it is here in voluntary forms of association that the foundations for participation and political protest are built. From the perspective of critical theory one of the central issues has been the implications of the changing character of civil society for the social actors within it (Keane 1984, 1988a, 1988b; Cohen and Arato 1992).

Mediational Inquiry: The Public Sphere
and Transformative Action

In a sense mediational analysis is to a great extent a special case of interpretive action analysis; the primary difference is that it involves the study of phenomena that are indicative of crucial moments of failed or successful social and cultural reproduction, hence the strategic interplay of structure and action. In the context of Western democracies the development of the *public sphere* of democratic debate has provided the central theme for mediational research on the state (Calhoun 1992b). Central to critical theory, especially in the wake of abandoning classical revolutionary theory, has been the problem of linking the empirical and normative aspects of a new theory of democracy (Frankel 1987; Held 1987). More generally, it has been argued that Habermas's account of the democratic public sphere needs to be corrected by empirical research in the sociology of culture that suggests that advances in universalistic rationality have not necessarily required decontextualized systems of discourse "conducted by talking heads in virtual isolation from the baser, quotidian realities that were essentially antithetical to discourse based on universalistic claims" (Zaret 1992, p. 23).

A landmark historical mediational study is E. P. Thompson's *The Making of the English Working Class,* a close analysis of the emergence of a self-conscious collective actor in British history (Thompson 1968). Similarly research on various types of contemporary class, racial, and gender movements has provided insights into the dynamics of the restructuring of democratic public life. For example, Eyerman and Jameson attempt to make a case for the *cognitive* dimension of the American civil rights movement and its impact on restructuring American democracy (Eyerman and Jameson 1991). The broader context of mediational analysis in political sociology revolves around the theme of the "democratic public sphere," a topic that has revitalized the discussion of democratic theory. Of course these issues cannot be separated clearly from cultural theory and the mass media. Similarly a concern of critical policy research has been on the interplay between planning practices and public participation (Kemp 1985; Forester 1985a; Chorney and Hansen 1993). The issues are parallel to those of many other domains of policy analysis

(Forester 1985c; Fischer and Forester 1987). Furthermore the debates on technology also suggest a *critical social ecology* that seeks to connect environmental debates with critical theory (Alford 1985; Luke 1987) and related work in *eco-feminist research* that seeks to reveal the links of historical gender characteristics and ways of understanding social relations to nature (Diamond and Orenstein 1990).

The central problematic of mediational research in this context—and one that spills over into the domains of cultural theory and social psychology—is the question of transforming these critiques into credible alternative strategies for organizing social relations. The difficulty stems, in part, from the high level of complexity of such innovative social relations and the forms of *collective learning* required for making social experiments both credible and potentially generalizable, a theme that has been discussed widely under the heading of "postindustrial utopians" (Frankel 1987). Germany may prefigure future developments here, given its current sociological preoccupation with the "crisis of the work society":

> Work has been reorganized to such an extent that the type of work represented by the working class has lost its critical place. . . . Thus the crisis of the working society is the crisis of a class that has lost its function and role as a historical actor. And it is with the crisis of the working class that the crisis of its opponent, the bourgeois class, is inextricably connected. (Eder 1992, p. 389)

Cultural Theory

Introduction: Mass Communications and Cultural Studies

The primary focus of variable-based research in the sphere of cultural sociology has been so-called "effects research" in the field of communications (Lowery and DeFleur 1983; Gitlin 1978). From this perspective, researchers attempt to link specific media events (e.g., violence) with concrete behavioral effects defined in experimental or quasi-experimental terms. Indeed for many years this linkage was synonymous with the "sociology of mass communications." The largely inconclusive results of such research contributed to the happy pluralist conclusion that the mass media were not the diabolic monsters portrayed by mass culture theorists and critical theory. In contrast early Critical Theory was associated with a version of the theory of mass culture that postulated a reductionist political economic thesis regarding the capacity of the "culture industries" to subvert protest potentials and reproduce false consciousness. Contemporary research, however, is concerned with overcoming the determinism of the older Critical Theory without rejecting altogether the decisive character of the mass media in the reproduction of contemporary societies; as such it is part of a more general revitalization of the sociology of culture that allows empirical correction of and constructive dialogue with questions originally posed in critical theory (Billington et al. 1991). In this context the work of Pierre Bourdieu in France and Norbert Elias—originally a student of Mannheim whose magnum opus was only translated belatedly (Elias 1978, 1982)—has proven especially influential in revitalizing the analysis of cultural production and consumption (Featherstone 1992).

Systemic Models:
The Dominant Ideology Thesis

The original impulse of Marxian-inspired research on culture is linked closely to the base-superstructure model and the method of political economic research. Internationally such research has been developed extensively in France (Mattelart 1979; Mattelart and Mattelart 1986, 1992) and Britain (Garnham 1990), as well as in North America (Smythe 1981; Schiller 1971, 1973, 1976; Ewen 1976).

The difficulty with such political economic research, however, is establishing the precise link between the economic infrastructure of communications and culture and the actual outcomes with respect to both content and ultimate effects on consumers. Pluralist defenders of commodified cultural systems claim, for example, that consumer sovereignty guarantees the owners of the media are in no position to "impose" their class interests and ideology on consumers. As a consequence, central to the revitalization of critical cultural research have been *cultural reproduction theories* that postulate some form of *dominant ideology* or a system of *cultural hegemony*. Under the general heading of the "dominant ideology thesis" such theories have been criticized for their functionalist method of argument.[5] In their more deterministic versions (as in the structuralist Marxism of Althusser) such theories attribute to culture a great deal of autonomy from immediate economic determination, but then argue that in the long run the ideological content of culture indeed does serve the interests of the reproduction of capital. The basis of the argument here is thus the functionalist assumption that capitalism has a "need" for a dominant ideology that the cultural system inevitably produces. From this perspective it becomes impossible to conceive how resistance to cultural domination might be mediated by actual subjects of social change (Connell 1983).

Yet if viewed in a more open and historically contingent manner, models of social and cultural reproduction can serve as a useful framework within which the relations between systemic integration and social integration can be conceptualized. Research in various domains based on such open models of systemic integration have produced a quite variegated picture of how the structures of domination operate over time. For example, the productivist ideology based on the reduction of workers to machines has been traced back to 19th-century liberal and Marxist thought alike, as well as 20th-century phenomena such as Fordism and Taylorism (Rabinbach 1992). Similarly studies of educational reproduction have moved away from an early focus on the "correspondence principle" rigidly linking the functions of education to the economy, to a more dynamic analysis of the relationship between education and power (Apple 1982; Whitty 1985; Cole 1988). These issues reappear in a somewhat different form in applied and professional fields, for example, the critical legal studies movement (Hutchinson 1989), radical social work (Wagner 1990), critiques of medicalization (Illich 1975), along with the feminist critiques cross-cutting and complementing all of these.

The implications of cultural hegemony as expressed in cultural products—as forms of discourse—have drawn particular attention. Despite the continuous risk of the formalism of synchronic analysis, structuralist-type methods have provided a crucial antidote to naive interactionism, social phenomenology, and conventional content analysis of media messages. Understood in more social and interactionist terms, such neostructuralist discourse analysis has explored a wide range of cultural phenomena. Especially valuable has been the notion of a *social semiotics* of hegemony (Hodge and Kress 1988; Gottdiener 1985a), a theme obviously central to communications studies but also such disparate domains as "promotional culture" (Wernick 1991), urban studies (Gottdiener and Lagopoulos 1986), geography, architecture, and the theory of complex organizations (Mumby 1988). Today these more structuralist approaches have moved, as in the case of state theory, toward more open, historically contingent models. A good example of this type of approach can be found in Douglas Kellner's focusing on the United States in *Television and the Crisis of Democracy*, which draws on a synthesis of critical theory and the Gramscian notion of *counterhegemony* (Kellner 1990).

Action Analysis:
Cultural Production and Reception

In response to the limits to the focus on the systemic imperatives of reproduction, *critical communications research* has moved beyond political economy by increasingly examining cultural processes at the action level—that is, as processes of production and reception (Hardt 1992). As in the case of the state, research on social integration in the context of culture and mass communications has been carried out effectively from a variety of perspectives, either in relation to the production of culture or its consumption (Curran and Gurevitch 1991). A central theme here has been the development of a theory of cultural consumption (Kellner 1989a, pp. 146-175). Sports and leisure research generally have emerged as sites where the issues of the relationship between constraint and agency have taken on strategic importance and increasingly global dimensions (Gruneau 1983; MacCannell 1992).

Much actor-oriented research in the area of cultural research remains primarily within the limits of interpretive and interactionist assumptions (Denzin 1992). Similar problems are especially evident in the most common traditional form of actor-oriented research in the analysis of media consumption: so-called *uses and gratifications research* based simply on asking people why they use the media—that is, the manifest needs that are gratified. This methodology largely uncritically accepts the manifest attitudes of actors as adequate for understanding consumption processes (Blumler and Katz 1974). In contrast, actor-oriented research embedded in or indirectly informed by a critical theory framework tends to construct analyses of both cultural production and consumption in a more potentially critical way by probing more deeply into the process of reception (Morley and Silverstone 1990). The crucial difference is that the assumption of constraints on cultural production becomes central to analysis, though not in the deterministic way assumed by political economy. Similarly research concerned with the study of the relationship between needs and commodities shifts attention to the agent as constrained by, but not a mere dupe of, the system of advertising (Leiss 1976, 1978; Leiss et al. 1986; Jhally 1987). Especially important in this context for questioning simplistic theories of hegemony has been research on the active character of the reception of popular culture by audiences (Radway 1984; Liebes and Katz 1990). Such interpretive *audience reception analysis* has called into question simplistic theories of cultural hegemony.

John Thompson attempts a more general account in his work on ideology in modern culture (Thompson 1990). Strongly influenced by Giddens and Habermas, Thompson develops an analysis of the "mediatization of culture" that stresses the "interactional impact of technical media," as well as its implications for the theory of ideology. In the context of education, theories of cultural reproduction have been recast in terms of open models that explicitly confront many of the issues posed by postmodernist critics of agency and representation (Aronowitz and Giroux 1991; Morrow and Torres Forthcoming). Mark Poster has sought to push critical media theory in an even more poststructuralist direction with analyses of what he calls the new "mode of information" that calls into question or points to the limits of the verbal bias and rationalism of theorists such as Habermas and Giddens. In contrast to earlier work on the role of the media in reproduction, domination, or eliciting resistance, Poster's "study of the mode of information is more concerned with the manner and forms in which cultural experience constitutes subjects"

(Poster 1990, p. 16). Electronically mediated phenomena such as advertising, databases, word processing, and computer science are analyzed from this perspective.

Mediational Inquiry:
Resistance and Transformation

The theorization of mediational-type analysis has been developed most extensively in the often overlapping fields of critical pedagogy, feminist theory, liberation theology, and studies of resistance in popular culture. Perhaps the most central theme in this kind of research is with the study of manifestations of *resistance,* a complex and contested term that refers to the ways actors actively come to terms with and potentially struggle against cultural forms that dominate them. A central shift visible here is the move from dogmatic toward more dialogical theories of ideology critique, partly under the influence of Gramsci, Habermas, and Bakhtin (Gardiner 1992), as well as on general efforts to develop *resistance theory* (Leong 1992). Indeed, it would be possible to broadly equate British style *cultural studies* research as increasingly mediational in character (Brantlinger 1990; G. Turner 1990; Agger 1992a; Easthope and McGowan 1992; Barker and Beezer 1992).

The point of departure for mediational analysis in *critical pedagogy* is the seminal work of Paulo Freire, a Brazilian educator whose theory of "conscientization" developed in the context of literacy training in Latin America (Freire 1970; Leonard 1990; Misgeld 1985). Adapted to advanced societies, critical pedagogy has been concerned especially with teachers as critical intellectuals (Giroux 1988a, 1988b, 1992) and the possibilities for curricular reform (Apple and Weis 1983). Habermas's work has been a focus for research in curriculum theory (Carr and Kemmis 1986), as well as a major reinterpretation of the pedagogical implications of Habermas's theory of communicative action (R. Young 1989). Education also has been a key site for critical ethnographic work (Kanpol 1992). One of the most widely cited examples of mediating critical research is that of Willis on *Learning to Labor,* an ethnographic study that powerfully captures the moment of failed resistance among working-class male youth in the transition from school to work (Willis 1981).

Cultural studies research has been especially influential in bringing the issues of critical theory to the study of popular culture (Gruneau 1988; Grossberg 1992; Grossberg et al. 1992). The range of research in this area suggests noting some representative themes. Popular music has been a particular focus of attention (Grossberg 1992; Middleton 1990). Hebdige's study of the origins of punk music in Britain provided the basis for widely cited ethnographic research on the interplay between working-class youth culture and race relations (Hebdige 1979). A suggestive analysis of the possibilities for consumer resistance has been developed in Grahame's research on "critical literacy" among consumers, evoking the educational literacy analogy in the sphere of consumption (Grahame 1985). Parallel concerns are evident in anthropological research on the relations between political economy and culture (Marcus 1990) and the nature of peasant resistance (J. Scott 1985; Nordstrom and Martin 1992).

Social Psychology

Introduction: Toward a Critical Social Psychology

As a subfield of psychology, *social psychology* has been described as a research tradition almost completely defined by variable-based experimental and quasi-experimental research. The primary exceptions to this description have been in sociology where symbolic interactionism and social phenomenology have been established as an often closely related framework for various microsociological investigations. Also psychoanalytic theory has been influential on the margins of sociology and centrally in feminist theory. At various points all of these latter interpretive approaches have proven useful for addressing the kinds of social psychological questions that have been of concern to critical social theory, for example, alienation and reification, theory of domination and social character, the psychodynamics of ideology critique and transformations of consciousness, and communicative interaction. Although aspects of such questions have been and still are translated into research projects based on statistical modeling, interpretive research has been more conducive to dealing with these questions.

The concept of a *critical social psychology* (or a "critical psychology" that is implicitly a *social* psychology) has at times been suggested as a framework for overcoming the various problems and limitations of the existing social psychological orientations (Sampson 1983; Wexler 1983; Boer 1983; Parker 1989). One of the characteristics of these concerns is that a wide range of approaches (e.g., interactionist, cognitive, developmental, psychoanalytic) have been brought to bear on social psychological problems put on the agenda of research by critical theories. Another aspect of such tendencies is a critique of existing psychological and social psychological work (Stam et al. 1987; Broughton 1987; Buss 1979).

The variety and range of these efforts defy easy summary. What we attempt instead is to review some of the representative contributions associated with the three modes of social psychological inquiry that naturally follow from the three moments of social reproduction: systematically oriented models concerned with the nature of domination, action-oriented accounts focusing on issues of agency and subjectivity, and mediational accounts attempting to capture aspects of the agency-structure dialectics in relation to resistance.

Systemic Models: Domination

The uses of systemic models in social psychological analysis is linked closely to early deterministic models of socialization. The early Frankfurt School research on the authoritarian personality in the German working class can be cited as a pioneering contribution in this context.[6] Later work in the United States suggested the partial compatibility of this type of research with conventional survey methods (Adorno et al. 1964; Forbes 1985). Through the influence of Erich Fromm, David Riesman's *Lonely Crowd* (Riesman 1961) provided a view of the socialization process whose concern with social character sharply differentiated it from then reigning functionalism and complemented the effort of Gerth and Mills to develop a historical social psychology (Gerth and Mills 1964). Riesman's distinction between tradition-, inner-, and other-direction was suggestive of the profound changes in the relations of social control as mediated through collective personality structures. In diverse and often conflicting ways this tradition of critical "historical social psychology" has been extended in various directions (Lasch 1979, 1984; Langman 1991; Langman and Kaplan 1981; Sennett 1977; Kreilkamp 1976).

At the same time, more theoretical inquiry has contributed to the question of the relationship between critical theory and psychoanalytic theory. Most importantly, some of the gender blindspots have been criticized in an effort to draw out further the interactive foundations of subjectivity and domination (Benjamin 1988). Other research has tackled a wide range of issues with respect to the relationship between childhood and the "relational preconditions of socialism" (Richards 1984). Another area of related inquiry has already been cited in connection with cultural theory: studies on the social psychology of consumption and its relation to human needs (Leiss 1976).

Research on alienation marked one of the first social psychological topics extensively drawn on for more conventional empirical research techniques (Blauner 1964; Seeman 1975). As critics have pointed out, however, the simplistic translation of alienation as a social psychological category of "powerlessness" defined by attitude scales undercuts the basic agency-structure dialectic (Schwalbe 1986). Research in this area has for some time formed the basis of a research area for the International Sociological Association (Schweitzer and Geyer 1976, 1981, 1989; Geyer and Heinz 1992).

The most popular way of getting around the limits of survey research to study these issues is evident in some uses of "discourse analysis" and narrative theory for a critical social psychology (Parker 1992). For example, Mumby has studied organizational cultures in terms of the discources of storytelling within bureaucracies to get at issues of domination and subject formation (Mumby 1988).

Action Analysis:
Agency and Autonomy

The limitation of domination theory in its various guises is its *negativity*—that is, a focus on the relation of power to subjugation and personality formation. This concern does not explicitly address what is presupposed by the notion of resistance to domination: a more generalized competence for interaction and communication that might prefigure the possibilities to be realized through transformative practices. One strategy of dealing with this topic has been recourse to theories of human "nature," issues that traditionally have been defined in the continental tradition as those of "philosophical anthropology." Traditional philosophical discourse attempted to deal with such issues in terms of speculative accounts of an invariant "human essence." Marxian accounts have remained ambivalent because, on the one hand, historical materialism necessarily insisted on the social structural determinants of individual social character; on the other hand, the thesis of alienation and revolutionary transformation presupposed some kind of essential, inherent possibilities that somehow escape historical determination. Critical theories have been central to formulating a conception of "historical anthropology" that relates universality and particularity in a more convincing manner (Honneth and Joas 1988).

As Habermas and Giddens have argued in somewhat different ways, the missing dimension of the Marxian theory of society was the absence of an adequate model of symbolic or communicative action. Otherwise the subject has been defined almost exclusively in negative terms as alienated or suffering from exploitation and false consciousness and yet able to act "progressively" because of utilitarian motives driven by material needs. The lack of an adequate theory of the subject led inexorably to Leninism, a vanguardist theory of revolution that turned over to the revolutionary experts the task of socializing "correct" consciousness through the erection of a bureaucratic apparatus ostensibly representing the objective will of the working class.

Habermas has been concerned particularly with integrating *competence models* of development (ego, moral, social) into a theory of the subject as understood by the theory of communicative action (Habermas 1984, 1987a). Consistent with his strong program for critical theory, various types of reconstructive or structuralist sciences (linguistics, developmental psychology) are taken as evidence of universal potentials inhibited or facilitated by social relations. Giddens, on the other hand, has not embraced a strong theory of the developmental subject in Habermas's manner. Instead he has been more concerned with the self and identity in high modernity, a theme reflected in much other recent work influenced by critical theory (Lash and Friedmann 1992). Paul Ricoeur's hermeneutic poststructuralism has been used to analyze discursive moments of identification in a manner that overcomes the neglect of agency in much social psychology (D. Brown 1994). Under the influence of Mikhail Bakhtin, others have sought to develop aspects of his dialogical theory of the self (Bakhtin 1981; Gardiner 1992). Finally, microsociological research has stressed the crucial importance of emotions to an interactionist theory informed by theories of power and status, a shift complementary to the further development of the critical theory of the subject (Kemper 1978; Hochschild 1983; Scheff 1990). This shift complements the long-standing interest in theories of the body and its relation to body politics (B. Turner 1984; O'Neill 1985; Morrow 1992b).

Attributing agency and knowledgeability to dominated subjects opens up new lines of inquiry that seek to establish the character of the experience of exploitation and alienation prior to postulating how and in what direction that change might or should take place. Indicative of the possibilities here is a recent ethnographic study of unemployment (Burman 1988) that explicitly orients itself in relation to Giddens's structuration theory, though focusing on the subjective dimensions of the experience of unemployment. Although this study otherwise resembles much good interpretive research carried out under the heading of symbolic interactionism and social phenomenology, it explicitly relates its object of study to questions of power and domination. Also much feminist research is concerned with portraying women who, despite their domination in relations of subordination, exhibit qualities of resourcefulness indicative of missed possibilities and potential transformations.

Mediational Inquiry: Changing the Subject

It is in the context of social psychological mediational analysis that the most fundamental issues of the subjective bases of social reproduction and change become apparent, though from a more individual perspective than the analysis of similar issues in the contexts of the state and culture. Studies of actors in this context typically focus on the tensions involved in resistance and situations in which new possibilities may be glimpsed momentarily and perhaps lost altogether, or consolidated as part of the cumulative change process. It is at these moments that it becomes possible to view agency/structure relations in their most dynamic form, especially in the context of the cultural politics of everyday life and social movements (Shotter 1993). Historically the Marxist tradition was limited by its focus on the working class and the absence of an adequate transformational social psychology, a problem exacerbated by individual-society dualisms (Henriques et al. 1984).

Theological critiques of Marxism always have been sensitive to these issues, and contemporary forms of "critical theology" (Baum 1975; Lamb 1982; McCarthy 1991, pp. 181-99) and "liberation theology" (Sigmund 1990; Leonard 1990, pp. 167-248) have provided important contributions to the reconciliation of critical theory and religion. Anthropological research on "resistance" has provided a needed comparative perspective on these issues (J. Scott, 1985, 1992; Nordstrom and Martin 1992). Critical pedagogy also has related its concerns directly to fundamental issues in critical social psychology (Sullivan 1990).

Another line of research strongly influenced by Michel Foucault has sought to underscore some of the problems of viewing "liberation" as merely a process of overcoming "domination" (P. Miller 1987). Here an important corrective is applied to the assumption that freedom and power are totally opposed, as if a society could be formed without power, and as if power were not essential to the very possibility of freedom. Such questioning provides insights into the more complex nature of resistance than implied by a focus on the problematic of rationality evident in Habermas. Such questions have been central to feminist debates about theories of the subject (Nicholson 1990; P. Smith 1988).

Probably the most important focus of work touching on mediational analysis has been related to research on *new social movements* involving, for example, women, racial and ethnic claims, and environmental concerns (A. Scott 1990). Whereas social class was the primary agent in classical Marxist theories of social reproduction, the diversity of social movements in civil society is the concern of critical theory (Cohen and Arato 1992). In certain contexts the study of movements in process cannot be separated readily from a research relationship that approximates an act of intervention. As we have seen with respect to critical ethnography, an inevitable tension exists between critical distance and engagement, a theme pursued in the final chapter in discussing research and practice. In this regard, however, reference to another context of mediational research helps underscore the importance of these issues.

Alain Touraine's method of "permanent sociology" is especially suggestive of the constructive role of critical research in relation to mobilizing practices. Touraine's method is of interest as well because it stops just short of the more directly engaged strategies of participatory action research. The primary reason is that the tensions between research and practice are made explicit: "The researcher, then, is neither external to the group nor identified with it. Rather, the researcher tries to have the focus on and clarify those meanings of its action which challenge the constraints on practical discourse and the active formation of political will" (Hearn 1985, p. 198). In general, therefore, this focus is consistent with Habermas's suggestion that critical research can serve only in an instructive or advisory capacity quite distinct from the practical decisions that have to be made by actors themselves.

Conclusion

The preceding survey could only serve to illustrate selectively the kinds of problems involved in the movement between a focus on systemic, actional, and mediational processes in social life in the domains of state theory, culture, and social psychology. In particular our discussion did not link up the details of the methodological techniques employed in the research alluded to, partly because they involved the full gamut of interpretive analytical techniques in intensive case studies and case study comparisons of a historical and ethnographic character, textual analysis, and even the occasional use of variable-based research. Systemic-level analyzes made extensive use of structural generalizations involving contradictions (as in state crisis theory) or the formation of new relationships between political publics and the state or audiences and the mass media. But these structural arguments retained—at least in their nonfunctionalistic variants—an interpretive dimension that acknowledges that the outcomes were always mediated in a contingent way in concrete circumstances by agents with at least partial awareness of their contexts of action.

Another central feature of critical research, however, is that empirical research is *not an end in itself.* Empirical research is typically theory-driven and, often as not, concerned with the further exemplification of already partly validated theory of cultural reproduction or change, rather than focusing strictly on confirmation or falsification as in the case of middle-range theories. Further, given its potential relation to practice, much critical research is more concerned with producing knowledge for the uses of particular publics and constituencies. This knowledge does not seek to be completely "original," so much as to extend and communicate what already is understood to audiences previously deprived of such knowledge. This communicative aspect is similar to many forms of applied research orientation, but with the crucial difference of a very different conception of the relationship between theory and practice—the theme of the final chapter.

Notes

1. These problems are not ones of ignorance, of course, but reflect the increasingly unmanageable nature of the material. Kellner thanks Giddens for his comments even though the latter does not figure in the study.

2. For the most sustained critical discussion of the uses and alleged abuses of the social versus system integration distinction by Habermas, Giddens, Lockwood, and others, see Mouzelis (1991), notwithstanding his intemperate impatience with Habermas's philosophical concerns.

3. It should be noted that for primarily circumstantial reasons Gottdiener's study was consulted only after the first draft of this manuscript was completed. Hence its exemplary status with respect to the themes of this book could be taken to suggest a broader convergence in critical theory about the understanding of theory and empirical research—one occurring independently in disparate, specialized areas.

4. Indeed the issues surrounding theories of the state have become so extensive and convoluted that many of the earlier distinctions between political economy

structuralist Marxism, critical theory, and so forth have become blurred as neo-Marxist approaches attempt to adjust to rapidly changing realities (Jessop 1990). The purpose of the present discussion is to assert the pioneering importance of the research questions posed by Habermas and Offe and their ongoing elaboration, refinement, and critique in subsequent debates about the welfare state (Held 1987; Frankel 1987; Pierson 1991).

5. To be sure, several variants of this type of argument have been subjected to extensive criticism with respect to some of the stronger claims made about their explanatory force in theories of social reproduction (Abercrombie et al. 1980). Many of these issues have been addressed, however, in more recent discussions about the theory of the public sphere (Calhoun 1992a).

6. More recently, the "interpellated subject" of Althusserian structuralism became for a time the basis of an even more deterministic model of social reproduction based on a fusion of Marxian and Freudian (Lacanian) structuralism. Although such contributions acknowledge the social psychological deficits of classical Marxism, they do so in a rather selective and problematic manner, but see Craib 1989; Elliott 1992; Fraser and Bartky 1992.

12

CRITICAL SOCIAL SCIENCE AND SOCIETY

Theory and Practice

The assumption that thought profits from the decay of the emotions, or even that it remains unaffected, is itself an expression of the process of stupefaction. (Adorno 1974, pp. 122-3)

In its proper place, even epistemologically, the relationship of subject and object would lie in the realization of peace among men as between men and their Other. Peace is the state of distinctness without domination, with the distinct participating in each other. (Adorno 1978, p. 500)

Thus the theory that creates consciousness can bring about the conditions under which the systematic distortions of communication are dissolved and a practical discourse can then be conducted; but it does not contain any information which prejudges the future action of those concerned. . . . Therefore theory cannot have the same function for the organization of action, of the political struggle, as it has for the organization of enlightenment . . . the vindicating superiority of those who do the enlightening over those who are to be enlightened is theoretically unavoidable, but at the same time it is fictive and requires self-correction: in a process of enlightenment there can only be participants. (Habermas 1973, pp. 38-41)

To this point we have not taken up the implications of this approach for the interplay between research and society, other than clearly differentiating between critical theory as a research program and ideologies as action-oriented belief systems. As noted, the post-Marxist context of contemporary politics dramatically alters the tasks of critical theory in ways that can at the moment only be vaguely anticipated. But Giddens's formulation of the stance of a weak program bears repeating here: "In being stripped of historical guarantees, critical theory enters the universe of contingency and has to adopt a logic that no longer insists upon the *necessary* unity of theory and practice" (Giddens 1987a, p. 337).

Not unlike the failure of economic depression to generate the revolutionary class consciousness anticipated by classical Marxism earlier in this century, the pervasive fiscal crisis of the contemporary capitalist state has resulted in an ambiguous *legitimation crisis* whose effects are contradictory and have called into question the very notion of progress. These circumstances have deepened the crisis of intellectuals with respect to the project of modernity, a project with which critical theory has been implicated from the outset (Boggs 1993). Having passed through the self-doubts of Adorno and Horkheimer's *dialectic of enlightenment*, however, critical theory accepted the absence of guarantees long ago; moreover, in its more recent forms it has rejected the simple choice between Dewey and Foucault as ingeniously formulated by the philosopher Richard Rorty:

> What Foucault doesn't give us is what Dewey wanted to give us—a kind of hope which doesn't *need* reinforcement from the "idea of a transcendental or enduring subject." . . . Foucault sees no middle ground, in thinking about the social sciences, between the "classic" Galilean conception of "behavioral science" and the French notion of "*sciences de l'homme.*" It was just such a middle ground that Dewey proposed, and which inspired the social sciences in America before the failure of nerve which turned them "behavioral." (Rorty 1982, p. 206)

This contention—characteristic of liberal, as opposed to technocratic, models of enlightenment—appears tenable at first glance. As Rorty continues, "Reading Foucault reinforces the disillusion which American intellectuals have suffered during the last few decades of watching the 'behavioralized' social sciences team up with the state" (1982, p. 207). But against Foucault he argues:

But there seems no particular reason why, after dumping Marx, we have to keep on repeating all the nasty things about bourgeois liberalism which he taught us to say. There is no inferential connection between the disappearance of the transcendental subject—of "man" as something having a nature which society can repress or understand—and the disappearance of human solidarity. Bourgeois liberalism seems to be the best example of this solidarity we have yet achieved, and Deweyan pragmatism the best articulation of it. (Rorty 1982, p. 207)

Even if bourgeois liberalism may be in some sense the best example of human solidarity, it has an increasingly precarious relationship to it. The mediating positions of Habermas and Giddens—between Dewey and Foucault—provide the most astute alernative in the form of a *postbehavioral* critical social science. That pragmatism's failure was not merely circumstantial and related to some endemic problems is glossed over by those neopragmatists (e.g., Shalin 1992) who jump on the postmodernist bandwagon as critics of critical theory, forgetting that it was critical theory that put pragmatism back on the agenda of late 20th-century philosophy and social theory (Joas 1993; Antonio, 1989; Morrow, 1983). How so? First, because critical theory provided the basis for a critical theory of society absent in pragmatism; and second, because in the form represented by Habermas's interpretation of Peirce (along with critical realism), it has provided the most forceful attempt to secure universalistic *ontological* grounds for reason and solidarity beyond the foundationalisms of a transcendental subject and the Marxian philosophy of history.

What often were seen to be some of the weaknesses of critical theory in the past can in the new context often be drawn on as resources. Given its strong metatheoretical orientation, capacity for theoretical renewal, and lack of compromising political affiliations, critical theory has been in a good position to redeploy the concepts of critical thought to deal with the emergent forms of crisis and the reorganization of the human sciences. In concluding we can only briefly touch on some of these issues in terms of three basic objectives. First, we attempt to locate our account of critical social research in relation to four conceptions of social science: the *technocratic, liberal enlightenment, critical-dialogical,* and *skeptical postmodernist* models.

Second, we examine the current historical context of critical research in advanced capitalist societies. Our task is not to define "what is to be done" in any concrete sense, a strategy that would involve a conjunctural diagnosis based on specific societies that is beyond the scope of this study. What we do attempt, however, is a limited, historically specific characterization of the position of critical research in relation to the current crisis of the welfare state and the New Right challenges to it. We stress in particular the confluence of three vocabularies of theoretical discourse that define this situation: the radicalized *rights-based discourse* emanating from liberal theory, the revised and pluralized discourse constituted by *counterhegemonic struggles* and cultural creation, and the unifying discourse directed toward the revitalization of the democratic public sphere and civil society.

Our third objective in this chapter is to extend the implications of this general critical model with respect to the different sites or locales of inquiry and practice. All too often statements about recommended relations of theory and practice are voiced in abstract terms without reference to particular contexts of practice. In the process we discuss three locales of inquiry, each with specific tasks: the relatively autonomous inquiries located in universities and other locations that encourage fundamental or relatively *autonomous research* oriented to relevant *scientific communities*; the interventions of *social criticism*—that is, forms of inquiry and advocacy primarily directed toward the *public sphere,* though also often involved in professional training associated with policy and social problems analysis; and *critical action research* directed toward informing the social *praxis* actually carried out by social agents. Although each of these is essential and some researchers may move between these three locales, it is misleading to reduce critical inquiry to any one or to see them as a hierarchy leading from theory down to practice.

Models of Social Science

The notion of the "myth of value-free" science extends beyond its impossibility. In practice, few social scientists have seen their work as ultimately without redeeming value; indeed the whole history of social science is caught up in the classic Enlightenment and modernist vision of reform and progress. What most people mean by the value-free doctrine is shared broadly even by critical researchers: that one should not allow one's personal values to distort or bias the conduct or interpretation of research. The primary difference is in how to achieve that goal. Positivists have tended to argue that it required some kind of ascetic commitments to impersonality; critical approaches argue that self-consciousness about values is the best way to be vigilant against such problems.

As a consequence the most crucial issue at stake is not whether to be value-free or not, but *how to connect values and research in rationally justifiable ways.* That statement implies specific models of the relationship between social research and society. Previously we have distinguished broadly between social engineering models of explanation and those of social theorizing. This type of distinction often has been the basis of a parallel distinction between technocratic and critical conceptions of applied knowledge in which the latent ideological implications of the former strategy are suppressed fully in the emulation of the engineering model. We find this heuristic schema a bit simplistic; accordingly we compare four basic models of applied social knowledge—the technocratic, liberal enlightenment, and critical dialogical and skeptical postmodernist models—in terms of three basic issues: (a) their metatheoretical assumptions about the nature of scientific knowledge, (b) their understanding of the theory/practice relationship—that is, account of the dynamics of the relationship between knowledge application and concrete social actors, and (c) their implicit or explicit utopian vision about the "good society."

Technocratic Models

Metatheory. A succinct definition of technocratic theorizing has been characterized as "the American ideology" (Wilson 1977, p. 15) because it would not

> have been possible at all had it not been for the emergence and coming of age of this "first new nation". . . This ideology is technocratic because it invokes science in order to justify policies aimed at realizing particular objectives. These policies take the form of allegedly neutral techniques whose origins and concerns are distended from

the interests they serve. It is science's effective condemnation of both critical reflection and common-sense thinking which makes such obfuscation possible. (Wilson 1977, pp. 15-7)

It is not necessary here to review again the epistemological foundations of such technocratic perspectives, whether in logical positivism or general systems theories (Bryant 1985).

Theory and Practice. Although technocratic models have never been consistently applied except under authoritarian political conditions, the form of criticism they represent has been a powerful tendency that pervasively has influenced postwar political culture. The technocratic impulse thus has shaped much contemporary discussion and contributed to the suppression of the political dimension of applied knowledge even though it never has been realized in a complete form. Habermas's discussion (1970) of the logic underlying the potential of science and technology to serve as a new form of ideology is instructive here regarding an emergent ideological tendency, though one that nowhere has been fully realized—partly because of the sustained critiques aligned against it.

Utopian Vision. Despite the austere implications of emulating the natural sciences, technocratic visions of the constructive potential of social knowledge have a decidedly utopian cast but primarily in the more pejorative sense of that term. A systems theoretical and behavioral version can be distinguished. Most systems analysis is wedded firmly to controlling change processes within the limits of the given, serving the powers that be (Boguslaw 1965; Hoos 1974; Lilienfeld 1978). For the most part, then, the utopian vision of technocratic approaches follows in the tradition of St. Simon in providing magical tools to bring to bear on controlling society in the name of whatever values are projected from the given official or popular culture. In this context the imagery of the metaphor of "social engineering" takes on a literal form.

Liberal Enlightenment Models

Metatheory. The epistemological foundations of an alternative to classical positivism in the social sciences can be found in

American *pragmatism*, especially as elaborated by Dewey and his followers (Kaplan 1964), as well as the *critical rationalism* associated with Karl Popper and his disciples.[1] These approaches generally acknowledge the distinctive features of the relationship between social technology and human actors, as opposed to technical control over nature, though references to analogies between the two (e.g., the notion of "piecemeal engineering" in Popper) often sound like more traditional technocratic conceptions. In American pragmatism, in particular, the social and political dimensions of applied knowledge are taken into account at the level of the theory of knowledge. But the result is a relatively narrow focus on the ethical implications of research (practical discourse) and the definition and resolution of social problems. Although this focus constitutes an advance over technocratic approaches, the resulting linkage of empirical and normative issues often remains superficial and unreflective. As Agger concludes: "Social problem-oriented scientism is still scientism, unable to understand its own constitution of, as well as its constitution by, the impermanent present. Freedom requires the lived experience of free thought as seeming social determinism is undone historically, not only in 'humanist' method—idealism" (Agger 1989, p. 15).

Theory and Practice. To their credit, liberal enlightenment models do not predicate their conception of critique on purely scientistic assumptions—that is, the denial of the political dimension of knowledge application or the suppression of value questions. Yet they do not entirely escape the dilemmas of what Habermas has referred to as a "positivistically bisected rationalism" (in the case of Popper) or a somewhat naive conception of the democratic public sphere (in the case of American pragmatism). The liberal conception of critique is based on the assumption that if a gap exists between the means and ends of policy, or in the workings of any social or cultural institution, there exists a rational basis for illuminating that discrepancy empirically (e.g., evaluation research or studies of institutions). Such criticism is recognized as the preliminary step in the definition of "social problems," hence the necessary point of departure for "problem solving." Although experts and technical professionals are acknowledged to be fallible and caught up in political processes, it is argued that professional ethics provide an adequate defense against abuses of power.

Such a position acknowledges the necessity of evaluative discourse in the social sciences, especially the applied domains, but contends that it can be conducted in a manner that escapes the dilemmas of traditional ideological confrontations (MacRae 1976; Rule 1978).

Utopian Vision. The liberal enlightenment model is considerably more cautious than its more optimistic technocratic counterpart. Although the metaphors of "social engineering" or "social technology" often are employed in this literature, they usually are deployed in an analogical rather than literal sense, as in the case of technocratic approaches. In other words, although liberal pragmatist strategies of reform may employ the scientific rhetoric of the dominant culture, projects of reconstruction clearly are conceived as having crucial political dimensions, and the differences between controlling natural processes and social ones are the subject of considerable attention.

Inevitably there is a considerable degree of convergence between the liberal enlightenment and critical enlightenment conceptions of democratic planning, but this should not obscure the fundamental differences. Despite overt intentions, liberal pragmatic models of planning veer off in an elitist direction.[2] The social psychological assumptions that guide such a liberal humanism are conveyed effectively with the theme of "public education." Education here is seen as a rational process of communicating information that culminates in the well-informed citizen necessary for liberal democracy. Such aware citizens thus become receptive to the definition of new social problems and the development of strategies of reform that guarantee continued progress. Chronic failure in achieving these ambitions, however, has left the liberal enlightenment perspective increasingly vulnerable to neoconservative criticism even if in some of its current versions (e.g., Rorty 1989) it can find ironic comfort in the paradoxes of postmodern contingency.

Critical Dialogical Models

Metatheory. The point of departure of critical social science is a critique of the uses of instrumental rationality as a process of domination over both external and internal nature (Leiss 1974; Held 1980). A much sharper distinction than that found in liberal pragmatism is made between the logic underlying the notion of control over natural processes and social ones. This theme is illustrated most effectively in Habermas's notion of *knowledge interests,* which distinguishes between empirical-analytical, hermeneutic-historical, and critical-emancipatory forms of knowledge. Whereas the first is based on the natural scientific notion of technical control, the latter two imply a fundamentally different relationship between knowledge and action. Most importantly, critical-emancipatory knowledge is viewed as having decisive significance for fundamental social change because it involves the fundamental transformation of individual and collective identities through liberation from previous constraints on communication and self-understanding. From this perspective the process of modernization has been mediated selectively by relations of power, rather than reflecting the natural logic of technological change. This approach opens the way for understanding the full implications of the diversity of critical methods and modes of discourse (practical, therapeutic, aesthetic) involved in social transformation.

Theory and Practice. On the one hand, critical theories do not deny or completely ignore the importance of empirically based analyses as the basis of a form of enlightenment. To that extent there is considerable continuity between the liberal and critical enlightenment models. On the other hand, critical theories do contend that liberal enlightenment models seriously underestimate the obstacles to reasoned dialogue, let alone either the implementation or application of pertinent forms of empirical research. In short, *liberal enlightenment models of critique simply do not take into account the full implications of the theory of ideology and its conception of the depth-structure of distorted communication.* It is for this reason that critical theory necessarily resists the dissolution of the tasks of critical intellectuals into the professional model (Gouldner 1975; Bauman 1987). Indeed the very possibility of exercising the tasks of critique presupposes a degree of marginality and risks of "unprofessional" conduct. As Agger laments: "They inevitably find us wanting—methodology, objectivity, reasonableness" (1989, p. 2). To that extent the professional model—its conception of "discipline"—inevitably contains a residue of positivism even if it moves beyond a purely technocratic self-understanding.[3]

Utopian Vision. The reconstructive project of contemporary critical social science is jeopardized at the outset because of its ambiguous relationship to the given sociohistorical context within which it seeks to speak: above all, deep-set doubts about the very historical possibility (and nature) of potential transformation. Still a certain broadly based consensus has emerged with respect to the contours that social transformation and reconstruction might embody; much more problematic is the degree to which they can be practically prefigured within, and hence might contribute to transforming, existing forms of society (Frankel 1987). The reconstructive utopian themes of critical theory thus are reflected most typically in the concepts of participatory democracy and critical pedagogy.

The ambivalence of planning concepts in critical theory—notions of how to practically construct a rational society—is linked closely to the recognition of the obstacles to *participatory democracy.* And yet there is a radical reformist side of critical social science that persists in evoking this notion as the basis of policy and planning research (Forester 1985c; Friedmann 1979, 1987). This strategy is based on the somewhat problematic assumption that participatory processes do—even if a failure in practice by technical standards—facilitate the formation of forms of consciousness and resistance necessary for fundamental change even though some populist responses may release a destructive *ressentiment.* A typical expression of this paradox is the examples of critical theorists who advocate participation in the electoral processes of party systems that give little immediate prospect of fostering fundamental transformations (Birnbaum 1988).

The point of departure of critical pedagogies is that the liberal humanistic notion of public education, however noble in its intention, has lost its grip on reality in the era of the decline of the public sphere, the emergence of massive cultural industries, and the failure of educational institutions to challenge effectively their reproductive functions. The alternative is a critical pedagogy that redefines the categories of public education in terms of such concepts as cultural hegemony and resistance attuned to the postmodern condition (Giroux 1992). However important the formation of a utopian *discourse of possibility* may be, the concrete prospects of the "researcher as social actor" requires a peculiar combination of detachment and engagement (Popkewitz 1984, pp. 183-202).

Skeptical Postmodernism: The End of Reason?

Metatheory. There are basically two readings of postmodernist social theory on of the issue of theory and practice. The first—variously described as critical, oppositional, and feminist—can be read in dialogical terms as both a critique of critical theory and yet complementary (reflecting thus self-criticisms immanent within it). Much postmodernist theorizing in this sense has been incorporated within critical theory. The second—variously described as relativist, nihilist, and skeptical—culminates in a variety of political positions that, at best, assume an ironic acceptance of the status quo or, at worst, suggest the futility of all projects of human transformation. Rather than attempt to map this complex terrain, we simply allude to the central challenges posed by skeptical postmodernism.[4] With respect to the epistemological foundations of inquiry, skeptical postmodernist social theory calls into question the very notion of an objective "representation" of reality, whether because of the reliance of science on language or because of the way the postmodern condition itself has undermined "grand narratives" of philosophy and social science (Lyotard) or has obscured the very relationship between the real and the hyperreal (Baudrillard).

Theory and Practice. Under the influence of Michel Foucault, knowledge and power are viewed as mutually implicated in their mutual constitution. To this extent knowledge is inseparable from domination, and any claim to expertise or knowledge—even in the name of emancipatory interests—is contaminated from the outset. In the process of this generalized struggle in which no participants have a privileged position in relation to truth, the notion of ideology disappears in a world of universalized, distorted communication. But whether viewed as an "endless conversation" (Rorty) or as interminable struggle, politics in the strong postmodernist interpretation can no longer be understood in terms that cumulatively relate to the needs of real people in existing communities who want to connect their personal problems with public troubles.

Utopian Vision. To the extent that any form of political or transformative practice becomes conceivable in skeptical postmodernist terms, it is completely cut off from transcendent or universal claims. The British sociologist David Silverman has aptly described the current crisis in terms of criticizing the "impossible dreams for reformism and romanticism." It is concluded that Foucault has moved beyond this through his deconstruction of the techniques based on such representations:

> This constitutes five challenges to the Enlightenment thinker: an onward march of Progress can no longer be assumed; politics is not reducible to the practices of the State, for power does not arise in any central point; power is seen in an incitement to speak as much as in censorship, repression, or exclusion; the human sciences are not free-floating critical apparatuses but are inside mechanisms of power; and finally, the "free individual" is a construction of power/knowledge, not its antithesis. (Gubrium and Silverman 1989, p. 5)

Redefining Counterhegemony and the Public Sphere

Two themes have emerged as central to a new conception of theory and practice and its relationship to social research: developing strategies for overcoming the fragmenting effects of the pluralization of counterhegemonic movements, and the development of incorporating rights-based claims as part of the normative theory.

Counterhegemony and Pluralism

Postmodernist critiques of the Enlightenment have important implications for critical theory, as does the parallel but different thesis that we have entered a new postmodernist cultural epoch and phase of economic organization. From this perspective the classic theory of counterhegemony (a universalizing social movement based on the working class) has lost its force. Critical theory no longer claims any kind of class-based Archimedean position that would justify such a universal class, and poststructuralist neo-Gramscian theory has been reworked to deal with many of these problems in ways that often converge with debates in contemporary critical theory (Laclau 1990; Golding 1992). In other words, although the result is a recognition of the plurality of forms of domination, this does not necessarily culminate in a form of liberal pluralism that endlessly fragments politics. As a consequence, regardless of the changes that might take place, the oppositional role of critical theory as distinct from liberalism will persist, albeit in new guises and perhaps under different names because of the transformation of counterhegemonic struggles.

Rights-Based Claims

The social problems focus of much applied sociology contributes to the tendency of normative debates (social criticism) to be couched in terms of the claims of specific groups in relation to university-based research (Trow and Nybom 1991). Despite the built-in liberal and social democratic bias of the sociological tradition, the normative justifications of such positions rarely have been the focus of systematic inquiry or debate within sociology. In the past, Marxist theory has been prone to dismiss theories of human rights and *rights-based claims* as a "bourgeois illusion" or mere ideology. For critical theory, in contrast, the principle of *immanent critique* has long been the basis of using liberal principles of rights as the basis of a critique of existent realities. But such concerns with normative theory have been difficult to assimilate within the sociological tradition or professional training. Otherwise normative questions are relegated to the dogmas of various ideological groupings (including theologies) and the political sphere. In short, despite being the cognitive center of cultural reproduction in advanced societies, universities—faithful to their secular status—at no point make training in skills related to normative reasoning a central part of the curriculum. Although some religiously affiliated institutions do have such requirements or options, they generally are tied to particular denominational concerns or, at best, an ecumenical religious perspective.

A fundamental shift in normative theory in critical theory is evident in acknowledgment that the theory of domination (hence theories of justice) does not provide a self-sufficient foundation for moral discourse. In Giddens this is reflected in the distinction between emancipatory politics and life politics; Fay points to the tension between the goals of clarity and autonomy and happiness; and Habermas acknowledges the contrast between the formal determinations of procedural ethics and the fact that "actual forms of life and actual life-histories are embedded in unique traditions" and that "the theory of social evolution permits no conclusions about orders of happiness" (Habermas 1982, p. 228). On this basis a communicative ethics is confronted with the crucial challenge of bridging the gap between the generalized and concrete "other" of rights-based claims, a theme of feminist contributions to the theory of communicative ethics (Benhabib 1986, 1992).

Intellectuals and Practice:
Contexts of Critical Research

Introduction

Unfortunately the crisis experienced by leftist intellectuals during the past few decades has contributed to an increasingly unproductive rift over issues of theory and practice. On one side are those who follow the thesis that in large measure the failure of the Left can be attributed to its academic institutionalization and the decline of public intellectuals (Jacoby 1987). Another version is the insistence in much feminist theory (Lather 1991) that immediate emancipatory relevance take methodological priority. However, without denying the latter as a legitimate goal of some forms of theory and research, it is possible to counter that immediacy of practice does not provide an adequate basis for the multiple possible and necessary relations between critical theory and its overall counterhegemonic project (Popkewitz 1990). Nor does this defense of the autonomy of critical inquiry entail some necessary capitulation to positivism, careerism, and reformism. The production and appropriation of these different forms of knowledge vary with the different social locations of intellectuals and their relation to the pertinent systems of social and cultural reproduction.

The consequence of the historicity of practice is that the fundamental ambivalence of critical theory is implicit in its conception of the unity of theory and practice. First, this unity is itself historically variable, taking on different meanings in different contexts. Second, critical theory's insistence on unifying critical intelligence and democratic participation results in an *aporia* or unresolvable logical problem. This issue becomes most apparent in discussions that define critical research as radical transformative praxis, as both immediately relevant to practice and based on a subject-subject relation that does not involve domination of those researched. But this is only an aspiration "in principle" given the realities of research, especially in the light of the divisions between the researchers and the researched. In response to this problem, one focus of critical research has been "concrete situations in which the differences between subject and object are minimized and where material circumstances pose least resistance to change" (A. Sayer 1992, p. 254). But these situations are few and far between in the present conjuncture. As a consequence most critical research is confronted with the risk that "the development of certain types of knowledge may (and often does) have the effect of reinforcing domination and subordination and hence opposing a general emancipation. Social divisions therefore frequently override the immanent link between knowledge and emancipation" (A. Sayer 1992, pp. 254-5). It can be argued that even Marx was confronted with this dilemma because the reformist responses of the dominant classes were based, in part, on the ways hegemonic bourgeois intellectuals took seriously much of his diagnosis of the contradictions of laissez-faire capitalism. The crucial issue is that the typical failure of the ideal of an immanent link between knowledge and emancipation in the practice of research cannot be resolved through a retreat from "knowledge" to immediate "practice" even if this step remains in some sense the central experimental premise of participatory action research.

One way to respond to these difficulties is to recognize that generalizations about theory and practice need to be contextualized strategically. It is useful here to distinguish three basic contexts—often overlapping—in which critical theory is implicated in social life: (a) its relation to scientific communities as relatively *autonomous research* in institutions such as the university, (b) its public functions in *policy analysis and social criticism*, and (c) its contributions to *action research* involving actual agents of change. Such a notion of a decentered research tradition requires a multiplicity of different relationships to theory, research, and practices. As a consequence it downplays glorification or demeaning of any of them. To this end it is instructive to contrast the constraining and enabling conditions characteristic of the three primary contexts of theory and practice.

Universities and the Critical Renewal of Traditions

Many—especially Marxist and New Left—critics of the Frankfurt tradition have remarked on the intellectual aloofness of people such as Theodor Adorno as a kind of betrayal of the theory/praxis orientation of critical theory. Often this aloofness is attributed to a kind of intellectual elitism that is used as the basis of ad hominem arguments against the validity of specific theoretical arguments. Much of this attitude reflects a hangover of the original New Left's ambivalence toward the university, culminating in its being labeled as the primary bastion of the "system" in the late 1960s.

But a more fundamental question is involved here: that the autonomy of even a critical research program points to limits of engagement and the primary responsibility of university-based research to the critical renewal of traditions. For this reason Habermas has made a sharp distinction between the science system and political organization:

> I don't think that we can ever again, or even that we should ever again, bridge the institutional differentiation between the science system and political agitation and political organization and political action. That is what Lenin tried to do. And I think that it's a part of the past that we don't want to retrieve. So there are just bridges between us as participants in some sort of political action and as members of the science community. I know that Horkheimer began his career with a famous article denying just this. (Habermas 1992b, p. 471)

On the other hand, an optimistic reading of the postempiricist, reflexive turn in science and technology studies has set the stage for a critical renewal of scientific traditions that goes beyond the momentary loss of confidence represented by skeptical postmodernism (e.g., Fuller 1993). This recognition of the "politics of knowledge" implied by social epistemologies need not result in the confrontation of simplistic politicization and postmodernist skepticism. Instead a deepening of the analysis of the problems linked to the democratization of the public sphere has been envisioned by the new science and technology studies. In this context the boundaries between scientific communities and the public sphere are blurred, but not obliterated. The original project of the Frankfurt School has been renewed and transformed in hopeful ways.

Policy Research and Social Criticism

Second, it is important to locate social criticism and forms of policy evaluation as a form of knowledge in their own right, forms that can neither be reduced to the empirical or elevated to the purely normative. This form of research and writing is associated with the notion of *social criticism* but needs to be given a stronger rationale as practically contextualized and empirically informed normative claims with political implications. From this perspective the strategic implications of non-empirical methods become central, rather than peripheral: the question of "knowledge for what" thus reverses the logical priority of the empirical and normative. Although some of this type of work is and can be undertaken in university contexts, its most central context of reference is the public sphere where "public intellectuals" have a particular part to play and radicalize the methodological issues otherwise hidden under technocratic notions of *evaluation research* (Fischer and Forester 1987; Guba 1990). In this context public intellectuals have a strategic place to play both with the university system and on the margins of the mass media (where critical voices often can be represented), as well as the various contexts where the educational tasks of revitalization of the public sphere may be realized.

Critical Action Research

The third context in which critical research intersects with society involves what is sometimes called *critical action research*, especially in education (Kemmis and McTaggart 1988a, 1988b; Carr and Kemmis 1986). Related notions include "participatory action research" and earlier associations with the notion of "conflict methodology" (T. Young 1976). It also is associated closely with feminist theory and feminist methodology generally (Lather 1991). Another version couples a "dialectical sensibility" with "radical empiricism" (Agger 1992a, pp. 239-268).

Although the term *action research* has its origins in the work of the cognitive social psychologist Kurt Lewin, in its contemporary radicalized form it often has been associated with forms of critical social theory:

> Action research is a form of collective self-reflective inquiry undertaken by participants in social situations in order to improve the rationality and justice of their own social or educational practices, as well as their understanding of these practices and the situations in which these practices are carried out. (Kemmis and McTaggart 1988b, p. 5)

Two types of situations are characteristic of action research. First, social movements are in a position to actively appropriate knowledge for their own purposes or to allow participant observers to make them into an object of inquiry on their own terms. In this first context involving social movements the diversity of the audiences for critical research becomes evident. The proliferation of interests represented in the new social movements is both a blessing and a curse. The blessing is perhaps obvious: Recognition of the multiplicity of sources of domination and distorted communication has allowed the voicing of many different types of suppressed anger and frustration. The curse is the other side: the babel of causes and practical consequences of the dissipation of energies in single-issue movements or awkward and artificially popular coalitions between them (Adam 1993).

Second, action research may at times be encouraged or tolerated within or on the margins of existing institutions as part of experimental programs. A limitation of focusing on new social movements is common to all analyzes of overt political action: the assumption that the political can be limited to participation in activities explicitly defined in such terms. A closer look suggests a number of other dialogical spaces where challenges to the dominant order have been mounted and visions of alternatives projected. One of the central themes uniting these often highly institutionalized domains is the question of "alternatives to bureaucracy." From this perspective the necessity of complex organization is acknowledged, but the reification of existing forms of administration and centralization are challenged in terms of alternative organizational strategies and modes of democratic representation within dominant institutions. In part, this challenge may be viewed as one context for what was labeled in the late 1960s as the "long march through institutions." Not surprisingly, therefore, a critical literature has emerged for virtually all of these institutional locations, for example, education, health and therapeutic professions, work, communities (rural, urban ghettoes, Natives and reserves), environmental issues, the family, intimate relationships, the media, religion, and last but not least—politics.

Conclusion: Beyond Fragmentation?

The debates about postmodernism have brought to the fore all of the accumulated issues suppressed by the positivist vision of restoring order through science following the collapse of the religious worldview. Given the waning of this totalizing modernist vision, we are confronted with its dialectical opposite: infinite fragmentation, difference, and particularity as ineluctable features of social life and foundational limits to social inquiry.

The perspective of critical theory involves an attempt to mediate between totalizing unification and anarchic fragmentation. The central claim of such a balancing act is that it is our historical understanding of social determination that allows us to envision alternative worlds. Critical methodology thus is concerned with careful explication of what *is* in order to ultimately liberate us from the destiny of what *has been:* "Reality as it is now needs reasons, legitimations for being thus and not otherwise—the way it concretely *could* be. As against the current scientific fatalism, motives like dreaming, hope . . . assume a *cognitive* function in a less zealously restrictive science" (Gebhardt 1978, p. 406). One task of such concrete utopian thinking was formulated long ago by an American associate of the Frankfurt Institute in its New York phase (Robert Lynd) by suggesting that "it should not be our only concern to ask whether a hypothesis is true, possible or realistic; we should, perhaps, also ask the other way around: 'what sort of earth' would it have to be in which this hypothesis (e.g., one describing a possible situation) *would be* realistic. Only history could verify such hypotheses—by realizing them" (Gebhardt 1978, p. 406). Perhaps the logics of experimentation are not that far from the *raison d'être* of critical theory which is, after all, nothing more and nothing less than a theory of the necessity of overcoming distorted communication as part of an endless process of collective learning.

Notes

1. The present analysis follows Stockman (1983, pp. 121-38) and others in acknowledging the distinctiveness of Popper's critical rationalism and the dangers of subsuming it within any narrow definition of positivism (or technocratic approaches generally). These issues have been discussed extensively within the German tradition, for example, Adorno et al. 1976.

2. Perhaps the most illuminating example of this can be found in the later work of Mannheim (1940) and the whole history of social democratic planning theory.

3. Needless to say, this presuppositions a conception of the role of contemporary intellectuals that cannot be developed here (Gouldner 1979; Lemert 1991; Bauman 1987; Eyerman et al. 1987; Jacoby 1987; Birnbaum 1988; Boggs 1993; B. Robbins 1993).

4. In so doing we are assuming that the debates stemming from critical postmodernist perspectives can be read as part of internal dialogue within the critical dialogical model. These complex debates—strongly shaped by feminist theory—go beyond the present discussion.

REFERENCES

Abel, Theodore. 1977. "The Operation Called Verstehen." Pp. 81-92 in *Understanding and Social Inquiry*, edited by Fred R. Dallmayr and Thomas A. McCarthy. Notre Dame, IN: University of Notre Dame Press.

Abercrombie, Nicholas, Stephen Hill, and Bryan S. Turner. 1980. *The Dominant Ideology Thesis*. London: Allen & Unwin.

———. 1988. *The Penguin Dictionary of Sociology*, 2nd. ed. Harmondsworth, UK: Penguin.

———, eds. 1990. *Dominant Ideologies*. London: Unwin Hyman.

Aboulafia, Mitchell. 1986. *The Mediating Self: Mead, Sartre, and Self-Determination*. New Haven, CT: Yale University Press.

Adam, Barry. 1993. "Post-Marxism and the New Social Movements." *Canadian Review of Sociology and Anthropology* 30:316-36.

Adorno, Theodor W. 1974. *Minima Moralia: Reflection From Damaged Life*, translated by E. G. Jephcott. London: NLB.

———. 1978. "Subject and Object." Pp. 497-511 in *The Essential Frankfurt School Reader*, edited by Andrew Arato and Eike Gebhardt. Oxford: Basil Blackwell.

———. 1991. *The Culture Industry: Selected Essays on Mass Culture*, edited by J. M. Bernstein. London: Routledge.

Adorno, Theodor W. et al. 1976. *The Positivist Dispute in German Sociology*, translated by Glyn Adey and David Frisby. London: Heinemann.

Adorno, Theodor W., Else Frenkel-Brunswick, Daniel J. Levinson, and R. Nevitt Sanford. 1964. *The Authoritarian Personality*. New York: John Wiley.

Agger, Ben. 1979. *Western Marxism: An Introduction: Classical and Contemporary Sources*. Santa Monica, CA: Goodyear.

———. 1989. *Socio(onto)logy: A Disciplinary Reading*. Urbana: University of Illinois Press.

———. 1990. *The Decline of Discourse: Reading, Writing, and Resistance in Postmodern Capitalism*. New York: Falmer.

———. 1991. "Critical Theory, Poststructuralism, Postmodernism: Their Sociological Relevance." Pp. 105-31 in *Annual Review of Sociology*. Vol. 17, edited by W. Richard Scott and Judith Blake. Palo Alto, CA: Annual Reviews.

———. 1992a. *Cultural Studies as Critical Theory*. London: Falmer.

_____. 1992b. *The Discourse of Domination: From the Frankfurt School to Postmodernism.* Evanston, IL: Northwestern University Press.

Alexander, Jeffrey C., ed. 1985. *Neofunctionalism.* Beverly Hills, CA: Sage.

Alexander, Jeffrey C. and Paul Colomy. 1990. "Neofunctionalism Today: Reconstructing a Theoretical Tradition." Pp. 33-67 in *Frontiers of Social Theory: The New Syntheses,* edited by George Ritzer. New York: Columbia University Press.

Alford, C. Fred. 1985. *Science and the Revenge of Nature: Marcuse and Habermas.* Tampa: University of South Florida Press.

Anderson, R. J., John A. Hughes, and W. W. Sharrock. 1986. *Philosophy and the Human Sciences.* London: Croom Helm.

Angenot, Marc. 1979. *Glossaire pratique de la critique contemporaine.* Montreal: Hurtubise HMH.

Ansart, Pierre. 1990. *Les sociologies contemporaines.* Paris: Seuil.

Antonio, Robert J. 1989. "The Normative Foundations of Emancipatory Theory: Evolutionary Versus Pragmatic Perspectives." *American Journal of Sociology* 94(4):721-48.

_____. 1990. "The Decline of the Grand Narrative of Emancipatory Modernity: Crisis or Renewal in Neo-Marxian Theory?" Pp. 88-116 in *Frontiers of Social Theory: The New Syntheses,* edited by George Ritzer. New York: Columbia University Press.

Antonio, Robert J. and Ronald M. Glassman, eds. 1985. *A Weber-Marx Dialogue.* Lawrence: University of Kansas Press.

Apel, Karl-Otto. 1975. *Der Denkweg von Charles S. Peirce.* Frankfurt am Main: Suhrkamp.

_____. 1984. *Understanding and Explanation: A Transcendental-Pragmatic Perspective,* translated by Georgie Warnke. Cambridge: MIT Press.

Apple, Michael W., ed. 1982. *Cultural and Economic Reproduction in Education: Essays on Class, Ideology, and the State.* London: Routledge & Kegan Paul.

Apple, Michael W. and Lois Weis, eds. 1983. *Ideology and Practice in Schooling.* Philadelphia: Temple University Press.

Arato, Andrew. 1978. "Political Sociology and Critique of Politics: Introduction." Pp. 3-25 in *The Essential Frankfurt School Reader,* edited by Andrew Arato and Eike Gebhardt. Oxford: Basil Blackwell.

Arato, Andrew and Paul Breines. 1979. *The Young Lukacs and the Origins of Western Marxism.* New York: Seabury.

Archer, Margaret. 1990. "Human Agency and Social Structure: A Critique of Giddens." Pp. 73-84 in *Anthony Giddens: Consensus and Controversy,* edited by Jon Clark, Celia Modgil, and Sohan Modgil. London: Falmer.

Arminger, Gerhard and George W. Bohrnstedt. 1987. "Making It Count Even More: A Review and Critique of Stanley Lieberson's *Making It Count: The Improvement of Social Theory and Research.*" *Sociological Methodology* 17:363-72.

Aronowitz, Stanley. 1981. *The Crisis of Historical Materialism: Class, Politics, and Culture in Marxist Theory.* New York: Praeger.

_____. 1988. *Science as Power: Discourse and Ideology in Modern Society.* Minneapolis: University of Minnesota Press.

Aronowitz, Stanley and Henry A. Giroux. 1985. *Education Under Seige: The Conservative, Liberal, and Radical Debate Over Schooling.* South Hadley, MA: Bergin & Garvey.

———. 1991. *Postmodern Education: Politics, Culture, and Social Criticism.* Minneapolis: University of Minnesota Press.

Ashmore, Malcolm. 1989. *The Reflexive Thesis: Wrighting Sociology of Scientific Knowledge.* Chicago: University of Chicago Press.

Atkinson, Paul. 1990. *The Ethnographic Imagination: Textual Constructions of Reality.* London: Routledge.

Babbie, Earl. 1983. *The Practice of Social Research.* 4th. ed. Belmont, CA: Wadsworth.

Bakhtin, M. M. 1981. *The Dialogic Imagination: Four Essays,* edited by Michael Holquist. Austin: University of Texas Press.

Baldamus, W. 1976. *The Structure of Sociological Inference.* London: Marin Robertson.

Ball, Terence, ed. 1987. *Idioms of Inquiry: Critique and Renewal in Political Science.* Albany: State University of New York Press.

Barker, Martin and Anne Beezer, eds. 1992. *Reading Into Cultural Studies.* London: Routledge.

Barthes, Roland. 1972. *Mythologies,* translated by Annette Lavers. New York: Hill & Wang.

Baugh, Kenneth, Jr. 1990. *The Methodology of Herbert Blumer: Critical Interpretation and Repair.* Cambridge, UK: Cambridge University Press.

Baum, Gregory. 1975. *Religion and Alienation: A Theological Reading of Sociology.* New York: Paulist Press.

Bauman, Zygmunt. 1987. *Legislators and Interpreters: On Modernity, Post-Modernity, and Intellectuals.* Ithaca, NY: Cornell University Press.

Baynes, Kenneth, James Bohman, and Thomas McCarthy, eds. 1987. *After Philosophy: End or Transformation?* Cambridge: MIT Press.

Beardsley, Philip L. 1980. *Redefining Rigor: Ideology and Statistics in Political Inquiry.* Beverly Hills, CA: Sage.

Beilharz, Peter, Gillian Robinson, and John Rundell, eds. 1992. *Between Totalitarianism and Postmodernity: Thesis Eleven Reader.* Cambridge: MIT Press.

Benhabib, Seyla. 1986. *Critique, Norm, and Utopia: A Study of the Foundations of Critical Theory.* New York: Columbia University Press.

———. 1992. *Situating the Self: Gender, Community, and Postmodernism in Contemporary Ethics.* New York: Routledge.

Benhabib, Seyla and Drucilla Cornell, eds. 1987. *Feminism as Critique.* Minneapolis: University of Minnesota Press.

Benhabib, Seyla and Fred Dallmayr, eds. 1990. *The Communicative Ethics Controversy.* Cambridge: MIT Press.

Benjamin, Jessica. 1988. *The Bonds of Love: Psychoanalysis, Feminism, and the Problem of Domination.* New York: Pantheon.

Benjamin, Walter. 1969. *Illuminations,* translated by Harry Zohn. New York: Schocken.

Benton, Ted. 1984. *The Rise and Fall of Structural Marxism: Althusser and His Influence.* New York: Macmillan.

Berger, Peter, and Thomas Luckmann. 1967. *The Social Construction of Reality.* Garden City, NY: Doubleday.

Berman, Russell A. 1989. *Modern Culture and Critical Theory: Art, Politics, and the Legacy of the Frankfurt School.* Madison: University of Wisconsin Press.

Bernstein, Richard J. 1971. *Praxis and Action.* Philadelphia: University of Pennsylvania Press.

_____. 1978. *The Restructuring of Social and Political Theory.* Philadelphia: University of Pennsylvania Press.

_____. 1983. *Beyond Objectivism and Relativism: Science, Hermeneutics, and Praxis.* Philadelphia: University of Pennsylvania Press.

_____, ed. 1985. *Habermas's and Modernity.* Cambridge: MIT Press.

_____. 1989. "Social Theory as Critique." Pp. 19-33 in *Social Theory of Modern Societies: Anthony Giddens and His Critics,* edited by David Held and John B. Thompson. Cambridge, UK: Cambridge University Press.

_____. 1992. *The New Constellation: The Ethical-Political Horizons of Modernity/Postmodernity.* Cambridge: MIT Press.

Bhaskar, Roy. 1979. *The Possibility of Naturalism: A Philosophical Critique of the Contemporary Human Sciences.* Brighton: Harvester.

_____. 1986. *Scientific Realism and Human Emancipation.* London: Verso.

_____. 1989. *Reclaiming Reality: A Critical Introduction to Contemporary Philosophy.* London: Verso.

_____. 1991. *Philosophy and the Idea of Freedom.* Oxford: Basil Blackwell.

_____. 1993. *Dialetic: The Pulse of Freedom.* London: Verso.

Billings, Dwight B. 1992. "Critical Theory." Pp. 384-90 in *Encyclopedia of Sociology.* Vol. 1, edited by Edgar Borgatta and Marie Borgatta. New York: Macmillan.

Billington, Rosamund, Sheelagh Strawbridge, Lenore Greensides, and Annette Fitzsimons. 1991. *Culture and Society: A Sociology of Culture.* New York: Macmillan.

Birnbaum, Norman, ed. 1977. *Beyond the Crisis.* New York: Oxford University Press.

_____. 1988. *The Radical Renewal: The Politics of Ideas in Modern America.* New York: Pantheon.

Blaikie, Norman. 1993. *Approaches to Social Enquiry.* Cambridge: Polity.

Blauner, Robert. 1964. *Alienation and Freedom: The Factory Worker and His Industry.* Chicago: University of Chicago Press.

Bleicher, Josef. 1980. *Contemporary Hermeneutics: Hermeneutics as Method, Philosophy, and Critique.* London: Routledge & Kegan Paul.

Bloor, David. 1991. *Knowledge and Social Imagery.* 2nd. ed. Chicago: University of Chicago Press.

Blumer, Herbert. 1969. *Symbolic Interactionism: Perspective and Method.* Englewood Cliffs, NJ: Prentice-Hall.

Blumler, Jay G. and Elihu Katz, eds. 1974. *The Uses of Mass Communications: Current Perspectives on Gratifications Research.* Beverly Hills, CA: Sage.

Boer, Theo de. 1983. *Foundations of Critical Psychology,* translated by Theodore Plantinga. Pittsburgh: Duquesne University Press.

Boggs, Carl. 1993. *Intellectuals and the Crisis of Modernity.* Albany: State University of New York Press.

Boguslaw, Robert. 1965. *The New Utopians: A Study of System Design and Social Change.* Englewood Cliffs, NJ: Prentice-Hall.

Bohman, James. 1991. *New Philosophy of Social Science.* Cambridge: MIT Press.

Bonß, Wolfgang. 1982. *Die Einübung des Tatsachenblicks: Zur Struktur und Veränderung empirischer Sozialforschung.* Frankfurt am Main: Suhrkamp.

_____. 1984. "Critical Theory and Empirical Social Research: Some Observations." Pp. 1-38 in *The Working Class in Weimar Germany,* edited by Erich Fromm. London: Berg.

Bottomore, Tom. 1975. *Marxist Sociology.* New York: Macmillan.

Bourdieu, Pierre. 1968. "Structuralism and Theory of Sociological Knowledge." *Social Research* 35:681-706.

_____. 1977. *Outline of a Theory of Practice,* translated by Richard Nice. Cambridge, UK: Cambridge University Press.

_____. 1982. *Leçon sur la leçon.* Paris: Minuit.

_____. 1984. *Distinction: A Social Critique of the Judgement of Taste,* translated by Richard Nice. Cambridge, UK: Cambridge University Press.

_____. 1988. *Homo Academicus,* translated by Peter Collier. Stanford, CA: Stanford University Press.

_____. 1989. *La noblesse d'état: Grandes écoles et esprit de corps.* Paris: Minuit.

_____. 1990. *In Other Words: Essays Towards a Reflexive Sociology,* translated by Matthew Adamson. Stanford, CA: Stanford University Press.

Bourdieu, Pierre and Jean-Claude Passeron. 1977. *Reproduction in Education, Society, and Culture,* translated by Richard Nice. Beverly Hills, CA: Sage.

Bourdieu, Pierre and Loïc J. D. Wacquant. 1992. *Réponses: Pour une anthropologie réflexive.* Paris: Seuil.

Boyne, Roy. 1990. "Culture and the World-System." Pp. 57-62 in *Global Culture,* edited by Mike Featherstone. London: Sage.

Braaten, Jane. 1991. *Habermas's Critical Theory of Society.* Albany: State University of New York Press.

Bramson, Leon. 1961. *The Political Context of Sociology.* Princeton, NJ: Princeton University Press.

Brand, Arie. 1990. *The Force of Reason: An Introduction to Habermas' Theory of Communicative Action.* London: Allen & Unwin.

Brantlinger, Patrick. 1990. *Crusoe's Footprints: Cultural Studies in Britain and America.* London: Routledge.

Braybrooke, David. 1987. *Philosophy of Social Science.* Englewood Cliffs, NJ: Prentice-Hall.

Broughton, John M., ed. 1987. *Critical Theories of Psychological Development.* New York: Plenum.

Brown, David D. 1994. "Discursive Moments of Identification." *Current Perspectives in Social Theory* 14.

Brown, Richard Harvey, ed. 1992. *Writing the Social Text: Poetics and Politics in Social Scientific Discourse.* Hawthorne, NY: Aldine.

Bruner, Jerome. 1990. *Acts of Meaning.* Cambridge, MA: Harvard University Press.

Bryant, Christopher G. A. 1985. *Positivism in Social Theory and Research.* New York: Macmillan.

Bryant, Christopher G. A. and David Jary, eds. 1991. *Giddens' Theory of Structuration: A Critical Appreciation.* London: Routledge.

Burman, Patrick. 1988. *Killing Time, Losing Ground: Experiences of Unemployment.* Toronto: Wall & Thompson.

Burrell, Gibson and Gareth Morgan. 1979. *Sociological Paradigms and Organizational Analysis.* London: Heinemann.

Buss, Allan R., ed. 1979. *Psychology in Social Context.* New York: Irvington.

Calhoun, Craig. 1991. "Morality, Identity, and Historical Explanation: Charles Taylor on the Sources of the Self." *Sociological Theory* 9:232-63.

_____, ed. 1992a. *Habermas and the Public Sphere.* Cambridge: MIT Press.

_____. 1992b. "Culture, History, and the Problem of Specificity in Social Theory." Pp. 244-88 in *Postmodernism and Social Theory,* edited by Steven Seidman and David G. Wager. Oxford: Basil Blackwell.

Calhoun, Craig, Edward Postone, and Moishe LiPuma, eds. 1993. *Bourdieu: Critical Perspectives.* Chicago: University of Chicago Press.

Carlin, Alan. 1991. *Social Division.* London: Verso.

Carr, Wilfred and Stephen Kemmis. 1986. *Becoming Critical: Education, Knowledge, and Action Research.* London: Falmer.

Caws, Peter. 1988. *Structuralism: The Art of the Intelligible.* Atlantic Highlands, NJ: Humanities Press.

Charlton, William. 1991. *The Analytic Ambition: An Introduction to Philosophy.* Oxford: Basil Blackwell.

Chorney, Harold and Phillip Hansen. 1993. *Toward a Humanist Political Economy.* Montreal: Black Rose.

Cicourel, Aaron. 1964. *Method and Measurement in Sociology.* New York: Free Press.

Clark, Jon, Celia Modgil, and Sohan Modgil, eds. 1990. *Anthony Giddens: Consensus and Controversy.* London: Falmer.

Clegg, Stewart. 1975. *Power, Rule, and Domination: A Critical and Empirical Understanding of Power in Sociological Theory and Organizational Life.* London: Routledge & Kegan Paul.

_____. 1989. *Frameworks of Power.* Newbury Park, CA: Sage.

Clifford, James and George E. Marcus, eds. 1986. *Writing Culture: The Poetics and Politics of Ethnography.* Berkeley: University of California Press.

Cohen, Bernard P. 1989. *Developing Sociological Knowledge: Theory and Method.* 2nd. ed. Chicago: Nelson-Hall.

Cohen, Ira H. 1982. *Ideology and Unconsciousness: Reich, Freud, and Marx.* New York: New York University Press.

Cohen, Ira J. 1989. *Structuration Theory: Anthony Giddens and the Constitution of Social Life.* New York: Macmillan.

_____. 1990. "Structuration Theory and Social Order: Five Issues in Brief." Pp. 33-46 in *Anthony Giddens: Consensus and Controversy,* edited by Jon Clark, Celia Modgil, and Sohan Modgil. London: Falmer.

_____. 1993. "Structuration." Pp. 649-50 in *The Blackwell Dictionary of Twentieth-Century Social Thought,* edited by William Outhwaite and Tom Bottomore. Oxford: Basil Blackwell.

Cohen, Jean. 1982. *Class and Civil Society: The Limits of Marxian Critical Theory.* Amherst: University of Massachusetts Press.

Cohen, Jean and Andrew Arato. 1992. *Civil Society and Political Theory.* Cambridge: MIT Press.

Cole, Mike, ed. 1988. *Bowles and Gintis Revisited: Correspondence and Contradiction in Educational Theory.* London: Falmer.

Cole, Stephen. 1980. *The Sociological Method: An Introduction to the Science of Sociology.* Chicago: Rand McNally.

Collins, Randall. 1986. *Weberian Sociological Theory*. Cambridge, UK: Cambridge University Press.

————. 1988. *Theoretical Sociology*. Orlando, FL: Harcourt Brace Jovanovich.

————. 1989. "Sociology: Protoscience or Antiscience?" *American Sociological Review* 54:124-39.

————. 1990. "Conflict Theory and the Advance of Macro-Historical Sociology." Pp. 68-87 in *Frontiers of Social Theory: The New Syntheses*, edited by George Ritzer. New York: Columbia University Press.

Connell, R. W. 1983. *Which Way Is Up? Essays on Sex, Class, and Culture*. London: Allen & Unwin.

————. 1987. *Gender and Power: Society, the Person, and Sexual Politics*. Stanford, CA: Stanford University Press.

Connerton, Paul, ed. 1976. *Critical Sociology: Selected Readings*. London: Penguin.

Cook, Judith A. and Mary Margaret Fonow. 1990. "Knowledge and Women's Interests: Issues of Epistemology and Methodology in Feminist Sociological Research." Pp. 69-93 in *Feminist Research Methods*, edited by Joyce McCarl Nielsen. Boulder, CO: Westview.

Cooper, David E. 1990. *Existentialism*. Oxford: Basil Blackwell.

Coser, Lewis. 1990. "The Virtues of Dissent in Sociology." Pp. 207-13 in *Sociology in America*, edited by Herbert Gans. Newbury Park, CA: Sage.

Craib, Ian. 1976. *Existentialism and Sociology: A Study of Jean-Paul Sartre*. Cambridge, UK: Cambridge University Press.

————. 1984. *Modern Social Theory: From Parsons to Habermas*. Brighton: Harvester.

————. 1989. *Psychoanalysis and Social Theory*. New York: Harvester.

————. 1992. *Anthony Giddens*. London: Routledge.

Crespi, Franco. 1992. *Social Action and Power*. Oxford: Basil Blackwell.

Culler, Jonathan. 1982. *On Deconstruction: Theory and Criticism After Structuralism*. Ithaca, NY: Cornell University Press.

Curran, James and Michael Gurevitch, eds. 1991. *Mass Media and Society*. London: Edward Arnold.

Dahmer, Helmut, ed. 1980. *Analytische Sozialpsychologie*. Frankfurt am Main: Suhrkamp.

Dallmayr, Fred R. 1987. *Critical Encounters Between Philosophy and Politics*. Notre Dame, IN: University of Notre Dame Press.

D'Amico, Robert. 1989. *Historicism and Knowledge*. London: Routledge.

Dant, Tim. 1991. *Knowledge, Ideology, and Discourse: A Sociological Perspective*. London: Routledge.

Denzin, Norman K. 1970. *The Research Act: A Theoretical Introduction to Sociological Methods*. Chicago: Aldine.

————. 1989. *Interpretive Interactionism*. Newbury Park, CA: Sage.

————. 1991. "Empiricist Cultural Studies in America: A Deconstructive Reading." *Current Perspectives in Social Theory* 11:17-40.

————. 1992. *Symbolic Interactionism and Cultural Studies: The Politics of Interpretation*. Oxford: Basil Blackwell.

Der Derian, James and Michael J. Shapiro, eds. 1989. *International/Intertextual Relations: Postmodern Readings of World Politics*. Lexington, MA: Lexington.

Derrida, Jacques. 1976. *Of Grammatology*, translated by Gayatri Chakravorty Spivak. Baltimore: Johns Hopkins University Press.

_____. 1991. *A Derrida Reader: Between the Lines*, edited by Peggy Kamuf. New York: Columbia University Press.

Dewey, John. 1938. *The Theory of Inquiry*. New York: Henry Hold.

Dews, Peter. 1987. *Logics of Disintegration: Post-Structuralist Thought and the Claims of Critical Theory*. London: Verso.

Diamond, Irene and Gloria Feman Orenstein, eds. 1990. *Reweaving the World: The Emergence of Ecofeminism*. San Francisco: Sierra Club.

Dilthey, Wilhelm. 1976. *Dilthey: Selected Writings*, edited by H. P. Rickman. Cambridge, UK: Cambridge University Press.

_____. [1910] 1981. *Der Aufbau der geschichtlichen Welt in den Geisteswissenschaften*. Frankfurt am Main: Suhrkamp.

Doyal, Len and Ian Gough. 1991. *A Theory of Human Need*. New York: Guilford.

Doyal, Len and Roger Harris. 1986. *Empiricism, Explanation, and Rationality: An Introduction to the Philosophy of the Social Sciences*. London: Routledge & Kegan Paul.

Drover, Glen and Patrick Kierans, eds. Forthcoming. *New Approaches to Social Welfare*. New York: Guilford.

Dubiel, Helmut. 1978. *Wissenschaftsorganisation und politische Erfahrung: Studien zur frühen Kritische Theorie*. Frankfurt am Main: Suhrkamp.

Dunn, William N. and Bahman Fozouni. 1976. *Toward a Critical Administrative Theory*. Sage Professional Papers in Administrative and Policy Studies, Vol. 3. Beverly Hills, CA: Sage.

Easthope, Antony and Kate McGowan, eds. 1992. *A Critical and Cultural Theory Reader*. Toronto: University of Toronto Press.

Eder, Klaus. 1992. "Culture and Crisis: Making Sense of the Crisis of the Work Society." Pp. 366-99 in *Theory of Culture*, edited by Richard Münch and Neil J. Smelser. Berkeley: University of California Press.

Edmondson, Ricca. 1984. *Rhetoric in Sociology*. New York: Macmillan.

Elias, Norbert. 1978. *The Civilizing Process: The History of Manners*, translated by Edmund Jephcott. New York: Random House.

_____. 1982. *The Civilizing Process: Power and Civility*, translated by Edmund Jephcott. New York: Random House.

Elliott, Anthony. 1992. *Social Theory and Psychoanalysis in Transition: Self and Society From Freud to Kristeva*. Oxford: Basil Blackwell.

Ewen, Stuart. 1976. *Captains of Consciousness: Advertising and the Social Roots of the Consumer Culture*. New York: McGraw-Hill.

Eyerman, Ron and Andrew Jamison. 1991. *Social Movements: A Cognitive Approach*. Cambridge: Polity.

Eyerman, Ron, Lennart G. Svensson, and Thomas Söderqvist, eds. 1987. *Intellectuals, Universities, and the State in Western Modern Societies*. Berkeley: University of California Press.

Fairclough, Norman. 1992. *Discourse and Social Change*. Cambridge: Polity.

Fararo, Thomas J. 1989. *The Meaning of General Theoretical Sociology: Tradition and Formalization*. Cambridge, UK: Cambridge University Press.

Fay, Brian. 1975. *Social Theory and Political Practice*. London: Allen & Unwin.

_____. 1987. *Critical Social Science*. Ithaca, NY: Cornell University Press.

Featherstone, Michael, ed. 1990. *Global Culture: Nationalism, Globalization, and Modernity*. London: Sage.

_____. 1992. "Cultural Production, Consumption, and the Development of the Cultural Sphere." Pp. 265-92 in *Theory of Culture*, edited by Richard Münch and Neil J. Smelser. Berkeley: University of California Press.

Feenberg, Andrew. 1991. *Critical Theory of Technology*. New York: Oxford University Press.

Fekete, John, ed. 1987. *Life After Postmodernism: Essays on Value and Culture*. Montreal: New World Perspectives.

Ferry, Jean-Marc. 1987. *Habermas: l'éthique de la communication*. Paris: Presses Universitaires de France.

Feyerabend, Paul K. 1975. *Against Method*. London: New Left Books.

Fischer, Frank and John Forester, eds. 1987. *Confronting Values in Policy Analysis*. Newbury Park, CA: Sage.

Forbes, H. D. 1985. *Nationalism, Ethnocentrism, and Personality: Social Science and Critical Theory*. Chicago: University of Chicago Press.

Ford, Julienne. 1975. *Paradigms and Fairy Tales: An Introduction to the Science of Meanings*. London: Routledge & Kegan Paul.

Forester, John, ed. 1985a. *Critical Theory and Public Life*. Cambridge: MIT Press.

_____. 1985b. "Introduction: The Applied Turn in Contemporary Critical Theory." Pp. ix-xix in *Critical Theory and Public Life*, edited by John Forester. Cambridge: MIT Press.

_____. 1985c. "Critical Theory and Planning Practice." Pp. 202-27 in *Critical Theory and Public Life*, edited by John Forester. Cambridge: MIT Press.

_____. 1985d. "The Policy Analysis-Critical Theory Affair: Wildavsky and Habermas as Bedfellows?" Pp. 258-80 in *Critical Theory and Public Life*, edited by John Forester. Cambridge: MIT Press.

Foucault, Michel. 1984. *The Foucault Reader*, edited by Paul Rabinow. New York: Pantheon.

Frankel, Boris. 1987. *The Post-Industrial Utopians*. Madison: University of Wisconsin Press.

Frankfurt Institute for Social Research. 1972. *Aspects of Sociology*, edited by Max Horkheimer and Theodor W. Adorno, translated by John Viertel. Boston: Beacon.

Fraser, Nancy. 1989. *Unruly Practices: Power, Discourse, and Gender in Contemporary Social Theory*. Minneapolis: University of Minnesota Press.

Fraser, Nancy and Sandra Lee Bartky, eds. 1992. *Revaluing French Feminism: Critical Essays on Difference, Agency, and Culture*. Bloomington: University of Indiana Press.

Freeman, Christopher. 1973. "Malthus With a Computer." Pp. 5-13 in *Thinking About the Future: A Critique of the Limits to Growth*, edited by H. S. D. Cole, Christopher Freeman, Marie Johoda, and K. L. R. Pavitt. London: Chatto & Windus.

Freire, Paulo. 1970. *Pedagogy of the Oppressed*, translated by Myra Bergman Ramos. New York: Seabury.

Friedmann, John. 1979. *The Good Society: A Personal Account of Its Struggle With the World of Social Planning and a Dialectical Inquiry Into the Roots of Radical Practice*. Cambridge: MIT Press.

_____. 1987. *Planning in the Public Domain: From Knowledge to Action*. Princeton, NJ: Princeton University Press.

Frisby, David and Derek Sayer. 1986. *Society.* London: Tavistock.

Fromm, Eric. 1970. *The Crisis of Psychoanalysis.* Greenwich, CT: Fawcett.

_____. 1978. "The Method and Function of an Analytic Social Psychology." Pp. 477-96 in *The Essential Frankfurt School Reader,* edited by Andrew Arato and Eike Gebhardt. New York: Urizen.

_____. 1984. *The Working Class in Weimar Germany: A Psychological and Sociological Study,* edited by Wolfgang Bonss, translated by Barbara Weinberger. Leamington Spa, UK: Berg.

Fuller, Steve. 1993. *Philosophy, Rhetoric, and the Ends of Knowledge: The Coming of Science and Technology Studies.* Madison: University of Wisconsin Press.

Gadamer, Hans-Georg. 1975. *Truth and Method,* edited and translated by Garrett Barden and John Cumming. New York: Seabury.

Galtung, Johan. 1977. *Methodology and Ideology: Essays in Methodology.* Vol. 1. Copenhagen: Christian Ejlers.

Gardiner, Michael. 1992. *The Dialogics of Critique: M. M. Bakhtin and the Theory of Ideology.* London: Routledge.

Garfinkel, Alan. 1981. *Forms of Explanation: Rethinking the Questions in Social Theory.* New Haven, CT: Yale University Press.

Garfinkel, Harold. 1967. *Studies in Ethnomethodology.* Englewood Cliffs, NJ: Prentice-Hall.

Garnham, Nicholas. 1990. *Capitalism and Communication: Global Culture and the Economics of Information.* Newbury Park, CA: Sage.

Gebhardt, Eike. 1978. "A Critique of Methodology: Introduction." Pp. 371-406 in *The Essential Frankfurt School Reader,* edited by Andrew Arato and Eike Gebhardt. Oxford: Basil Blackwell.

Geertz, Clifford. 1973. *The Interpretation of Cultures.* New York: Basic Books.

_____. 1983. *Local Knowledge: Further Essays in Interpretive Anthropology.* New York: Basic Books.

_____. 1988. *Works and Lives: The Anthropologist as Author.* Stanford, CA: Stanford University Press.

Gerth, Hans and C. Wright Mills. 1964. *Character and Social Structure: The Psychology of Social Institutions.* New York: Harcourt, Brace & World.

Geyer, Felix and Walter R. Heinz, eds. 1992. *Alienation, Society, and the Individual: Continuity and Change in Research.* New Brunswick, NJ: Transaction Books.

Giddens, Anthony. 1971. *Capitalism and Modern Social Theory.* Cambridge, UK: Cambridge University Press.

_____. 1973. *The Class Structure of the Advanced Societies.* London: Hutchinson.

_____, ed. 1974. *Positivism and Sociology.* London: Heinemann.

_____. 1976. *New Rules of Sociological Method.* London: Hutchinson.

_____. 1977. *Studies in Social and Political Theory.* New York: Basic Books.

_____. 1979. *Central Problems in Social Theory: Action, Structure, and Contradiction in Social Analysis.* Berkeley: University of California Press.

_____. 1981. *A Contemporary Critique of Historical Materialism.* Vol. 1. Berkeley: University of California Press.

_____. 1982a. *Profiles and Critiques in Social Theory.* Berkeley: University of California Press.

_____. 1982b. *Sociology: A Brief but Critical Introduction.* Orlando, FL: Harcourt Brace Jovanovich.

_____. 1984. *The Constitution of Society*. Berkeley: University of California Press.

_____. 1987a. *A Contemporary Critique of Historical Materialism*. Vol. 2, *The Nation-State and Violence*. Berkeley: University of California Press.

_____. 1987b. "Structuralism, Post-Structuralism, and the Production of Culture." Pp. 195-223 in *Social Theory Today*, edited by Anthony Giddens and Jonathan H. Turner. Stanford, CA: Stanford University Press.

_____. 1989a. "A Reply to My Critics." Pp. 249-301 in *Social Theory of Modern Societies: Anthony Giddens and His Critics*, edited by David Held and John B. Thompson. Cambridge, UK: Cambridge University Press.

_____. 1989b. *Sociology*. Oxford: Basil Blackwell.

_____. 1990a. *The Consequences of Modernity*. Stanford, CA: Stanford University Press.

_____. 1990b. "Structuration Theory and Sociological Analysis." Pp. 297-315 in *Anthony Giddens: Consensus and Controversy*, edited by Jon Clark, Celia Modgil, and Sohan Modgil. London: Falmer.

_____. 1991a. *Modernity and Self-Identity: Self and Society in the Late Modern Age*. Stanford, CA: Stanford University Press.

_____. 1991b. "A Reply to My Critics." Pp. 249-301 in *Social Theory of Modern Societies*, edited by David Held and John B. Thompson. Cambridge: Cambridge University Press.

_____. 1992. *The Transformations of Intimacy: Sexuality, Love, and Eroticism in Modern Societies*. Stanford, CA: Stanford University Press.

_____. 1993. "Introduction to the Second Edition." Pp. 1-15 in *New Rules of Sociological Method*. 2nd. ed. Stanford, CA: Stanford University Press.

Giroux, Henry. 1981. *Ideology, Culture, and the Process of Schooling*. Philadelphia: Temple University Press.

_____. 1988a. *Schooling and the Struggle for Public Life: Critical Pedagogy in the Modern Age*. Minneapolis: University of Minnesota Press.

_____. 1988b. *Teachers as Intellectuals: Toward a Pedagogy of Learning*. Granby, MA: Bergin & Garvey.

_____. 1992. *Border Crossings: Cultural Workers and the Politics of Education*. London: Routledge.

Gitlin, Todd. 1978. "Media Sociology: The Dominant Paradigm." *Theory and Society* 6:205-53.

Golding, Sue. 1992. *Gramsci's Democratic Theory: Contributions to a Post-Liberal Democracy*. Toronto: University of Toronto Press.

Goldmann, Lucien. 1959. *Recherches dialectiques*. Paris: Gallimard.

_____. 1969. *The Human Sciences and Philosophy*, translated by Hayden White and Robert Anchor. London: Jonathan Cape.

Goodin, Robert E. 1988. *Reasons for Welfare: The Political Theory of the Welfare State*. Princeton, NJ: Princeton University Press.

Görtzen, René, ed. 1982. *Jürgen: Eine Bibliographie seiner Schriften und der Sekundärliteratur 1952-1981*. Frankfurt am Main: Suhrkamp.

_____. 1990. "Jürgen Habermas: A Bibliography." Pp. 114-40 in *Reading Habermas*. Oxford: Basil Blackwell.

Gottdiener, Mark. 1985a. "Hegemony and Mass Culture: A Semiotic Approach." *American Journal of Sociology* 90:979-1001.

_____. 1985b. *The Social Production of Urban Space.* Austin: University of Texas Press.

Gottdiener, Mark and Alexandros Lagopoulos, eds. 1986. *The City and the Sign: An Introduction to Urban Semiotics.* New York: Columbia University Press.

Gouldner, Alvin. 1971. *The Coming Crisis of Western Sociology.* New York: Basic Books.

_____. 1975. *For Sociology: Renewal and Critique in Sociology Today.* Harmondsworth, UK: Penguin.

_____. 1976. *The Dialectic of Ideology and Technology: The Origins, Grammar, and Future of Ideology.* New York: Seabury.

_____. 1979. *The Future of the Intellectuals and the Rise of the New Class.* New York: Seabury.

_____. 1980. *The Two Marxisms.* New York: Seabury.

Grahame, Peter. 1985. "Criticalness, Pragmatics, and Everyday Life: Consumer Literacy as Critical Practice." Pp. 147-74 in *Critical Theory and Public Life,* edited by John Forester. Cambridge: MIT Press.

Gramsci, Antonio. 1971. *Selections From the Prison Notebooks,* edited and translated by Quintin Hoare and Geoffrey Nowell Smith. New York: International Publishers.

Green, Bryan S. 1988. *Literary Methods and Sociological Theory: Case Studies of Simmel and Weber.* Chicago: University of Chicago Press.

Gregory, Derek. 1978. *Ideology, Science, and Human Geography.* London: Hutchinson.

Griswold, Wendy. 1987. "A Methodological Framework for the Sociology of Culture." *Sociological Methodology* 17:1-36.

Grossberg, Lawrence. 1992. *We Gotta Get Out of This Place: Popular Conservatism and Postmodern Culture.* London: Routledge.

Grossberg, Lawrence, Cary Nelson, and Paula Treichler, eds. 1992. *Cultural Studies.* London: Routledge.

Grumley, John E. 1989. *History and Totality: Radical Historicism from Hegel to Foucault.* London: Routledge.

Gruneau, Richard. 1983. *Class, Sports, and Social Development.* Amherst: University of Massachusetts Press.

_____. 1988. "Introduction: Notes on Popular Culture and Political Practices." Pp. 11-32 in *Popular Culture and Political Practices,* edited by Richard Gruneau. Toronto: Garamond.

Guba, Egon G., ed. 1990. *The Paradigm Dialog.* Newbury Park, CA: Sage.

Gubrium, Jaber F. and David Silverman, eds. 1989. *The Politics of Field Research: Sociology Beyond Enlightenment.* Newbury Park, CA: Sage.

Gutmann, Amy, ed. 1988. *Democracy and the Welfare State.* Princeton, NJ: Princeton University Press.

Habermas, Jürgen. 1970. *Toward a Rational Society: Student Protest, Science, and Politics,* translated by Jeremy J. Shapiro. Boston: Beacon.

_____. 1971. *Knowledge and Human Interests,* translated by Jeremy J. Shapiro. Boston: Beacon.

_____. 1973. *Theory and Practice,* translated by John Viertel. Boston: Beacon.

_____. 1975. *Legitimation Crisis,* translated by Thomas McCarthy. Boston: Beacon.

_____. 1976. "The Analytical Theory of Science and Dialectics." Pp. 131-62 in *The Positivist Dispute in German Sociology*, edited by Theodor W. Adorno et al., translated by Glen Adey and David Frisby. London: Heinemann.

_____. 1979. *Communication and the Evolution of Society*, edited and translated by Thomas McCarthy. Boston: Beacon.

_____. 1982. "A Reply to My Critics." Pp. 219-83 in *Habermas: Critical Debates*, edited by John Thompson and David Held. Cambridge: MIT Press.

_____. 1983. "Interpretive Social Science vs. Hermeneuticism." Pp. 251-67 in *Social Science as Moral Inquiry*, edited by Norma Haan, Robert N. Bellah, Paul Rabinow, and William M. Sullivan. New York: Columbia University Press.

_____. 1984. *The Theory of Communicative Action*. Vol. 1, *Reason and the Rationalization of Society*, translated by Thomas McCarthy. Boston: Beacon.

_____. 1986. *Autonomy and Solidarity: Interviews*, edited by Peter Dews. London: Verso.

_____. 1987a. *The Theory of Communicative Action*. Vol. 2, *Lifeworld and System: A Critique of Functionalist Reason*, translated by Thomas McCarthy. Boston: Beacon.

_____. 1987b. *The Philosophical Discourse of Modernity*, translated by Frederick Lawrence. Cambridge: MIT Press.

_____. 1988. *On the Logic of the Social Sciences*, translated by Shierry Weber Nicholsen and Jerry A. Stark. Cambridge: MIT Press.

_____. 1989. *The New Conservatism*, edited and translated by Shierry Weber Nicholsen. Cambridge: MIT Press.

_____. 1990. *Moral Consciousness and Communicative Action*, translated by Christian Lenhardt and Shierry Weber Nicholsen. Cambridge: MIT Press.

_____. 1992a. "Further Reflections on the Public Sphere." Pp. 421-61 in *Habermas and the Public Sphere*, edited by Craig Calhoun. Cambridge: MIT Press.

_____. 1992b. "Concluding Remarks." Pp. 462-79 in *Habermas and the Public Sphere*, edited by Craig Calhoun. Cambridge: MIT Press.

Hall, John R. and Mary Jo Neitz. 1993. *Culture: Sociological Perspectives*. Englewood Cliffs, NJ: Prentice-Hall.

Hall, Stuart. 1992. "Cultural Studies and Its Theoretical Legacies." Pp. 277-94 in *Cultural Studies*, edited by Lawrence Grossberg, Cary Nelson, and Paula Treichler. London: Routledge.

Hall, Stuart, David Held, and Tony McGrew, eds. 1992. *Modernity and Its Futures*. Cambridge, UK: Open University Press.

Halliday, Terence C. and Morris Janowitz, eds. 1992. *Sociology and Its Publics: The Forms and Fates of Disciplinary Organization*. Chicago: University of Chicago Press.

Hamel, Jacques, ed. 1992. "The Case Method in Sociology." *Current Sociology* 40:1.

Hammersley, Martyn. 1992. *What's Wrong With Ethnography?* London: Routledge.

Hanen, Marsha and Kai Nielsen, eds. 1987. *Science, Morality, and Feminist Theory*. Calgary: University of Calgary Press.

Hardt, Hanno. 1992. *Critical Communications Studies: Communication, History, and Theory in America*. London: Routledge.

Harré, Rom. 1986. *Varieties of Realism: A Rationale for the Natural Sciences*. Oxford: Basil Blackwell.

Harris, David. 1992. *From Class Struggle to the Politics of Pleasure: The Effects of Gramscianism on Cultural Studies.* London: Routledge.

Harvey, David. 1989. *The Condition of Postmodernity.* Oxford: Basil Blackwell.

Harvey, Lee. 1990. *Critical Social Research.* London: Unwin Hyman.

Haugaard, Mark. 1992. *Structures, Restructuration, and Social Power.* Aldershot, UK: Avebury.

Hearn, Frank. 1985. *Reason and Freedom in Sociological Thought.* London: Allen & Unwin.

Hebdige, Dick. 1979. *Subculture: The Meaning of Style.* New York: Methuen.

Heidegger, Martin. 1962. *Being and Time,* translated by John Macquarrie and Edward Robinson. New York: Harper & Row.

Hekman, Susan J. 1986. *Hermeneutics and the Sociology of Knowledge.* Notre Dame, IN: University of Notre Dame Press.

Held, David. 1980. *Introduction to Critical Theory: Horkheimer to Habermas.* Berkeley: University of California Press.

———. 1983. "Frankfurt School." Pp. 182-88 in *A Dictionary of Marxist Thought,* edited by Tom Bottomore et al. Cambridge, MA: Harvard University Press.

———. 1987. *Models of Democracy.* Stanford, CA: Stanford University Press.

Held, David and John B. Thompson, eds. 1989. *Social Theory of Modern Societies: Anthony Giddens and His Critics.* Cambridge, UK: Cambridge University Press.

Henriques, Julian, Wendy Hollway, Cathy Urwin, Couze Venn, and Valerie Walkerdine. 1984. *Changing the Subject: Psychology, Social Regulation, and Subjectivity.* New York: Methuen.

Hiley, David R., James F. Bohman, and Richard Shusterman, eds. 1991. *The Interpretive Turn: Philosophy, Science, Culture.* Ithaca, NY: Cornell University Press.

Hochschild, Arlie Russell. 1983. *The Managed Heart: Commercialization of Human Feeling.* Berkeley: University of California Press.

Hodge, Robert and Gunther Kress. 1988. *Social Semiotics.* Ithaca, NY: Cornell University Press.

Hohendahl, Peter Uwe. 1991. *Reappraisals: Shifting Alignments in Postwar Critical Theory.* Ithaca, NY: Cornell University Press.

Holenstein, Elmar. 1975. *Roman Jakobsons phänomenologischer Strukturalismus.* Frankfurt am Main: Suhrkamp.

Holsti, Ole R. 1969. *Content Analysis for the Social Sciences and Humanities.* Reading, MA: Addison-Wesley.

Holub, Robert C. 1991. *Jürgen Habermas: Critic in the Public Sphere.* London: Routledge.

Holy, Ladislav, ed. 1987. *Comparative Anthropology.* Oxford: Basil Blackwell.

Honneth, Axel. 1987. "Critical Theory." Pp. 347-82 in *Social Theory Today,* edited by Anthony Giddens and Jonathan H. Turner. Stanford, CA: Stanford University Press.

———. 1991. *The Critique of Power: Reflective Stages in a Critical Theory of Society,* translated by Kennth Baynes. Cambridge: MIT Press.

———. 1993. "Frankfurt School." Pp. 232-35 in *The Blackwell Dictionary of Twentieth-Century Social Thought,* edited by William Outhwaite and Tom Bottomore. Oxford: Basil Blackwell.

Honneth, Axel and Hans Joas. 1988. *Social Action and Human Nature,* translated by Raymond Meyer. Cambridge, UK: Cambridge University Press.

Honneth, Axel, Thomas McCarthy, Claus Offe, and Albrecht Wellmer, eds. 1992. *Philosophical Interventions in the Unfinished Project of Enlightenment,* translated by William Rehg. Cambridge: MIT Press.

Hoos, Ida R. 1974. *Systems Analysis in Public Policy: A Critique.* Berkeley: University of California Press.

Horkheimer, Max. [1937] 1972a. *Critical Theory: Selected Essays,* translated by Matthew J. O'Connell. New York: Herder & Herder.

———. 1972b. *Sozialphilosophische Studien.* Frankfurt am Main: Suhrkamp.

Horkheimer, Max and Theodor W. Adorno. 1972. *Dialectic of Enlightenment,* translated by John Cumming. New York: Herder & Herder.

Hunter, Albert, ed. 1990. *The Rhetoric of Social Research: Understood and Believed.* New Brunswick, NJ: Rutgers University Press.

Husserl, Edmund. 1970. *The Crisis of the European Sciences and Transcendental Phenomenology,* translated by David Carr. Evanston, IL: Northwestern University Press.

Hutchinson, Allan C., ed. 1989. *Critical Legal Studies.* Totowa, NJ: Rowman & Littlefield.

Illich, Ivan. 1975. *Medical Nemesis: The Expropriation of Health.* Toronto: McClelland & Stewart.

Ingram, David. 1987. *Habermas and the Dialectic of Reason.* New Haven, CT: Yale University Press.

Irvine, John, Ian Miles, and Jeff Evans, eds. 1979. *Demystifying Social Statistics.* London: Pluto.

Izenberg, Gerald N. 1976. *The Existentialist Critique of Freud: The Crisis of Autonomy.* Princeton, NJ: Princeton University Press.

Jacoby, Russell. 1987. *The Last Intellectuals: American Culture in the Age of Academe.* New York: Basic Books.

Jameson, Fredric. 1990. *Late Marxism: Adorno, or, The Persistence of the Dialectic.* London: Verso.

———. 1991. *Postmodernism, or, The Cultural Logic of Late Capitalism.* Durham, NC: Duke University Press.

Jary, David and Juali Jary. 1991. *Collins Dictionary of Sociology.* Glasgow: HarperCollins.

Jay, Martin. 1973. *The Dialectical Imagination: A History of the Frankfurt School and the Institute of Social Research, 1923-1950.* Boston: Little, Brown.

———. 1984. *Marxism and Totality: Adventures of a Concept From Lukacs to Habermas.* Berkeley: University of California Press.

———. 1985. *Permanent Exiles: Essays on the Intellectual Migration From Germany to America.* New York: Columbia University Press.

———. 1988. *Fin-de-siècle Socialism and Other Essays.* London: Routledge.

———. 1993. *Force Fields: Between Intellectual History and Cultural Critique.* London: Routledge.

Jenks, Chris, ed. 1993. *Cultural Reproduction.* London: Routledge.

Jessop, Bob. 1990. *State Theory: Putting the Capitalist State in Its Place.* Cambridge: Polity.

Jhally, Sut. 1987. *The Codes of Advertising: Fetishism and the Political Economy of Meaning in the Consumer Society.* New York: St. Martin's.

Joas, Hans. 1985. *G. H. Mead: A Contemporary Re-examination of His Thought*, translated by Raymond Meyer. Oxford: Basil Blackwell.

_____. 1990. "Giddens's Critique of Functionalism." Pp. 91-102 in *Anthony Giddens: Consensus and Controversy*, edited by Jon Clark, Celia Modgil, and Sohan Modgil. London: Falmer.

_____. 1993. *Pragmatism and Social Theory*. Chicago: University of Chicago Press.

Johnson, Terry, Christopher Dandeker, and Clive Ashworth. 1984. *The Structure of Social Theory*. New York: Macmillan.

Kalberg, Stephen. 1992. "Culture and the Logic of Work in Contemporary Western Germany: A Weberian Configurational Analysis." Pp. 324-65 in *Theory of Culture*, edited by Richard Münch and Neil J. Smelser. Berkeley: University of California Press.

Kanpol, Barry. 1992. *Towards a Theory and Practice of Teacher Cultural Politics: Continuing the Postmodern Debate*. Norwood, NJ: Ablex.

Kaplan, Abraham. 1964. *The Conduct of Inquiry: Methodology for Behavioral Science*. San Francisco: Chandler.

Keane, John. 1984. *Public Life and Late Capitalism: Towards a Socialist Theory of Democracy*. Cambridge, UK: Cambridge University Press.

_____, ed. 1988a. *Civil Society and the State*. London: Verso.

_____. 1988b. *Democracy and Civil Society*. London: Verso.

Keat, Russell and John Urry. 1982. *Social Theory as Science*. 2nd. ed. London: Routledge & Kegan Paul.

Kellner, Douglas. 1989a. *Critical Theory, Marxism, and Modernity*. Baltimore: Johns Hopkins University Press.

_____. 1989b. *Jean Baudrillard: From Marxism to Postmodernism and Beyond*. Stanford, CA: Stanford University Press.

_____, ed. 1989c. *Postmodernism, Jameson, Critique*. Washington, DC: Maisonneurve.

_____. 1990. *Television and the Crisis of Democracy*. Boulder, CO: Westview.

Kelly, George Armstrong. 1969. *Idealism, Politics, and History: Sources of Hegelian Thought*. Cambridge, UK: Cambridge University Press.

Kelly, Michael, ed. 1990. *Hermeneutics and Critical Theory in Ethics and Politics*. Cambridge: MIT Press.

Kemmis, Stephen and Robin McTaggart, eds. 1988a. *The Action Research Planner*. 3rd. ed. Victoria, Australia: Deakin University Press.

_____, eds. 1988b. *The Action Research Reader*. 3rd. ed. Victoria, Australia: Deakin University Press.

Kemp, Ray. 1985. "Planning, Public Hearings, and the Politics of Discourse." Pp. 177-201 in *Critical Theory and Public Life*, edited by John Forester. Cambridge: MIT Press.

Kemper, Theodore D. 1978. *A Social Interactional Theory of Emotions*. New York: John Wiley.

Kilminster, Richard. 1979. *Praxis and Method: A Sociological Dialogue with Lukacs, Gramsci, and the Early Frankfurt School*. London: Routledge & Kegan Paul.

_____. 1991. "Structuration Theory as a World-view." Pp. 74-115 in *Giddens' Theory of Structuration: A Critical Appreciation*, edited by Christopher G. A. Bryant and David Jary. London: Routledge.

Kirby, Sandra and Kate McKenna. 1989. *Experience, Research, Social Change: Methods From the Margins.* Toronto: Garamond.

Kotarba, Joseph A. and Andrea Fontana, eds. 1984. *The Existential Self in Society.* Chicago: University of Chicago Press.

Kreilkamp, Thomas. 1976. *The Corrosion of the Self: Society's Effects on People.* New York: New York University Press.

Kuhn, Thomas. 1970. *The Structure of Scientific Revolutions.* Chicago: University of Chicago Press.

Kurzweil, Edith. 1980. *The Age of Structuralism: Lévi-Strauss to Foucault.* New York: Columbia University Press.

Kymlicka, Will. 1990. *Contemporary Political Philosophy.* Oxford: Oxford University Press.

Laclau, Ernesto. 1990. *New Reflections on the Revolution of Our Time.* London: Verso.

Laclau, Ernesto and Chantal Mouffe. 1985. *Hegemony and Socialist Strategy: Towards a Radical Democratic Politics.* London: Verso.

Lakatos, Imre. 1970. "Falsification and the Methodology of Scientific Research Programmes." Pp. 91-196 in *Criticism and the Growth of Knowledge,* edited by Imre Lakatos and Alan Musgrave. Cambridge, UK: Cambridge University Press.

Lamb, Matthew L. 1982. *Solidarity With Victims: Toward a Theology of Social Transformation.* New York: Crossroad.

Langman, Lauren. 1991. "From Pathos to Panic: American Character Meets the Future." Pp. 165-241 in *Critical Theory Now,* edited by Philip Wexler. London: Falmer.

Langman, Lauren and Leonard Kaplan. 1981. "Political Economy and Social Character: Terror, Desire, and Domination." *Current Perspectives in Social Theory* 2:87-115.

Larrain, Jorge. 1983. *Marxism and Ideology.* New York: Macmillan.

Lasch, Christopher. 1979. *The Culture of Narcissism: American Life in an Age of Diminishing Expectations.* New York: Warner.

_____. 1984. *The Minimal Self: Psychic Survival in Troubled Times.* New York: Norton.

Lash, Scott and Jonathan Friedman, eds. *Modernity and Identity.* Oxford: Basil Blackwell 1992.

Lash, Scott and John Urry. 1987. *The End of Organized Capitalism.* Madison: University of Wisconsin Press.

Lather, Patti. 1991. *Getting Smart: Feminist Research and Pedagogy With/In the Postmodern.* London: Routledge.

Laudan, Larry. 1977. *Progress and Its Problems: Towards a Theory of Scientific Growth.* Berkeley: University of California Press.

Lawson, Hilary and Lisa Appignananesi, eds. 1989. *Dismantling Truth: Reality in the Post-Modern World.* London: Weidenfeld & Nicolson.

Layder, Derek. 1993. *New Strategies in Social Research.* Cambridge: Polity.

Leiss, William. 1974. *The Domination of Nature.* Boston: Beacon.

_____. 1976. *The Limits to Satisfaction: An Essay on the Problem of Needs and Commodities.* Toronto: University of Toronto Press.

_____. 1978. "Needs, Exchanges, and the Fetishism of Objects." *Canadian Journal of Political and Social Theory* 2:27-48.

_____. 1990. *Under Technology's Thumb*. Montreal: McGill-Queen's University Press.

Leiss, William, Stephen Kline, and Sut Jhally. 1986. *Social Communication in Advertising: Persons, Products, and Images of Wellbeing*. New York: Methuen.

Lemert, Charles C., ed. 1981. *French Sociology: Rupture and Renewal Since 1968*. New York: Columbia University Press.

_____, ed. 1991. *Intellectuals and Politics: Social Theory in a Changing World*. Newbury Park, CA: Sage.

Lengermann, Patricia M. and Jill Niebrugge-Brantley. 1990. "Feminist Sociological Theory: The Near-Future Prospects." Pp. 316-44 in *Frontiers of Social Theory: The New Syntheses*, edited by George Ritzer. New York: Columbia University Press.

Leonard, Stephen T. 1990. *Critical Theory in Political Practice*. Princeton, NJ: Princeton University Press.

Leong, Laurence Wai-Teng. 1992. "Cultural Resistance: The Cultural Terrorism of British Male Working-Class Youth." *Current Perspectives in Social Theory* 12:29-58.

Lepenies, Wolf. 1988. *Between Literature and Science: The Rise of Sociology*, translated by R. J. Hollingdale. Cambridge, UK: Cambridge University Press.

Levine, Andrew. 1989. "What Is a Marxist Today?" Pp. 29-58 in *Analyzing Marxism*, edited by Robert Ware and Kai Nielsen. Calgary: University of Calgary Press.

Lévi-Strauss, Claude. 1967. *Structural Anthropology*, translated by Claire Jacobson and Brooke Schoepf. Garden City, NY: Anchor.

Li, Peter S. and B. Singh Bolaria, eds. 1993. *Contemporary Sociology: Critical Perspectives*. Toronto: Copp Clark.

Lichtman, Richard. 1982. *The Production of Desire: The Integration of Psycho-analysis Into Marxist Theory*. New York: Free Press.

Lieberson, Stanley. 1984. *Making It Count: The Improvement of Social Theory and Research*. Berkeley: University of California Press.

Liebes, Tamar and Elihu Katz. 1990. *The Export of Meaning: Cross-Cultural Readings of Dallas*. New York: Oxford University Press.

Lilienfeld, Robert. 1978. *The Rise of Systems Theory: An Ideological Analysis*. New York: John Wiley.

Linklater, Andrew. 1990. *Beyond Realism and Marxism: Critical Theory and International Relations*. New York: Macmillan.

Little, Daniel. 1991. *Varieties of Social Explanation: An Introduction to the Philosophy of Social Science*. Boulder, CO: Westview.

Livesay, J. 1985. "Normative Grounding and Praxis." *Sociological Theory* 3:66-76.

Lockwood, David. 1964. "Social Integration and System Integration." Pp. 244-57 in *Explanations in Social Change*, edited by G. K. Zollschan and W. Hirsch. London: Routledge & Kegan Paul.

Longhurst, Brian. 1989. *Karl Mannheim and the Contemporary Sociology of Knowledge*. New York: Macmillan.

Lowery, Shearon and Melvin L. DeFleur. 1983. *Milestones in Mass Communication Research: Media Effects*. New York: Longman.

Löwith, Karl. [1932] 1982. *Max Weber and Karl Marx*, edited by Tom Bottomore and William Outhwaite, translated by Hans Fantel. London: Allen & Unwin.

Lukacs, Georg. [1923] 1968. *History and Class Consciousness,* translated by Rodney Livingstone. London: Merlin.

Luke, Timothy W. 1987. "Social Ecology as Critical Political Economy." *The Social Science Journal* 24:303-15.

———. 1990. *Social Theory and Modernity: Critique, Dissent, and Revolution.* Newbury Park, CA: Sage.

Lüschen, Günther, ed. 1979. *Deutsche Soziologie seit 1945.* Opladen: Westdeutscher Verlag.

Lyotard, Jean-François. 1984. *The Postmodern Condition: A Report on Knowledge,* translated by Geoff Bennington and Brian Massumi. Minneapolis: University of Minnesota Press.

MacCannell, Dean. 1992. *Empty Meeting Grounds: The Tourist Papers.* London: Routledge.

MacRae, Duncan, Jr. 1976. *The Social Function of Social Science.* New Haven, CT: Yale University Press.

Mancias, Peter T. 1987. *A History and Philosophy of the Social Sciences.* Oxford: Basil Blackwell.

Manganaro, Marc, ed. 1990. *Modernist Anthropology: From Fieldwork to Text.* Princeton, NJ: Princeton University Press.

Mannheim, Karl. 1936. *Ideology and Utopia,* translated by Edward Shils. New York: Harcourt, Brace & World.

———. 1940. *Man and Society in the Age of Reconstruction: Studies in Modern Social Structure,* translated by Edward Shils. New York: Harcourt, Brace & World.

———. 1952. *Essays on the Sociology of Knowledge,* edited by Paul Kecskemeti. London: Routledge & Kegan Paul.

Manza, Jeff. 1992. "Classes, Status Groups, and Social Closure: A Critique of Neo-Weberian Social Theory." *Current Perspectives in Social Theory* 12:275-302.

Marcus, George E. 1990. "Once More Into the Breach Between Economic and Cultural Analysis." Pp. 331-352 in *Beyond the Marketplace: Rethinking Economy and Society,* edited by Roger Friedland and A. F. Robertson. New York: Aldine de Gruyter.

Marcus, George E. and Michael M. J. Fischer. 1986. *Anthropology as Cultural Critique: An Experimental Moment in the Human Sciences.* Chicago: University of Chicago Press.

Marcuse, Herbert. [1941] 1960. *Reason and Revolution: Hegel and the Rise of Social Theory.* Boston: Beacon.

———. 1966. *One-Dimensional Man: Studies in the Ideology of Advanced Industrial Society.* Boston: Beacon.

Marshall, Barbara L. 1991. "Re-Producing the Gendered Subject." *Current Perspectives in Social Theory* 11:169-96.

———. Forthcoming. *Engendering Modernity: Feminism, Social Theory, and Social Change.* Cambridge: Polity.

Mattelart, Armand. 1979. *Multinational Corporations and the Control of Culture: The Ideological Apparatuses of Imperialism,* translated by Michael Chanan. Atlantic Highlands, NJ: Humanities Press.

Mattelart, Armand and Michèle Mattelart. 1986. *Penser les médias.* Paris: Éditions la Découverte.

_____. 1992. *Rethinking Media Theory,* translated by James A. Cohen and Mariana Urquidi. Minneapolis: University of Minnesota Press.

McCarthy, Thomas. 1978. *The Critical Theory of Jürgen Habermas.* Cambridge: MIT Press.

_____. 1991. *Ideals and Illusions: On Reconstruction and Deconstruction in Contemporary Social Theory.* Cambridge: MIT Press.

Meinhof, Ulrike. 1993. "Discourse." Pp. 161-62 in *The Blackwell Dictionary of Twentieth-Century Social Thought,* edited by William Outhwaite and Tom Bottomore. Oxford: Basil Blackwell.

Meja, Volker, Dieter Misgeld, and Nico Stehr, eds. 1987. *Modern German Sociology.* New York: Columbia University Press.

Merton, Robert. 1968. *Social Theory and Social Structure.* New York: Free Press.

Meyer, Michel. 1986. *From Logic to Rhetoric.* Philadelphia: John Benjamins.

Middleton, Richard. 1990. *Studying Popular Music.* Cambridge, UK: Open University Press.

Miliband, Ralph. 1987. "Class Analysis." Pp. 325-46 in *Social Theory Today,* edited by Anthony Giddens and Jonathan H. Turner. Stanford, CA: Stanford University Press.

Miller, Peter. 1987. *Domination and Power.* London: Routledge & Kegan Paul.

Miller, Richard W. 1987. *Fact and Method: Explanation, Confirmation, and Reality in the Natural and the Social Sciences.* Princeton, NJ: Princeton University Press.

Mills, C. Wright. 1967. *The Sociological Imagination.* New York: Oxford University Press.

Misgeld, Dieter. 1985. "Education and Cultural Invasion: Critical Social Theory, Education as Instruction, and the 'Pedagogy of the Oppressed.' " Pp. 77-118 in *Critical Theory and Public Life,* edited by John Forester. Cambridge: MIT Press.

Morley, David and Roger Silverstone. 1990. "Domestic Communication—Technologies and Meanings." *Media, Culture, and Society* 12:31-55.

Morrow, Raymond A. 1982a. "Théorie critique et matérialisme historique: Jürgen Habermas." *Sociologie et Sociétés* 14:97-111.

_____. 1982b. "Deux pays pour vivre: Critical Sociology and the New Canadian Political Economy." *Canadian Journal of Political and Social Theory* 6:61-105.

_____. 1983. "Habermas et le pragmatisme américain." *Communication et Information* 5:187-214.

_____. 1985. "Critical Theory and Critical Sociology." *Canadian Review of Sociology and Anthropology* 22:710-47.

_____. 1986. "Marcel Rioux: Critiquing Quebec's Discourse on Science and Technology." *Canadian Journal of Political and Social Theory* 10:151-73.

_____. 1991a. "Critical Theory, Gramsci, and Cultural Studies: From Structuralism to Poststructuralism." Pp. 27-70 in *Critical Theory Now,* edited by Philip Wexler. London: Falmer.

_____. 1991b. "Introduction: The Challenge of Cultural Studies to Canadian Sociology and Anthropology." *Canadian Review of Sociology and Anthropology* 28:153-72.

_____. 1991c. "Toward a Critical Theory of Methodology: Habermas and the Theory of Argumentation." *Current Perspectives in Social Theory* 11:197-228.

_____. 1992a. "Marxist Sociology." *Encyclopedia of Sociology*, edited by Edgar Borgatta and Marie Borgatta. New York: Macmillan.

_____. 1992b. "Patriarchal Bodies and Pre-Modern Subjects: Grotesque Realism and Domination in García Márquez's *El Otoño del patriarca*." Pp. 29-57 in *Literature and the Body*, edited by Anthony Purdy. Amsterdam: Rodopi.

_____. 1993. "Introducing Critical Sociology." Pp. 24-45 in *Contemporary Sociology: Critical Perspectives*, edited by Peter S. Li and B. Singh Bolaria. Toronto: Copp Clark.

Morrow, Raymond A. and Carlos Alberto Torres. 1994. "Education and the Reproduction of Class, Gender, and Race: Responding to the Postmodern Challenges." *Educational Theory* 44: 43-61.

_____. Forthcoming. *Social Theory and Education: A Critique of Social and Cultural Reproduction Theories*. Albany: State University of New York Press.

Mouzelis, Nicos P. 1991. *Back to Sociological Theory*. New York: Macmillan.

Mueller-Vollmer, Kurt, ed. 1988. *The Hermeneutics Reader*. New York: Continuum.

Mumby, Dennis K. 1988. *Communication and Power in Organizations: Discourse, Ideology, and Domination*. Norwood, NJ: Ablex.

Münch, Richard and Neil Smelser, eds. 1992. *Theory of Culture*. Berkeley: University of California Press.

Murphy, Raymond. 1988. *Social Closure: The Theory of Monopolization and Exclusion*. Oxford: Clarendon.

Neuman, W. Lawrence. 1991. *Social Research Methods: Qualitative and Quantitative Approaches*. Boston: Allyn & Bacon.

Nicholson, Linda J., ed. 1990. *Feminism/Postmodernism*. London: Routledge.

Nielsen, Greg Marc. 1985. "Communication et esthétique culturelle dans deux sociologies critiques: J. Habermas et M. Rioux." *Sociologie et Sociétés* 17:13-26.

_____ 1993a. "Critical Theory." Pp. 527-28 in *Encyclopedia of Contemporary Literary Theory*, edited by Irena A. Makayryk. Toronto: University of Toronto Press.

_____. 1993b. "Frankfurt School." Pp. 60-4 in *Encyclopedia of Contemporary Literary Theory*, edited by Irena A. Makayryk. Toronto: University of Toronto Press.

Nielsen, Greg Marc and Raymond A. Morrow, eds. 1991. "Special Issue on Cultural Studies in Canada." *Canadian Review of Sociology and Anthropology* 28:153-298.

Nielsen, Joyce McCarl, ed. 1990. *Feminist Research Methods: Exemplary Readings in the Social Sciences*. Boulder, CO: Westview.

Noble, David F. 1977. *America by Design: Science, Technology, and the Rise of Corporate Capitalism*. Oxford: Oxford University Press.

Nordstrom, Carolyn and JoAnn Martin, eds. 1992. *The Paths to Domination, Resistance, and Terror*. Berkeley: University of California Press.

Norris, Christopher. 1990. *What's Wrong With Postmodernism: Critical Theory and the Ends of Philosophy*. Baltimore: Johns Hopkins University Press.

O'Connor, James. 1987. *The Meaning of Crisis: A Theoretical Introduction*. Oxford: Basil Blackwell.

Offe, Claus. 1984. *Contradictions of the Welfare State*, edited by John Keane. London: Hutchinson.

_____. 1985. *Disorganized Capitalism: Contemporary Transformations of Work and Politics*, edited by John Keane. Cambridge: MIT Press.

Ollman, Bertell. 1993. *Dialectical Investigations*. London: Routledge.

O'Neill, John. 1972. *Sociology as a Skin Trade: Essays Towards a Reflexive Sociology*. London: Heinemann.

_____. 1985. *Five Bodies: The Human Shape of Modern Society*. Ithaca, NY: Cornell University Press.

Outhwaite, William. 1987. *New Philosophies of Social Science: Realism, Hermeneutics, and Critical Theory*. New York: Macmillan.

Outhwaite, William and Tom Bottomore, eds. 1993. *The Blackwell Dictionary of Twentieth-Century Social Thought*, edited by William Outhwaite and Tom Bottomore. Oxford: Basil Blackwell.

Parker, Ian. 1989. *The Crisis in Modern Social Psychology—and How To End It*. London: Routledge.

_____. 1992. *Discourse Dynamics: Critical Analysis for Social and Individual Psychology*. London: Routledge.

Parkin, Frank. 1979. *Marxism and Class Theory: A Bourgeoisie Critique*. London: Tavistock.

Patterson, Orlando. 1982. *Slavery and Social Death: A Comparative Study*. Cambridge, MA: Harvard University Press.

Pawson, Ray. 1989. *A Measure for Measures: A Manifesto for Empirical Sociology*. London: Routledge.

Pettit, Philip. 1977. *The Concept of Structuralism: A Critical Analysis*. Berkeley: University of California Press.

Phillips, Derek L. 1971. *Knowledge From What? Theories and Methods in Social Research*. Chicago: Rand McNally.

Piaget, Jean. 1970. *Structuralism*, translated by Chaninah Maschler. New York: Harper Torchbooks.

Pierson, Christopher. 1991. *Beyond the Welfare State? The New Political Economy of Welfare*. Cambridge: Polity.

Polanyi, Michael. 1962. *Personal Knowledge: Towards a Post-Critical Philosophy*. Chicago: University of Chicago Press.

Polkinghorne, Donald. 1983. *Methodology for the Human Sciences: Systems of Inquiry*. Albany: State University of New York.

_____. 1988. *Narrative Knowing and the Human Sciences*. Albany: State University of New York Press.

Popkewitz, Thomas S. 1984. *Paradigm and Ideology in Educational Research: The Social Functions of the Intellectual*. London: Falmer.

_____. 1990. "Whose Future? Whose Past? Notes on Critical Theory and Methodology." Pp. 46-66 in *The Paradigm Dialog*, edited by Egon G. Guba. Newbury Park, CA: Sage.

Popper, Karl. 1965a. *Conjectures and Refutations: The Growth of Scientific Knowledge*. New York: Harper Torchbooks.

_____. 1965b. *The Logic of Scientific Discovery*. New York: Harper Torchbooks.

Porpora, Douglas V. 1987. *The Concept of Social Structure*. New York: Greenwood.

Poster, Mark. 1975. *Existential Marxism in Postwar France: From Sartre to Althusser*. Princeton, NJ: Princeton University Press.

_____. 1984. *Foucault, Marxism, and History: Modes of Production Versus Mode of Information*. Oxford: Basil Blackwell.

_____. 1989. *Critical Theory and Poststructuralism: In Search of a Context.* Ithaca, NY: Cornell University Press.

_____. 1990. *The Mode of Information: Poststructuralism and Social Context.* Chicago: University of Chicago Press.

Potter, Jonathan and Margaret Wetherell. 1987. *Discourse and Social Psychology: Beyond Attitudes and Behavior.* Newbury Park, CA: Sage.

Pusey, Michael. 1987. *Jürgen Habermas.* London: Tavistock.

Rabinbach, Anson. 1992. *The Human Motor: Energy, Fatique, and the Origins of Modernity.* Berkeley: University of California Press.

Rabinow, Paul and William M. Sullivan, eds. 1987. *Interpretive Social Science: A Second Look.* Berkeley: University of California Press.

Rachlin, Allan. 1991. "Rehumanizing Dialectic: Toward an Understanding of the Interpenetration of Structure and Subjectivity." *Current Perspectives in Social Theory* 11:255-69.

Radnitzky, Gerard. 1973. *Contemporary Schools of Metascience.* Chicago: Henry Regnery.

Radway, Janice A. 1984. *Reading the Romance: Women, Patriarchy, and Popular Literature.* Chapel Hill: University of North Carolina Press.

Ragin, Charles C. 1987. *The Comparative Method.* Berkeley: University of California Press.

Ragin, Charles C. and Howard S. Becker, eds. 1992. *What Is a Case? Exploring the Foundations of Social Inquiry.* Cambridge, UK: Cambridge University Press.

Rasmussen, David M. 1990. *Reading Habermas.* Oxford: Basil Blackwell.

Richards, Barry, ed. 1984. *Capitalism and Infancy.* Atlantic Highlands, NJ: Humanities Press.

Ricoeur, Paul. 1965. *De l'interpretation: essai sur Freud.* Paris: Seuil.

_____. 1974. *The Conflict of Interpretations,* edited by Don Ihde. Evanston, IL: Northwestern University Press.

_____. 1981. *Hermeneutics and the Human Sciences,* edited and translated by John B. Thompson. Cambridge, UK: Cambridge University Press.

Riesman, David. 1961. *The Lonely Crowd: A Study of the Changing American Character.* New Haven, CT: Yale University Press.

Rioux, Marcel. 1978. *Essai de sociologie critique.* Montreal: Hurtubise HMH.

Ritzer, George. 1991. *Metatheorizing in Sociology.* Lexington, MA: D. C. Heath.

_____. 1992. *Contemporary Sociological Theory.* 3rd. ed. New York: McGraw-Hill.

Robbins, Bruce. 1993. *Secular Vocations: Intellectuals, Professionalism, Culture.* London: Verso.

Robbins, Derek. 1991. *The Work of Pierre Bourdieu: Recognizing Society.* Boulder, CO: Westview.

Roberts, Julian. 1992. *The Logic of Reflection: German Philosophy in the Twentieth Century.* New Haven, CT: Yale University Press.

Rochberg-Halton, Eugene. 1986. *Meaning and Modernity: Social Theory in the Pragmatic Attitude.* Chicago: University of Chicago Press.

Rockmore, Tom. 1989. *Habermas on Historical Materialism.* Bloomington: Indiana University Press.

Roderick, Rick. 1986. *Habermas and the Foundations of Critical Theory.* New York: St. Martin's Press.

Roemer, John, ed. 1986. *Analytical Marxism*. Cambridge, UK: Cambridge University Press.

Romm, Norma R. A. 1991. *The Methodologies of Positivism and Marxism: A Sociological Debate*. New York: Macmillan.

Rorty, Richard. 1979. *Philosophy and the Mirror of Nature*. Princeton, NJ: Princeton University Press.

_____. 1982. *Consequences of Pragmatism*. Minneapolis: University of Minnesota Press.

_____. 1989. *Contingency, Irony, and Solidarity*. Cambridge, UK: Cambridge University Press.

_____. 1991. *Essays on Heidegger and Others*. Philosophical Papers, vol. 2. Cambridge: Cambridge University Press.

Rosenau, Pauline Marie. 1992. *Post-Modernism and the Social Sciences: Insights, Inroads, and Intrusions*. Princeton, NJ: Princeton University Press.

Rosenberg, Alexander. 1988. *Philosophy of Social Science*. Boulder, CO: Westview.

Rossi, Ino, ed. 1982. *Structural Sociology*. New York: Columbia University Press.

Roth, Michael S. 1988. *Knowing and History: Appropriations of Hegel in Twentieth-Century France*. Ithaca, NY: Cornell University Press.

Rule, James B. 1978. *Insight and Social Betterment: A Preface to Applied Social Science*. New York: Oxford University Press.

Sabia, Daniel R., Jr. and Jerald Wallulis, eds. 1983. *Changing Social Science: Critical Theory and Other Critical Perspectives*. Albany: State University of New York Press.

Sampson, Edward E. 1983. *Justice and the Critique of Pure Psychology*. New York: Plenum.

Sartre, Jean-Paul. 1963. *Search for a Method*, translated by H. E. Barnes. New York: Knopf.

Sayer, Andrew. 1992. *Method in Social Science: A Realist Approach*. 2nd. ed. London: Routledge.

Sayer, Derek. 1983. *Marx's Method*. 2nd. ed. Brighton: Harvester.

_____. 1987. *The Violence of Abstraction: The Analytic Foundations of Historical Materialism*. Oxford: Basil Blackwell.

_____. 1991. *Capitalism and Modernity: An Excursus on Marx and Weber*. London: Routledge.

Scheff, Thomas J. 1990. *Discourse, Emotion, and Social Structure*. Chicago: University of Chicago Press.

Schiller, Herbert I. 1971. *Mass Communications and the American Empire*. Boston: Beacon.

_____. 1973. *The Mind Managers*. Boston: Beacon.

_____. 1976. *Communication and Cultural Domination*. White Plains, NY: M. E. Sharpe.

Scholte, Bob. 1974. "Toward a Reflexive and Critical Anthropology." Pp. 430-58 in *Reinventing Anthropology*, edited by Dell Hymes. New York: Vintage.

Schroyer, Trent. 1975. *The Critique of Domination: The Origins and Development of Critical Theory*. Boston: Beacon.

Schutz, Alfred. 1967. *The Phenomenology of the Social World,* translated by George Walsh and Ferderick Lehnert. Evanston, IL: Northwestern University Press.

Schwalbe, Michael L. 1986. *The Psycosocial Consequences of Natural and Alienated Labor.* Albany: State University of New York.

Schweitzer, David and Felix R. Geyer, eds. 1976. *Theories of Alienation: Critical Perspectives in Philosophy and the Social Sciences.* Leiden: Martinus Nijhoff.

———. 1981. *Alienation: Problems of Meaning, Theory, and Method.* London: Routledge & Kegan Paul.

———, eds. 1989. *Alienation Theories and De-Alienation Strategies.* Northwood: Science Reviews.

Scott, Alan. 1990. *Ideology and the New Social Movements.* London: Unwin Hyman.

Scott, James C. 1985. *Weapons of the Weak: Everyday Forms of Peasant Resistance.* New Haven, CT: Yale University Press.

———. 1992. "Domination, Acting, and Fantasy." Pp. 55-84 in *The Paths to Domination, Resistance, and Terror,* edited by Carolyn Nordstrom and Martin JoAnn. Berkeley: University of California Press.

Seeman, Melvin. 1975. "Alienation Studies." *Annual Review of Sociology* 1:91-123.

Seidman, Steven and David G. Wagner, eds. 1992. *Postmodernism and Social Theory.* Oxford: Basil Blackwell.

Sennett, Richard, ed. 1977. *The Psychology of Society: An Anthology.* New York: Vintage.

Sewell, William, Jr. 1992. "A Theory of Structure: Duality, Agency, and Transformation." *American Journal of Sociology* 98:1-29.

Shalin, Dimitri N. 1992. "Critical Theory and the Pragmatist Challenge." *American Journal of Sociology* 98:237-79.

Sherman, Howard J. 1987. *Foundations of Radical Political Economy.* Armonk, NY: M. E. Sharpe.

Shils, Edward. 1980. *The Calling of Sociology and Other Essays on the Pursuit of Learning.* Chicago: University of Chicago Press.

Shotter, John. 1993. *Cultural Politics and Everyday Life.* Toronto: University of Toronto Press.

Sigmund, Paul E. 1990. *Liberation Theology at the Crossroads: Democracy or Revolution?* Oxford: Oxford University Press.

Silverman, David. 1985. *Qualitative Methodology and Sociology.* Aldershot: Gower.

———. 1989. "Introduction." Pp. 30-48 in *The Politics of Field Research: Sociology Beyond Enlightenment,* edited by Jaber F. Gubrium and David Silverman. Newbury Park, CA: Sage.

Simonds, A. P. 1978. *Karl Mannheim's Sociology of Knowledge.* Oxford: Oxford University Press.

Simons, Herbert W., ed. 1989. *Rhetoric in the Human Sciences.* Newbury Park, CA: Sage.

———, ed. 1990. *The Rhetorical Turn: Invention and Persuasion in the Conduct of Inquiry.* Chicago: University of Chicago Press.

Singer, Burton and Margaret Mooney Marini. 1987. "Advancing Social Research: An Essay Based on Stanley Liberson's *Making It Count.*" *Sociological Methodology* 17:373-92.

Sjoberg, Gideon and Roger Nett. 1968. *A Methodology for Social Research.* New York: Harper & Row.

Skinner, Quentin, ed. 1985. *The Return of Grand Theory in the Human Sciences.* Cambridge, UK: Cambridge University Press.

Skocpol, Theda, ed. 1984. *Vision and Method in Historical Sociology.* Cambridge: Cambridge University Press.

Smart, Barry. 1983. *Foucault, Marxism, and Critique.* London: Routledge & Kegan Paul.

_____. 1985. *Michel Foucault.* London: Tavistock.

_____. 1992. *Modern Conditions, Postmodern Controversies.* London: Routledge.

Smith, Dorothy E. 1990. *The Conceptual Practices of Power: A Feminist Sociology of Knowledge.* Toronto: University of Toronto Press.

Smith, Paul. 1988. *Discerning the Subject.* Minneapolis: University of Minnesota Press.

Smith, Tony. 1991. *The Role of Ethics in Social Theory: Essays From a Habermasian Perspective.* Albany: State University of New York Press.

_____. 1993. *Dialectical Social Theory and Its Critics: From Hegel to Analytical Marxism and Postmodernism.* Albany: State University of New York Press.

Smythe, Dallas W. 1981. *Dependency Road: Communications, Capitalism, Consciousness, and Canada.* Norwood, NJ: Ablex.

Soja, Edward W. 1989. *Postmodern Geographies: The Reassertion of Space in Critical Social Theory.* London: Verso.

Söllner, Alfons. 1979. *Geschichte und Herrschaft: Studien zur materialistischen Sozialwissenschaft 1929-1942.* Frankfurt am Main: Suhrkamp.

Sperber, Irwin. 1990. *Fashions in Science: Opinion Leaders and Collective Behavior in the Social Sciences.* Minneapolis: University of Minnesota Press.

Stam, Henderikus J., Timothy B. Rogers, and Kenneth J. Gergen, eds. 1987. *The Analysis of Psychological Theory: Metapsychological Perspectives.* Cambridge: Hemisphere.

Stinchcombe, Arthur. 1968. *Constructing Social Theories.* New York: Harcourt, Brace & World.

Stockman, Norman. 1983. *Antipositivist Theories of the Sciences: Critical Rationalism, Critical Theory, and Scientific Realism.* Dordrecht, The Netherlands: D. Reidel.

Sullivan, Edmund. 1990. *Critical Psychology and Pedagogy: Interpretation of the Personal World.* New York: Bergin & Garvey.

Swingewood, Alan. 1977. *The Myth of Mass Culture.* Atlantic Highlands, NJ: Humanities Press.

Taylor, Charles. 1989. *Sources of the Self: The Making of Modern Identity.* Cambridge, MA: Harvard University Press.

Therborn, Göran. 1976. *Science, Class, and Society: On the Formation of Sociology and Historical Materialism.* London: New Left Books.

Thomas, David. 1979. *Naturalism and Social Science: A Post-Empiricist Philosophy of Social Science.* Cambridge: Cambridge University Press.

Thompson, E. P. 1968. *The Making of the English Working Class.* Harmondsworth, UK: Penguin.

Thompson, John B. 1981. *Critical Hermeneutics: A Study in the Thought of Paul Ricoeur and Jürgen Habermas.* Cambridge, UK: Cambridge University Press.

_____. 1984. *Studies in the Theory of Ideology.* Berkeley: University of California Press.

_____. 1990. *Ideology and Modern Culture: Critical Social Theory in the Era of Mass Communication.* Stanford, CA: Stanford University Press.

Thompson, John B. and David Held, eds. 1982. *Habermas: Critical Debates.* Cambridge: MIT Press.

Toulmin, Stephen. 1958. *The Uses of Argument.* Cambridge, UK: Cambridge University Press.

Touraine, Alain. 1977. *The Self-Production of Society,* translated by Derek Coltman. Chicago: University of Chicago Press.

_____. 1981. *The Voice and the Eye: An Analysis of Social Movements,* translated by Alan Duff. Cambridge, UK: Cambridge University Press.

_____. 1986. "Sociologies et Sociologues." Pp. 134-43 in *L'État des sciences sociales en France.* Paris: La Decouverte.

Trigg, Roger. 1985. *Understanding Social Science: A Philosophical Introduction to the Social Sciences.* Oxford: Basil Blackwell.

Trow, Martin and Thorsten Nybom, eds. 1991. *University and Society: Essays on the Social Role of Research and Higher Education.* London: Jessica Kingsley.

Tucker, Robert C., ed. 1978. *The Marx-Engels Reader.* New York: Norton.

Turner, Bryan S. 1984. *The Body and Society: Explorations in Social Theory.* Oxford: Basil Blackwell.

Turner, Graeme. 1990. *British Cultural Studies: An Introduction.* London: Unwin Hyman.

Unger, Roberto Mangabeira. 1986. *The Critical Legal Studies Movement.* Cambridge, MA: Harvard University Press.

van den Berg, Axel. 1980. "Critical Theory: Is There Still Hope?" *American Journal of Sociology* 86:449-78.

Volosinov, V. N. 1986. *Marxism and the Philosophy of Language,* translated by Ladislav Matejka and I. R. Titunik. Cambridge, MA: Harvard University Press.

Wachterhauser, Brice R., ed. 1987. *Hermeneutics and Philosophy.* Albany: State University of New York Press.

Wagner, David. 1990. *The Quest for a Radical Profession: Social Service Careers and Political Ideology.* Lantham, NY: University Press of America.

Wajcman, Judy. 1991. *Feminism Confronts Technology.* Cambridge: Polity.

Wallace, Walter L. 1971. *The Logic of Science in Sociology.* Chicago: Aldine.

Wallerstein, Immanuel. 1990. "Culture as the Ideological Battleground of the Modern World-System." Pp. 31-56 in *Global Culture,* edited by Mike Featherstone. London: Sage.

Walzer, Michael. 1987. *Interpretation and Social Criticism.* Cambridge, MA: Harvard University Press.

Warnke, Georgia. 1987. *Gadamer: Hermeneutics, Tradition, and Reason.* Cambridge: Polity.

Wartenberg, Thomas E. 1990. *The Forms of Power: From Domination to Transformation.* Philadelphia: Temple University Press.

Waters, Malcolm. 1994. *Modern Sociological Theory.* Thousand Oaks, CA: Sage.

Weber, Max. 1949. *The Methodology of the Social Sciences,* translated by Edward A. Shils and Henry A. Finch. New York: Free Press.

Wellmer, Albrecht. 1971. *Critical Theory of Society*, translated by John Comming. New York: Seabury.

Wernick, Andrew. 1991. *Promotional Culture: Advertising, Ideology, and Symbolic Expression*. Newbury Park, CA: Sage.

Wexler, Philip. 1983. *Critical Social Psychology*. London: Routledge & Kegan Paul.

_____, ed. 1991. *Critical Theory Now*. London: Falmer.

White, Stephen K. 1987. "Toward a Critical Political Science." Pp. 113-36 in *Idioms of Inquiry: Critique and Renewal in Political Science*, edited by Terence Ball. Albany: State University of New York Press.

_____. 1988. *The Recent Work of Jürgen Habermas: Reason, Justice, and Modernity*. Cambridge, UK: Cambridge University Press.

Whitty, Geoff. 1985. *Sociology and School Knowledge: Curriculum Theory, Research, and Politics*. New York: Methuen.

Wiggershaus, Rolf. 1987. *Die Frankfurter Schule*. Munich: Carl Hanser Verlag.

Wiley, Norbert, ed. 1987. *The Marx-Weber Debate*. Newbury Park, CA: Sage.

Willis, Paul. 1981. *Learning to Labor: How Working Class Kids Get Working Class Jobs*. New York: Columbia University Press.

Wilson, H. T. 1977. *The American Ideology: Science, Technology, and Organization as Modes of Rationality in Advanced Industrial Societies*. London: Routledge & Kegan Paul.

Wilson, Thomas P. 1987. "Sociology and the Mathematical Model." Pp. 382-404 in *Social Theory Today*, edited by Anthony Giddens and Jonathan H. Turner. Stanford, CA: Stanford University Press.

Wimmer, Roger D. and Joseph R. Dominick. 1983. *Mass Media Research: An Introduction*. Belmont, CA: Wadsworth.

Winch, Peter. 1958. *The Idea of a Social Science and Its Relation to Philosophy*. London: Routledge & Kegan Paul.

Wittgenstein, Ludwig. 1974. *Philosophical Investigations*, translated by G. E. M. Anscombe. Oxford: Basil Blackwell.

Wood, Ellen Meiksins. 1986. *The Retreat From Class: A New "True" Socialism*. London: Verso.

Woolgar, Steve. 1988. *Science: The Very Idea*. London: Tavistock.

Wright, Erik Olin. 1985. *Classes*. London: Verso.

_____. 1989. *The Debate on Classes*. London: Verso.

Yin, Robert K. 1984. *Case Study Research: Design and Methods*. Beverly Hills, CA: Sage.

Young, Robert E. 1989. *A Critical Theory of Education: Habermas and Our Children's Future*. New York: Harvester.

Young, T. R. 1976. Some Theoretical Foundations for Conflict Methodology. *Sociological Inquiry* 46:23-9.

Zaret, David. 1992. Critical Theory and the Sociology of Culture. *Current Perspectives in Social Theory* 12:1-28.

INDEX

Critical social psychology, 294-298
Critical Social Research, 61n.
Critical social science, 18, 32n., 163
Critical social theory (*see* Critical
    theory), 6
Critical sociology, 18, 23, 32n., 132
    (French)
Critical structuralism, 132, 135-137,
    194n.
Critical theology, 296
Critical theory:
    and cultural Marxism, 18
    and ideology, 26-27
    as a research program, 85-111
    (passim.), 141-194, 241ff., 269-
    271, 274-275
    concept of, 7-12, 241-244
    critique of, 240-241
    definition of, 12, 16
    of methodology, 38-40
    of technology, 282
    origins of, 12-16
    strategy of introducing, xii-xv
    supradisciplinary character of, 12,
    274
Critical-dialectical perspective, 58
Critical-dialogical model (of social sci-
    ence), 304, 309-312
Criticism:
    conventionalized, 71
    literary, 31n.
    of critical theory, xiv, 26-30
    scientific, 70ff.
    social and cultural, 11, 47, 50, 152
Critique, 7, 109, 174-175, 254-255
    cultural, 255
    immanent vs. transcendent, 263
    intellectual, 174
    moral, 174
    of ideologies, 95, 149-150, 162-
    163, 174
    of technology, 101
    practical, 174
    sociocultural, 10
Crozier, Michel, 132
Crucial experiments (*see* Falsifica-
    tionism), 85

Culler, Jonathan, 129, 246n.
Cultural:
    anthropology, 148
    arbitrary, 133
    capital, 134
    change, 218
    criticism, 47
    critique, 254-255
    Marxism, 18
    materialism, 18
    sciences, 92-93
    studies, 11, 18, 61n., 105 (and
    Horkheimer), 189-190 (British),
    258, 292
    theory, 99, 272n., 273, 274, 287-
    292
Cultural reproduction
    (*see* Reproduction)
Culture:
    elite, 265
    mass, 98
    popular, 98, 265
    sociology of, 47, 249, 263-264,
    271n., 286-291
Culture industries (*see also* Mass
    media), 15, 106, 286, 311
Curran, James, 290
Curriculum theory, 291

Dahmer, Helmut, 103
Dallmayr, Fred R., 11, 17, 152, 240
D'Amico, Robert, 95
Dant, Tim, 263
Data (*see also* Sense-data), 43-44
Davies, Ioan, 17
Death (of the subject), 124
Deconcentration (of urban spaces),
    276ff.
Deconstruction, 122, 128, 129, 201,
    202, 227, 237, 246n.
    (definitions of)
Deconstructive argumentation, 232
Deduction, 66
Deductive logic, 228
Deductive-nomological model, 46,
    66ff., 78

ABOUT THE AUTHORS

Raymond A. Morrow is Associate Professor of Sociology, University of Alberta, Edmonton, where he has taught since 1984. His graduate training included an MA at the University of British Columbia, study at the Free University of Berlin, a Ph.D. at York University (1981), and postdoctoral research at the Université de Montréal. He also has taught at the University of Manitoba and the University of Western Ontario. He teaches primarily in the areas of sociological theory and cultural sociology (especially in relation to mass communications and education) and has published articles and chapters in critical theory and cultural studies. He recently completed a book on social theory and education (with Carlos Alberto Torres, Graduate Faculty of Education, UCLA), and is working on a project on theories of social psychology.

David D. Brown completed his Ph.D. in sociology at the University of Alberta in 1990. His thesis was titled *Ricoueur's Narrative Methodology and the Interpretation of Life History Texts*. He is an Associate Professor of Sociology at the University Lethbridge, where he teaches in the areas of contemporary theory and research methodology. He recently published an article titled "Discursive Moments of Identification" in *Current Perspectives in Social Theory*. He is the organizer of an internet electronic discussion group called Narrative-L which provides an international forum for scholars concerned with narrative in everyday life. He is a principal researcher with the University of Lethbridge Regional Center for Health Promotion and Community Studies and he is currently conducting research into narrative-based identification within communities and support groups.

381